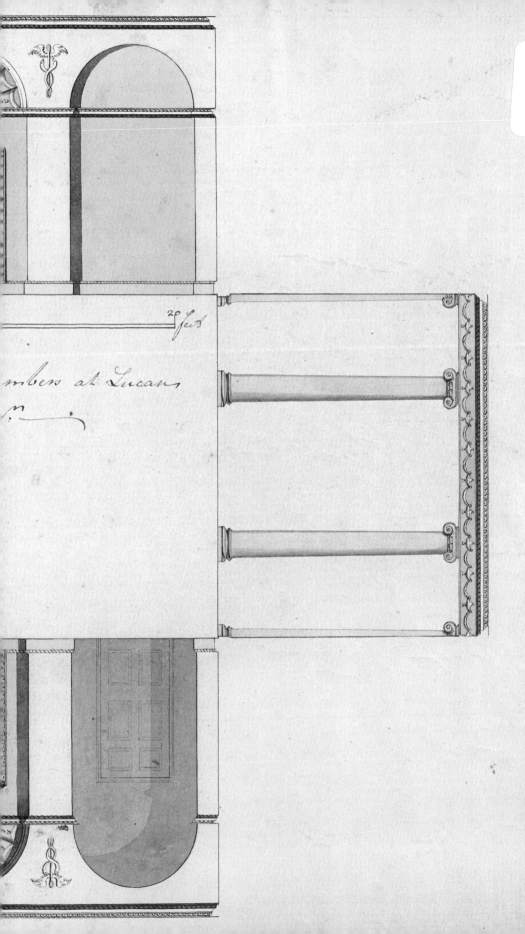

mbers at *Lucan*

20 feet

Life in the Country House in Georgian Ireland

Patricia McCarthy

Life *in the* Country House *in* Georgian Ireland

published for
The Paul Mellon Centre for Studies in British Art
by Yale University Press, New Haven and London

This publication has been supported generously by the Marc Fitch Fund, the Irish Georgian Society and the Paul Mellon Centre for Studies in British Art.

Designed by Sophie Sheldrake
Printed in China

The Library of Congress has catalogued the hardcover edition as follows
Names: McCarthy, Patricia, 1947- author.
Title: Life in the country house in Georgian Ireland / Patricia McCarthy.
Description: New Haven : Paul Mellon Centre BA, 2016. | Based on the author's
  thesis (Ph. D.--Trinity College, 2009) under title: Planning and use of
  space in Irish houses 1730–1830. | Includes bibliographical references and index.
Identifiers: LCCN 2016001892 | ISBN 9780300218862 (hardback)
Subjects: LCSH: Country homes--Ireland. | Country life--Ireland. | Domestic
  space--Ireland. | Ireland--Social conditions--18th century. |
  Ireland--Social conditions--19th century. | BISAC: HISTORY / Europe /
  Ireland. | HISTORY / Modern / 18th Century. | ARCHITECTURE / Buildings / Residential.
Classification: LCC DA985 .M39 2016 | DDC 941.507--dc23
LC record available at: http://lccn.loc.gov/2016001892

Endpapers
Thomas Penrose, *Lobby to the Bed Chambers at Lucan for Ag. Vesey Esqr.* (detail), April 1776
(*see* fig. 70).

Frontispiece
George Barret RA (*c.*1728/32–1784), *A View of Powerscourt, Co. Wicklow* (detail), 1760–2;
oil on canvas. Yale Center for British Art, Paul Mellon Collection (*see* fig. 22).

Page v
Thomas Cooley, elevation of wall of study with bookcases at Mount Kennedy, n.d.
(*see* fig. 172).

Page vi
Design for plasterwork for the ceiling of the ground-floor dining room at Leinster House
(detail), attributed to Filippo Lafranchini, *c.*1760 (*see* fig. 94).

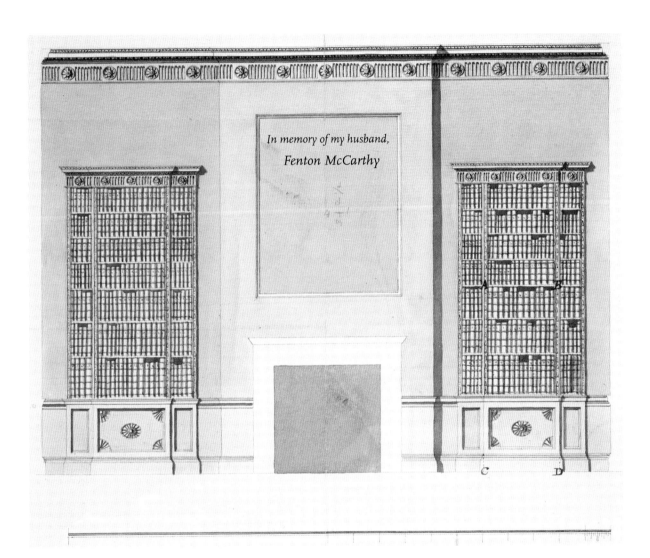

In memory of my husband,
Fenton McCarthy

Contents

Acknowledgements

This book has been quite a long time in the making, a statement with which my family, friends and colleagues would concur. I have, however, enjoyed every step of the journey and am privileged to have been accompanied and encouraged by many wonderful people, who were happy to share their knowledge and expertise with me.

Many years ago, when I was searching for a subject for my undergraduate dissertation, Dr Edward McParland suggested, among other possibilities, the idea of looking at the interior planning of Irish country houses, how the spaces were named and used. Ignoring the suggestion at that point, I returned to it, some years later, as the subject for my doctoral thesis, under Eddie's supervision. He exhorted me to 'read promiscuously', and the late Knight of Glin, Desmond FitzGerald, suggested that Irish novels of the Georgian period would throw light on how spaces were used. They were so right. I cannot overstate the support and encouragement received from Eddie McParland, and his many introductions to people working in my field (often over delicious suppers in his rooms at Trinity College Dublin), were invaluable.

The Knight was encouraging and interested from the beginning, generously passing on useful information as he received it, as he did for many others, and he invited me to root through his archive at Glin Castle, which was hugely rewarding, and for which I am very grateful. John Cornforth, former architectural editor of *Country Life*, is also no longer with us, but I had the benefit of his vast knowledge of country houses and their interiors, in both

Opposite
The gallery at Carton, early nineteenth-century (present drawing room) (*see* fig. 130).

Ireland and Britain, not only through his books and articles, but also personally, all of which I greatly appreciate. Kevin Mulligan introduced me to Ballyfin many years ago when we collaborated on a study of Dominick Madden, an earlier architect for the house. A mine of information on Ireland's architecture and hugely generous with his time and knowledge, from which I have greatly benefited, Kevin also arranged for me to use the series of architectural drawings for Ballyfin which are an important part of this book: my sincere thanks to him. For images other than architectural plans, I cannot thank William Laffan enough for his knowledge of Irish art and where it is located, the range of contacts from whom he managed to obtain permissions for me to publish, and perhaps above all, for his prompt responses to my emails, usually by return! Thank you, William!

Mark Girouard's seminal *Life in the English Country House* (1972) has been a valuable point of reference throughout this project. When I began my research, Eddie McParland encouraged me to consult the work of Dr Toby Barnard. Toby's scholarship has been an inspiration to me: he has been generous with his suggestions and I have valued his interest in my work. I am very grateful too to David Griffin for allowing me to tap into his vast knowledge of Irish houses, and for reading the final draft of the book. The staff of the Irish Architectural Archive, the Library of Trinity College Dublin and the National Library of Ireland have been particularly helpful, and mention must be made of Colum O'Riordan, Eve McAulay, Aisling Dunne, Anne Henderson, Simon Lincoln, Paul Doyle and Tom Desmond. Many people have helped to bring this book to fruition: Charles Benson, Christine Casey, Charles and Sally Clements, Alec Cobbe, Hugh Cobbe, Antoinette Dornan, Jane Fenlon, Alison Fitzgerald, Robert Ganly, Patrick Guinness, Susan Keating, Frank Keohane, Rolf Loeber, Conor Lucey, Ross McCarthy, Anthony Malcomson, John Montague, Christopher Moore, Michael Murphy, Aidan O'Boyle, Finola O'Kane, Brendan Rooney, Regina Sexton, David Sheehan, Ruth Sheehy and David White. My thanks to all, and particularly to Livia Hurley for her ongoing support, and my apologies to anyone I may have inadvertently left out. I am also grateful to the Irish Georgian Society and the Marc Fitch Foundation for their welcome grants towards this publication.

The readers of Yale University Press responded positively and with constructive criticism and I believe the book is improved by their valuable comments. It has been further improved by Hester Higton's diligent copy-editing. Special thanks to Sally Salvesen and to the book's designer, Sophie Sheldrake, for shepherding the process with patience and good humour. Without the moral and financial support of my late husband, Fenton, I could not have pursued this path: he accompanied me for as much of the journey as he could, and I will forever be grateful to him. Our children, Simon, Ross and Kate, have encouraged me all the way, and our grandchildren, Ben, Luke, Harry, Hugo, Molly and Keelin, have added a new and very welcome dimension to my life as well as much fun along the way.

Introduction

The building of Castletown House by William Conolly (1662–1729), Speaker of the Irish House of Commons (1715–29), and considered to be the richest man in Ireland, was a pivotal event in the history of Irish domestic architecture. Its designer, Alessandro Galilei, was Italian, and Sir Edward Lovett Pearce, a neo-Palladian and a cousin of Sir John Vanbrugh, supervised its building. He was also responsible for the design of the entrance hall and the curved Ionic colonnades. Like Inigo Jones a century before, Pearce had made the Grand Tour annotating Palladio's *Quattro Libri* as he travelled, and Castletown is Ireland's first, and arguably finest, Palladian house. It set a pattern for large and medium-sized houses in Ireland for decades, establishing the country house practice of Pearce and, after his death in 1733, of his assistant Richard Castle.

Palladianism revolutionised Irish and British domestic architecture in the eighteenth century. The trend began later in Ireland, but it also lasted longer there, where it was enthusiastically embraced by landowners who found that the Palladian layout allowed them a satisfyingly extended frontage to their house, the safety of having the kitchen and services at a remove in one pavilion, and the convenient location of the stables in the other.

The interaction between social and architectural history first employed by Mark Girouard in *Life in the English Country House* (1978) allows us to explore the ways in which landowners, together with their architects, planned houses for themselves, their families and their servants to live in, and in which they would entertain. The period covered in this book runs from the building of Castletown in 1720, through the building boom that followed the Act of Union between England and Ireland in 1800 to the Great Famine (1845–9) and the subsequent sharp decline in building activity.

As might be expected, Irish domestic architecture and interiors owe much to British practice: many trends that began in Britain found their way to Ireland, but they were not slavishly followed. Architecture in eighteenth-century Ireland was less academic than that in England and more eclectic, perhaps because there was less pressure on either the patron or architect to prove their learning.[1] In domestic architecture, many ideas were borrowed and then adapted to an Irish way of living by those who were building. With constant streams of traffic between the two islands, and many landowners in Ireland having homes and also relatives in Britain, it is not surprising that a number of British architects, including James Wyatt, Sir William Chambers, Robert Adam and Isaac Ware, supplied plans for Irish patrons.

As the result of a commission for a drawing of a chimneypiece for Henry Fox in London, Isaac Ware was introduced by Fox to his brother-in-law, the earl of Kildare (later the duke of Leinster), for whom Ware produced plans for both Carton, the earl's country seat, and Kildare (later Leinster) House in Dublin. Kildare and Fox were married to, respectively, Ladies Emily and Caroline Lennox, daughters of the 2nd duke of Richmond. A third sister, Lady Louisa, was married to the wealthy Thomas Conolly MP, of Castletown House. With strong (sometimes family) links to the vice-regents in residence at Dublin Castle, Emily FitzGerald and

1
George Barret RA (*c*.1728/32–1784), *View of Castletown*; oil on canvas. Private collection.

Louisa Conolly were leaders of fashion in Ireland, and were well informed and enthusiastic about architecture and interior decoration. It was through family and social connections such as these that architectural ideas were disseminated in Ireland.

Wealthy, ambitious collectors and prospective house-builders arriving in Rome as Grand Tourists found it a convenient meeting place where artists, architects, and agents were ready to provide whatever services and introductions were required. Like the British, many members of the nobility and gentry in Ireland were part of this milieu, with much business promised and often carried out. In this way, ideas from Italy and France were adopted. Many of those Irish who travelled and were in a position to build felt an obligation to promote better building practice in Ireland and were happy to dispense advice to others on their return. It was a mark of a gentleman to be acquainted with architecture.[2] Architectural books and prints, published in Ireland and abroad, were therefore much-valued additions to Irish domestic libraries.

The eighteenth century was a time of peace in Ireland. After the political unrest and destruction of buildings in the country throughout most of the seventeenth century, building began in earnest, not only in domestic architecture but also in the development and expansion of towns. At the beginning of the eighteenth century most Irish country houses were castles, or, perhaps more appropriately, towerhouses, many having been built by Norman-Irish families. These towerhouses had often been extended to provide further accommodation in semi-fortified structures where large windows contrasted with the vertical narrow openings in the attached towerhouse. At Leamaneh Castle, Co. Clare, the primary seat of the O'Briens in the seventeenth century, the family attached a four-bay three-storey extension with large windows to the towerhouse.[3] Springhill in Co. Derry, originally a modest house built *c*.1680, was surrounded by a defensive bawn, or walled courtyard with corner towers.

In choosing a site for a house in the first half of the eighteenth century, the priority was generally that they were built 'where new timber could flourish'. Display and aspect only became a requirement in the second half of the century, when elevated sites with views of the surrounding countryside were important.[4] Politically, these houses demonstrated the power, wealth and ambition of their owners. Architecturally, they represented the transition from the defensive towerhouse to the 'polite' country house.

A rise in rental income between 1710 and 1730, largely due to the falling in of long-term leases, enabled landlords to increase rents for the first time in a long while. More rental increases occurred in the 1740s and again in the last quarter of the eighteenth century.[5] With money at the owners' disposal, houses that were not deemed fashionable enough were rebuilt, extended or improved. During the eighteenth century Springhill's bawn was swept away, two single-storey and free-standing wings of stone were built facing each other, creating a broad forecourt, and, later still, single-storey wings with canted bays were attached to the house. A fairly common practice in Ireland, rather than attaching wings, was to build a new front, so that the original house became the back section.[6]

For the most part, the plans in this book deal with the major political houses in Ireland in the Georgian period. According to John Bateman's *Great Landowners of Great Britain and Ireland* (published in the 1870s), the largest land holdings in Ireland by the patrons discussed here were held by the duke of Leinster (Carton and Leinster House), the earl of Clanrickarde (Portumna Castle), Viscount Powerscourt (Powerscourt), Viscount Dillon (Lough Glynn) and Viscount Lorton (Rockingham) – all of whose Irish estates were valued at over £50,000.[7] Of the thirty-one patrons for whom figures were published, twenty-five held land valued at over £10,000. Only one landlord, Frederick Hervey, earl-bishop of Bristol, had his principal residence in England.

Using a number of types of evidence it is possible to discover something about how patrons and their architects visualised the house being used, not just on a day-to-day basis but as a stage for entertaining. We can investigate the extent to which the design determined the function of the spaces or conversely how a perceived function might determine the design. Other specifications might include the number and names of rooms that were required, or their location within the plan, as well as the orientation of particular rooms. Was it, for example, important that the breakfast room faced the morning sun, or that the library was north-facing to protect the books? Were separate bedrooms required for the owner and his wife, and was any thought given to sleeping accommodation for servants?

Annotated architectural drawings where room names are indicated have provided much evidence. These plans were not all executed, while some of the houses have disappeared or have been greatly altered, but the drawings give an idea of how the house was meant to function at a certain time. It is has been possible to locate more than two hundred plans for fifty-eight houses, among which are eighty-one ground-floor plans. These range in date from 1730 to 1840 and vary in size from a seven-bay villa to a thirteen-bay house. It is from this body of evidence that conclusions are drawn as to how spaces were arranged within the house.

Household inventories of the period and estimates and invoices for furniture and furnishings bought can provide important information about the contents of specific rooms. The majority of the inventories were made for probate valuations; others were connected to the rental or leasing of the property, or were produced for auctions. Where no reason is given, it is likely that an inventory was made for insurance purposes, and as a record when a person owned more than one house and items were moved between them. Such inventories might be taken by a housekeeper or another member of the household, or by an 'upholder' or valuer in the case of contents being assessed for auction.

Valuers often lumped together numerous items in one room, making it difficult to interpret the purpose of that room. Furthermore, it is not always apparent when an entire room has been ignored, perhaps because the contents belonged to somebody other than the owner of the property, such as the widow. It cannot be assumed, therefore, that an inventory will give a full picture. Nonetheless, these vivid evocations of eighteenth- and nineteenth-century furniture, fittings, fabrics and artworks add colour to our understanding of domestic life of the period and its material culture.[8]

Other sources – letters, diaries, journals and account books – yield immense riches. The ubiquitous Mrs Delany, with her keen eye for detail, regularly goes so far as to give measurements of rooms, and the novels of Maria Edgeworth, Lady Morgan, Anthony Trollope and others are important, particularly for social history.[9]

The Irish way of life in big houses during the long eighteenth century is an essential part of this book. The Irish were particularly renowned for their hospitality and for the numbers of servants they had in their homes. Travel journals are filled with accounts of invitations to dine in houses where tables groaned under the weight of food sufficient for more than twice the number of guests. Large dining room furniture, such as the long sideboards to be seen regularly nowadays in auction houses throughout the country, indicates the importance attached to entertaining in Ireland, as did the inscribed stone on the road close to Clodagh Castle, Co. Cork, belonging to the MacSweeney family, that directed all travellers to repair to Mr Edmund MacSweeney's house for hospitality. Even perfect strangers who desired to 'view' a house and/or its improvements, often without previous notice, were usually welcome.

Sadly, as the Knight of Glin and James Peill point out in *Irish Furniture* (2007), it is rare to find a house in Ireland with a muniment room: the great families of Ireland did not place much importance on the preservation of papers for posterity, with one writer going so far as to say that they disliked showing them to the interested scholar. As a result, a large body of documentation on the building, decorating and furnishing of Irish country houses is lost to researchers. Nevertheless, those documents that are extant paint a broader picture of how owners and their families lived in the Irish country house, how they utilised and furnished the spaces, and how these houses were used for their own entertainment and for that of their friends.

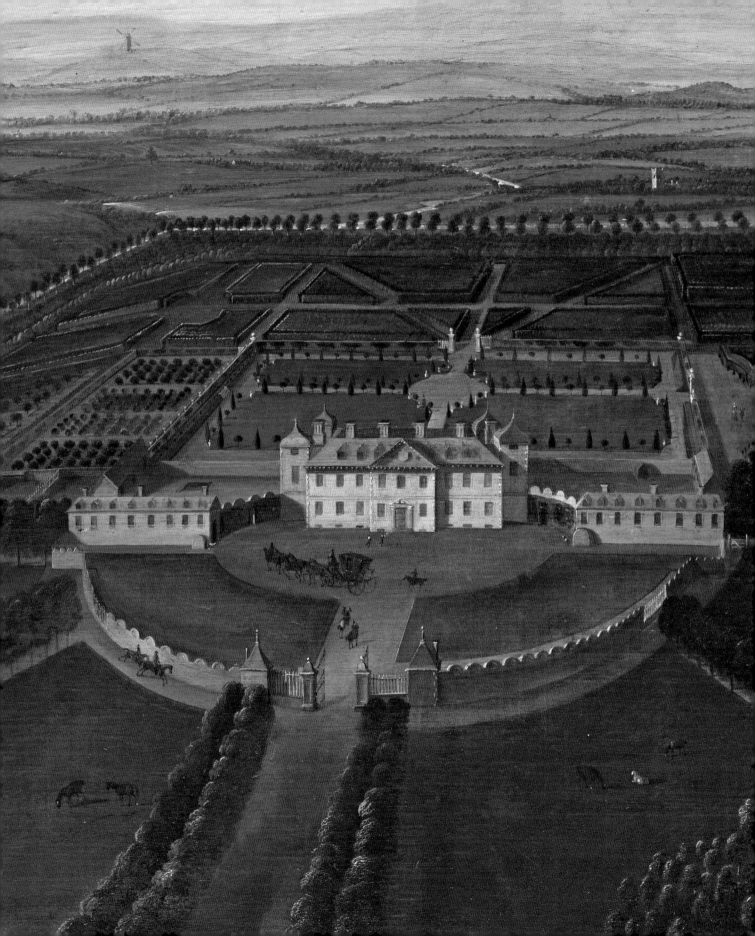

One

Approaching and Arriving

The eighteenth-century country house – the primary home of members of the nobility and gentry – was the centrepiece of a planned landscape, within an estate that included buildings such as stables, outbuildings, follies, gardens (both open and walled) and, often, a planned village at or close to one of its entrance gates. The house in its landscape was the result of a collaboration between architects, landscape theorists, practical gardeners, poets, politicians and artists, where 'layered images, frames and views contrived to augment the intellectual and sensual experience'.[1] This awareness of the location of a house within its surrounding landscape was already well established in England by the beginning of the century. As the century progressed, owners of country houses in Ireland similarly became more conscious of the impression that landscape made on visitors to their houses, gardens and demesnes. Natural landscapes were tailored to the requirements of the created landscape as promoted by the English landscape architect Capability Brown from the mid-century, when follies, rustic cottages and even lakes were built to create interest. The strategic placement of these in laying out walks and the creation of new routes for the entrance avenue all contributed to what was virtually a theatrical experience and a manipulation of viewpoints for visitor and occupier alike. The building of large and small country houses, together with the development of the landscape surrounding them, thus epitomised a provincial mentality or, as the Irish historian Roy Foster put it, 'the Georgian Ascendancy's obsession with laying ostentatious claim to the land'.[2]

Together with its estate, the country house was not only home to the owner and his family, who took up residence only at certain times during the year, but also a destination for visitors, both welcome and unwelcome. These included both those formally invited to stay and friends travelling to and from other parts of Ireland, to whom the overnight hospitality of the house was extended. Unexpected visitors bearing letters of introduction were also generally welcomed, fed and sometimes given a bed for a night. Less welcome, particularly when the family was in residence, might be house tourists: strangers (who sometimes arrived without warning) requesting permission to view the grounds and often the interior of the house.

Gates and lodges

Arrival at a country house invokes feelings of anticipation and expectation in the visitor. The walls surrounding private grounds protect the mystery and exclusivity of the place and the privacy of its owner. During the eighteenth century it became increasingly popular to inject drama into the design of the approach route to the house. From the gate and its (often eye-catching) lodge, picturesque snapshots revealed themselves along an avenue with tantalising glimpses of follies, bridges, lakes and plantations that culminated in the appearance of the house itself.

Even before reaching the gates, visitors were made aware of the presence of the country house by a change in the landscape, with dense plantations of trees set behind the high stone walls that enclosed the demesne. In many cases there was a relationship between the town and the demesne's entrance, such as that at Strokestown Park, Co. Roscommon, where the exceptionally wide main street in the town, laid out by Thomas Mahon MP, 2nd Lord Hartland, in the early nineteenth century, terminates with an impressive Gothic triumphal-arched gateway that leads to the house. Other examples of some degree of formal planning in the relationship of entrance and village are found in Mitchelstown, Co. Cork, Castletown and Carton (both in Co. Kildare) and Glin Castle, Co. Limerick.

The gates and lodges of a country house 'were not merely garden structures, they were designed as entrances, garden buildings on the perimeter to lure respectable visitors to view similar pleasures within' (fig. 2).[3] They played a significant role at a time when appearances were of the utmost importance as a prologue to the main event: in this case, the house. An

2
Entrance gateway to Glananea, Co. Westmeath, watercolour, 1796, signed by the architect Samuel Woolley.

'Tiara' lodge at one of the entrances to Rockingham, Co. Roscommon, built in 1810 to designs by John Nash for the 1st Viscount Lorton.

early reference to a gate lodge was made by the writer and politician Robert Molesworth in a letter to his wife in 1716 about the laying out of the main avenue to their new mansion at Breckdenston, in Swords, Co. Dublin, in which he proposed to construct a 'house by [the] Dublin gate . . . as 'tis done in places of 40 times greater resort all about London and Hampton Court'.[4] This indicates that a gate lodge was an innovation at the time, though the gatehouse has a long history as a defensive building.

There was usually more than one entrance to a large demesne, allowing for a certain amount of architectural variety in gateways and lodges. Rockingham, Co. Roscommon has a two-storey castellated main entrance gateway and lodge combined, and a classical subsidiary entrance gateway behind which is the 'Tiara' lodge with its curved pediment (fig. 3). The variety of gate lodge types demonstrates that owners did not feel it necessary to mimic the architectural style of the house that they guarded. This was the case with the gothick gateways at Ardfert Abbey, Co. Kerry, Castle Martyr, Co. Cork and Tollymore Park, Co. Down. The Rev. Daniel Augustus Beaufort, rector of Collon, Co. Louth and a 'gentleman architect', made a number of tours in Ireland between 1765 and 1810, sometimes accompanied by his wife, Mary, and their daughter, Louisa. In 1788 he described the 'large Gothick gateway' at the entrance to Ardfert Abbey as 'not of a piece with the rest of this old-fashioned place' (figs 4, 5). And he pulled no punches about the earl of Shannon's gateway at Castle Martyr, 'lately built in a very bad stile', nor about the approach and the house itself: 'The Coupe d'oeil on the first entrance is very pleasing but as you advance, the river . . . appears too artificial, the grounds too flat, the woods too young and the adjacent country too poor and flat. The house is very large but not at all handsome—Regular at the front, but not at all so to the lawn.'[5]

The triumphal arch was a popular style of gateway; at houses such as Russborough, Co. Wicklow (built from 1741 by William Leeson, later 1st earl of Milltown), it reflects the classicism of the house itself. The most common style of gate lodge was the classical temple form,

usually to be found, as the majority of lodges were, tucked away inside the gate. However, in Ireland one frequently finds the lodge located on the opposite side of the public road and facing into the gateway, as at Killua Castle, Co. Westmeath, Loughcrew, Co. Meath and Johnstown Castle, Co. Wexford. This was one way of solving the problem of single lodges for a Georgian mind-set ruled by symmetry, and it gained some favour but was rare outside Ireland. Another option was to have a pair, such as those at Beardiville, Co. Antrim, where

4
Gateway to Ardfert Abbey, Co. Kerry.

5
Ardfert Abbey, Co. Kerry, built in the late seventeenth century by Sir Thomas Crosbie, MP and altered in 1720 and 1830.

the single-storey lodges with large Diocletian windows are linked by a pedimented archway. The architect James Gandon's drawing for Emo Court, Co. Laois, dated 1780, shows a pair of lodges complete with smoking chimneys linked by a classical arched gateway, and a design by Thomas Owen for a 'Lodge and Entrance to the Cottage and Plantations at Waterstone' on the Carton estate in Co. Kildare shows a plan of the twin rectangular lodges. At Portumna Castle, Co. Galway, built by Richard de Burgo, 4th earl of Clanrickarde, and completed by 1618, a gothic gateway with twin lodges was installed before 1808 at the end of the axial approach. Another example can be seen in a painting by Robert Woodburn, *The Gates of Belline* (1800), where the gates are attached to two octagonal two-storey stone buildings with central chimneys; smoke is emanating from one chimney and a woman is entering the same building, indicating that it was inhabited (fig. 6). Such pairs were referred to as 'inkpots' and could be found at Ballymenoch and Belvoir Park, both in Co. Down.[6]

In 1787, Beaufort described a gateway to Downhill, Co. Derry (dem.), the palace of Frederick Hervey, 4th earl of Bristol and bishop of Derry, as 'a sort of chinese wooden one only between two piers of two columns and a niche each', which is perhaps more likely to have been the Lion Gate, with statues of snow leopards on top of the piers, than the elegantly classical Bishop's Gate (*c.*1784), which has a lodge placed at rightangles to it. Beaufort's daughter, Louisa, writing in 1807, compared the view of Downhill from three miles away to 'an hospital on the top of a bare hill' and found 'the Avenue most absurd, [the] steepness and length of the ascent to the house, is dangerous . . . a few trees at the gate which is handsome, but the Lodge is gothick'.[7] Near Lismore in Co. Waterford are the turreted gates and castellated bridge of Ballysaggartmore, built by the owner, Arthur Keily, to designs by his gardener (fig. 7). It was intended that this extravagant entrance would lead to a castle, built to upstage the nearby Strancally Castle, which belonged to Mrs Keily's brother-in-law, but by the time that the gateway was complete the money had run out and it appears that the proposed house was never built. A novel idea was found at Affane House, Co. Waterford in the 1790s, where the jawbones of a whale formed the sides and arch of a gateway 'large enough for a coach to drive through'.[8]

6
Robert Woodburn, *The Gates of Belline*, 1800, oil on canvas. Private collection.

7
Ballysaggartmore, Co. Waterford, part of the elaborate gate lodge and folly bridge, 1847.

Avenues and settings

From the early years of the eighteenth century it became fashionable to alter the direction of the main avenue leading to a country house. The axial approach to the baroque house gave way at this time to a more picturesque one, usually from one side, with the house ultimately revealed to the visitor, such as at Castletown and along all 700 feet of Russborough's façade. However, this trend was realised only gradually. Mrs Catherine O'Brien, who managed the O'Brien estates in Co. Clare during her son's minority, was not at the vanguard of fashion at Dromoland House, where, in about 1720, she designed 'a straight Avenue to ye Hall door'.[9] The approach to the old house at Stradbally, Co. Laois as depicted in a painting dating to about 1740 was similarly designed (figs 8, 9). A carriage and entourage can be seen making their way from the road, along an avenue leading to a gateway (consisting of a curved wall and two gateposts) which gives access to the main avenue. This avenue, on the axis of the house, has a low wall on each side and extends to a gateway to one side of the house which opens into a large courtyard, beyond which are the stables. The parkland and garden, it will be noted, are designed to emphasise the new house (built by the owner, Pole Cosby, in the 1730s), with its pedimented front, projecting end bays and Venetian windows, as their

8

*Stradbally House, Co. Laois, c.*1740, oil on canvas. Private collection.

9
Detail of *Stradbally House, Co. Laois.*

10
Portumna Castle, Co. Galway, built 1618 by Richard Burke, 4th earl of Clanrickarde. Aerial view showing two of the three courts at the entrance front.

centrepiece, shifting the old-fashioned tower with its tower house (dating to *c.*1699) to one side. This gave the house two entrances, one in the tower house, the grander one, to the new house, approached through a gateway in the wall separating the old from the new forecourt. The axial arrangement can still be seen at Portumna Castle, where the approach is 'through a progression of three courts entered by stone gateways of different architectural periods' (fig. 10).[10]

At Breckdenston, the approach to the old house was an axial one from the west, but in 1716 (probably the same time that the Palladian house was built) Robert Molesworth replaced it as the principal approach by a curving route lined with lime trees from the south-west of the demesne, where curved walls and gates were set back from the Dublin road.[11] All of this served not only to give greater privacy to the house but to manage the approach route in such a way that visitors, as they made their way to the heart of the estate, would be impressed by the improvements made by the owner.

Unlike at Breckdenston, where Molesworth chose not to link his house directly to the village of Swords, Castletown, the largest and the earliest of Ireland's Palladian houses, (begun in 1722, to designs by Alessandro Galilei and Edward Lovett Pearce, and built for William Conolly MP, Speaker of the Irish House of Commons), and Carton, the country seat of the FitzGeralds, earls of Kildare and later the dukes of Leinster (remodelled in 1739 by Richard Castle), both in Co. Kildare, are connected by avenues of lime trees to their respective estate towns of Celbridge and Maynooth. Both originally had axial approaches from the south (fig. 11). In the 1750s Emily FitzGerald, the young countess of Kildare, wrote that her husband had recently 'cut down the avenue south of the house' at Carton, making 'a very fine lawn before [it]'; in the 1760s a new approach route from Dublin was created, diluting the importance of the Dunboyne avenue to the north, which then became a service

11

William van der Hagen (d. 1745), *View of Carton, Co. Kildare,* showing the early house prior to its remodelling in 1739 to designs by the architect Richard Castle. Private collection.

2

Belvedere, Co. Westmeath, built *c.*1740 by Richard Castle for Robert Rochfort, later 1st earl of Belvedere.

entrance.[12] Emily's sister, Lady Louisa Conolly, built the Batty Langley lodge in 1772 at the entrance to Castletown from the Dublin road, making this the main entrance from the capital, and one that meandered sufficiently to give visitors ample opportunity to admire their surroundings.[13] Such an approach was similarly experienced by a visitor to Bellamont Forest, Co. Cavan in 1778, who described the avenue there as 'more than a mile long . . . on the right a small but pleasing lake almost surrounded with wood and when you lose sight of that a river on your left opens to your view and forms itself into a vast lake'.[14]

The lime trees that had frequently lined early avenues like rows of soldiers became unfashionable in the face of the more informal, though still contrived, landscapes. However, Lord Chief Baron Edward Willes wrote in 1762 that the two-mile-long avenue leading to Rockfield, Seapoint in Co. Dublin had 'a cut-hedge on each side'. This sounds rather unusual, but hedging was often used to camouflage the shoots that frequently grew from the trunks of lime trees. Willes's two-mile stretch of avenue pales into insignificance when compared to that of the MP and landowner Richard Martin at Ballynahinch Castle in Connemara, Co. Galway: he owned so much of Connemara that he could boast of having an approach from his gatehouse to his house of twenty-six miles. At Belan, Co. Kildare, seat of the earls of Aldborough, there were six avenues of approach, each a mile in length and with two porter's lodges to each gateway.[15]

Many visitors remarked on the position of country houses and the views they had, and also supplied a general, or frequently particular, impression of the architecture. Invariably, comparisons were drawn with English counterparts. George Hardinge, the English judge and writer, compared Irish seats favourably to those in England: 'I see as much taste and as much <u>neatness</u> without or within to the full as in <u>England</u> accompanied with <u>more</u> beauty of <u>exterior</u> for they are <u>all</u> of them white and grey – slated at the top seldom irregular and hardly ever ill situated.'[16] The agriculturalist Arthur Young thought Lord Belvedere's villa on the shores of Lough Ennell in Co. Westmeath as impressive a combination of house and setting

as any he had ever seen (fig. 12).[17] Lord Shannon's seat at Castle Martyr was admired by the French tourist the Chevalier de Latocnaye in the 1790s as 'one of the most beautiful and best cared-for places, not merely in Ireland, but, perhaps, in Europe', but Daniel Beaufort was not overly impressed, describing it in 1806 as 'well-dressed and in nice order, but totally destitute of picturesque beauty'.[18]

A few travellers, such as the Beauforts, left interesting accounts of buildings that sometimes included observations on the interior layouts, while many commented on the general appearance of a house within its landscape. Mary Beaufort described Portumna Castle as 'an immense pile of Building', but she liked the forecourts and gates, especially the 'Gate of entrance from the road, very pretty and light'. Her daughter, Louisa, was economical with words, in 1807 summarising Lord Gosford's house in Co. Armagh as: 'house seems indifferent, gateway frightful . . . stands low, has no view of the mountains . . . very old, plan odd, ill furnished'.[19] In an amusing passage in her memoir, the writer Frances Power Cobbe, a descendant of the archbishop and primate of Ireland Charles Cobbe, contrasts the appearance of Newbridge, the family home in Co. Dublin, with Turvey, a house belonging to Lord Trimleston on the adjoining estate, in anthropomorphic terms: Newbridge 'is bright and smiling and yet dignified; bosomed among its old trees and with the green, wide-spreading park opened out before the noble granite perron of the hall door . . . it has as open and honest a countenance as its neighbour has the reverse'; Turvey, however, 'is really a wicked-looking house with half-moon windows which suggest leering eyes' (figs 13, 14).[20]

13
Turvey, Donabate, Co. Dublin.

14
Newbridge, Donabate, Co. Dublin.

CURRAGHMORE.Co.WATERFORD.74.W.L.

5
Curraghmore, Portlaw, Co. Waterford. Entrance
through the double row of offices admired by
Daniel Beaufort.

The house entrance

Before moving on to the entrance to the house itself, mention should be made of the fore-court at Curraghmore, Co. Waterford (seat of the marquess of Waterford), designed by John Roberts 1750–60 and described as the finest in Ireland (fig. 15).[21] Beaufort admired it too: 'The Entrance now is through the double row of Magnificent Offices each side containing 26 doors and windows one great gate and four coach houses.'[22] It dates from the mid-eigh-teenth century, is French in style and is unique in Ireland: a counterpart in Britain would be Seaton Delaval in Northumberland.[23] The effect of the house, with its central three-storey tower crowned with a stag (the family emblem), wings projecting forward and the stable ranges on each side with massive central triumphal-arched gateways, is much in the ba-roque style of the architect Sir John Vanbrugh.

Mrs Mary Delany was another eagle-eyed reporter on architectural details and an avid let-ter-writer.[24] In 1744 she described her Dublin house, Delville, in Glasnevin, in a letter to her sister as standing 'on a rising ground', with an ample forecourt, 'large enough for a coach and six to drive round commodiously'; the house was five bays wide and of two storeys, with six steps leading to a hall door beneath a portico.[25] A drawing dated 1754 (fig. 16) shows the

pedimented 'portico' as one bay wide and apparently projecting over the steps, but it is similar to what would later be called a porch. Mrs Delany describes the practical value of her portico in sheltering visitors from rain, enabling them to step out of their carriage at the foot of the steps directly under cover and so up to the hall door.

Not many owners of 'middle-sized' houses could afford a portico.[26] It was the feature of the great English Palladian houses that gave them their air of grandeur, and, being designed for an Italian climate, it was an asset in sunny weather when one could sit beneath it, shaded from the sun. Furthermore, the shade it provided protected the furniture and furnishings in the rooms behind from fading. However, it had drawbacks that may have been observed by the Irish: in the wet Irish (and English) climate it made the rooms behind it dark, and it dripped rain, creating a slippery flight of steps for the visitor.[27] A tripartite elevation, with a concentration of architectural detail on the central section, was therefore generally preferred to a giant order of columns or a portico, this treatment being given to many of his houses by the architect Richard Castle.[28] But eighteenth-century examples of the free-standing portico are to be found at Bellamont Forest (*c.*1728; fig. 17) and at Seafield, Donabate, Co. Dublin (begun between 1737 and 1741).

A solution that eliminated the problems caused by wind and rain can be seen in an unexecuted plan by the Scottish architect James Byres for Charles William Bury, 1st earl of Charleville, at Charleville Forest, Co. Offaly, which dates to 1789. On it is inscribed 'Passage with a landing under cover for Carriages': the carriage could make its way across the broad forecourt and into an opening in the curved and covered corridor that linked the house with the stable pavilion, deposit its passengers and continue into the stable yard (fig. 18).

Porticoes became a little more common in the following century at houses such as Garbally, Co. Galway (1819), Ballyfin, Co. Laois (1822) and Loughcrew (1823) and Annesbrook

16
Letitia Bushe (d. 1757), *A View of Delville from beyond the Ever-Green Grove*, 1754. Bushe was an intimate friend of Mary Delany.

17
Bellamont Forest, Co. Cavan (*c.*1728), often described as a perfect Palladian villa, was designed by Sir Edwa Lovett Pearce for Thomas Coote, Lord Justice of the King's Bench in Ireland.

18
James Byres (1734–1817), unexecuted ground-floor plan of Charleville Forest, Tullamore, Co. Offaly, 178 for the 1st earl of Charleville. The entrance for the carriage into the covered passage can be seen in the left-hand quadrant.

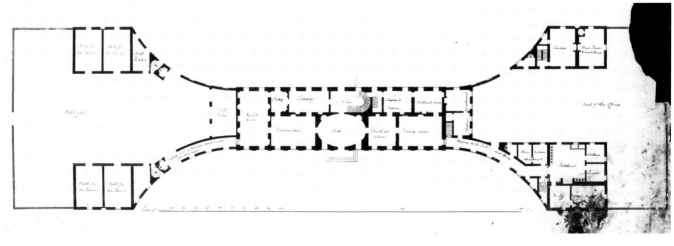

(where a Georgian front was added to an earlier house), both in Co. Meath. Towards the middle of the nineteenth century, many porticoes were added to houses that their owners believed were old-fashioned, lending them a stylish neo-classical air.[29] The double-height portico at Mount Shannon, Co. Limerick (remodelled after 1813 by the 2nd earl of Clare) was large enough to act as a porte-cochère, as were those at Rockingham (added *c*.1822) and Baronscourt, Co. Tyrone (*c*.1835). In the same county, at Killymoon Castle (built in 1803 for William Stewart MP and described as 'one of the most brilliant examples of the Picturesque Castle style evolved by John Nash and one of the earliest'[30]), the porte-cochère (fig. 19) made quite an impression on Louisa Beaufort in 1807: 'the grand entrance is a portico so large that the carriage drives under it and receives its company dry, it is formed by two highly ornamented pillars, fluted and supported by octagonal bases of rougher free stone, the pillars are dressed smooth'.[31] The north-facing entrance front at Sir Robert Gore-Booth's Lissadell, Co. Sligo (1831–3, designed by the London architect Francis Goodwin) has been described as 'a classical temple front adapted, and naturalised, to Atlantic instead of Mediterranean conditions' (fig. 20).[32] Its porte-cochère was designed to lessen the effects of such weather by being, if necessary, entirely enclosed. Its functionality was noted with approval by a visitor shortly after it was built: 'there is a most comfortable covered landing place for carriages

19

Killymoon Castle, Cookstown, Co. Tyrone, designed by John Nash, *c*.1801–3.

Francis Goodwin, 'Lissadell. The Seat of Sir Robert
Gore Booth, Bart', 1833. Francis Goodwin, *Rural
Architecture* (2nd edn, London 1835), pl. 32.

(with folding doors and 3 windows) so that your horses may wait for the ladies in great comfort, if the wind and rain come from the north and south at the same moment. You descend upon a marble slab and marble steps lead up to the door.'[33]

Arriving in pouring rain at houses such as Castletown and Russborough, and endeavouring to mount their flights of steps to the entrance, must have been uncomfortable, particularly for women. A visitor to Castletown in 1797 described the 'grand stone steps, about twenty in number, fifty feet wide, and a balustrade at each side, projecting boldly from the house into the lawn; upon each side of the hall door, when you ascend these steps, is a green garden chair, each capable of affording rest to six persons'.[34] Even with the help of an umbrella held by a servant, it would have been challenging. Umbrellas were used for ladies from the beginning of the eighteenth century: Jonathan Swift refers to one in 'A Description of a City Shower', printed in *The Tatler* in October 1710:

The tuck'd up seamstress walks with hasty strides
While streams run down her oil'd umbrella's sides.

However, as late as the 1790s it was still considered effeminate for a man to carry an umbrella (at least in Ireland), though the French traveller de Latocnaye was unperturbed to find himself an object of ridicule when he carried his.[35]

In late seventeenth- and early eighteenth-century houses in Britain the main (hall) doors were surprisingly little used, with most visitors entering through a side door or at a lower level. This left the forecourt free from the sounds of horses and from the marks of coach wheels, and the windows free from overlooking such comings and goings. The arrangement was also convenient from an interior planning point of view as it gave more direct access to the everyday parts of the house, leaving the more formal rooms undisturbed.[36] At Stradbally House, for example, it would appear from the painting (*see* figs 8, 9) that only the most

21
Anon., *A Bird's Eye View of Howth Castle*,
Co. Dublin (detail), n.d. Private collection.

formal occasion would warrant an arrival at the main door, as the forecourt is almost closed off by what look like two rectangles of grass, and is terminated by a canal. In a painting of Howth Castle, Co. Dublin (home to the St Lawrence family for eight centuries and enlarged by William St Lawrence, 14th Baron Howth), a generous forecourt can be seen, extending from which is an ornamental garden with pond and gravel walk terminated, as at Stradbally, by a canal (fig. 21). Some people on horseback have already entered the forecourt and look as if they are about to ride across it to the opposite gate, while a lone horseman approaches the first gate. The man standing just inside the gate at the arched doorway of a square tower, behind which is the stable yard, may be the stable hand or groom, waiting to take the horse from the rider.

The amateur architect and writer Roger North, writing at the end of the seventeenth century, refers to entrances other than the principal one while making it clear that he does not approve of 'keeping company from the forecourt', thinking it absurd that a stranger arriving at the house, and finding the main entrance closed, has to find another. He believes that the forecourt requires a 'higher pitch of neatness' than does the stable yard, so it should 'endure comon using'. He is also in favour of a back entrance, not only for the servants' use but also important for the master to survey the comings and goings of his staff, and to deal with them (and 'other mean persons') without bothering his guests or interfering with the more formal part of his house. Stressing the need for the back entrance to be 'cheerfull', as it will be used by the family, North says that it should be located so that, in the event of heavy rain, a coach can conveniently draw close to it and pick up or deposit a visitor.[37]

22

George Barret RA (*c.*1728/32–1784), *A View of Powerscourt, Co. Wicklow*, 1760–2, oil on canvas. Yale Center for British Art, Paul Mellon Collection.

Of course, North was writing at a time before the Palladian plan – with a main block and two wings – came into fashion in the 1720s in England. The pavilions at Castletown accommodate the kitchen to one side and the stables to the other, the purposes assigned to them by Palladio in his sixteenth-century villas in the Veneto, a custom that was followed in Ireland but not generally in England.[38] Here, 'for such guests as arrived late on horseback, or required a meal before making an early start', there was a doorway from the stable yard into the colonnade, leading to a room, probably in the east pavilion.[39] Beaufort mentions that the 'usual' entrance to Downhill was by the back door, under the staircase, leading into a corridor which ran the length of the house.[40]

In Britain, a separate entrance for family and informal occasions was often to be found at a lower level, a point that deserves a brief digression. The 'lower level' is understood to

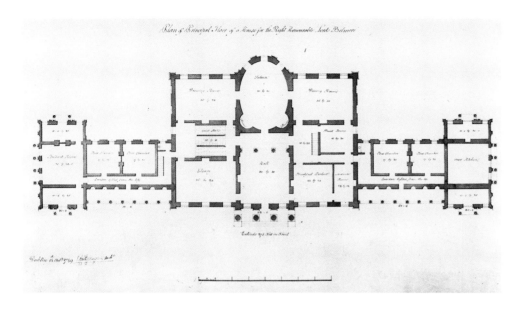

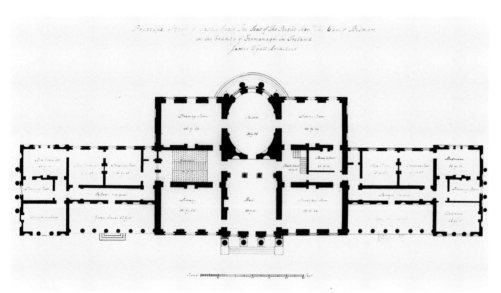

mean, in this case, the ground floor of a house, or 'the rustic[k]' as it was frequently called in England, where the *piano nobile* is on the first floor and a flight of steps leads to the main door at that level. This was not at all common in Ireland, where the 'lower level' meant a basement. In Britain, family rooms and rooms for informal entertaining were often at ground level, leaving the rooms of parade upstairs for formal use. An example of this was Colen Campbell's Wanstead House, London (from 1713), where a doorway was placed at the centre of the rusticated base and a staircase on each side led to the temple front and the main door.[41] The English architect Isaac Ware describes a basement that is 'not under ground entirely, it is let in some feet below the surface and usually and very properly built in front with rustick work'. This is a kind of half-basement that keeps the first-floor apartments free from

23
Richard Johnston (1759–1806), *Plan of Principal Floor of a House for the Right Honorable Lord Belmore* (Castle Coole, Co. Fermanagh), 1789.

24
James Wyatt (1746–1813), *Principal Story of Castle Coole the Seat of The Right Honbl. The Earl of Belmore*, 1790.

5

mes FitzGerald, earl of Kildare (later 1st duke of
einster), plan of Carton, Co. Kildare, 1762.

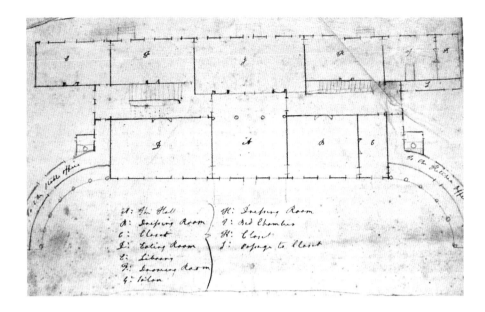

25
James FitzGerald, earl of Kildare (later 1st duke of Leinster), plan of Carton, Co. Kildare, 1762.

damp, while the lower floor is used for everyday family life and 'keeps the servants near the body of the house'.[42] It seemed of no concern to Ware that the family might have to endure damp quarters. The Irish basement may have had a triple origin – partly defensive, partly as a type of damp course and partly as a plinth. In classical architecture the plinth supports the order, but in Ireland that is more often notional rather than expressed by columns or pilasters.[43] An exception is perhaps at Powerscourt, Co. Wicklow (built 1731–40 to the design of Richard Castle, for Richard Wingfield, MP, later 1st Viscount Powerscourt), where the main entrance is in the centre of the rusticated plinth that supports the order, and the *piano nobile* is on the floor above (fig. 22).

There can be no doubt that, in the majority of cases, there were side entrances into houses for the use of the family and those calling on business, but there is not much documentary evidence to support this in the architectural plans under consideration. There are also very few back or garden entrances on the plans, which might lead one to the conclusion that these were implied – that a window opening could easily be converted into a doorway. A Scottish visitor to Ireland, Robert Graham, mentions a separate entrance into the family apartments at the earl of Belmore's Castle Coole, Co. Fermanagh from the west colonnade, which can be seen on the drawings by both Richard Johnston (1789) and the architect who replaced him in 1790, James Wyatt (figs 23, 24).[44] In an early drawing for the same house by Richard Castle, dated to after 1730, there are doorways from the stable yards into the sides of the house.[45] Some plans for Carton also show side entrances. In a plan purported to be by Lord Kildare and dated to 1762 (fig. 25), access points to the house from the stable yard are clear;[46] in another plan, which was closest to what was built, the house has acquired a doorway and flight of steps to the centre of its west side (fig. 26). Another plan by Castle, for Lord Headfort's eponymous seat in Co. Meath (unexecuted, fig. 27), shows the 'Great Gate into the Stable yard' to the right of the forecourt, and a 'back entry' from the 'arcade of communication' on that side, leading into the east wing. A plan by Sir William Chambers, also for Headfort (unexecuted, fig. 28), shows side entrances to the house from the forecourt, one in each quadrant, up double flights of steps, as well as access from the stable yard to the house via a curved passage behind the east arcade.

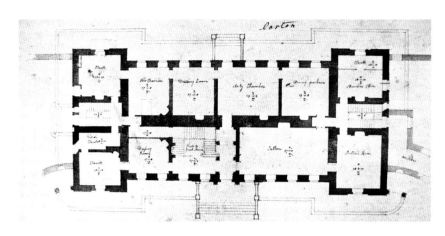

Carton

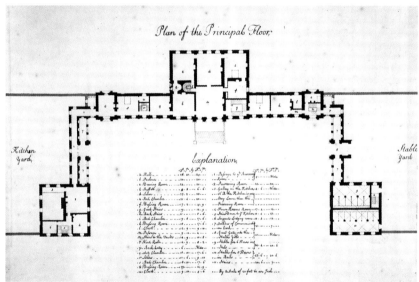

Plan of the Principal Floor.

Explanation.

Kitchen Yard,

Stable Yard,

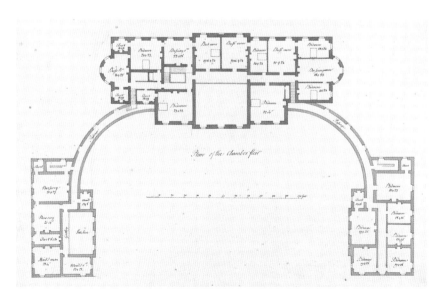

Plan of the Chamber floor

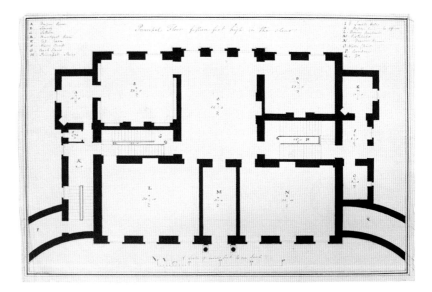

Frequently the owner of the house would ensure that his dressing room or study was close to the side or back entrance, so that people coming to the house on business were not required to use the main entrance. At Ardbraccan, Co. Meath (1773–4, palace of the Church of Ireland bishops of Meath), the plan of the principal or ground floor has a door on the east side leading into a 'small hall' (fig. 29), off which to one side is a water closet and to the other a 'Coffee Room', where the bishops of Meath might have conducted some business, rather than bringing visitors to the library and dressing room at the far side of the house.

The family

Families moved from the city to the country (or vice versa) or from England to their Irish house(s) at different times in the year. They might, for example, stay in Dublin when parliament was sitting, where they could enjoy the social whirl that went hand in glove with it, transferring to the country for hunting, shooting and, usually, to celebrate Christmas. Moving from one house to another meant travelling as a small cavalcade with servants. Often items such as linen and pieces of furniture and furnishing were transported in advance. When Lord Buttevant (heir to the earl of Barrymore) and his lady were removing from Dublin to Castle Lyons, Co. Cork in 1738, he travelled with a friend in a chaise and six, while Lady Buttevant was accompanied by her maid in a landau and six, 'with led horses alongside and three or four servants'.[47] Dean and Mrs Delany journeyed from their Dublin home to that in Co. Down in three conveyances – they in their chaise, the cook and housemaid in the coach and four, and another maid 'in a car we have had made for marketing and carrying luggage when we travel'.[48] But sometimes the cavalcade was not so small. According to a newspaper report (probably from the early nineteenth century) on the Hamiltons' month-long journey between Baronscourt, Co. Tyrone and London, their suite consisted of thirty-three persons in a cavalcade of four carriages and ten outriders. The latter comprised grooms and footmen whose job was to ride ahead of the carriages to ensure that all was in order at

26
Richard Castle (d. 1751), plan of Carton, Co. Kildare, 1739.

27
Richard Castle (d. 1751), plan of the principal floor (Headfort, Kells, Co. Meath), unexecuted, n.d.

28
Sir William Chambers RA (1723–96), plan of the chamber floor (Headfort), unexecuted, 1765.

29
Thomas Cooley (?1742–84), ground-floor plan of Ardbraccan, Co. Meath, 1773–4.

the various inns at which they stayed; the major domo and cook would arrive at the inn in the morning.[49]

    The domestic arrangements put in place to prepare for expected arrivals, whether the family, a bride or a viceroy, were fairly standard. Correspondence between owner and steward (or housekeeper) gives a good idea of the minute detail of the instructions given, so that little was left to chance. In anticipation of one of his rare visits to Baronscourt, the 8th earl of Abercorn, an absentee landlord, wrote from England to his agent in Tyrone in September 1745 with instructions for his arrival due to take place in the late spring or early summer, following a week or so spent in Dublin.[50] The agent was to 'employ either one of the workmen's wives whom you can trust, or some other discreet body, to make fires once a week, or as often as there may be occasion, to keep the house well aired all this winter'. In February 1745/6 turf was to be cut for fires in the house 'that it may be dry early', and the following month a ship was secured that could take Abercorn's coach and most, if not all, of his horses to Dublin. Ale and small beer was to be brewed at the house and two maids were to be engaged. The earl also urged his agent to check that the road leading to his demesne was now complete for the safety of his coach. Securing suitable accommodation for the family's stay in Dublin was difficult, not only because parliament was sitting (when prices 'are vastly extravagant') but 'especially as they must be furnished with table linen which is as I am informed seldom expected, and will much enhance the price'. Abercorn's Dublin agent was eventually successful, and gave instructions for hay, straw, beer and coals to be laid in and for the bedchambers to be aired for a couple of days before the earl's arrival. In April 1749 the earl instructed his agent at Baronscourt to buy two cows and to order poultry 'to be fatted for me', and to keep fires in the saloon and his bedchamber every day until his arrival. Similar instructions were sent in advance almost sixty years later in 1807 by his nephew and heir (created 1st marquis of Abercorn in 1790). Along with fatting the calf and filling the cellars,

Carton, Co. Kildare, original entrance front.

EMILY, COUNTESS OF KILDARE.   JAMES EARL OF KILDARE.

more mundane orders had to be fulfilled, such as the 'half a ton of good soap to be season-
ing against yr Lordship's coming over, which with 8 hundred weight sent before, will . . . be a
pretty good stock', and six hundredweight of 'different sizes of candles to be drying'.[51]

Cold and damp were persistent problems in houses. Many references are made by travellers in journals and correspondence regarding damp beds in both inns and houses.[52] At
Dublin Castle in 1758 the surveyor general, Thomas Eyre, worried that the new state apartments would not be sufficiently dry for the return of the viceroy, the duke of Bedford. As soon
as the roof went on he kept fires in every room day and night and even had workmen sleep in
the rooms, as a test. A further test involved the use of paper: 'I find that Paper pinned against
the Wall all Night, contracts so little Dampness or Moisture therefrom, that it is perfectly
dry and fit to be wrote upon the Next Day without the Ink sinking into it.'[53] Emily Fitzgerald,
duchess of Leinster, implored her daughter Lucy to delay her arrival at Leinster House in
Dublin until her bed there had been aired by the housekeeper, who was instructed to sleep
in it for a week before her arrival.[54] Following that, a maid should sleep in it for a couple of
nights, after which she should bring word to Lucy of its condition.[55] The Fitzgeralds preferred to spend their time at their much-loved country house, Carton, on which Emily spent
time and money creating a comfortable and beautiful home and demesne for her family (figs
30, 31). Her granddaughter Lady Isabella FitzGerald remembered with fondness the delight
of the family's arrival at Carton every spring, describing it as 'remarkably well situated . . . a
pleasing object from every part of the Park where it could be seen'.[56]

Though his episcopal residence was in Elphin, Co. Roscommon, Bishop Edward Synge's
homecoming was to his house in Kevin Street, Dublin, where his motherless young daughter, Alicia, lived with a governess/companion and a full staff. He ran the house from his
bishop's palace by proxy through numerous letters to Alicia. While this was not a country
house, it is worth investigating because it helps us to understand the context of the country
house as an occasional residence (or, in this case, an official residence and the bishop's place
of work), and there are similarities in the preparations for impending visits regarding food,
wines and silver. The difference is the fact that Synge sent these instructions to his daughter
and included some rather personal requests that might be more conveniently carried out at

his Dublin residence. A man of taste and learning, his main concern for his homecoming was for the provision of food and silver for his table, and the brewing of quantities of ale for his cellar, where his discerning taste in wine and champagne was evident. His instructions regarding the brewing were precise in the letter about his imminent arrival in September 1750. The brewer was to 'lay in some Ale . . . try to prevail on him to brew some Ale on purpose, such as you know I like, pale, soft, smooth, and not too bitter and lay in some, three or four half Barrels, as soon as brew'd and continue afterwards to lay in one every week to be ready to succeed them'.

Synge's stay in Dublin each autumn prompted a similar letter every year: John (his steward at Kevin Street) was to be given the receipt from 'one of the little Drawers in the Scriptoire' with which to collect the 'Plate-chest' from Lennox's (where it was presumably in safe keeping); beef had to be ordered; in 1749 there was a very specific request for Will (Alicia's manservant) to 'secure Hamilton the Corn-cutter to be with me on Sunday morning. Both my Toes and Hair will want his hand.' On the day of his arrival, he told his daughter, he would dine with her at about 4 pm: 'some Sole, Whiting, or other good Sea Fish will be a treat' but there must also be roast mutton and a couple of roasted fowl. She was also required to 'provide plentifully for the Servants who will be hungry'. Synge cautioned her against a youthful, enthusiastic welcome for him, telling her not to run out into the courtyard to greet him but to 'have a good fire in the great parlour, and there receive me'.[57] His letters to Alicia are very tender, as he, conscious of her lack of a mother's hand, gently guided her into adulthood and maturity, and, of course, towards a suitable marriage.

The servants

For servants the house was their workplace and, in many cases, where they lived. They could gain access to it through the kitchen and stable yards. Most country houses had farms attached to them, often literally, and it would not do to have various errands connected to the running of the farm displayed in full view from the elegant interiors of the mansions. Underground tunnels were therefore provided to prevent such eyesores. One leading from the area to the offices is indicated on Lovett Pearce's plan for Bellamont Forest (*c.*1728), an early example of what became 'a well-established Irish device' by the end of the century.[58] It was not, however, unknown in England: examples were to be found at Petworth, West Sussex, Wolterton Hall, Norfolk and Belton House, Lincolnshire. At Ardbraccan the stable and farm yards are joined by a tunnel running under the garden terrace; one leads from the kitchen in Castle Coole to stables and offices, and there is a similar arrangement at Strokestown Park (fig. 32).[59] Also in Roscommon, Rockingham (designed by John Nash for General Robert King, 1st Viscount Lorton) had a complex series of subterranean tunnels. One led from the house to the lakeside, where fuel arrived by boat; another was for goods arriving by land, its entrance 100 yards away from the house; the third was for servants.[60] Robert Graham describes how the turf made its journey to the fireplaces of the house: 'There is a canal of communication with the bog, from which the supply of turf comes and which is brought in through the lake by a subterranean communication, which ends at a square shaft by which the fuel may be hoisted up by machinery thro' the interior of the house.'[61] At Pakenham Hall (later Tullynally Castle), Co. Westmeath, a special tunnel was created that bypassed the stable yard in order to prevent flirting between laundry maids and stablehands.[62] Maria Edgeworth, in her novel *Ormond* (1817), describes how, after his death, Sir Ulick O'Shane's body was carried through the underground passage that led to the stables and out by the lane to the churchyard.[63] Tunnels were not unknown in Dublin houses either:

32

Strokestown Park, Co. Roscommon, service tunnel from the stable yard to the side of the house.

33
Francis Wheatley, *The Earl of Aldborough Reviewing
Volunteers at Belan House, County Kildare*, 1782
(later changes *c.*1787; later extensions *c.*1810);
oil on canvas; Waddesdon, The Rothschild Collection
(The National Trust).

number 25 Merrion Street (now 5 Upper Merrion Street) was connected to the mews at the rear by an underground passage.

The advantages to owners of houses such as Rockingham, Bellamont Forest, Castle Coole and Lissadell were that, like pieces of sculpture, their properties were designed to be seen 'in the round', with servants and offices firmly out of sight and from every window a view of the surrounding countryside, as the poet William Butler Yeats wrote:

> The light of evening, Lissadell
> Great windows open to the south.[64]

Ceremonial arrival

Edward Augustus Stratford, 2nd earl of Aldborough, left nothing to chance when arranging his homecoming to Belan, Co. Kildare following his marriage in 1788 (fig. 33). In a letter to his agent he wrote that he and his new bride, Anne Elizabeth, daughter of Sir John Henniker and niece of the duchess of Chandos, together with members of her wealthy family, would expect an appropriate welcome. The party were to be 'received at Ballimore [*sic*] by a small corps of Light Horse, at Stratford by a ditto of Light Foot, at Baltinglass, by a ditto of Artillery, and escorted from thence to Belan by a ditto of Grenadiers and Light Horse; or

the Grenadiers at Ballimore, and the Light Horse to go from Baltinglass . . . they need not consist of more than twelve each corps and the officers'. Anxious not to lose face before his new in-laws, Aldborough listed the entertainment required, beginning with theatricals: 'two Tragedies, two Comedies, two Musical and two other farces, the choice I leave to yourselves, but beg you'll all be up in your parts, and no disappointment'. While amateur theatricals, with parts played by the members of the family and their friends, were very popular in the latter part of the century, the players in this case were to be from among the earl's company of soldiers.[65] He required 'balls as usual, some Concerts, and a Fête Champêtre . . . I hope my towns of Stratford and Baltinglass will make a figure as they pass through, be neat and clean, the . . . church covered in, and Baltinglass new bridge completed.' With a month's notice, it seemed a rather tall order for the agent, but then the new countess brought with her 'Fifty thousand pounds hard cash down, and will at her Father's and Aunt's death succeed to one hundred and fifty thousand more'.[66]

To impress his bride, Valentine Lawless, 2nd Baron Cloncurry, who was returning to Ireland in 1805 after a sojourn on the Continent, planned a somewhat different arrival at his house, Lyons, Co. Kildare (fig. 34): it was to be at night. His agent was instructed to have each window to the front of the house lit with five candles of tallow, making a total of 190, while all thirty candles in the dining room and the library were to be of wax: 'that will cost about £40 or thereabouts'.[67] But it meant that the local populace – tenants, villagers, servants and

34
Aerial view of Lyons, Co. Kildare, built 1797 for Nicholas Lawless, 1st Baron Cloncurry.

Castletown House, Celbridge, Co. Kildare.

labourers – were deprived of the more customary, daytime arrival of a bride, when all could see her.

In 1733, the newly married Lady Anne Conolly, daughter of the 1st earl of Strafford, of Wentworth Castle in Yorkshire, arrived in Ireland with her husband, William, and proceeded to Castletown, the house that William was to inherit on the death of the formidable Mrs Katherine Conolly, the widow of his uncle, Speaker Conolly (fig. 35). No description of her arrival at the house has come to light but she apparently settled in remarkably well, according to a letter written by William to her father after their arrival: 'Lady Anne and I have continued here with the good old Lady, ever since we landed and I can with pleasure say that your daughter has quite got the length of her foot.'[68] Bearing in mind Lady Anne's background, her description of Castletown at about this time is of interest, as the house was begun eleven years earlier: '[It] is so very unfinished without doors, I don't think the place very pleasant, though the house is really a charming one to live in . . . [the] front is quite without ornaments of any sort, not even so much as pediments over the windows . . . altogether it looks very well. At least here it does, where there are but few places any way like a seat.'[69]

The viceroy

Members of the upper class were regular attendees at functions at Dublin Castle, where they could and did extend invitations to the lord lieutenant and his wife to visit their homes. In many cases, these invitations would be accepted in due course, with prior notice sent to the prospective host. It was considered a great honour to welcome the viceroy to one's house. Sometimes it was intended as an informal visit, such as dropping in to Mrs Delany's house for breakfast with little notice; at other times it was a formal arrival, complete with lavish entertainment laid on (at huge expense). Mrs Delany was not too perturbed when the viceroy and his wife, Lord and Lady Chesterfield, sent word early on 21 October 1745 that they would like to breakfast with her and Dean Delany at Delville, Glasnevin, at eleven o'clock that morning: 'To work went all my maids, stripping covers off the chairs, sweeping, dusting, and by eleven my house was as spruce as a cabinet of curiosities, and well bestowed on their Excellencies, who commended and admired, and were as polite as possible. They came soon after eleven in their travelling coach, with only two footmen [and two guests] . . . They staid till near two, and my Lord Lieut and the Dean had a great deal of conversation.' Before his departure from Ireland in April 1746, Lord Chesterfield desired to bid a personal farewell to the Delanys by dining with them, for which they had one day's notice, received while dining at the bishop of Clogher's residence. Mrs Delany immediately dispatched a messenger to Delville, with a note to her housekeeper to inform her that she was to prepare for a dinner the following day 'of seven and nine' (the number of dishes, for two courses), and a dessert. Chesterfield's successor (and half-brother), William Stanhope, earl of Harrington, also breakfasted with the Delanys. He came in October 1747 with two attendants, to be met at the 'street-door' by the dean and at the bottom of the stairs by Mrs Delany. As was customary,

36
V. Green, *Mary Isabella, duchess of Rutland*; mezzotint after Sir Joshua Reynolds, 1780.

37
W. Dickinson, *Charles Manners, 4th duke of Rutland*; mezzotint after Sir Joshua Reynolds, 1791.

she went next day to Dublin Castle to thank the viceroy for honouring them with a visit. In 1752 Mrs Delany proposed to invite the duke and duchess of Dorset to breakfast rather than dinner, providing the weather was fine. Dinners, she felt, 'are grown such luxurious feasts in this country that we do not pretend to show away with such magnificence, and our viceroy loves magnificence <u>too well</u> to be pleased with our way of entertaining company'.[70]

In 1785 another vice-regal couple, the rather extravagant and fun-loving 4th duke of Rutland and his duchess (figs 36, 37), expressed a desire to visit Cork, but only if they were invited. This caused alarm among members of the city council, one of whom expressed the opinion that 'there is neither place or person here fit to entertain her [the duchess, daughter of the 4th duke of Beaufort], nor even to invite her . . . [she] must fix her residence at Castle-martyr [seat of the earl of Shannon], or at some of the great houses in the neighbourhood'.[71] In the event, they stayed at Castle Martyr. Two years later, in 1787, the duke made a three-month tour of the country, during which he and his retinue enjoyed lavish entertainment provided by hosts who feared loss of face by not doing so.[72]

In the autumn of 1809 the then lord lieutenant and his wife, the duke and duchess of Richmond, together with a large retinue, made a prolonged tour in the south of Ireland, lodging as guests with families in each area. At Mount Shannon, Co. Limerick, the seat of the late lord chancellor, John FitzGibbon, earl of Clare, his widow, with the seventeen-year-old 2nd earl, hosted the party for four nights in early October. A newspaper description of the visit was given under the heading 'The Irish Court at Mount Shannon': 'This princely mansion, so often visited by the reps of his Majesty in this country, was now again dignified by the reception of the illustrious House of Richmond and the Irish Court, while, on the part of the accomplished Countess who received them and of her noble son nothing was wanting that was due to such a visit, to themselves or to the magnificent memory of the late Earl of Clare.'[73] The earl and his mother, accompanied by 'leading gentlemen of the neighbourhood', met the party on their way to Mount Shannon and accompanied them to the house.

Charleville Forest in Co. Offaly (fig. 38) was another house visited on this tour. On arrival (as was customary for honoured guests), the horses were removed from the viceroy's

38
Catherine Maria Bury, Countess of Charleville,
Charleville Forest, Co. Offaly, 1812/20.

carriage and it was dragged manually from the lodge at the gate of the park to the house, where two bands played *God Save the King*. Yeomanry were ranged on either side of the hall door, officers and people on horseback walked about and the crowds cheered. The cost of such a visit in time, effort and money was substantial. In a letter to her son prior to the visit, the countess of Charleville wrote that 'magnificent' full-dress liveries were made for the servants and, for the upper male servants, a uniform of blue and scarlet: 'it ought to go off handsome for money has not been spared'.[74]

Country house 'tourism'

Another type of visitor was not always welcome, particularly when the family was in residence in the country: the house tourists, strangers who sometimes arrived without warning, requesting permission to view the grounds and often the interior of the house. The suggestion has been made that the royal progresses of Queen Elizabeth I to noblemen's houses throughout her kingdom had the effect of encouraging a building mania among her courtiers, and of instituting a custom that continues to the present day – that of country house visiting.[75] Another writer, however, is of the opinion that country house tourism was unknown until the Restoration, when social change and the rise of a wealthier class encouraged a new desire to travel for its own sake.[76] Whatever the case, by 1700 it was evident from the publication of travel journals and diaries by people such as John Evelyn and Celia Fiennes that country house tourism in England was well established, and conducted not only by the aristocracy but by the gentry too. It became a pastime (as it is today), a way of gathering material for publication, or a means to satisfy the fashionable eighteenth- and nineteenth-century pursuit of filling one's journal. Roads were being improved by this time, gazetteers were making their appearance and, between 1715 and 1725, Colen Cambell's three volumes of *Vitruvius Britannicus* – promoting neo-Palladianism as an architectural ideal for the English country house – was published.[77] Architecture became a recreational pursuit for men and women, as house-owners vied with each other in building or altering their houses and improving their demesnes. As early as 1718 Robert Molesworth advised his wife to view the Southwells' landscaping at Clontarf in Dublin because 'they are well laid out and worthy of our imitation in due course'.[78]

From the beginning of the century in England, steady streams of visitors familiarised themselves with the building progress of large country houses. At Blenheim in 1711 it was found necessary to place a man at every doorway 'to keep people back from Crowding in with my Lord Duke', while small fences were put in place in front of windows to protect the glass.[79] Pole Cosby of Stradbally Hall, who visited Blenheim with his father in 1721, found a printed guide to the as yet unfinished house.[80] By the 1770s the 'Tour of Norfolk', which included houses such as Houghton, Holkham, Blickling, Felbrigg and Raynham, had become obligatory for the curious, while at Kedleston, Derbyshire a hotel for visitors was built at the same time as the house, overlooking the park.[81]

In July 1757, the countess of Kildare encouraged her husband to take a look at houses in Yorkshire while he was there: 'You will get so much pleasure in seeing all those fine seats . . . to my taste there is no entertainment equal to it, particularly at this fine time of the year.'[82] Visiting houses in England was one way in which architectural and landscaping ideas were disseminated in Ireland: like many others, Pole Cosby was influenced by what he saw and put many of these ideas into practice at Stradbally. A note of caution for potential house tourists in Ireland was sounded in the *Dublin Journal* of 1725, however, when it reported that 'On Sunday last Mr Butler, a gentleman belonging to his Excellency the Lord Cartert [*sic*], fell

39
W.H. Brooke, *Tourists in Ireland*; after Crofton Croker.

from a Scaffold and dashed his Brains out, as he was viewing the fine house at Castletown, now building by the Rt Hon William Connolly [*sic*], Esq.'[83]

It was not until the middle of the eighteenth century that house tourism became popular in Ireland (fig. 39). For those living at a distance from Dublin – for example, in places such as counties Galway, Clare and Sligo – the occasional visit from any respectable-looking traveller was a godsend, and they were more than happy to offer hospitality and to conduct tours of their property personally. It was also a way of letting others know of the architectural and landscape improvements that were being made by a great number of owners. These visitors were viewed in various ways by the different house-owners: some did not admit strangers; others found them a necessary evil whose visits had to be endured (after all, it was flattering if someone was curious or interested enough to desire admittance to see the interior) but who brought with them the possibility of relaying news of new building or improvements made to other country houses; still others were simply delighted to have the company.

As in England, so in Ireland travel had become easier: roads had improved and maps were available, such as those by Taylor and Skinner (published in 1778) which identified the seats of noblemen and the gentry; carriages were more comfortable and post chaises and horses could be hired. By the end of the century, mail or stage coaches connected many towns. Swift's declaration that the English knew little more of Ireland than they did of Mexico might not have been true by 1800.[84] Travellers such as John Loveday and Richard Pococke made tours in 1732 and 1752 respectively; Lord Chief Baron Edward Willes wrote his account of Ireland in a series of letters between 1757 and 1762; and the account of Richard Twiss's Irish tour was published in 1776.[85] Most of these earlier tourists concentrated on the antiquities and geology of Ireland, and made general comments on the state of the country, both politically and geographically. Arthur Young was particularly interested in the agricultural improvements (or otherwise) being made by landlords throughout the country in his account published in 1780, and he was warmly welcomed and given tours of their estates by those who were making efforts to improve their land.[86] But not many writers gave details of the houses they visited, apart from comments on their location and aspect within the demesne and in the context of the surrounding countryside, noting the plantations and other physical features, and the type of stone used in the building. Nevertheless, there are some travellers' accounts that yield much interesting information on the country house and its use. With the prevalence of grand tours and the rise of connoisseurship, there was a great deal of interest not only in architectural pursuits but also in collections. Visiting houses and taking note of the architecture, furniture, furnishings, pictures, sculptures, garden layouts and so forth was the way that information was disseminated and gave ideas to others. There was an amount of rivalry involved here, both friendly and otherwise.

40
Two sides of coin used for admission to Rathfarnham Castle.

41
Rathfarnham Castle, Co. Dublin, garden front.

non., *Luggala, Roundwood, Co. Wicklow*;
atercolour, n.d.

It was not difficult to gain entry to houses and gardens so long as one was well dressed and well mounted, unlike the 'unpretending appearance' of the German Prince Pückler-Muskau and his friend who, in their opinion, were 'most discourteously denied admittance' to the earl of Meath's seat at Kilruddery, Co. Wicklow in 1829.[87] Robert Graham had no such problem there six years later, noting in his travel journal how impressed he was with the housekeeper, 'a very sensible woman . . . almost the only housekeeper I have met with who would not take money for a great deal of trouble in showing her charge'.[88] It was usually sufficient to tip the housekeeper or gardener, or both, to gain entrance, but sometimes there were systems in place to control the numbers. At Rathfarnham Castle, Dublin, a silver ticket in the shape of a coin, dating to 1780–90, was inscribed 'This ticket admits four persons to see Rathfarnham on Tuesdays only' on one side; the reverse, below Lord Ely's coronet, was marked 'This ticket to be left at the porters lodge' (figs 40, 41).[89] Close to the porter's lodge at Castle Howard, Co. Wicklow was a small cottage where parties were allowed to 'take their repast', and where a book was kept into which the names of those in the party and the date of their visit were entered.[90] Castletown was open to the public on Sundays from 11 am to 3 pm; at Bellevue, the La Touche seat in Co. Wicklow, visitors were admitted to view the grounds on Mondays.[91] By the 1850s, Sir Charles Domville of Santry House, Dublin had special cards printed admitting parties of four or fewer to view his house on Tuesdays and Fridays between 2 pm and 5 pm.[92]

Many owners were remarkably hospitable: Peter La Touche allowed his hunting box, Luggala at Roundwood, Co. Wicklow, to be used by 'respectable strangers wherein the spirit of Irish hospitality, beds and attendants are provided' (fig. 42).[93] Robert Graham provides information on how the system worked on his visit to Luggala, when he encountered 'a party of ladies and gentlemen who had arrived in a coach-and-four, but not being armed with the right of entry, could not venture farther. Mr Latouche is ready to give access, and even the liberty of fishing, to any gentle party who asks for it [presumably in advance], but he is most exclusive to other intruders and interdicts his servants from any power of admission. The Powerscourt family, in the same way, require special applications and printed notices are put up, stating that the servants are debarred from taking money under the penalty of dismissal.'[94] Whether it was due to the numbers arriving at Carton or because produce was being stolen or trampled upon, in 1767 the duke of Leinster was forced to erect a notice there with instructions that none were to be admitted to the kitchen garden.[95] However, he was content to allow respectable visitors to ride or drive through his grounds, and he gave keys to local gentlemen to open gates on the demesne.[96]

The novelist Anthony Trollope, in *The Kellys and the O'Kellys* (1848), wondered why Lord Cashel would advertise the fact that his house was open to the public on two days a week, given the nature of the attractions there, which, in his opinion, were negligible. Furthermore, he explained, those who handed over half-a-crown to the housekeeper, 'for the privilege of being dragged through every room in the mansion', were sure to be disappointed and frustrated by the fact that one room, that of Lord Cashel's daughter, Lady Selina, was kept locked: 'many a petitionary whisper is addressed to the housekeeper on the subject, but in vain; and, consequently, the public too often leave Grey Abbey dissatisfied'.[97]

Whether the family was in residence or not while these tours were going on did not seem to matter greatly at most country houses in Ireland. When Daniel Beaufort and his party arrived at Muckross, Co. Kerry in 1788, the family had just departed for England; as one of the party expressed a wish to see Mr Herbert's collection of drawings, permission was granted by a neighbour who had accompanied them to Muckross, where they spent two hours enjoying the works of Sandby, Rowlandson, Calendar and others.[98] Robert Graham walked through Lord Kingsborough's house in his absence, 'with the exception of his book rooms, which, his attendants say, no one must enter'.[99] At Carton, on the other hand, he and his party were rushed through the principal rooms because it was almost dinner time 'and two gentlemen were already in the library where they meet before dinner. There was a very small dinner table so we concluded that the duke only was at home.'[100] Lady Clanrickarde was at home at Portumna Castle when the Beauforts visited it in 1808: back in the hall after the housekeeper had shown them around, she wordlessly 'crossed the hall graciously bowing as she passed'.[101]

Any discomfort that the owners might experience with these visitors might have been increased had they been aware of the business-like approach adopted in Britain by the countess (later duchess) of Northumberland, who, in 1760, began one of her travel journals with a sizeable questionnaire to help in her observations of the houses she visited. Her queries opened with 'what is the situation of the House good or bad sheltered or exposed', continued to 'Is the Furniture rich plain neat mean Elegant Expensive' and arrived, 150 enquiries later, at 'How much meat wine malt liquor coals charcoal corn butter do they usually consume'.[102] Perhaps the inquisitive tourist would have had second thoughts about producing a list of questions when their tour guide was the owner, many of whom took pleasure in personally showing off their houses and grounds to visitors and demonstrating their improvements to their estates. In Waterford Lord Grandison took Richard Pococke in his carriage to show him the town he had created near Dromana, called Villierstown; at Russborough a visitor remarked of Lord Milltown that 'he takes a pleasure in shewing his house and paintings himself to all who have curiosity to see them'.[103]

Some owners even invited their visitors to dine, and provided overnight accommodation. In 1752 Pococke experienced such hospitality at Hazelwood in Sligo (built 1731 for

Owen Wynne to designs by Richard Castle), where, in the absence of his father, the eldest son showed him over the house, insisted that he stay for dinner and invited him to remain for two or three days, while Beaufort was similarly entertained by Colonel William Stewart, owner of the newly built Killymoon Castle, in 1807.[104] This hospitality was welcome, given the general lack of comfort provided by inns, particularly in the early eighteenth century: in 1717 the bishop of Killala, Co. Mayo reported that, for the last forty miles of his journey from Dublin, 'if two Gent: on ye road did not allow strangers to make Inns of their Houses, it would be a difficult matter to get Lodging or other Necessarys'.[105]

While most visitors to houses in Ireland and Britain would not have adopted the clinical approach of the duchess of Northumberland, these details were, and indeed still are, savoured by those who visited. There were at least some advantages for all involved: the owners were flattered that people desired to view their houses; the visitors satisfied their curiosity, whether they liked the house or not; and the servants conducting the tours were in receipt of a tip.

Two

Crossing the Threshold

For visitors to the country house, expectations must have been high when, having negotiated the gateway, the lodge (with possibly a porter) and the meandering avenue, they found themselves finally stepping through the main entrance and into the hall. In its original form the hall was a room of entertainment where the family, guests and servants gathered together to eat and to enjoy music and dancing. But by about 1670 servants had been moved to the basement, and the hall had become a room of entry and a means of gaining access to other parts of the house. As such, it became an important introduction to the house, particularly to its public rooms. At the same time, new arrangements, which incorporated passages or corridors in the plan, created some flexibility with regard to the location of the staircase and allowed for new types of furniture to be created specifically for these spaces.

The hall and its adjuncts

As the main point of access to the house, it was important that the impact on the visitor made by the hall would be favourable and impressive. The architect Francis Goodwin, however, who designed Lissadell, urged caution: 'The entrance hall offers a richer architectural *coup d'œil* than it is always advisable to make at first; because whatever may be urged in favour of first impressions in architecture, they may be rendered too forcible and too favourable, and so occasion comparative disappointment in what follows.'[1] As a rule, that impact

Opposite
The staircase at Townley Hall, Co. Louth (*see* fig. 58).

was made more by the architecture of the space than the contents. The size of the hall and often how well it was lit provided the overall impression for visitors, followed by its architectural decoration, which might include the use of orders, niches, galleries and chimneypieces. It is these architectural elements that mark the transition from outdoors to indoors. Use of the classical orders increased as the eighteenth century progressed, with the availability of treatises, books on architecture and foreign travel. In his newly built house, Castle Durrow, Co. Laois (1716–18), William Flower announced the importance of his hall by the incorporation of oak panelling rather than deal, which was used in the rest of the house. In contrast, from the 1730s the great reformer the Rev. Samuel Madden promoted the employment of stucco decoration for walls and cornices in place of timber wainscoting as it reduced the risk of fire, praising Brockhill Newburgh MP, owner of Ballyhaise, Co. Cavan (*c.*1733) for doing this.[2]

Visitors such as the Rev. William Henry and the Beaufort family were quite knowledgeable on matters architectural and were not slow to give their opinions. Henry described the hall at Hazelwood, Co. Sligo in the 1730s shortly after it was built: 'The Hall is about 20ft square lighted by a large Venetian Window, whereof the Hall Door is the middle part. The Floor Chequered with Marble. The sides and Ceiling of this, as of all the rooms, Stucco Work with Cornishes of different orders, all exceedingly well executed.'[3] Mary Beaufort was struck by just two things in the hall at the earlier Muckross House, Co. Kerry in 1810, describing it as 'small and floor'd with brick'.[4] The hall in the semi-fortified Portumna Castle was deemed 'capacious' in 1808 and Mary observed that 'an ornamental skreen had been begun of carved wood to separate the doorway and keep off any wind from the fireplace'.[5]

43
Hamwood, Dunboyne, Co. Meath, built in 1775 for Charles Hamilton, agent to the duke of Leinster at Carton.

Ballyfin, Co. Laois.

Rather than the combined layout of hall and stairs within the one space, most of the plans under discussion show a preference for a self-contained square or rectangular space for the hall, located at the centre of the front of the house, flanked by windows. Some entrances into halls were off-centre as, for example, at Marlay, Co. Dublin (late 1700s) and Coolattin, Co. Wicklow (1804); others were on the short side of the house, as at Rockingham, Co. Roscommon (1809, destroyed by fire 1957) and Roxborough Castle, Co. Tyrone (remodelled 1841, destroyed by fire 1922). The main entrance at Hamwood, Co. Meath (1770s) is possibly unique, being situated in the western of the two octagonal pavilions and linked by a curved corridor to the main block, where the entrance hall is located (fig. 43).[6] Not many imitated the shape of James Gandon's hall at Emo Court, Co. Laois (c.1790), which is rectangular with curved ends, nor the circular domed hall proposed by James Lewis for Coole House, Co. Galway in the 1780s.[7] The oval halls (on the long axis) created by Richard Morrison at Castlegar, Co. Galway (1801) and proposed by James Byres at Charleville Forest in 1789 did not blaze a trail either.[8]

In 1807, Louisa Beaufort gave her first impression of Killymoon Castle, where 'the Hall into which you first enter is small square and somewhat dark – opposite the great door you go to the staircase, it is of Portland stone, very handsome, and lighted from the top by four gothick windows which form a Lanthorn with painted narrow border of violet and yellow round each window'.[9] Her comment about the hall is interesting, anticipating Goodwin's comments made years later. While the porte-cochère could have the effect of darkening the entrance hall, the architect John Nash might have been providing what Horace Walpole referred to as 'gloomth', the ambience of neo-gothic architecture.[10] Louisa admired the brightness and quality of the narrow staircase that connects the porte-cochère, the main hall and the stair hall, all on one axis, which revealed itself to her as she progressed into the house.

This type of 'prelude' to the main event was achieved at Ballyfin (1822; fig. 44). There, the architects Richard and William Vitruvius Morrison's aim of delaying spatial excitement until the entrance hall had been passed through was annotated on one of the plans: 'The saloon, vestibule and Grand Staircase united, make a Room 80 feet in length, lighted from above – the effect of which will be very striking' (fig. 45). In the large number of drawings for Ballyfin, dating to c.1822, the hall is consistently rectangular and centrally placed: as built, it is not at

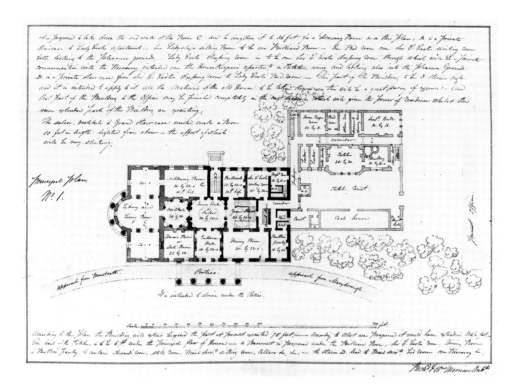

45
Richard and William Morrison, ground-floor plan
of Ballyfin, *c.*1822.

all dark, but it does not prepare the visitor for the treat to come. The owners, Sir Charles and
Lady Coote, worked with the architects, adjusting and fine-tuning the design to get what they
wanted. It is worth looking at a few of the plans to see how that goal was achieved.

The hall at Ballyfin remains behind the portico in all of the drawings, varying only slightly in size. The earliest plan shows the centre of the house taken up by the hall (with a door to
each side giving access to reception rooms), a 'Vestibule' behind a screen, and an imperial
staircase in a deep projection to the rear (fig. 46). A later drawing shows the staircase pulled
into the main block, a spacious 'Gallery or Inner Hall' with columnar screens on all four
sides, and no vestibule. As built, the hall has a fireplace, and there is no access to the adjoining dining room and 'Music Room or Anti-Room'. The door on axis to the entrance leads into
the large 'Inner Hall or Saloon', from which a screen of columns leads to the staircase on the
right and to a circular vestibule on the left, continuing into the bow-sided 'Library and Living
Room'.[11] In all of their proposals for the house, the Morrisons used either top-lighting or a
Wyatt window for the grand staircase. This conformed to their preference for the drama of
a staged progress through a building, reinforced by the small, single-storey, unpretentious
hall, in which a single door leads to the sumptuous double-height top-lit saloon and enfilade
that Richard Morrison had admired so much.

The low ceiling of the hall at Powerscourt, Co. Wicklow is of interest. The house incorporates an ancient castle on a U-shaped plan, with forward-projecting wings that formed
a court. Richard Wingfield MP, later Viscount Powerscourt, commissioned Richard Castle
to design a Palladian-style house around it. The front wall of the house was built across the
court (1731–40), creating the entrance hall and, above it, the wonderful double-height saloon.[12] Mention was made in the previous chapter of the main entrance here into the 'rus-
tics'. This led into the long, low, arcaded entrance hall with a coffered ceiling (fig. 47). On

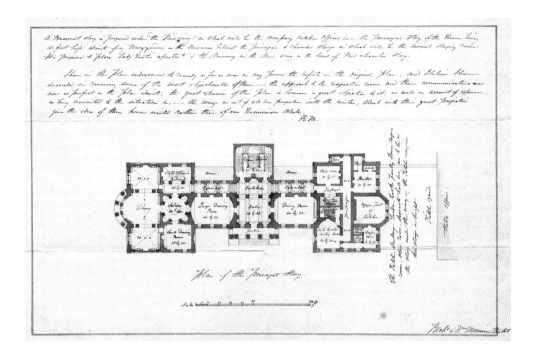

axis with the hall was Lord Powerscourt's study rather than, as was the usual practice, the saloon.[13] To the right on entering was a waiting room, and beyond this an opening to the great
staircase. Daniel Robertson's plan of 1843 shows this ground-floor level as the private part of
the house and the place where business was conducted. Privacy and business will be considered in later chapters.

The two-storey saloon and hall were advocated by William Chambers in his *Treatise on
Civil Architecture*, published in 1759: 'The usual method, in buildings where beauty and magnificence are preferred to oeconomy [*sic*], is to raise the Hall and Salon higher than the other
rooms, and make them occupy two Stories.'[14] Isaac Ware agreed with Chambers that height
was important: particularly in the country, where there were other ways into the house, 'the
hall may be an elegant room, and it is there we propose its being made large and noble'.[15] The
two-storey hall manifested itself in the last quarter of the seventeenth century and at the beginning of the eighteenth in a number of the great houses of England, such as Chatsworth,
Castle Howard and Blenheim. According to one writer, in a house 'of any pretension' (in the
early Georgian period), the entrance 'was directly into a great hall of two-storey height, and
richly decorated'.[16] However, despite Chambers's preference for the double-height hall, it
was a feature of baroque architecture that went out of fashion in England in the 1740s.

There are no houses in Ireland to match the scale of those mentioned above, but it is no
surprise to see double-height halls in big houses such as Castletown and Leinster House,
the Dublin mansion of the duke of Leinster. What is interesting is the number of two-storey
halls in houses that would seem unlikely to contain them because of their small size. Much
space was required, the decoration was expensive and they would have been difficult, if not
impossible, to heat. However, it is worth looking at some of them, many of which are remarkable for the variety of their architectural handling, including their galleries.

Among these examples, the earliest are at Platten Hall, Co. Meath, which dates to *c.*1700
(fig. 48), and Beaulieu, Co. Louth, built in the 1660s but largely rebuilt between 1710 and

1720 to designs by John Curle.[17] The joinery in the spacious panelled double-storey hall, the staircase and the gallery at Platten Hall is finely executed, and paired Corinthian columns are superimposed on Ionic columns. The decoration at Beaulieu is old-fashioned for its date, having a baroque, even Scottish, feel to it, with carved wood military trophies in the arches over two of the doors in the hall and an amount of heraldry on the walls. Two other overdoors contain trophies of musical instruments (fig. 49), all reminiscent of those at the Royal Hospital Kilmainham, Dublin (now the Irish Museum of Modern Art), probably carved by James Tabary between 1680 and 1684.[18] An impressive central doorway leads to a small room at the rear. The staircases adjoin each side of the saloon, the principal one leading to the first floor only.[19] As the hall is self-contained and has a massive chimneypiece (in which is set a view of Drogheda, Co. Louth, reputedly by Van der Hagen), it may have been used by its owners as a music room and/or sitting room; it would have been quite comfortable, as the sash windows that overlook the hall from the gallery are closed.

The two-storey hall at Castletown was certainly the most elegant Irish example, designed by Edward Lovett Pearce in the mid-1720s. Aptly described as 'both monumental and fes-

47
The lower hall at Powerscourt, Co. Wicklow. The main block of the house was gutted by an accidental fire in 1974.

48
Entrance Hall at Platten Hall, Co. Meath,
T. U. Sadleir and P. L. Dickinson, *Georgian Mansions
in Ireland* (Dublin 1915).

49
Beaulieu, Drogheda, Co. Louth, tympanum over-
door in hall. *The Georgian Society Records of Eighteenth
Century Domestic Architecture and Decoration in
Ireland*, vol. 5 (Dublin, 1913).

tive', the three-bay space has a gallery carried on a screen of Ionic columns, and a complete
entablature is supported by this and by half-columns (fig. 50).[20] The upper storey is unexpectedly different: the tapering square columns (with baskets of flowers in place of capitals)
that support a carved frieze and cornice suggest a certain playfulness in juxtaposing two different moods. A doorway on axis with the entrance leads into what was probably the great
parlour or saloon. The space extends seamlessly through an opening to the right of the entrance that leads into the staircase hall, creating a spectacular *coup d'œil* for the visitor (fig.
51). The Palladian hall gives way to the Lafranchini rococo decoration of the stair hall, and the
black and white stone floor flows through both spaces. Here the family portraits incorporated in the plasterwork look down on their visitors as they mount the Portland stone staircase
with its elegant brass banisters.[21]

At Gloster, Co. Offaly (late 1600s/early 1700s) the hall is panelled with strongly articulated plasterwork, with niches for busts on the upper part. A three-bay arcaded gallery at
first-floor level opens, unusually, into an upper hall to the rear decorated in the same style,
this time with a Doric entablature and a barrel-vaulted coffered ceiling. The three-bay hall
at Seafield, Donabate, Co. Dublin (probably late 1730s) spans the full depth of the house, an
unexpected Palladian touch, lit by windows to the front and rear; fluted Ionic and Corinthian
pilasters separate a series of painted grisaille classical figures on both storeys, probably added later in the eighteenth century.[22]

Behind the arcaded screen that separates the hall (a 32-foot cube) from the imperial staircase in John Aheron's plan for Dromoland House, Co. Clare (*c.*1741, for Sir Edward O'Brien)

are doorways into the formal rooms to the left and into the private wing to the right (figs 52, 53). The screen supports a balustraded gallery and an arcade articulated with doubled Corinthian pilasters on plinths.[23] The lower arcade is rusticated, an idea that might have come from Edward Lovett Pearce's Court of Requests at the Parliament House (now the Bank of Ireland) in Dublin.[24] The hall here, at Platten Hall, and that at Roundwood, Co. Laois (*c.*1750) are the only two-storey halls under discussion that contain staircases, both of which are on the imperial plan. At Roundwood the staircase is on axis with the entrance but it is the gallery and its fretwork rail that give the space its charm. This type of bridge occurs in at least three other houses: Ballinlough Castle, Co. Westmeath (reconstructed in the 1730s), Drewstown, Co. Meath (*c.*1745; fig. 54) and Raford, Co. Galway (1750s).[25]

Before we examine staircases in a little more detail, consideration of the spaces that adjoin the hall might put into context the route taken by visitors. Many houses had a saloon adjoining the hall to the rear on the short axis, such as has been seen at Castletown.[26] These are the earliest examples of this configuration, together with two plans for Headfort by Richard Castle dating to *c.*1750 (fig. 27) and one by John Ensor (after 1751).[27] An early drawing for the enlargement of the house at Carton by Castle (*c.*1739) shows a variation of this treatment: the hall takes up a four-bay space to the right on entering; on axis with the entrance is a door, through which the four-bay saloon is similarly to the right. This may have been due to the constraints of the thick interior walls that remain from the original early seventeenth-century house. The configuration of the centrally placed hall and saloon remained popular in houses designed during the second half of the eighteenth century. Screens were often incorporated in the hall to provide the desirable effect of the columns framing the centralised doorway into the saloon.

The information gleaned from annotations on the plans about the location of rooms to each side of the hall is inconclusive. No real trend appears between 1730 and 1830, apart from the prevalence of the 'parlour' (which might be on either side of the entrance), a space that had often become a 'breakfast' or 'morning' room by the beginning of the nineteenth century, when the 'parlour' all but disappeared from country houses. From 1750 there was

50
Castletown, Co. Kildare, entrance hall showing the double-height hall and columnar screen, and the archway to the staircase.

51
Castletown, Co. Kildare, staircase with brass baluster 1760.

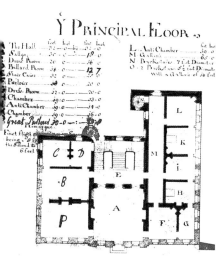

52

ohn Aheron, section of Dromoland House.

3

ohn Aheron, plan of the principal floor.
Dromoland House, Co. Clare, *c.*1741.

4

he staircase at Drewstown, Co. Meath.

VIEW OF THE HALL AND PRINCIPAL STAIRCASE OF LISSADELL, NEAR SLIGO, IRELAND.

The Seat of Sir Robert Gore Booth, Bart.

NOW ERECTING BY THE AUTHOR.

also an increase in rooms called, variously, 'study', 'own room' and 'office' (all for the same purpose), added to which could be the 'book room' or 'library', spaces that the master of the house might use as a study. Placing a study at the front of the house meant that any visitors could wait in the hall, rather than being allowed to wander through the house. This will be examined in more detail in Chapter 3.

55
Francis Goodwin, 'View of the Hall and Principal Staircase of Lissadell, near Sligo, Ireland'. Francis Goodwin, *Rural Architecture* (2nd edn, London, 1835) pl. 33.

While the hall was the first space encountered in the house, the staircase was also important and it too merited comment by the Beauforts, as we have seen. Louisa judged the staircase at Hazelwood to be 'large and handsome'; in contrast, her father voiced his reservations at Castlegar, Co. Galway: 'The new house very pretty but unfinished, with much too fine a staircase – for its purpose.'[28] It is unclear what he meant by this comment: was a 'fine staircase' unnecessary because all the reception rooms were on the ground floor? Was it too grand for a house of its quite modest size? Or was there a perception that the Mahon family were getting above their station?

The location of the main staircase varied only slightly in ground-floor plans up to 1840.[29] Prior to 1750 a slight majority favoured one or other side of the hall at the front of the house, followed closely by a location directly behind the hall to the rear. During the period 1750 to 1800, a majority preferred the spinal corridor for the staircase, evenly divided between left and right, while the location directly behind the hall was the second choice. But between 1800 and 1840 the great majority opted for it being directly behind the hall. Most staircases took the shape of the open-well design, and Aheron's imperial design for Dromoland found only a few followers, probably because it took up too much space and was expensive. The first known house in Ireland to have an imperial staircase was Eyrecourt Castle, Co. Galway, built in the 1670s, where the rather low hall and the staircase behind it took up the entire centre third of the house. The grandeur of such a large space, and the exceptionally fine carved woodwork of the staircase with its broad steps and its gradual ascent, must have impressed visitors as they made their way to the reception rooms, which were on the first floor.[30]

John Ensor proposed an imperial staircase for Headfort, possibly in the 1750s; at Castle Coole both Richard Johnston and James Wyatt included them in their plans, in 1789 and 1790 respectively, and one also appears in a plan in Richard Morrison's book.[31] Two early drawings by Morrison for Ballyfin employed an imperial staircase and Francis Goodwin designed one for Lissadell in 1883 (fig. 55). A visitor to the latter shortly after the house was built was critical of the staircase, describing it as 'of black marble, supported upon high and solid pilasters below . . . The aim of this staircase gives you the idea of a house the size of Althorp at least and, in point of material, is only to be met with I suppose, in the foreign palaces. Though a very handsome thing in itself, [it] is totally out of keeping with the series of very nice small comfortable bedrooms that it leads to.'[32] These were interesting observations in view of Goodwin's comments mentioned earlier. The hall at Lissadell is one of the few among the plans that has no light flowing directly into the space, owing to the porte-cochère. Natural light, however, comes from the roof over the staircase, to the left of the entrance.

The same visitor admired the progression of spaces on entering Rockingham, Co. Roscommon (figs 56, 57), from a small entrance hall to a grand gallery (or 'gallery of communication', as John Nash annotated his plan of 1809), lighted from above with stained glass, with the 'handsome' imperial staircase to the right of the centre.[33] Other such staircases are at Colebrooke, Co. Fermanagh, Dunkettle, Co. Cork (where it is framed by a wide elliptical arch in the hall) and Kilmore See House, Co. Cavan.[34] A late-eighteenth-century reverse imperial staircase, on axis with the entrance hall, is found at Glin Castle, Co. Limerick, seat of the Knights of Glin.

Arguably the most spectacular main staircase is at Townley Hall, Co. Louth (1790–4), designed in the neo-classical style for Blayney Townley Balfour by Francis Johnston. It is contained within a rotunda lit by a glazed dome, and an elegant restraint is maintained in the decoration, which is largely architectural on the upper level, with apses, niches and arched recesses (fig. 58). Among other remarkable staircases are those at Kilshannig (1765–6) and Vernon Mount (c.1784), both in Co. Cork, Farnham, Co. Cavan (c.1802), Pollacton, Co.

56
John Nash, ground-floor plan of Rockingham, Boyle, Co. Roscommon.

57
Rockingham, Co. Roscommon.

58
At Townley Hall, Co. Louth, the staircase curves around the wall of the central rotunda.

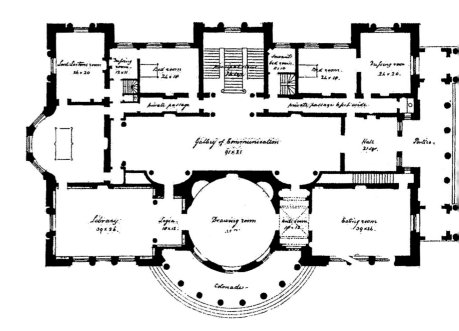

Carlow (*c*.1802, dem.) and Castle Howard (*c*.1811), Co. Wicklow. Equally spectacular is the free-standing flying staircase of wood with wrought-iron balustrades (fig. 59) at Woodbrook, Co. Wexford (1827).

The two-storey hall almost disappeared after the mid-eighteenth century, but the columnar screen, seen first in Ireland at Castletown, gained in popularity throughout the period under discussion. Plans show that, during the second half of the century, Lord Kildare proposed one for Carton and Sir William Chambers for Headfort, while Davis Ducart provided one at Castletown Cox, Co. Kilkenny, as did Agmondisham Vesey for his house at Lucan (after consulting with Chambers, James Wyatt and Michael Stapleton). The screen also appears in Mount Kennedy, Co. Wicklow (figs 60, 61; to plans by James Wyatt (1772), executed by Thomas Cooley in 1781), in plans for Castle Coole by both Johnston and Wyatt (1789 and 1790 respectively; figs 23, 24) and in James Gandon's proposal for Carriglas, Co.

59
The swirling staircase at Woodbrook, Killane, Co. Wexford.

60
The columnar screen in the hall at Mount Kennedy, Co. Wicklow.

61
William Ashford (1746–1824), *Mount Kennedy,
Co. Wicklow,* 1785; oil on canvas. Yale Center for
British Art, Paul Mellon Collection

Entrance hall at Fota House, Co. Cork.

Longford (*c*.1794–6). In the first half of the nineteenth century screens were to be found at Ballycurry, Co. Wicklow (1807 and 1808), Roxborough Castle (1841) and Castle Dillon, Co. Armagh (1842). Richard Morrison, in his re-modelling of the late eighteenth-century Mount Bellew, Co. Galway (before 1820) and, with his son William, of the former hunting box Fota House, Co. Cork (*c*.1825; fig. 62), opened the existing walls to the rooms on each side, replacing them with lateral screens of columns.[35]

Corridors, vestibules and lobbies

Other features that Castletown shares with Leinster House are the axial vaulted corridors that appear on all floors, lit by windows at each end of the house.[36] The earl's plans for Carton, those for Castle Coole and Chambers's plan for Headfort show a similar corridor in which the main and secondary staircases are located.[37] Barbavilla, Co. Westmeath (*c*.1730) has a broad corridor which contains a staircase, and it appears to terminate at each end with a door to the garden. The ample transverse corridor at Portumna Castle contains two staircases.

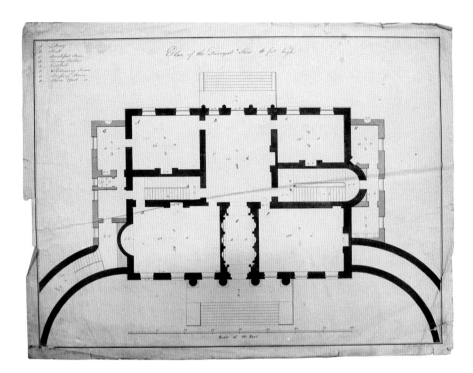

63
Daniel Augustus Beaufort (1739–1821), proposed
ground-floor plan for Ardbraccan, Co. Meath, 1774.

References are made in many plans to vestibules and lobbies – spaces between which there appears to have been no clear dividing line. Roger North, writing in the 1690s, described a 'moderate sized room which the French call a vestibule' where visitors might adjust their clothes before entering the hall.[38] On the face of it, this sounds like a reasonably good idea, particularly if guests or visitors had to make their way up a long flight of steps in rain to get to the door. But in practice, certainly in Ireland, the few houses among the plans under discussion that had long flights of steps did not possess such a facility, leaving visitors with no choice but to arrive in the hall possibly in some disarray from travel, and/or dripping rain onto the floor.[39] However, in plans for Ardbraccan, Co. Meath by both Thomas Cooley and Daniel Beaufort (the latter dated 1774), a narrow 'vestibule' leads on axis from the main entrance to a large rectangular hall, located to the rear of the house between the library and the breakfast room.[40] Beaufort's drawing (fig. 63) shows a highly decorated vestibule with niches and engaged columns that would be in line with North's suggested decoration for this space: 'the ornaments most proper to it are niches, and statues'.[41] However, these two rooms together were probably seen as a waste of living space. In a drawing of the plan as executed, no 'hall' appears but the narrow 'vestibule' to the front of the house is retained (with no access to the adjoining rooms, as at Ballyfin), playing the part of a hall that leads on axis into a saloon (fig. 29). The vestibule appears to be poorly lit, with a small rectangular window over the entrance door and light transmitted from the rear window through the internal fanlight over the door to the saloon.

The words 'vestibule' and 'lobby' are used in other plans to indicate small spaces that communicate with rooms or apartments in the house (not dissimilar to the purpose of the hall). They seem to mean something similar, both being forms of ante-room, but the plans show that a 'vestibule' is often a larger space than a 'lobby', which can frequently take the form of a short corridor. However, it should be noted that the sizeable 'hall' at the late twelfth-century Killeen Castle, Co. Meath, seat of the earls of Fingall, is referred to as a 'lobby' in

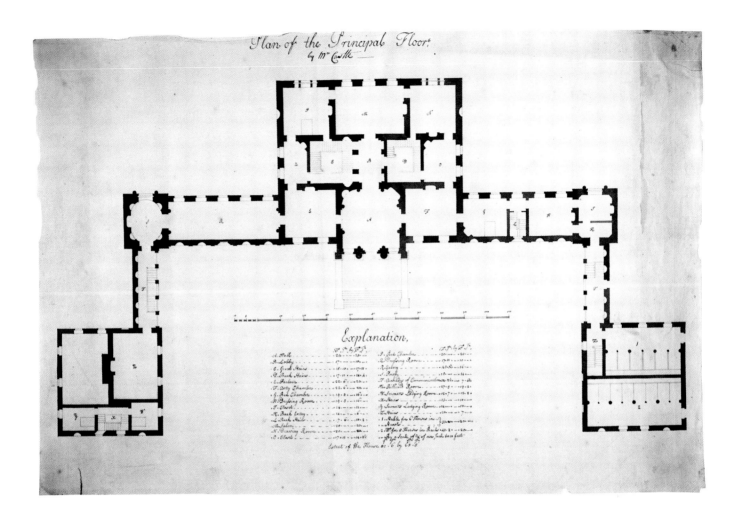

Plan of the Principal Floor
by Mr. Castle

Explanation,

4

Richard Castle, *Plan of the Principal Floor*
(ground floor), Headfort, Co. Meath, *c.*1750.

Francis Johnston's plans to transform the tower house into a Gothick castle (1802–3), and this is a name that must go back at least to 1735/6, when it is mentioned in the inventory.[42] At Headfort (*c.*1750; fig. 64), Richard Castle, using the traditional double-pile layout, describes as a 'lobby' the fairly generous space that emphasises the main cross-axis of the house between the entrance hall and the saloon. Here a screen of columns gives access on one side to the main staircase, while a doorway opposite the screen leads to the back stairs. Meanwhile, John Aheron defines a lobby as an 'Anti-chamber' where, in noble houses, 'Strangers stay till such time as the Party to be spoken with is at Leisure'.[43]

The 'vestibule' was a space that appealed to Richard Morrison, though he used both it and 'lobby' to describe a similar space in two of his designs published in 1793.[44] He provided a space for 'Vestibule and Billiards' behind a screen of columns to the rear of the centrally placed staircase at Castlegar (1801), and in another drawing for the house located a vestibule with curved ends behind the hall's columnar screen.[45] At Mount Bellew he proposed (*c.*1810) an oval vestibule that linked the Library with the Book Room, giving access to stairs leading to the gallery of the Book Room on one side and a doorway to the garden on the other. With his son William, he created the circular, top-lit vestibule at Ballyfin that has been discussed above (while in other plans he calls this identical space a 'saloon').

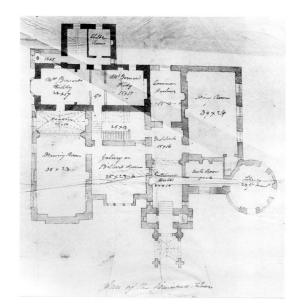
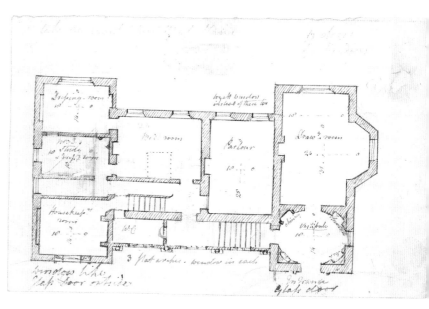

In his Tudor Revival plan for Castle Bernard, Co. Offaly (1833; fig. 65), the architect G.R. Pain shows an elongated route, similar to that at Roxborough Castle, into the body of the house, from the porte-cochère into the front part of the hall, up a flight of six steps to the main part, and continuing under an arch to the vestibule, from where access could be gained to other rooms. Finally, an unsigned and undated drawing from the Townley Hall Collection shows an entrance through a glass door into an oval vestibule (measuring 18 feet × 14 feet, with a fireplace and niches for seating) that leads directly into the drawing room (fig. 66).[46]

There is another lobby that seems to be peculiar to Irish houses: John Cornforth says that it is never to be seen in an English house but he describes it as 'one of the happiest features in Irish country houses'.[47] It is a space on an upper floor (usually the first that is not a landing), top-lit (often via an opening in the ceiling by a lantern in the floor above), self-contained and from which access is gained to bedrooms and other rooms. It can be quite a spacious room, like that on the first floor at Castle Coole, which is two storeys high and lit by an oval skylight (fig. 67). Robert Graham described it in the 1830s: 'There is one open space communicating to all the bedrooms on the principal floor with a gallery of communication to the rooms on the attick floor. This is handsome but, as I understand, is an objectionable arrangement in consequence of the noise of the servants passing and re-passing to the rooms in the morning.'[48]

A similar type of lobby designed by Richard Castle one hundred years earlier at Hazelwood was described thus: 'a small Stair Case ascends to the Attick story, and lands in an Octagon Lobby, from each side of which a door opens into a Bed Chamber. This Octagon is Illuminated by a large Lanthorn on the Roof[;] in the midst of the Octagon is a Well, with a Ballastrade around which gives light to the Stairs.'[49] This form of lobby was first used by Edward Lovett Pearce at Bellamont Forest (fig. 68); later by Richard Castle at Russborough (fig. 69), at Bellinter, Co. Meath (*c.*1750) and in unexecuted plans for Headfort; and in a drawing by Thomas Penrose for Lucan House (fig. 70). It is a space often articulated through highly architectural decoration, with the use of glass, columns, stucco and ironwork. Examples can be seen at Vernon Mount, Co. Cork (where the doors of the lobby

65

G.R. Pain, ground-floor plan for Castle Bernard (now Kinnity Castle), Co. Offaly, 1833.

66

Ground-floor plan of a house, possibly by Anne Mar. Balfour, sister of the owner, and a talented draughtswoman.

57
Bedroom lobby at Castle Coole, Co. Fermanagh.

58
Bedroom lobby at Bellamont Forest, Co. Cavan.

59
Bedroom lobby at Russborough, Co. Wicklow.

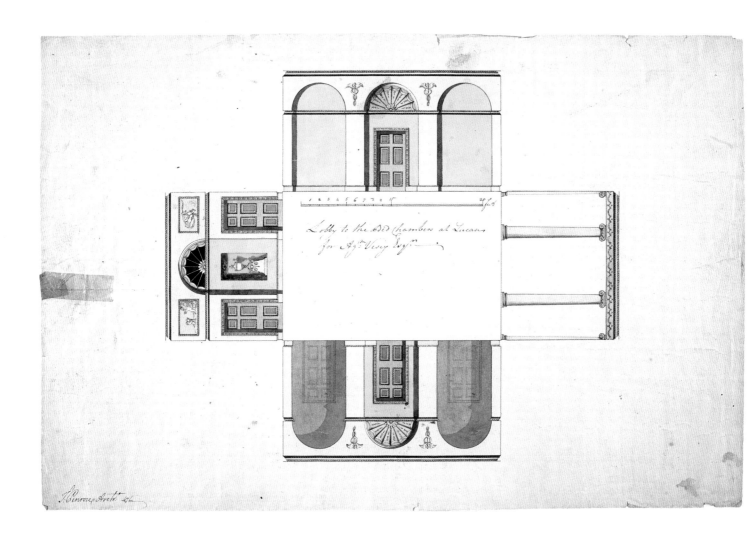

are painted as *trompe l'oeil* niches in monochrome with statues and urns by the Cork artist Nathaniel Grogan (*c.*1740–1807)), at Edermine, Co. Wexford, at Mount Henry, Co. Laois
(where small bedroom lobbies were located behind screens of Doric columns) and at Mount
Kennedy, Co. Wicklow.[50] Such lobbies were also a feature in some town houses, for example
at the Provost's House at Trinity College, Dublin (1759).

70

Thomas Penrose, *Lobby to the Bed Chambers at Lucan
for Ag. Vesey Esqr.*, April 1776.

Using the hall

Apart from its role as the room of entrance to the house, the hall served other purposes. The
Rev. John Payne, writing in 1753, reminds his readers that 'both formerly and at this Day,
the Hall, when it is large enough, was and is the chief Place of Entertainment'.[51] This refers
to the hall of the country house rather than that in town, about which Ware sounds dismis-
sive: 'In town a hall is a place of reception for servants; therefore, in this, neither magnitude
nor elegance are needful.' But he agrees with Payne regarding the hall in the country, calling it a multi-purpose space, serving as 'a summer-room for dining; it is an anti-chamber in
which people of business, or of the second rank, wait and amuse themselves; and it is a good

apartment for the reception of large companies at publick feasts'.[52] According to the diary of the countess of Roden, Easter religious services were conducted in the hall at Castletown in 1799 and 1800.[53] The writer Dorothea Herbert describes the large hall at Desart Court, Co. Kilkenny in 1774, 'where in my Grandfathers time the family met and dined round a blazing Wood fire after the Manner of Old Times'.[54] Fireplaces are present in almost all of the plans under consideration, and in some cases two appear, placed opposite each other (for example, Aheron's plan for Dromoland and Chambers's for Headfort).

Mrs Delany stayed at Dangan, Co. Meath in 1732 and described 'a charming large hall with an organ and harpsichord, where all the company meet when they have a mind to be together, and where music, dancing, shuttlecock, draughts, and prayers, take their turn. The hall is so large that very often breakfast, battledore and shuttlecock, and the harpsichord, go on at the same time without molesting one another.'[55] Twenty years later she found the hall at Mount Usher, Co. Wicklow used in a similar fashion, though apparently not for eating: 'The house is a very good one, old fashioned, convenient, and comfortable, the hall very large, in which is a billiard-table and harpsichord, and a large desk filled with books . . . the amusements belonging to it make us give it the preference to all the other rooms.'[56] The entrance hall at Glin Castle (1780s) was the scene in 1814 of 'sumptuous entertainment', with 'the choicest delicacies of the season', provided in an elegant manner, 'so characteristic . . . of the ancient House of Glin'; on another occasion, the countess of Dunraven described guests dancing in the same hall.[57]

While there is evidence that meals were served in halls in England, there appear to be few accounts of such festive occasions there. The situation seems to have been quite different in Ireland, however, where the hall may well have been considered the most appropriate place for parties as the stone floors were hard-wearing, the walls were generally covered with a cheaper (and neutral) paint, and the room did not contain many of the owners' treasures. There are descriptions of generous amounts of alcohol being consumed in Ireland at Castle Hume, Co. Fermanagh, where Lord Ely entertained his tenantry in January 1770, as was customary at Christmastime.[58] On 6 January the tenants from Castle Hume Manor were invited; 120 of them drank nineteen gallons of rum, six gallons of whiskey and two barrels of ale. Similar parties for tenants were held on 8 and 10 January. Dining or entertaining in the hall would have been perfectly simple to manage as these rooms were generally spacious, while niches, frequently part of the architectural decoration of halls, could be used for the display of dishes.[59] Some halls even contained unexpected features to aid entertainment: when the Smythes at Barbavilla, Co. Westmeath dined in their hall, it must have given their guests a start to see the servants emerge from the basement into the hall by means of a trapdoor.[60]

According to the inventories of the period, there was no shortage of tables and chairs in halls, but there was a lack of the musical instruments that one might expect to find from Mrs Delany's descriptions. One cannot help feeling that the 'french horn' mentioned in 'ye Grand Hall' at Barbavilla in 1742–3 had a use other than for the provision of music, as the hall was almost a minor armoury. A 'harpsichord with stand' is listed at Baronscourt (inv. 1782); at Newbridge House (inv. 1821) the 'Barrell Organ' in the Middle Hall completes the number of musical instruments to be found in halls among the inventories.[61] There was a long-standing tradition in old Irish dwellings of a fiddler playing while people ate and danced or sang.[62] In an article in the *Kerry Evening Post* of 1894 the writer describes how the itinerant fiddler 'was occasionally utilized for a carpet dance in a gentleman's country house', and recalls one occasion in Kerry where the shabbily dressed blind fiddler took his place 'in the shade in the hall'.[63] In one of the Irish author Sydney Owenson's books (writing as Lady Morgan), the son of an English earl describes a hospitable evening at a house in Ireland where 'during dinner the door was left open' for a fiddler and a piper, and later, after the gentlemen had joined the ladies for tea, 'the piper struck up in the hall and in a moment everyone was on their feet'.[64] Mrs Delany frequently had fiddlers and harpers to entertain her and her friends: in 1745 she wrote 'We have got an Irish harper in the house, who plays a great variety of tunes very well; he plays to us at our meals, and to me whilst I am drawing.'[65] It seems that the musician took his instrument with him to different parts of the house and was not confined to the hall, assuming that he was more suitably attired than the Kerry fiddler. As musical instruments appear in the inventories in other rooms, their portability, even including harpsichords, would have allowed for such occasions.

Contents

Until 1750 most halls contained tables: from the inventories, it appears that the average was three, mostly oval in shape and of oak. It is not until about 1750 that a table for a specific use is mentioned, when, in the Great Hall at Howth Castle, a 'square breakfast table' of deal was to be found.[66] After this date mahogany emerged as the most-favoured wood: in 1755 in the Marble Hall at Dromana, Co. Waterford there were a 'Large Mahogany two-leaved dining table with frame do.' and '2 Ovil do. of a smaller [size]'; in a passage adjoining the Hall was another dining table and a 'long two-leaved breakfast table', also of mahogany. At Lord Londonderry's seat, Mount Stewart, Co. Down, in 1821, '6 Dinning [*sic*] Tables of different sizes' are listed, which seems excessive and begs the question of whether they were leaves rather than tables. The same might be asked of the set of four dining tables found in the Back Hall at Doneraile Court, seat of the St Legers, Viscounts Doneraile. Dining tables continued to be found in halls throughout the Georgian period, sometimes with their own covers of 'green cloth' (baize?) and leather. Carton's inventory of 1818 lists 'Two Dinner Canterburys'

71
The scagliola table-top was the largest of three purchased by Joseph Leeson of Russborough while in Italy. It was executed by Don Pietro Belloni, a monk at the monastery of Vallambrosa near Florence, and completed in 1750.

and 'Two mahogany wine tables', with a large oval table in the same wood in the 'Inside Hall and Stairs'.[67] Dumb waiters were to be found in the halls at (old) Townley Hall (inv. 1773) and Carton (two in inv. 1818). This proliferation of dining and breakfast tables in the halls seems to confirm that meals were taken there, at least sometimes, but it is possible that tables were stored in halls and not necessarily used there.

Marble-topped tables appear in the hall infrequently: there was one at Baronscourt and two at Lord Wicklow's Shelton House, Co. Wicklow (inv. 1816); an 'inlaid marble table' at the earl of Leitrim's seat at Killadoon, Co. Kildare was acquired in 1829; and Russborough boasted a magnificent scagliola table by Don Pietro Belloni (1750; fig. 71).[68] Carton had '2 white carved frames with composition slabs'; and an auction of furniture at Altadore, Co. Wicklow in 1835 included '2 elegant marble tables on stands, surmounted by large figures for lights'.[69] Apart from their role as items of furniture to impress visitors, some of these marble tables will have functioned as side-tables for dining purposes.

Card tables were common in other rooms but first appeared in the hall in the 1755 inventory for Dromana; (old) Townley Hall had one in 1773, together with 'baggamon tables'; Prospect (later called Ardgillan Castle), Co. Dublin had two card tables, as had Doneraile Court (fig. 72). It is, of course, possible that there were card parties in the halls of country houses, as card-playing was a fairly incessant occupation in Irish houses. Only two inventories – for Newbridge House (1821) and Convoy House, Co. Donegal (*c.*1844) – list a billiard table in the hall. Carton's is noted in the Billiard Room (which was also the hall after the 1815 alterations by the Morrisons) and an old photograph shows one in in the hall at Bellamont (fig. 73).[70]

While cane- and rush-seated chairs enjoyed great popularity in their time they were quite old-fashioned by the mid-eighteenth century but continued to be used.[71] Barbavilla had

ish George III red walnut foldover card table,
e top inset with counter wells and candle stands.

'6 cain Arm Chairs' in the hall in 1742–3 and one has to wonder at the '24 Rush Bottom Cheeres' and 'two do. Easey do. with cushions' at Knapton, Co. Laois in 1763. The eighteen oak chairs in the Great Hall at Howth Castle, while numerous, might seem appropriate for a castle.[72] Two 'black oak seats with cane seats' in the lobby of the staircase at Mount Stewart in 1821 might signify an appreciation of old furniture at this late date, bearing in mind that by the middle of the eighteenth century the hall chair was a most desirable item of hall furniture. Eleven of the latter, with a crest and Lord Londonderry's coronet, stood proudly in the entrance hall at Mount Stewart.

The hall chair, which became fashionable from about 1730, was designed specifically for use in the entrance hall and was usually hard, with a shaped back bearing a crest or a coat of arms. The earliest mention of chairs with crests among the inventories is at Dromana in 1755, where there were fourteen in the hall. An estimate for Caledon, Co. Tyrone (the newly built house of James Alexander, later 1st earl of Caledon), dated 1783, lists for the hall and vestibule '8 Hall Chairs painted, Crests &c in the backs' at 2 guineas each.[73] James Wyatt designed a set of mahogany armchairs with crest and coronet for the hall at Castle Coole *c.*1790.[74] Less sophisticated and undoubtedly less expensive were the '8 mahogany Hall chairs with painted crests' at £8 9s. od. bought in 1808 by Thomas Hynes from Eggleso's of Dublin for his recently purchased Brook Lodge, Co. Galway.[75] Sets of Irish mahogany crested chairs also appear at Killadoon in 1807 (fig. 74), at Shelton House, Co. Wicklow and at Newbridge House, where sixteen chairs are divided between the Entrance and Middle Halls. It is surprising that crested chairs do not appear in the Carton inventory, where, in the 'Hall and Billiard Room', there are '8 mahogany X [curved] chairs'.

Hall chairs are usually associated with servants, though it is unclear whether this means the servants of the house, the servants of visitors or both. They were also used by people wait-

4
Killadoon, Co. Kildare. Seen here are five of the eight Irish mahogany hall chairs that bear the Clements crest below an earl's coronet and are mentioned in the 1807 inventory. The red moreen drapery listed in the 1812 inventory was restored in recent years.

ing to see the owner. Such visitors included those coming on matters of business, for reasons of national and local politics, and on estate matters, agents and/or stewards, tenants, petitioners, tailors, peruke-makers and tradespeople in general. At least in some cases there existed a pecking order as to where people waited. In recommending a ground-floor location for a man's dressing room (later generally referred to as a 'study' or 'own room'), Ware suggested that next to it should be a waiting room where business callers with a previous

appointment, and 'of better rank than to be left in the hall', might wait to see the master.[76]
The Irish playwright Richard Brinsley Sheridan (fig. 75), who was constantly in debt, worked
this system to perfection in his London home, presumably with the help of his servants:

> Sheridan's habit was to keep his visitors distributed variously, according to their rank
> and intimacy with him. Some . . . penetrated into the library; others tired the chairs in
> parlours; and tradesmen lost their time in the hall, the butler's room and other sceni-
> cal divisions of the premises. A door opening above stairs moved all hopes below; but
> when he came down his hair was drest for the day, and his countenance for the occa-
> sion; and so cordial were his manners, his glance so masterly and his address so capti-
> vating, that the people, for the most part, seemed to forget what they actually wanted,
> and went away as if they had only come to look at him.[77]

It is evident that the more important the visitor, the more comfortable were their surroundings and particularly the seat on which they waited: those seated on the hard hall chairs were
being kept in their place.

Other types of seating, such as benches and stools, were to be found in the hall. William
Kent's simplified version of the Italian Renaissance *sgabello* designed as a hall seat, which be-
came standard in England throughout the eighteenth century, does not seem to have made
an impact in Irish houses. The earliest mention of a bench or a 'form' is at the duke of
Ormonde's house at Clonmel in 1675, where there were 'Two jointed formes long' and 'three
short forms' in the hall.[78] Powerscourt, Co. Wicklow had a large deal bench 'with back'. At
Stackallen, Co. Meath (fig. 76) in 1757 there were '2 raled Seats painted Green' in the Stone
Hall and another in the Great Staircase Hall.[79] Two green benches appear in the hall at
Prospect, Co. Dublin in 1795. Stools in the hall are quite rare in the inventories, appearing
only at Baronscourt and at Killadoon in the 1807 and 1812 inventories. In an estimate for hall
furniture for Castlegar, together with a large mahogany table 'for [the] centre' of the room,
were '8 roman Chairs' and '4 roman stools'.[80]

Owners were security-conscious: some of the earlier inventories list locks, bolts and keys,
which were important and probably costly items. At Dublin Castle the duchess of Ormonde,
when supervising the removal of the Ormonde goods after the duke was relieved of his duties as lord lieutenant in 1669, was optimistic that her husband's replacement would buy for
his use 'the bedsteads for servants, tables and such lumber . . . all the locks and keys I like-
wise paid for, and particularly those belonging to my Lord's closet and my own chamber'.[81]
Similarly in England, the duchess of Marlborough, having fallen out with Queen Anne, was
forced to give up her lodgings in St James's Palace but was careful to remove from them the
brass locks 'of my own buying and which I never heard that anybody left for those that were
to come after them'.[82] The typical Irish hall-door lock that can be still seen in many town and
country houses is of mahogany with decorative brass mountings, manufactured in Dublin,
Limerick and elsewhere (fig. 77).[83] Locks were a selling point in an advertisement for the sale
by raffle of Lady Eustace's house at Montpelier in Dublin in 1724.[84] At Conyngham Hall, Co.
Meath in 1710 not only were the hall locks listed but so was the door knocker. Apart from
brass locks and bolts mentioned in the inventories, '2 iron barrs with screwes to windows'
were in each of the two halls at Dromana in 1755, where the hall door was armed with '2 iron
barrs three bolts with a stock lock & key and large brass knocker'.

A number of the halls contained arms and sports equipment, used as much for decoration as for recreation or defence. The judge and MP Sir Jonah Barrington described his

75
C. Turner, *The Right Honourable Richard Brinsley
Sheridan*; mezzotint after Sir Joshua Reynolds.

5
ackallen House, Co. Meath (1712), attributed to
hn Curle.

7
ish Georgian mahogany and brass lock.

grandfather's home at Cullenaghmore, Co. Laois: 'The walls of the large hall were decked (as was customary) with fishing-rods, fire-arms, stags' horns, foxes' brushes, powder-flasks, shot-pouches, nets and dogs' collars; here and there relieved by the extended skin of a kite or a king-fisher, nailed up in the vanity of their destroyers.'[85] At Newbridge House a basement corridor was hung 'from end to end with arms intended for defence'.[86] The trophies of arms as depicted in woodcarvings over the doors at Beaulieu have already been mentioned, but the real thing was at Tarbert House, Co. Kerry, where there are carved wooden bayonet-holders with the Leslie coat of arms over each of the four doors leading off the hall, with arched elements securing the bayonets, creating fan effects as overdoors.[87] In 1742 Barbavilla had a large array of arms, including 'mahogany sheelds with 12 Pistols, 2 gun racks with 20 guns, 3 yew Bow Harrows [*sic*], 1 Cross Bow, 2 hallberts and 4 half picks', while at Howth Castle, in 1746, apart from the 'great sword of Howth' and a couple of other swords and forty-seven bayonets, there were '5 pairs of stags' horns, 2 pairs of elk horns' and '3 pieces of old armour'.

With such decoration the hall might not have been the most comfortable place for a visitor to wait, nor, indeed, for a servant to sleep. In Dublin houses it was not uncommon for a servant to sleep on a settle bed in the hall. By the beginning of the eighteenth century, however, beds for servants were not commonly found in halls: at Powerscourt, Co. Wicklow there was a deal settle bed in the Boarded Hall and one in the Stone Hall, and a 'table bed' in the lobby of Killeen Castle.[88] While sleeping accommodation for servants was at a premium in Dublin houses, with the result that some slept wherever they found a space in the service area, a servant sleeping in the hall was probably a security measure that, together with the presence there of arms, allowed the family to rest easy.

The hall was both a fashionable and a practical place for a clock (many called '8-day clocks', some in walnut or oak cases) and barometers. Other practical items are listed in inventories – 'hat hooks' at the entrance and back halls at Clogrenane Lodge (dem.), Co. Carlow and '2 ranges of Brass Hat Hooks' at Carton; '2 brass hoops for umbrellas' at Killadoon (1829); and letter boxes and foot brushes at Killadoon and at Doneraile Court. Letter boxes were provided for incoming and outgoing post, the latter being delivered by a servant either personally (if the address was local) or to the nearest post stage. An interesting item that appears in the hall in some Dublin inventories, but not in country houses, is 'a writing slate for names': presumably the butler, a footman or, indeed, the visitor wrote his or her name on it, to be announced. This begs the question of whether there was a difference in the ritual of visiting between town and country.

Decoration

Stone colour or 'buff' was generally regarded as an inexpensive, hard-wearing colour for wall paint in circulation spaces such as halls, staircases and corridors but was not often to be found in the more formal rooms in the house. As early as 1728, 'buff' was used on the staircase walls at Marble Hill, Twickenham, the quintessential villa, believed to be designed by Henry Herbert, 9th earl of Pembroke.[89] At Headfort, Robert Adam's colour for the entrance hall was a mid-grey and white. A paint called 'Portland Stone' was used in Carton in 1820 for passages on the bedchamber storey, a shade that was also apparently used on the 'Garret Story, Attic Story, Grand Staircase, North & South Staircases, Corridore Between Grand and South Staircase'.[90] Interestingly, the hall at Castletown has always been painted white.[91]

The prevalence of black and white stone floors in the halls of large houses throughout Ireland in the period under discussion reflects the similarity with Britain, where that style of floor had become popular from the early seventeenth century. Pattern books such as C. A. d'Aviler's *Cours complet d'architecture* (1691), which contains Roman floor designs with advice on construction, and later designs published by James Gibbs (1728), J. Carwitham (1739) and Batty Langley (1736 and 1740) wielded a great deal of influence.[92] While surviving plans of houses frequently indicate the design for the ceiling, it is not often that designs for floors are to be found: perhaps their very popularity made drawings redundant. There is, however, a drawing for the floor of the hall at Leinster House, possibly by Castle and dating to *c*.1745, which shows a diagonal pattern of large white and small black flagstones, similar to that found at many houses, including Bellamont Forest, Kilshannig, Co. Cork and Castletown Cox, Co. Kilkenny.[93] Another plan for 'Flagging for Genl. Cuningham's Hall at Mt. Kennedy', dated August 1793 and drawn by Thomas Cooley, is of interest as a working drawing indicating how the flagstones were to be arranged around crucial areas such as the columnar screen and the fireplace with its 'Portland Slab' (fig. 78).[94] Similar floors are at Abbeyleix, Co. Laois and Florence Court, Co. Fermanagh. Houses such as Castletown and Newbridge, both in

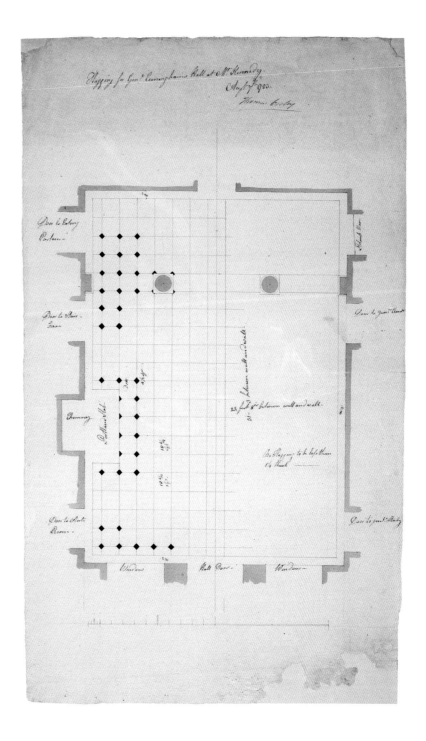

Thomas Cooley, *Flagging for Genl. Cuningham's Hall
t Mt. Kennedy, Aug 7th, 1783.*

Co. Kildare, and Rathbeale Hall, Co. Dublin had their halls paved with alternate black and
white slabs of similar size. The paving was sometimes extended to adjoining areas, with the
effect of uniting the halls, as at Castletown and Florence Court.

    Mention should also be made of the *trompe l'œil* (or three-dimensional) effect of the floor
at Powerscourt House, Dublin, of black Kilkenny marble and grey and white limestone,

reputed to be unique in the city. At Leixlip Castle the terracotta squares in the hall were painted black and white to mimic this pattern, as was the hall at Tarbert House, Co. Kerry.[95] The
elaborate geometrical design of the Portland stone floor in the staircase hall at Townley Hall
is superb. Lord Leitrim recommended Portland stone for the floor of his son's hall at Lough
Rynn, Co. Leitrim 'and a white flag which is much cheaper and which I believe comes from
Yorkshire, for the kitchen and servants' room, such as I lately laid down in the kitchen at
Killadoon'.[96]

A wooden floor in a hall is quite unusual in an Irish country house. However, Russborough, Co. Wicklow and Belvedere, Co. Westmeath are both in this category, and the parquetry of the floors in Russborough, as well as at Ballyfin and the Casino at Marino, Dublin
(designed by Sir William Chambers for the earl of Charlemont), is remarkably accomplished
(the latter two are renowned for the quality and variety of decorative materials used throughout the building). The entrance hall floor at Ballyfin is not of wood but of a richly patterned
antique Roman tessellated pavement, one of the art treasures bought by Sir Charles Coote on
his Grand Tour in 1822, surrounded by marble inlay (fig. 79).[97] However, the circular vestibule in the same house has a richly designed parquetry floor of Moorish influence, probably
devised by the Morrisons and based on the Lion Court of the Alhambra Palace in Granada.[98]

Other materials were frequently used for flooring, such as stucco, which 'when well
worked and laid makes a very beautiful floor, some of it looking like porphyry' (a form of polished composite similar to scagliola or terrazzo).[99] Such floors were common all over Europe
and could be elaborately patterned and highly polished.[100] Plaster floors were laid in passages and in upper rooms, and the *Builder's Dictionary* of 1734 gives directions for making
up the composition.[101] It would seem likely that in Ireland there were similar floors: Daniel
Beaufort described the floors at the earl of Clanbrassill's house, Tollymore, Co. Down, as 'all
tiled or stucco *à l'Italienne*'.[102] Brick was used in the hall floor at old Muckross House, described by Beaufort in 1788 as 'flagged with red and white marble of Mucrus [*sic*], of which
there is a great Quarry'.[103]

79
Ballyfin, Co. Laois, Roman pavement in entrance hall

Stone and wood floors have been looked at in an architectural context, but what of floor coverings? From the early part of the eighteenth century, painted canvas floor cloths were a popular and cheap substitute for carpets and remained so until the advent of linoleum in 1860. They were widely used in halls in Ireland, where they could be painted to resemble marble pavements (as they were in Caledon (1785), when Mayhew & Ince of London supplied James Alexander with '40 sq. yds of diamond matt pattern oil cloth'), on stairs, in passages and, as will be seen later, around sideboards to protect the floor of the dining room. They were made from wide sheets of seamless canvas which were stretched on a frame, painted on both sides with many layers of pigment mixed with linseed oil (hence the term 'oyle' cloth used commonly in Irish inventories) and left to dry for several months.[104] The earliest reference to these cloths in England is in 1736 but they are mentioned in the halls at Killeen Castle in 1735.[105] Christopher Dillon Bellew ordered floor cloths in 1810 for Mount Bellew, Co. Galway, including a 'large octagon' with a scarlet Allegro border around it; at Doneraile Court (c.1830) 'tarpaulin' covered the hall floor and the stairs.[106] In 1836 at Killadoon a 'piece of oil cloth' was kept in the passage leading to the offices, which reached from the door there to the dining room door.

The first mention of carpet in the inventories is at Barbavilla (1742/3), where there was a large carpet 'in ye coridore' and a 'carpet for church', possibly used to protect feet from the cold floor.[107] There was an increased use of carpets from the first quarter of the century, however, and, according to Ware, fitted carpets were usual by the 1750s: 'it is the Custom almost universally to cover a room entirely'.[108] Many of the staircases were covered in carpet, held in place by brass rods. A note among the Mahon Papers is interesting: the stairs at Castlegar were 4 feet 9 inches wide, on which carpet with a width of 27 inches 'will look much better than if it covered more of each step – handsome Portland stone stairs are I believe seldom quite covered by wide carpeting, the boarded stairs are sometimes'.[109]

Most country houses had 'hall lanterns' of glass, and brass, gilt or glass sconces in the hall in addition to the lantern, and up the staircase, in which candles were placed. The descriptions of the light fittings suggested in the estimate of furniture for Caledon House in 1783 are worth relating for their sophistication: '4 Antique Therms with paintings in medallions on the Shafts supporting Globe Lamps mounted in brass work & burners in do. £42.0s.0d.; A brass fram'd & pendant Lanthorn & brass chain to do. £25.0s.0d.; 2 Therms & lights for best Staircase £10.10s.0d.; 3 bell Lamps with Arms to the handrail to back Stairs £3.15s.0d.'[110] One is tempted to think that these may have been the eponymous new oil lamps designed by Aimé Argand in 1782 that had a cylindrical wick. It was said that these lamps gave light equal to that of ten candles. They became so popular in Ireland that one Dublin supplier had a cistern capable of holding 2,000 gallons of lamp oil.[111] At Newbridge House, the Entrance and Middle Halls each boasted '1 Bronze Figure with Lamp'.

All of the halls and most of the staircases had a degree of natural light from either windows or fanlights. Among the inventories there are no curtains for these windows until 1763 at Knapton, when they are mentioned in the hall. The Killadoon inventories are revealing: with a series dated 1807, 1812, 1830, 1836, 1844 and 1855, they demonstrate how furnishings and works of art were acquired over the years. For example, in 1807 '4 mahogany shutters for door & windows' of the hall are mentioned: by 1812 'scarlet moreen curtains [trimmed with black velvet] which formed a dominating continuous drapery across the entrance wall, whose colour was picked up by a scarlet hearth rug' have been added, a similar curtain on the staircase, an iron chest used as a window stool with cushion and frame covered to match the curtains, and, in 1836, a 'scarlet silk bell pull with tassel'. By 1844 a Turkey carpet had been laid with a hearth rug to match, 'Fossil elk horns' had been hung, and Grand Tour

fragments, such as a piece of marble from the Temple of Jupiter at Athens and two fragments of a statue from the Temple of Venus, had been acquired (fig. 74).[112] Scarlet moreen
was also used at the hall door and the stair window of Ashfield, Co. Cavan in 1843. Moreen
was a hardwearing fabric suitable for a hall: in choosing it in scarlet, the Clements of both
Killadoon and Ashfield combined economy with fashion.

At Newbridge House there was a green baize curtain on the hall door and a red curtain
on the window of the Inner Hall. Similar items are to be found in other sources. An estimate for curtains for the windows and door of the hall at Castlegar from Morgan of Henry
Street, Dublin in *c*.1791 shows that the Mahons were enquiring about more expensive fabrics: moreen would cost £57 11s. 0d.; if the curtains were made of velvet, the additional cost
would be £23 8s. 0d.; and if 'fine Scarlet cloth' were used, it would add '£37 extra to the
cost of Morin'.[113] In 1821, Viscount Doneraile bought from the London upholsterers Pryer
& Mackenzie a 'large size transparent blind for upper stair window with rich border' for 8
guineas.[114] Finally, in the furniture auction at Altadore (1835), 'elegant Morocco hangings'
and curtains from the hall were advertised.

Apart from scarlet curtains and the green baize already mentioned, there is very little information on colours in a hall area, except at Carton in 1818, where the 'drab Morine curtains
and cornices' in the inner hall and stairs did not add much colour, but the four windows in
the Hall and Billiard Room each had a 'flower Damask festoon' curtain and a 'linen spring
blind'.

While it is not the function of this book to analyse the paintings and prints to be found
in country houses, they form a small part of the inventories and, just as arms appear in halls
and not, for example, in other rooms in the house (except for the male dressing room or
study), so certain types of pictures sometimes appear in certain rooms. Not many pictures
are listed for the hall among the inventories and it is impossible to see a pattern emerging
from such a motley collection. At Manor Waterhouse, Co. Fermanagh, the home of the Rev.
Samuel Madden, in the 1739s the hall was 'almost covered with fine pieces of painting, several of which are originals, done by the names that have been most famous over Europe'.[115]
The Baronscourt inventory (1782) lists '2 heads and 4 figures over door Capes' in the 'Grate'
Hall, which might mean six pictures, two bust-length and four full-length, placed over the
doors. In the Marble Hall at Dromana (inv. 1755) were '11 long pannels of Indian paper pictures in mahogany frames, 4 smaller do. over doors', while in the passage leading to Lady
Grandison's dressing room there were eleven portraits of family and others, '2 Dutch pieces',
landscapes, still lifes and prints.

Decorative painting, particularly in monochrome that simulated low-relief sculpture, had
a following in Irish town and country houses. In the mid-eighteenth century, the walls of
the entrance halls at Ardfert Abbey (fig. 80), Seafield and Whitfield Court, Co. Waterford
were lined with life-size classical figures. In the hall at Lisreaghan House (also known as
Bellevue), Co. Galway a large-scale wall painting entitled *View of General de Burgh Inspecting
the Bellevue or Lawrencetown Volunteers at Birr 30 September 1784* was executed by John Ryan
(*fl*.1784–96), who, in the same county, painted four brown monochrome figures in the oval
hall at Lisdonagh House representing the cardinal virtues, set in *trompe l'oeil* niches.[116]

A small number of maps were hung in the halls of Barbavilla (1742/3), Stackallen (1757)
and Knapton (1763), and one (of Portugal) in the staircase and lobby area at Mount Stewart
(1821), where five pictures also appear, together with a number of busts. Circular niches for
busts occur in the halls at Bellamont (figs 73, 81) and Russborough. Four busts and brackets
and '3 composition figures' were in the entrance hall at Shelton House and '6 Bronze figs –
Bear, Bull & Lion' in the inner hall and stairs at Carton. The Killadoon inventories document

The painted entrance hall, Ardfert Abbey, Co. Kerry.

1
he hall at Bellamont Forest, Co. Cavan.

the expansion of the Clements' collection and the influence of the Grand Tour. In 1807 there was a bronze head of Lord Chesterfield on a stand in the hall; by 1812 a bust of 'Mr Fox by Nollekens', three white marble statues (including one of Apollo and one of Bacchus) and 'two Egyptian granite (porphry) plinths' had been added. By 1830 china vases and jars were listed; in 1836, '3 Maltese stone sarcophagi with rich arabesque ornament' and two flower stands of the same stone appear, with more china and a 'white marble sleeping child' with bow and arrow on a slab of black marble, bought by Lord Leitrim in 1820. In 1844 a bust of Earl Grey on a marble pedestal was added to all of the above, though Lord Chesterfield's 'head' had disappeared.

No paintings appear in the hall of Killadoon until 1905, but four portraits and seven views of Malta are listed in the Inner Hall in 1836. Similarly, none appear in the Entrance Hall at Newbridge House, though along the stairs in the Middle Hall were seventeen pictures (no details given) and there were four pictures in the Inner Hall, where two marble figures were placed in the niches. On the subject of marble or stone figures, according to local legend, after the suppression of the monasteries in the 1530s by Henry VIII, statues of the twelve apostles were removed by Edward Moore (or one of his descendants) from the church at Mellifont Abbey, Co. Louth, and placed in the hall of his mansion, clothed in red uniforms with muskets on their shoulders.[117]

Opposite
he drawing room (formerly the dining room)
Dowth Hall, Co. Meath (*see* fig. 95).

Three

Dining

Parlours, breakfast rooms and their contents

In Chapter 2 it was noted that the parlour is frequently the first room to the right or left off the hall on entering. In English houses this was known as a 'common' parlour, a description that is distinctly *uncommon* in Irish houses, where there is neither a shortage of parlours nor of adjectives by which they can be described. The parlour has a very long history; the earliest mention of the term was in the thirteenth century, according to the *OED*, where it is stated that it was 'the ordinary sitting room of the family which, when more spacious and handsomely furnished, is usually called the drawing room'. It was also very much an eating room. However, it was a room that changed over the eighteenth century from one that contained no comfortable, upholstered-seat furniture to being almost always a sitting room, before disappearing from country houses.[1] Among the plans and inventories in this study the term 'parlour' tended to attract a qualifying adjective in Irish houses: apart from dining and eating parlours, which are self-explanatory, there are 'parlours', 'grand' and 'great' parlours, 'big' and 'large' parlours, 'small', 'little' and 'lesser' parlours, 'common', 'gilt' and even 'out' parlours. In town houses it was simpler: there was the front or street parlour and the back parlour, while the breakfast parlour was a later addition to both country and town residences.

In contrast with the specialisation of rooms that began in the second half of the eighteenth century and culminated in the Victorian era, the parlour seemed to be almost a 'catchall' term in the late seventeenth century and well into the following one. With the exception of the 'great' or 'grand' parlour, parlours (and there were sometimes up to three in a house) were informal rooms for the family, where they ate, relaxed and received company.[2] Smaller rooms that were easier to heat and light were necessary for comfort, particularly in large houses. It is interesting to note that in Scotland, throughout the early eighteenth century, a room often called the 'family chamber' was used in a similar way to the parlour in Ireland. The main difference between parlour and 'family chamber' was that the latter contained a bed: these had disappeared from most parlours in Ireland by the early decades of the century.[3]

There are numerous references to rooms as parlours in inventories throughout the eighteenth century, probably owing to the fact that, once a room is called by one name, it can be difficult to break the habit. This might be particularly so in the case of the parlour, a family room that may not have had to endure as many changes of decor over the years as a more formal room might. As noted above, in Britain this room was most popularly called the 'common' (in the sense of everyday) parlour. It was recommended that the room should not be too big and should be located with a view of both front and back of the house in order to keep an eye on all activities surrounding it. Furthermore, the walls of the room should be lined with cupboards 'for the laying by books, swords, cloaks, and other things' in daily usage, and it should have at least one other door from it for the sake of privacy 'for it is unpleasant to be forc't to cross people, when one has not a mind to it'.[4] The only use of the term 'common parlour' in Ireland in the eighteenth century on the plans and inventories surveyed is at Lucan House and on a plan for Ardbraccan, both dating to the 1770s. It also appears in plans for Cloncarneel, Co. Meath in 1801 and Castle Bernard, Co. Offaly in 1833.[5]

The fact that the parlour does not appear to have moved upstairs on plans underlines its genesis as an eating room for upper servants (a small parlour) at ground level, where the great parlour was traditionally located directly below the great chamber on the upper floor.[6] By the beginning of the eighteenth century few such great or grand parlours were to be found in Irish houses. Pole Cosby, however, proudly recorded how his father in 1699 built 'the Big house, that is the Hall, Big Staircase and Big Parlour' at Stradbally Hall, Co. Laois, a phrase that seemed to define the house for him.[7] The 'Big Parlour' in this case surely ranks alongside the great or grand parlours.

In England it was common practice to locate great and common parlours on opposite sides of the hall.[8] This was the case in the plan for Dromoland House (*c.*1741; fig. 52), to the front of the house, as also for the Great Parlour in Conyngham Hall, Slane, Co. Meath (*c.*1710).[9] Among the inventories, a great parlour is mentioned at Powerscourt, Co. Wicklow (1728/9), as is a dining room, but, apart from the fact that the parlour had four pairs of curtains and the dining room five, there is no indication of where either was located, though the Great Parlour might have become the later Great Saloon.

It seems clear that, with its location immediately off the hall of entrance, the parlour was a convenient informal room used by the family as a living room, where items used on a daily basis were stored; it could also be used to entertain friends and as a comfortable waiting room for visitors. The last option seems to have been the object in one of Richard Castle's plans for Leinster House, Dublin in 1745, when he located the parlour to the right of the hall, where the earl could receive callers on business, usually in the mornings (fig. 82). There is, however, another parlour on this plan, overlooking the garden to the east. This appears to have been part of the formal suite of rooms, between the Great Dining Room (on the garden front) and a dressing room, with a bowed end screened by columns.[10] This parlour and the adjacent dressing room would have been used on formal occasions as sitting rooms.[11]

82
chard Castle, ground-floor plan of Leinster House
d offices, *c.*1745.

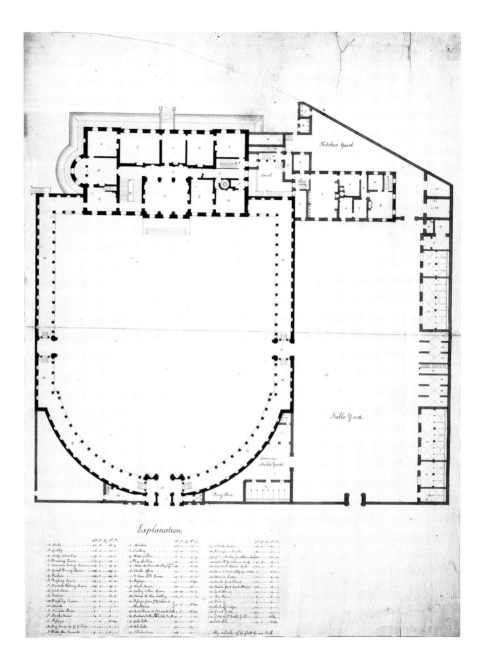

In a proposed plan for Castle Coole (*c.*1730?; fig. 83), and in one from the Charleville Forest Collection (undated), Richard Castle locates the parlour at the rear of the house. In the first plan it is directly behind the vaulted hall and is used as a drawing room (in the absence of such a room) as it is next to a two-storey dining room. In the second plan, the parlour is in addition to the drawing and dining rooms, but is smaller, and the back stairs next to it serve it and the dining room with equal ease.

There appears to be some ambiguity in architects' employment of the word 'parlour' even in the later eighteenth century. The terms 'parlour' and 'dining parlour' were used to describe the same space (that is, the main eating room) at Headfort in plans by Castle (*c.*1740s;

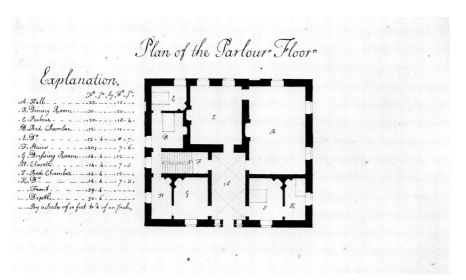

fig. 27) and by John Ensor (1750s?), both of whom located it to the left of the hall. As there
was no other named dining area on these plans, formal meals may have been served there
or, as was often the case in the early part of the century, in the saloon.[12] In 1765 Sir William
Chambers's plans for Headfort clarified the distribution slightly by leaving the parlour to the
left of the entrance and locating a dining room across the hall from it (fig. 28). In Richard
Morrison's book published in 1793, it appears that either he could not make up his mind
between the terms 'parlour' and 'dining room' or he might have been appealing to differing
tastes.[13] In one of his two largest house plans the eating room is called a parlour. Bearing in
mind that it is the biggest room and that in the same house are a billiard room, a study and
a breakfast parlour (all room names that are associated with lately built houses), a 'parlour'
was at this time rather *passé* in the country house. In the second plan he calls the same space
a 'dining room', the 'study' has become a 'library' and the 'breakfast parlour' is now a 'breakfast *room*'. It might also be worth noting that, in plans for Castle Coole, Richard Johnston
has a 'Breakfast *Parlour*' to the right of the hall (1789), whereas James Wyatt, in his plans for
the same house (1790; fig. 24), calls that space a 'Breakfast *Room*'.

While the parlour began to disappear from new houses in Britain in the 1740s and was
out of fashion by the 1750s, the same could not be said of Ireland. One is to be found on a
plan of Lucan House in the 1770s; at Cloncarneel as late as 1801 (as has been seen), Francis
Johnston has a parlour and a common parlour, the former clearly a dining room. A parlour
is also included on his drawings for Killeen Castle, (1803) and Pakenham Hall (Tullynally
Castle), Co. Westmeath (gothicised 1801–6) but perhaps, like Horace Walpole at Strawberry
Hill in 1754, the owners wanted room names that resonated with the past, particularly if
their house was in the castle style.[14] Among the plans examined, the parlour is markedly ab-
sent from houses newly built or altered extensively after the Act of Union in 1800, such as
Rockingham (1809), Ballyfin (1822), Emo Court (1821), Lissadell (1833) and Adare Manor,
Co. Limerick (1834), all newly built, and the refurbished Castlegar (1801), Mount Bellew
(1805), Castle Howard (gothicised *c*.1811) and Carton (*c*.1815).

Despite the ambiguity mentioned above, it appears that the parlour for informal use in
the country house was usually located to the right or left of the hall to the front. A look at the
furniture that was contained in 'informal' parlours might throw more light on the activities

pursued there. Jane Austen's description of a visit to a 'great house' might be a good starting point. There, paying a visit to their friends, Anne Elliot and her sister sat 'the full half hour in the old-fashioned square parlour, with a small carpet and shining floor, to which the present daughters of the house were gradually giving the proper air of confusion by a grand piano-forte, and a harp, flowerstands, and little tables placed in every direction'.[15] Given the emphasis here on musical instruments, it is surprising how few appear among the inventories.[16] Austen also mentions that the room is wainscoted, which seems to have been common in parlours.[17] In his specification for a house in Bristol in the early decades of the eighteenth century, the builder recommended wainscoting for the parlour, with no mention of the same for the dining room.[18] Mrs Mary Delany, in a letter from Dublin to her sister in 1750, supposed that 'when you turn your kitchen into a parlour, you will fit the wainscot of the best bedchamber there, and hang the bedchamber with paper', the latter being more fashionable by then.[19]

The Great Parlour in Powerscourt, Co. Wicklow (1728) has already been mentioned as having four windows; these were hung with scarlet paragon. There were twenty-four 'fine Walnut chairs with Barbary Leather Seats & loose covers of leather' (to protect them when not in use and/or to ring seasonal changes); the oak dining table was oval and there was a sideboard. For relaxation, the family could amuse themselves with the pair of backgammon tables, a pair of globes and a card table. The contents of the parlour at the (old) Bishop's Palace at Elphin, Co. Roscommon in 1740 were fewer but not dissimilar, with evidence for eating, drinking tea and playing cards. No curtains are listed, but there was a 'looking glass' and the ten leather chairs were similar to those itemised in the Dining Room. At Howth Castle in the mid-eighteenth century, the contents of the Out Parlour (the name possibly indicating its proximity to a back door) are rather ambiguous: a dining table, fourteen walnut chairs covered with Spanish leather and a 'large black & white marble table, mahogany frame'. It may have been used as a waiting room and for eating in.

It is important to note that, in the eighteenth century, room usage was fairly flexible. It is therefore not surprising that some rooms appear by their contents (or lack of them) to have had no clear purpose. In Co. Meath, Stackallen (inv. 1757; fig. 76) had a Small Parlour and a Large Parlour; the smaller, with green paragon curtains on the windows, was an informal eating room with two armchairs covered to match the curtains, twelve rush-bottomed chairs, an oval mahogany dining table 'with skelliton feet', an 'old octagonal table with slate top' and a tea table. The furniture in the Large Parlour gives little information about its use; apart from the '2 walnut armchairs with cane bottoms and backs', it had two card tables and an eight-leaved gilt leather screen, no other chairs and no curtains.[20] Nine panels of its wainscot were covered with India paper and the only picture was a portrait of 'King George'. It sounds rather like the description by Jonah Barrington of the parlours at his grandfather's house, Cullenaghmore, Co. Laois, where 'A large parlour [was] on each side of the hall, the only embellishments of which were some old portraits, and a multiplicity of hunting, shooting and racing prints, with red tape nailed round them by way of frames.'[21] Finally, in the 1783 estimate of furniture from the London firm of Mayhew & Ince for the 'Common Parlour' at Caledon, Co. Tyrone, it is evident that the room was for family eating, with mahogany dining and breakfast tables, a 'mahogany circular sideboard table between doors', six mahogany chairs with stuffed seats and two elbow chairs to match.[22] It would seem unlikely that the chairs were covered to match the white window curtains, but perhaps they matched the trimmings, a green fringe and tassels, and toned in with the 'Turkey carpet'.

Decoration of a somewhat different type was to be found in the Painted Parlour at Quilca, in Co. Cavan, the home of the actor and theatre manager Thomas Sheridan (fig. 84), father of Richard Brinsley Sheridan. Jonathan Swift made much fun of Quilca, where he was a

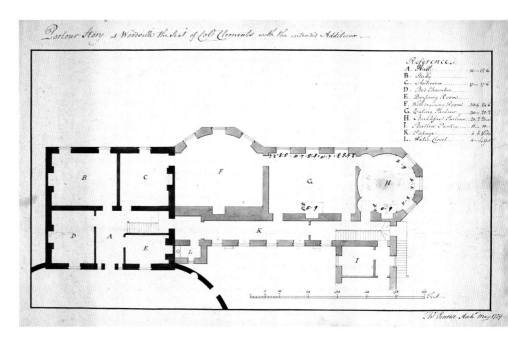

regular visitor, memorably in his poem 'To Quilca, a country house of Dr Sheridan, in no
very good repair'.[23] According to a visitor writing in 1852, a canvas had been spread on the
coved ceiling of the parlour, onto which John Lewis (*fl.*1740–1769), the painter and scene-
painter for Sheridan, painted a sky and clouds. Under this, on each of the four walls, contained within large medallions, were portraits of Milton, Shakespeare, Swift and Doctor
Sheridan. Apparently 'these were supported by allegorical figures, and set off by draperies,
and a goodly-sized sphinx or two, for the corners. The whole was cleverly and artistically
done, and had a vivid effect.'[24]

The breakfast room is one that leaves us in no doubt as to its purpose. As it appears in
the inventories of Lord Howth's Dublin house in St Mary's Abbey in 1751 and of Dromoland
House in 1753, it would seem that the arrival of such a specialised space was discernible as
early as the 1740s.[25] Among the plans, we find a Breakfast Room at Headfort, made by either
Richard Castle or John Ensor, possibly in the 1750s.[26] The fact that there is then an almost
twenty-year gap until the appearance of the next breakfast room/parlour indicates that it was
not widely copied at this time but that it had its followers from the second half of the eighteenth century. Apart from a breakfast room located, unusually, between two bedroom suites
on the first floor at Pollacton, Co. Carlow (1803), there is no discernible difference among
the plans between the location of the breakfast room and that of a parlour. The question of
whether or not serving breakfast was the only function fulfilled by this room would probably
depend on the size of the house, but breakfast was an informal affair and flexible, particularly when entertaining: it could be taken any time between 9 am and 11.30 am or later; it was
also perfectly acceptable to have it served in one's room. While staying with friends in Co.
Meath in 1733, Mrs Delany (or Mrs Pendarves, as she then was) and her fellow guests met at
breakfast at about 10 am. At Carton, 'we breakfast between ten and eleven tho it is called half
past nine. We have an immense table—chocolate—honey—hot bread—cold bread—brown
bread—white bread—green bread—coloured breads and cakes. After breakfast . . . the chaplain reads a few short prayers, and then we go as we like.'[27]

84
Engraving of Dr Thomas Sheridan, illustration to his
Life of Swift, 1784.

85
Thomas Penrose, *Parlour Story at Woodville, seat of
Col. Clements with the intended Additions*, 1779.

There can be no doubt that at Ardbraccan the patron required a breakfast room, as it appears in all of the plans. Thomas Penrose's elongated extension to one side of Woodville, Co. Dublin (1779, dem.; fig. 85) for the Clements family includes a circular Breakfast Room with three windows, linked by an enfilade along the garden front to the Eating Parlour, the Withdrawing Room and the 'Antiroom'. Access to the back stairs and kitchen from both eating rooms was adjacent to them. Blayney Balfour and his sister Anne played with the idea of a breakfast parlour at Townley Hall, Co. Louth from about 1790, but obviously abandoned it: no parlour of any description appears in James Playfair's proposals for the house (1792), nor in the house as built. In his 1789 plan for Charleville Forest, James Byres created an enfilade from one side of the main block to the other: off the oval hall to the right is the Breakfast Parlour, through which guests must go to gain access to the Dining Room beyond it (fig. 18).[28] An unusually shaped breakfast room at Brook Lodge in Galway (1776) had an apsidal end, a doorway in its centre that led to the dining room and a niche on one side of the apse, answered on the other by a curved tripartite window.[29] Curiously, in Richard Morrison's book, 'parlours' appear in smaller houses, while the larger houses have 'breakfast parlours'.[30]

A new space called a 'Morning Room' emerged on a plan by Francis Johnston dating to 1790; it was a large room to the right of the hall, located in a space that might previously have been called a parlour.[31] The *OED* defines such a room as one 'used as a sitting room during the early part of the day'. They never became common in Ireland and appear in few ground-floor plans, among which are Castlegar (1801), Castle Howard (1811), Dromoland Castle (*c*.1826) and Castle Dillon, Co. Armagh (1842). At Killeen Castle (1803; fig. 86) there is one on the second floor, 'Lady Fingall's Morning Room', where it is part of the earl and countess of Fingall's private bedroom suite (fig. 87).[32] Both breakfast and morning rooms appear on plans of Emo Court (1821) and of Mount Bellew (1817).[33] It is interesting to note that on all plans containing morning rooms there is direct access from them to the entrance hall, thus indicating that this was where visitors were received in the mornings. Morning rooms are not mentioned among the inventories.

W. Slater, watercolour of Killeen Castle, Co. Meath,
09. Private collection.

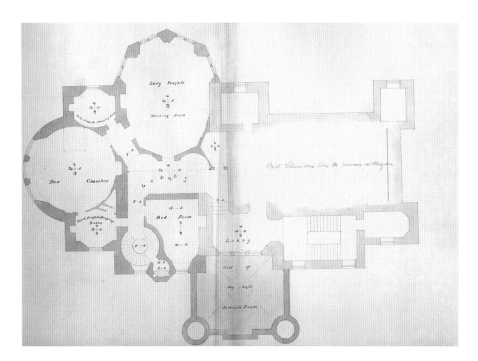

87
Francis Johnston, plan of second (bedchamber) floor
at Killeen Castle, Co. Meath, 1803.

On a visit to a country house, Lady Morgan's eponymous hero O'Donnel (1814) finds 'a kind of bar' (perhaps a type of buffet?) adjoining the breakfast room, 'where breakfast was prepared and served according to orders', noting that, from there, trays were dispatched to guests' dressing rooms.[34]

The contents of the eighteenth-century breakfast rooms are, on the whole, not impressive, and it is difficult to glean any information from them as to their use other than for a quick breakfast, perhaps even taken standing up. As well as a breakfast table, a card table, a desk and a mirror, there were a 'Settee and 8 Chairs Covered With Cross Stitch' at Dromoland House in 1753.[35] Baronscourt (inv. 1782) had a marble table-top on a frame, an oval mirror, a picture over the chimneypiece, a Pembroke table and seven elbow chairs covered with red and white check cases. On the 1787 inventory for Gaulston, Co. Westmeath (dem.), where the '3 large mahogany oval tables' in the breakfast room were presumably shared with the dining room, were ten rush-bottomed chairs painted green and white, a type of oven and a collection of items described as oval-shaped – two mirrors with gilt frames, sixteen portraits and a map, also with gilt frames.[36]

The later inventories are more interesting and indicate a greater degree of comfort and colour coordination in breakfast rooms. For example, in Clogrenan, Co. Carlow (*c*.1810) there were green moreen curtains, a 'Large settee and cuichens [cushions] with green check covers', six green and white chairs, and '2 green silk curtains to Lettice doors' (unclear, unless there were lattice doors on an item of furniture not listed). On the floor was a 'matt to cover whole room'; there were two tables and hanging on the walls were '23 French prints from Don Quixote'. The presence of a piano indicates that the room's use was not confined to the morning, confirmed by the press bed with 'feather bed boulster' (which might have been used as a day bed). Castle Coole's breakfast parlour in 1802 contained an exotic touch in its twelve chairs 'with Chinese covers'.[37] As at Clogrenan, green is also found in Shelton House (1816), where the mahogany sofa and eight armchairs were upholstered in green leather; the carpet covering the floor, the silk on the two firescreens and most probably the 'linen calico' curtains were also green. There were two oval dining tables, a card table and '59 framed and glazed engravings different subjects' on the walls. No colour is mentioned at Moore Abbey, Co. Kildare (inv. 1826), but it sounds like a comfortable room with (apart from tables and chairs) two sofas, cushions and covers, a Turkey carpet, a mirror over the fireplace, a pier glass and two oval mirrors, possibly hanging over the two pier tables. At Ashfield, Co. Cavan (inv. 1829) was a sofa complete with cushions, a 'lounger arm chair', two armchairs with cushions and two French armchairs. Apart from three tables, there was a work table, a book-case and '6 shelves for books'. By 1843 there were a few additions, among them a small otto-man, a ladies cabinet, lots of 'chimney ornaments', eleven prints and two bronze inkstands.

These later inventories indicate the same sort of comfort that has been seen in parlours that were used throughout the day as family sitting rooms. It is not clear if the analogy with a parlour stretched to the evening – did occupants abandon the breakfast/morning rooms at some point during the day and retire to another room? In the absence of a parlour, where did the family relax and entertain their friends? It would appear that the drawing room or the library, if there was one, fulfilled this need; alternatives were dressing rooms and closets.[38] Mrs Delany and her friends constantly entertained each other in these latter rooms, and it will be seen in Chapter 4 that in many houses a dressing room formed part of the suite of reception rooms.

The dining room

Up to *c.*1730, and following the French custom, the saloon was sometimes used as a dining room in Britain, particularly when catering for large numbers.[39] The earliest example is an-notated on Richard Castle's plans for Carton dating to 1739, where, as a dining parlour ad-joined it, the Saloon was unlikely to have been used on a regular basis for eating. The same might be said of two other early saloons – John Aheron's at Dromoland (where there were two parlours) and Castle's at Headfort (one parlour). But it is entirely possible that the saloon was still used for eating when entertaining large numbers of guests.

There is a great deal of inconsistency in the terminology used during the eighteenth cen-tury to describe a formal room for eating, as has been seen, with the word 'parlour' being used infrequently but regularly for the main eating room into the second half of the century, and sometimes even longer, especially in some 'castle-style' houses. The terms that were most commonly used for the main or formal eating rooms were 'dining room' and 'dining parlour'. Other terms relating to this space include 'eating room' and 'eating parlour'. The point has been made that 'dining parlour' was used from before the mid-seventeenth cen-tury, at the time that beds were disappearing from the principal parlour, and the new phrase underlined the exclusive use of this room for eating and entertaining rather than for sleep-ing.[40] As the eighteenth century progressed all of these terms, with the exception of 'dining room', became old-fashioned and were used only occasionally. Inconsistencies are found too in architects' use of the terms (the English architect John Nash used the term 'eating room' in his plan of Rockingham as late as 1809), but the choice of room names was likely to have been that of the client in many cases. For the sake of clarity, the term 'dining room' will be applied consistently here to cover the various names used. As the dining room is part of the formal rooms of a house, its functioning belongs to Chapter 4; here it will be examined as an architectural space, together with its contents.

It is surprising how early the term 'dining room' was used in Ireland compared to Britain: there is a reference to one ('dyneinge') at Croghan Castle, Co. Offaly in 1636; in an Ormonde inventory of 1639 for Kilkenny Castle; and in houses in Dublin belonging to the earls of Cork (1645, 'Dyneing') and of Kildare (1656).[41] In Britain the earliest use of the term is quoted as being in an inventory for Ham House dating to 1677.[42] Though not often found before the mid-1730s in England, the appearance of the term in an advertisement in a Dublin newspaper in June 1711 points to it being in fairly common usage in Ireland.[43] That said, according to the plans under discussion it was only in the second half of the century that it became a common term, as Mrs Delany acknowledged in 1755, referring to 'My "dining room", vulgarly so called'.[44]

The importance of the dining room has been acknowledged by a number of writers. Mark Girouard says that from the early decades of the century the dining room 'was always one of the best and biggest rooms in the house', and Isaac Ware said of the spacious dining room on one of his plans that measured 40 feet × 23.5 feet: 'this . . . gives a very noble room; it may be properly the capital apartment of the house, and may be called the great dining-room'.[45]

An interesting observation was made by Robert Adam on the reason why the dining room in France never achieved the importance that the English (and the Irish) attached to it: 'our manners prevent us from imitating them. Their eating rooms seldom or never constitute a piece in their great apartments, but lie out of the suite, and in fitting them up, little attention is paid to beauty'; the antechambers they used as dining rooms were usually decorated quite simply.[46] But Adam explained that the French used their dining room purely for eating in, that they 'trust to the display of the table for show and magnificence', not to the decor, and that, as soon as they had eaten, they retired to the 'rooms of company'. He goes on,

> It is not so with us. Accustomed by habit, or induced by the nature of our climate, we indulge more largely in the enjoyment of the bottle. Every person of rank here is either a member of the legislation, or entitled by his condition to take part in the political arrangements of his country . . . these circumstances lead men to live more with one another, and more detached from the society of the ladies. The eating rooms are considered as the apartments of conversation, in which we are to pass a great part of our time. This renders it desireable to have them fitted up with elegance and splendor, but in a style different from that of other apartments. Instead of being hung with damask, tapestry, &c. they are always finished with stucco, and adorned with statues and paintings, that they may not retain the smell of the victuals.[47]

There are a number of points in this quote that will be revisited. In his final comment about fabrics retaining the smell of food, Adam reiterates the advice given in 1702 by the Swedish architect Daniel Cronström, who recommended panelling in the room and approved of gilt leather for the same reason.[48] It was the gilt leather hangings in the Great Dining Room of Kilkenny Castle that caught the attention of John Dunton when he visited there in 1686.[49]

John Cornforth made some interesting observations after a visit to Castletown, noting that what would have been the common parlour (the room to the left on entering the house) had been extended into the dining room. He believed that the Green Drawing Room there was originally the Great Parlour, a belief that was reinforced when he discovered that 'when the silk was [taken] down, the walls were panelled and there were traces of pilasters – and pilasters confirm that it was not a drawing room'.[50] Generally, he explains, when a 'dining room' made its appearance, the great parlour became a withdrawing room or a saloon, but it retained its panelling (or stucco decoration).[51]

The importance of the dining room and the open hospitality extended there by the Irish gentry has often been commented upon. In 1732 John Loveday remarked upon their 'continually feasting with one another', but that they 'always praise the dishes at their own tables' and expected the same from their guests.[52] Mrs Delany thought the dinners were rather excessive: 'you are not invited to dinner to any private gentleman of a thousand a year or less that does not give you seven dishes at one course, and Burgundy and Champagne: and these dinners they give once or twice a week'.[53] Richard Pococke describes in detail a 'Milesian feast' in Ireland on his travels, the remnants of which were dished up for breakfast the next morning.[54] At Quilca, Thomas Sheridan entertained lavishly 'in the manner of the ancient Irish' with the floor of his dining room strewn with rushes and his table spread with 'antique dishes and cuisinage obsolete'. He enjoyed the effect on his guests of producing on the table a massive meal, 'till he made them all sick with "swilled" mutton, or a sheep roasted whole, and stuffed with geese, turkeys and chicken packed in vegetables; when lo! all was taken away, and the best of modern dinners served up with plenty of claret and champagne, to wash away unsavoury memories'.[55]

It is interesting to note how frequently visitors to houses relate the measurements of some of the reception rooms: was it something that the owner proudly boasted of or was it a talent that visitors had developed? Isaac Ware commented on the 'addition of a great room now [1756] to almost every house of consequence'.[56] Mrs Delany is quite informative on this point in her correspondence, giving precise measurements of numerous rooms in which she entertained or was entertained. In Scotland Lord Garlies, heir to the 5th earl of Galloway, stressed to the amateur architect Sir John Clerk in 1737 that, while he required a drawing room of about 16 feet square, the dining room should be 'as good as could be got not above 24 or 27 at most'.[57] And the bishop of Dromore, writing to a friend in 1793 about renting a house in Dublin, required 'a Dining Parlour large enough to give a Dinner to a Dozen Persons'.[58] It appears that the largest dining room was at Carton, to designs by Richard Morrison c.1815, at 50.4 × 24 feet (fig. 89). Next in size was in Thomastown House, Co. Tipperary, measuring 50 × 20 feet, suitable no doubt for the extravagant hospitality that was carried on there. This was followed by the dining room of Headfort at 48 × 24 feet and that at Curraghmore, Co. Waterford at 40 × 26 feet, 'fine and painted in great taste' according to Daniel Beaufort.[59] Among the plans on which the size is annotated, the average size for the eighteenth century (from the earliest plan, c.1709 for Old Castle Coole, to the end of the century) is 28 × 21.5 feet; from 1800 to 1842 it is 36 × 23.5 feet. The growth in size in the nineteenth century is not surprising as it coincides with a time when people travelled more, in better-sprung carriages and on improved roads, stopping to eat or to stay with friends en route.

Between 1763 and 1767 Lady Louisa Conolly (fig. 88) created a 'great room' at Castletown. This was the dining room, mentioned earlier, made out of two adjoining rooms to the left of the hall (fig. 90). It was a major job, as the dividing walls were removed through three floors to roof level, a false wall was built to the west to centre the windows, and fireplaces and flues were repositioned. Similarities between Leinster House and Castletown have been found: not surprisingly, as the duke of Leinster appears to have been responsible for the redecoration of the room, as implied by Louisa in a letter to her sister Sarah in 1767: 'The Duke of Leinster and my sister dined here the other day it was the first time that he had dined here since our new dining room was made which he had the making of, I may say, for it was him that persuaded Mr Conolly to do, he liked it vastly.'[60] Behind the false wall, the two closets became serving rooms with a lead sink and stoves that kept the food warm, after it was brought along the colonnade and in through a side door from the kitchen in the west pavilion.[61]

88
Stephen Catterson Smith the Elder (1806–72), *Portrait of Lady Louisa Conolly*, after a portrait by Sir Joshua Reynolds, c.1775; oil on canvas.

There was an amount of flexibility regarding the location of the dining room, with the majority favouring the front of the house.[62] The rooms are divided into two main types – those
that are part of an enfilade and those that are not. It is notable that, in the first type, such as
at Carton (*c*.1739, and Morrison's 1815 plan), Rockingham (1809; fig. 56), the Johnston and
Wyatt plans for Castle Coole (1789 and 1790; figs 23, 24), one of the Pain brothers' plans for
Dromoland Castle (*c*.1826), Lissadell (1833) and Ballyfin (*c*.1822; fig. 46), the dining room often terminates the enfilade. Given the use of the room, this makes sense. It is not a room of
'transit', a room through which a guest might 'parade', but a destination.

In 1807, when Louisa Beaufort visited Lissanoure Castle, Co. Antrim, she noted that all
of the rooms opened in to each other, that 'in going from the parlor to the drawing room you

89
Dining room at Carton, Co. Kildare, part of addition
to the house by Richard Morrison *c*.1815.

ining room at Castletown House.

pass through all of them – parlor and drawing room are square octagons 26 feet each way'. She mentions that the 'dining parlor' was located elsewhere – in other words, not in the enfilade.[63] In plans for Headfort, Castle and Chambers both locate the dining room at the front of the house, off the hall (figs 27, 28). There were also some rather odd arrangements. For example, at Charleville Forest (1789; fig. 18) and Mount Bellew (*c*.1805) the hall and breakfast room are located mid-enfilade: while the hall might be called part of the reception rooms, the breakfast room would not, and it would seem a little odd that guests had to walk through this room to gain access to the dining room.

But was there a relationship between the location of the dining room and its proximity to the kitchen? A study of the plans shows that, in the vast majority of cases, access to the kitchen was fairly close to the eating room, usually by a back staircase next to or close to the dining room, and often with a door into the room for the use of servants. There were three main reasons for such an arrangement: servants did not have to make their way across the hall carrying dishes and leaving a smell of food in their wake; the food arrived efficiently and still warm; and it avoided collisions between servants and guests or hosts in the door-way. But in some cases food had to be brought to the dining room from the wing halfway across the house; in other instances, the back staircase is on the opposite side of the hall.[64] In all of the early Headfort plans (Castle, Ensor, Chambers) there was a long journey from the pavilions to the parlour/dining room: Ensor's dining parlour was to the west of the hall while the kitchen was in the east wing; in Chambers's plan the opposite was the case, but the parlour was closer, to the west of the hall (fig. 28).

On an interesting Francis Johnston plan for Killeen Castle (fig. 91; 1802), there is a spiral back staircase rising into a lobby outside the dining room, and a small space to the right on entering the room is marked 'This recess arched over and enclosed by a curtain festooned up'. It is not clear whether this might have been a servery or somewhere for a collection of plate or desserts to be displayed with a flourish. Such serving spaces were included at both Lough Glynn, Co. Roscommon (*c.*1830) and Lissadell (1833), with back staircases conveniently adjacent to them. The French architect Jacques François Blondel preferred to have a small room or servery next to the dining room where food could be warmed up and glasses washed in a cistern, rather than in the dining room itself, to save the diners the irritating clatter.[65]

Whatever the requirements of serving food, one has to wonder just how accurate is one writer's assertion that, in the eighteenth century, 'in most country houses in Ireland there was a cellar underneath the dining room. By means of a trap-door, the host could descend and bring up bottle after bottle of wine.'[66] This architectural innovation was mentioned in the previous chapter at Barbavilla, Co. Westmeath, when the Smythes dined in their hall. Apparently when a visitor to the house 'saw the good beer rise from under ground up to his nose, [he] cried out good God did you Ever see the like!'[67]

While stucco panelling in dining rooms was not unusual in Ireland, there was nothing to rival the finest examples in England and Scotland, such as the Marble Parlour (later the State Dining Room) at Houghton Hall, Norfolk, and the all-over stucco at The Drum, Midlothian (1726). However one of the great dining rooms of the first half of the eighteenth century in

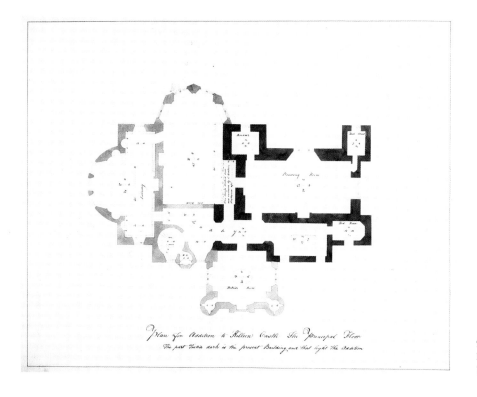

91

Francis Johnston, *Plan for Addition to Killeen Castle The Principal Floor*, 1802.

these islands, already noted for its large size, is that at Carton, designed by Richard Castle in 1739 and now called the Saloon.[68] Here the deeply coved ceiling of the double-height room was decorated with baroque exuberance by the Lafranchini brothers, Paolo and Filippo, who also executed the wall drops on the window side (fig. 92).[69] Another baroque coved dining room ceiling can be seen in Russsborough (fig. 93), also designed by Castle and begun 1741; at the earlier Bellamont Forest (c.1728), designed by Sir Edward Lovett Pearce, the ceiling is coved and coffered in the Palladian manner. For Leinster House, two drawings attributed to Filippo Lafranchini and dating to c.1760 show designs for plasterwork for the walls of the ground-floor dining room, and one for the ceiling (fig. 94).

Lady Kildare's brother-in-law, Henry Fox, was critical of Isaac Ware's scheme for the coved State Dining Room (later the Saloon) at Leinster House, suggesting that 'the walls

would be better without compartments that the pictures may be hung at discretion', a point that was ignored in the execution.[70] However, where there was a dearth of paintings, 'compartments' were a convenient method for decorating walls. Dado rails might also add interest, as in the dining room at Ardbraccan, where the rail is trimmed with pewter, as are the chimneypieces in some of the bedrooms and dressing rooms.[71] While Lord Cloncurry had other plans for the walls of his dining room at Lyons, Co. Kildare (as shall be seen), among the many pieces of sculpture acquired on his Grand Tour were three marble relief panels of classical subjects executed by Acquisti, placed as overdoors in this space.[72] Notable too is the mid-eighteenth-century French *boiserie*-type decoration of shallow stucco panels with foliate designs in eating rooms in two Dublin houses, Charlemont House and No. 86 St Stephen's

4
Design for plasterwork for the ceiling of the ground-
floor dining room at Leinster House, attributed to
Filippo Lafranchini, *c*.1760.

Green, and at Dowth Hall, Co. Meath (fig. 95).[73] As the dining room was generally considered a 'male' space, given that men spent more time in it than women did, and that French rococo (together with *chinoiserie*) was a style more usually associated with women for their dressing rooms and boudoirs – and even at mid-century for a drawing room – it seems an unusual choice of decoration for a dining room.[74]

Other ways of achieving architectural interest in dining rooms included the use of bows, bays, columnar screens and niches. Maurice Craig is of the opinion that the bow 'is so marked a feature of mid eighteenth-century Irish houses that its ancestry should be enquired into'. He also claims that Richard Castle's bowed saloon at Ballyhaise of *c*.1733 is the earliest example of this in Ireland and in Britain, and that the bow is a feature that is 'entirely absent from Dublin (apart from the backs of Dublin town houses) though not from Cork'.[75] The bow enjoyed popularity in Ireland from the first half of the century. With reference to dining rooms, it is seen to superb effect in Belvedere, the villa built for Robert Rochfort, later 1st earl of Belvedere, to designs by Castle in *c*.1740 (fig. 12), where both the dining and drawing rooms are in the curved end bays of the house, with rococo ceilings by the stuccadore Barthelemy Cramillion.[76] Other bow-ended dining rooms include those in James Playfair's plan for Townley Hall, Co. Louth (1792), Lyons (1797), Markree Castle, Co. Sligo (1803), Castle Howard (*c*.1811), Powerscourt, Co. Wicklow (1731–40) and Oakpark, Co. Carlow (remodelled 1832).

The countess of Shelburne described 'two very good rooms on each side of a spacious hall, the one a drawing room the other a parlour where we dined' at Dawson Court in Co. Laois in 1769.[77] She noted that the two were of similar size and 'have bow windows with this only difference that the window of one is circular, the other in angles – the circular one has a much better effect and gives such a look of space to the room that it is hardly possible to

95
French *boiserie* decoration in the drawing room
(formerly the dining room) at Dowth Hall,
Co. Meath.

believe them to be the same size – Kiloine Hill is the principal object of this room and ye whole country in general'.[78] From her description it seems more likely that the room with the view – and the bow – was the drawing room, while the canted bay was in the dining room. Such canted bays also had a substantial following but rectangular bay windows were less common. Mrs Delany's dining room had a sizeable one at Delville, the room being described by her in 1744 as '26 feet long and 16 feet and a half wide, with the projection in the middle, which opens thirteen foot and is eight foot deep, with three windows, and large enough for two sideboards, one window between the tables and one at each side, which lights the room very agreeably'.[79]

By the mid-1720s the columnar screen in British dining rooms had gained in popularity since Vanbrugh proposed one in an unexecuted plan for Blenheim in 1705, and William Adam provided one at Hopetoun, Midlothian in the early 1720s.[80] The screen of columns and accompanying frieze in the dining room at Bellamont Forest were added in *c*.1770 (fig. 96), below the original coved ceiling: as the columns are engaged, they are a purely decorative fea-

Dining Room at Bellamont Forest, Co. Cavan.

ture. While a screen was a decorative feature, there was a practical side to it, in that it could provide a service area in which the servants operated, frequently with a door leading to the back stairs. Such an arrangement can be seen in a Samuel Chearnley plan (1745–6), where an accompanying note explains that the back stairs are 'Private ways from the Kitchen to bring up Dinner'; a spiral staircase close to it leads directly into the wine cellar below.[81] In his published plans Richard Morrison, for whom columnar screens became a leitmotif, shows one that is too shallow for a service area but is designed to frame the sideboard set into a recess.[82] The plan contrasts with the convenience of Chearnley's: to get to the kitchen, servants in the Morrison design have to make their way across the vestibule to the other side of the house, where the back stairs were located.

A more convenient plan by Morrison for Mount Bellew (c.1805) has a door from the service area leading into the 'lobby and stairs for serving dinner'. In the new dining room at Carton in c.1815 he placed a screen at each end: the route to the kitchen was somewhat circuitous but, as the butler's pantry was across a passage from the service area, it was possible that food was kept warm there. The dining rooms created by Morrison, with his son William, at Borris House, Co. Carlow (*c.*1813), Ballyfin (1822) and Fota House, Co. Cork (*c.*1825) have in common screens of scagliola columns and friezes of swagged bucrania.[83] At Ballyfin the dining room is some distance from the kitchen, which is in a service block linked to one side of the house, but at Fota House a jib door in the service area leads into a butler's pantry or servery, while the opposite door leads to a lobby, the wine cellar and ultimately the kitchen.

From an aesthetic point of view, the columnar screen had the effect of framing the sideboard (the *buffet* in French houses) on which the family plate was often displayed. Prior to his departure for his Dublin residence at Kevin Street, Bishop Edward Synge of Elphin always insisted that his plate chest be collected from the bankers, Lennox and French of Lower Ormond Street ('the receit for the chest is in the Scriptoire') and cautioned his daughter Alicia to 'have a care that a larger Table does not crowd the place, tho' it may shew your plate to more advantage'.[84] Also displayed on the sideboard might be a 'pyramid' of fruits grown in hothouses in the walled gardens of country and large town houses, probably what Bishop Synge was referring to in a letter to Alicia in June 1747: 'I take it for granted that now fruits are coming in, you'll provide largely for Pyramids to be looked at. I'll allow you as much sugar as you please.'[85]

On the subject of desserts, plans for Headfort (*c.*1750) and for Castle Coole (1789 and 1790) are of interest. A small apsed space that separates the parlour from the drawing room (and with access to both) is called a 'Buffett' on Castle's Headfort plan (fig. 27). Here the ladies and later the gentlemen could pass through into the drawing room. The apse is back to back with the semicircular back staircase. Similarly, next to and connected with the dining room at Castle Coole, Richard Johnston locates a 'Dessert Room', beside which is a back staircase to the basement leading to the kitchen in the east wing (1789, fig. 23). One year later, in his plan for the same house, and with a similarly located staircase, Wyatt called this space a 'Beaufetteer'.[86] It is not clear how exactly these rooms were used: did guests move from the table into here for dessert? It would seem highly unlikely that a buffet laden with the Belmore silver would be hidden away from prospective admirers.[87] It is possible that the sideboard, on which the sugared desserts or pyramids were displayed, was wheeled into the dining room at the appropriate time or, simply, that the room was used by servants for last-minute preparation and checking of the food before serving. That the use of the room at Castle Coole was connected with dessert is confirmed by the list of contents there in an 1802 inventory taken by the housekeeper after Lord Belmore's death. In this she lists in the Dessert Room '14 dessert china dishes, 4 dozen and 4 dessert plates, 2 pails for ice, 2 glass sugar bowls and 11 common china froot dishes'.[88]

The dessert course for formal dinners was serious business, underlined by the appearance of a 'Confectioners Room' in the basement of Leinster House in Castle's plan of 1745: it is the largest space at that level.[89] There is no mention of such a room in the basement at Castle Coole, but there was one at Norfolk House in London in the 1750s, suggesting 'the elaborate desserts issuing from a room probably adjacent to the [ground-floor] Dining Room'.[90] While more will be said about formal dining in the next chapter, Joseph Farington's description of the dessert table (fig. 97) at a dinner with the Norfolks gives an example of what an ingenious confectioner could produce and it is worth relating at this point: 'The table was Prepar'd for Desert [*sic*], which was a Beautiful Park, round the edge was a Plantation of Flowering Shrubs, and in the middle a Fine piece of water, with Dolphins spouting out water, & Dear [*sic*] dispersed Irregularly over the Lawn, on the Edge of the Table was all the Iced Creams, & wet & dried Sweetmeats, it was such a piece of work it was all left on the Table till we went to coffee.'[91] In an advertisement in the *Dublin Journal* in October 1749, Elizabeth

Table setting at Fairfax House, York, with sugarwork
centrepiece by Ivan Day.

O'Brien, 'flower maker from London', informed readers that at her shop in Capel Street she 'makes and sells all kinds of artificial Flowers, Trees, Hedges and Arches for Deserts [*sic*]'.

There is a dearth of information on wall colour for dining rooms, though Mrs Delany hung hers in 1755 'with mohair cafoy paper, (a good blue)'.[92] In 1794 at Dorothea Herbert's home at Carrick, Co. Kilkenny, a rather Adam-style colour scheme was adopted when no less than 'a Head painter [was employed] to paint [the large Parlour] green with a beautiful lilac Cornice'. Whether Adam would have approved of the 'scarlet marine curtains' bought for the room by her mother is another matter.[93] His Eating Parlour at Headfort has now been restored to its original mid- and dark-green colour scheme (figs 98, 99, 100).[94] The Dining Room and the Ante Room (also used as a servery) at Baronscourt were to be painted 'light green in oil', according to instructions in 1795.[95] Also painted green was (at least part of) the Eating Parlour at Caledon in 1799, listed in an invoice from the painter as 'fine' green, while the frieze was 'picked in fancy colours'.[96] As late as 1835, in a furniture auction at Altidore, Co. Wicklow, 'rich red morocco hangings' (matching the chairs) were listed in the dining room.[97]

98
The coved ceiling of the eating parlour at Headfort, a double cube of two storeys, decorated to designs by Robert Adam (1728–92) between 1771 and *c*.1775.

99
Detail of paintwork in the eating parlour showing how the paint was originally applied to the decoration.

Design for finishing the Chimney side of the Eating Parlor. For The Right Hon.ble The Earl of Bective.

Adelphi Dec.r 2.d 1775.

obert Adam (1728–92), *Design for finishing the*
imney side of the Eating Parlor. For The Right
on.ble *The Earl of Bective*, Headfort, Co. Meath, 1775.
le Center for British Art, Paul Mellon Collection

At Lyons, the panoramic views executed by Gaspare Gabrielli (1770–1828) on opposite walls of the dining room must have been a talking point: the Bay of Naples on one side, Dublin on the other (fig. 101).[98] For General Cunninghame's dining room at Mount Kennedy, the Flemish artist Peter de Gree (1751–89) painted eleven grisaille medallions of various sizes, illustrating the arts, sciences and elements, all inserted in plaster frames (fig. 102). De Gree was associated with decorative schemes by the architect James Wyatt at Abbeyleix, Co. Laois, Lucan House and Curraghmore, Co. Waterford, where he and the Venetian artist Antonio Zucchi (1726–1795) painted roundels, panels and lunettes for the Dining Room. Zucchi was also responsible for five paintings that form part of the Robert Adam decoration of the Eating Parlour at Headfort.

101

The drawing room at Lyons, Co. Kildare is decorated with murals of idealised landscapes painted in tempera by Gaspare Gabrielli (1770–1828), signed and dated 1806.

102

Dining room at Mount Kennedy, showing four of Peter de Gree's medallions, *c.*1785.

While there is not a great deal of information about curtain colour and fabric in Irish houses, there is sufficient to ascertain a definite trend: of fifty-six inventories for dining rooms, only twenty-four mention colour and twenty-five record the type of fabric.[99] Of these, the predominant colour for curtains was red, used in fourteen dining rooms, and broken down as follows: crimson (seven), scarlet (six) and 'rich red' (one); in the hierarchy of colours, red has the grandest associations, with crimson used in state apartments of royal palaces from the seventeenth century. The next most popular colour was green, of which there are four examples.[100] In Britain by the end of the eighteenth century plain reds and greens were favoured for decorating the walls and the upholstery of dining rooms.[101] In the Great Dining Room at Howth Castle (inventories 1746–52) the predominant colour was yellow and the fabric damask; the three pairs of curtains were lined and had tassels and 'six lace bridles' (tie-backs); the walnut chairs in the same fabric also had yellow serge cases, as had the two settees. The rest of the furniture indicates that this room was also used as a drawing room.

Turning to the type of fabric used, damask (variously described as 'India', 'Genoa' and 'Nassau') is listed in sixteen of the twenty-five rooms, followed by moreen in seven and caffoy and calamanco (each in one room).[102] A description of '3 parlour curtains' dated 1808 from Eggleso's in Dublin shows how dramatic these must have looked: 'with parisian draperys on poles, of unwatered Scarlet morin bordered and bound with black velvet and rich corner pieces draperys fringed compleat'.[103] In many cases the covering of the dining room chairs is not specified (though many were covered in leather, which was easy to clean and would not retain odours). There was an effort to co-ordinate colour schemes at Killeen Castle in 1735/6, where the rooms were called after the predominant colour there, so it would seem likely that the seat colour of the '12 Oake Chairs fineer'd with wallnutt' matched the 'Green Callamanco' curtains and the green velvet cover on the card table.

Dining room contents

As might be expected, the contents of the formal dining room do not differ in essentials from those in the family parlour: in most cases they contain tables (or tables stored in the hall were moved into them when required), chairs, sideboards or side-tables and a number of screens and mirrors (fig. 103). The only record of a bed in the dining room is in the 1717 inventory of Corofin House, Co. Clare.[104]

Great numbers of chairs were to be found in country houses, particularly in the dining room or parlour. For dining rooms throughout the period, 'stuff'd' chairs (including tapestry, 'work'd', horsehair and leather) were by far the most popular, with fewer examples of cane- or rush-bottomed chairs.[105] In the dining room at Mount Stewart (inv. 1821), sixteen chairs were of mahogany with leather seats and fourteen were painted bamboo chairs with cane seats; for Rockingham, '28 small & 2 arm chairs in scarlet morocco & callico cases' were ordered from John Preston of Dublin in 1814, while in 1806, '6 Chinese back cane seat chairs painted' were ordered from Mack & Gibton for Castlegar, Co. Galway.[106] Invoices or estimates from cabinet-makers sometimes give detailed descriptions of the type of chair. One example is in an invoice from Mayhew & Ince of London for Caledon (1785) for '18 neat mahogany parlour chairs, carved, bannister backs, shaped hollow seats & fluted feet, stuffed with the best curled hair in strong linen, covered with fine green morocco leather & finished with the best burnished brass nails'.[107] Similar lists of furniture ordered for various houses in the early nineteenth century bear this out.

The earliest mention of a mahogany dining table was in 1728 at Powerscourt House, Dublin in the Large Street Parlour. Up to then the tables were of oak or of walnut. More

103
Irish Rococo giltwood pier mirror.

than one table was the rule in Irish dining rooms from the early eighteenth century: at Dromoland House (inv. 1753) a selection of tables is listed – 'One Long Mahogany table, 2 Round Mahogany Tables, One Oval Oak Table, One Round Yeagh [Yew] Table [and] One Little Mahogany Table'. Mrs Delany remarked in 1752 how the recently deceased Mrs Conolly at Castletown generally had 'two tables of eight or ten people each' to dine.[108] Such an arrangement, with two oval tables rather than a large table, was more usual in the first half of the century, the longer, rectangular table with removable leaves being a post-1760 development.[109] This potentially longer table did not necessarily mean a reduction in the number of dining tables in the room; at Woodville, Co. Dublin in 1797 for example, six mahogany tables are listed, and this is not exceptional. The new table with leaves was often called a 'set' or 'sett', and a good description of one is given in the invoice from Mayhew & Ince for Caledon: 'A large sett of Mahogany dining tables, of extra good Jamaica wood in 4 divisions, with 2 circular framed ends, and made to join together, and separate, in divisions, with slip hinges, brass bolts and fastenings & on therm feet.'[110]

Up to the early nineteenth century chairs were ranged around the walls; because of this, stuffed-backed chairs often had a cheaper fabric on the back. Before 'sets' of tables came into fashion, gate-leg tables which could fold neatly were also placed against the walls or in the hall or passage outside the dining room, being brought in as needed.[111] When the 'sets' of pedestal-type tables became fashionable, they could be dismantled and the two ends used as pier tables or, as Jane Austen described in a letter in 1800, 'The two ends put together form one constant table for everything, and the centre-piece stands exceeding well under glass.'[112] According to the inventories, there was a 'sett of dining tables, thin tables and four leaves' at Shelton House in 1816, and a 'Sett of Mahogany Pillar Tables (Consisting of 8)' at Carton in 1818.

More unusual tables are those found in dining rooms in Howth Castle (inv. 1746–52) and in Antrim House, Dublin (inv. 1801).[113] At Howth is a 'round mahogany drinking table' and a mahogany 'bottle-tray', indicating, as one writer put it, 'the habits of the time'; it may have incorporated a mechanism that enabled the bottle-tray to be moved about the table in relative safety.[114] An army officer staying near Limerick, described how, after the ladies had departed the table, 'a horse-shoe table, of curious workmanship, was placed before the spacious dining-room fire, and the master of the house sat in the centre of his friends' with a large cooper of claret at his feet.[115] In the Back Parlour at Antrim House, Dublin there was a 'Horse shoe table' in 1801, and Sir Charles Coote of Ballyfin purchased one for £23 2s. 0d. at a furniture sale at Dawson Grove, Co. Monaghan in 1827.[116] Also referred to as claret-tables, these horseshoe tables became fashionable towards the end of the eighteenth century for after-dinner drinking round the fire (fig. 104). Some had folding screens to protect the drinkers from the heat of the fire, and a net bag in the centre for biscuits (or discarded bottles) was common, 'while coasters attached to a metal rod, or sliding in a well, were provided to hold the bottles'.[117] One appears in Gillows's costbooks in 1801, described as a 'social table', fitted with japanned ice pails. On these, bottles might be contained in two metal coasters hinged to a brass rod.[118] James Dowling Herbert, in his book published in 1836, described how, when the tablecloth was removed after a dinner at Kilkenny Castle, 'the table changed to a horse shoe form near the fire, [where] the flow of soul succeeded the feast of reason'.[119]

Mention has been made of the buffet as either a space in itself or a type of sideboard on which silver, glass, china or desserts could be displayed.[120] The precursor to the sideboard (in its modern-day meaning) was the marble-topped side-table on a wooden frame, frequently mentioned in inventories (fig. 105). While this continued to be part of the dining room furniture throughout the period under discussion, the first time that a sideboard of wood is listed (mahogany) is in the Big Parlour at Knapton, Co. Laois in 1763. Often, as has been seen above, they were set into a recess in the room. The recess at Baronscourt was one foot deep, according to John Soane's superintendent there, Robert Woodgate, who describes the two (very long) sideboards as '10 (?) feet by 2 foot 6 inches at the bottom on each side the window recess one foot into the wall, that they may project only 1 foot 6 inches into the room'.[121] But even these did not appear to be sufficient for the Abercorns. Woodgate goes on: 'There are marble slabs in this house; two may be placed in the piers (?) to assist the sideboards which I think will be sufficient for the room, especially as the ante room is so convenient.'[122]

A 'sideboard suite' was made for the dining room at Castle Coole, together with two pier tables, to designs by James Wyatt.[123] This consisted of a plain mahogany sideboard, to show off the family silver, flanked by urns on pedestals with painted tôle medallions (fig. 106). Under the sideboard was a fluted sarcophagus wine cooler with a lion mask and a tôle medallion; when filled with crushed ice it could keep wine cold, or it could be filled with water for rinsing glasses. The suite is similar to that at Kedleston, Derbyshire, designed by Robert Adam in the 1760s, which was fitted into a domed apse in the dining room.

From the 1780s a great many more sophisticated items – such as mahogany plate buckets, wine coolers (fig. 107), bottle, glass and knife trays, cisterns, and mahogany and 'japann'd' plate warmers – became commonplace. An invoice among the De Vesci Papers lists '2 neat mahogany pedestals one fitted up as a plate warmer', and one from Gillows for Castlegar describes the 'mahogany sideboard with cupboards, one fitted up with warming plates lined with tin' (both dated 1809).[124] Mahogany pedestals and vases 'for warming Plates and holding Water &c' appear on an estimate for Caledon in 1783 and at Ashfield Lodge, Co. Cavan in 1808.[125] For the St Legers of Doneraile, Co. Cork in 1821, '2 rich oval coolers of fine Spanish mahogany on rich carved feet with scrolls, massive handles and covers all carved and lined inside with stout lead' were purchased for £55 10s. 0d. Adding to their already richly furnished dining room at Killadoon, in 1836 the Clements acquired a mahogany carved sarcophagus, an inlaid mahogany stand for a silver cistern, four bronze ormolu lamps for the sideboard and a 'cord from bell pull to table'.[126]

The Scottish architect William H. Playfair designed dining room furniture for Mr and Mrs Maxwell Close at Drumbanagher House, Co. Armagh (fig. 108) in 1833–4. His design for the sideboard is interesting: it has a shallow step on its back for the display of plate 'characteristic of Scottish sideboards', and the slatted 'Openings for Hot Air' (noted on the drawings) in each end compartment 'probably reflect the client's enthusiasm for central heat-

104
Drinking or claret table, attributed to Gillows of Lancaster and London. The demi-lune leaf is removable, and the hinged flaps can be folded down, as below.

105
Mid-eighteenth-century Irish carved mahogany side-table with marble top.

06

he sideboard and urns designed by James Wyatt
r the dining room at Castle Coole can be seen
ehind the dining table.

07

ineteenth-century mahogany wine cooler,
eputedly from Thomastown Castle, Co. Tipperary,
here Richard Morrison transformed the house into
Gothic castle in 1812. Thomastown was renowned
r the generous hospitality extended to all by the
wner, 'Grand George' Mathew.

108
Drumbanagher House, Co. Armagh, designed
by William H. Playfair.

ing rather than being an example of the built-in plate-warmers incorporated in some late Georgian sideboards'.[127] Playfair also designed the chairs for the room and, to ensure quality control, he not only sent full-size drawings for a chair but recommended that, instead of a drawing, he would get a 'Pattern chair' made in Scotland and send it over for approval. That the architect was less than confident in the abilities of an Irish tradesman might well be valid, but Playfair was known for being meticulous over every detail in his work, so would not trust an indigenous craftsman. If the English architect Francis Goodwin was the perfectionist that Playfair appeared to be, he would have been rather annoyed to find that the sideboard ordered for Lissadell, and attributed to Williams & Gibton, was too wide for the recess provided by him; channels on each side had to be hacked off the plaster to allow it to fit in (fig. 109).

A sideboard on wheels could be used in the manner of a dumb waiter. A combination of table and dumb waiter was apparently also available: 'a large mahogany Octagon Table on hollow Claw and a Dumb Waiter to fix on the Centre' was ordered by the De Vescis in 1809.[128] Dumb waiters could be placed next to the table, laden with wines and decanters when left with the gentlemen after dinner, or with plates, dishes and cutlery when the company simply wanted to help themselves, thereby dispensing with the services of a servant. It was considered a boost to the need for privacy that was perceived throughout the eighteenth century.[129] The fact that so few dumb waiters are listed in the inventories in either parlours or dining rooms might indicate that families living in Ireland did not mind the presence of servants (who probably knew all of their business anyway). It could also indicate an attitude of provincialism or, as with colonial societies such as those in the West Indies and later in India, that they simply enjoyed being waited upon.

As one would expect among the items of furniture in dining rooms, there were also numerous screens, sometimes used to shield the diners from the activities of servants. Another type of screen, only one of which (surprisingly) is found among the inventories – in the Delamain house in Cork City in 1763 – is a fire- or chimney-board, a decorative painted

MANOR HOUSE EDGEWORTHSTOWN Co. LONGFORD. 9982. W.L.

09
Detail showing how the niche for the custom-made
sideboard in the dining room at Lissadell,
Co. Sligo was adjusted to fit.

10
Edgeworthstown House, Co. Longford. The early
eighteenth-century house was greatly enlarged after
1770 by Richard Lovell Edgeworth, father of the
writer Maria Edgeworth.

screen that was made to fit the fireplace opening. It was convenient in rooms where a fire-place remained unused over long periods. Such screens often depicted a large vase of flow-ers, which, in some American examples at least, was surrounded on three sides with simu-lated delft tiles, like those used in fire surrounds.[130] Grates and locks were not mentioned (except rarely) in inventories after the 1760s, when they became 'fixed' rather than mov-able. They were nevertheless still considered among the 'removable fixtures' in house leases, along with bells, cisterns and other items, according to one writer in 1790.[131]

The inventor and writer Richard Lovell Edgeworth, father of Maria, was more preoccupied with comfort in his home than with where each piece of furniture was to be placed. Daniel Beaufort was greatly impressed with the early form of central heating at Edgeworthstown, Co. Longford (fig. 110) when he visited in 1787: 'Every chimney emits warm air from over the mantelpiece into all the rooms and in the Eating Room the warm air comes from the Kitchen it passes through a [place?] where plates are put to heat'. Here, too, he found both the sideboard and supper table were on wheels 'extremely easily moved and convenient'.[132]

In Chapter 2 the question of oil-cloth flooring was examined in some detail. Unsurprisingly they crop up again in the dining room, for the obvious reason that they would protect the carpet (frequently Turkey carpets) or flooring from food or grease stains.[133] In Britain it was apparently often the practice to cover the carpet with an oil-cloth on which was painted the pattern of that carpet, before dining tables were set up and the chairs brought forward from the walls.[134] An American visitor to a house in Cork in the first decade of the nineteenth century noted that 'under the table was green cloth spread fine enough for coats'.[135] According to a note among the Mahon of Castlegar papers, a piece of oil-cloth 'the length of the pier' (presumably that between the windows in the dining room) and half a yard wide would be required, bearing in mind that at one end of the table, 'which always stands in the Pier . . . is placed the Knife boxes for dirty Knives during dinner time', while the other end held 'the Camp table & tray for the dinner dishes when removed from the dinner table', so that the carpet at both ends of the table would be subject to grease stains.[136]

In the 1782 inventory for Baronscourt there was a Turkey carpet on the floor of the Dining Room. Nine years later, during the remodelling of the house, Woodgate made some suggestions about coverings for the carpet there, advising Lord Abercorn against his proposal to use baize with a lining:

> unless it was a very strong 'linning' the baize being 'lymp' would give way with the feet and be very uncomfortable and likewise be very expensive . . . When I was in Dublin at a carpet warehouse I saw a pattern for a carpet that would . . . suit your Lordships ideas and would come cheap; its ground was green, with a dark spot about the size of a half crown, not very frequent and promiscuously placed; it was 4/6 per yard. A carpet 30 by 20 would cost about £17. I know not the price of the baize but I think by the time it is lined and made up it will be as expensive as the carpet and not one quarter the wear in it.[137]

Drugget, a coarse woollen carpeting stuff, was also used on floors: grey drugget was found at Carton in 1818, along with a Turkey rug, a Turkey carpet and '2 Farmed Sheep Skins'. At Dromana in 1755, in contrast, a 'Large Irish carpet' covered 'the whole intire floore'.[138]

The orientation of the dining room was mentioned occasionally in architectural writings, where it was noted that it was not desirable that it would be exposed to much sun, not only because that would damage the furniture and furnishings but also because it would not be pleasant for some of the guests to have sun in their faces. Lord Lyttleton was probably right when he wrote that a dining room facing north 'will be best'.[139] Roger North thought that 'cupolo-lights' were perfect for the dining room because 'they are indifferent to all the company, and promote society by equall observation to and of all. In a side-light room, those that sitt averse are not observable to and of all. And a raised light is an advantage to feature, for it lays the shaddow of the prominencys downewards, and strong, which setts off the lights in each object.'[140] Robert Woodgate puts forward an argument, in his letter to Lord Abercorn, for the re-opening of the window that separated the two sideboards at Baronscourt, so that 'if ever the sun be so powerful as to oblige the [three] windows in the west [of the room] to be blinded this will be free; its small projection into the room will be a relief to the side-boards and give a pleasing effect to the end of the room'.[141] Blinds reduced the tendency of the sun to bleach wood and textiles and to damage paintings. Roller blinds were available from 1700, and Venetian blinds were fashionable by 1760.[142] Despite the dire warnings about the retention of food smells in fabrics, most Irish dining rooms had curtains. The festoon curtain became fashionable after 1720 and was listed in 1751 at Lord Howth's Dublin house in St Mary's Abbey ('crimson Nasaw draw-up') and at Caledon in 1785 ('146 yds rich drab stripe sattin damask . . . curtain lined, fringed & finished, to draw up in festoons complete with a pully lath . . . a rich silk tassel with button hangers').[143]

The inventories imply that there were many well-furnished and luxurious dining rooms in Irish houses. With lots of money expended on rather large pieces of furniture for this room, it is no surprise to find that much time was spent there, particularly by men. It is no great wonder, therefore, to read that, when Robert Graham visited Drumbanagher in 1835, although the house was still being built, 'the dining room was finished'.[144] Obviously William Playfair's furniture was in place by then, and perhaps Mrs Close, 'my Lady Patroness in Architecture' (as he chose to call her), took his advice on how to 'finish' the dining room in a letter sent (together with sketches) in June 1833:

> the floor is of oak . . . all the woodwork in imitation oak, walls to be covered with flock paper or to be painted in oil without any gloss upon the paint, and in either case to be of a beautiful warm brown tone of colour. The ceiling to be a light shade of the same, several of the mouldings to be gilded. Chimney-piece of Black and Gold marble. All the handles of Doors to be of black polished horn . . . The curtains to be of brown or red Cloth or Moreen and the Chairs and Tables of Mahogany and the chairs with red or green leather. A mirror over the fireplace, another one over the Side Board and another over the marble slab opposite the Fireplace. Pictures by the Old Masters, so as to balance the effect of the mirrors properly. In this way I conclude, with all submission to your better judgement, that the room will be properly finished.[145]

Not all dining rooms were like that. Many were probably similar to Elizabeth Connor (*née* Longfield)'s description of her grandfather's house at Longueville, Co. Cork when she visited it in the early nineteenth century, where there was a 'large dining room very scantily furnished, curtains that didn't reach the ground and no drapery, a carpet just the size of the dining table, a spindled-legged sideboard and chairs, and a large four-leaved screen covered with silk or what I think was called taffeta'.[146] In this context, the earl of Longford's comment on the luxurious furnishings at Inverary, Argyllshire in Scotland in 1793 (where the decoration of the drawing room alone cost 4,000 guineas) is of interest.[147] The dining room there, he says, was 'finished in the first style of superb elegance . . . the furniture is all suitable. However, I should be very sorry to be the master of such rooms or such furniture, for the thoughts of making any use [of] them which might endanger their being damaged or dirtied would set me distracted.'[148]

One inventory that stands out, because of its almost disarming frankness about the condition of the goods listed, is that of Stackallen, dated 1757. Here the emphasis is on how old, worn and broken the objects are, and on the sparseness of furniture. In the 'Dineing Room' were: '15 long backed chairs with cane bottoms, backs and frames worm-eaten; 2 ordinary square tables; large settee mahogany frame covered with green . . . and 6 pillows'; twelve pictures and a brass lock completed the list. The 'Smal Parlour' must have been used for eating as it contained an oval dining table and twelve rush-bottomed chairs, with two similar armchairs covered with green paragon '& Bottoms out'. The matching green window curtains, 'much worn & faded and each curtain lengthened by added pieces', bring to mind the dining room at Longueville. In this case, however, the inventory was attached to a lease made between Richard Hamilton of Stackallen and a John Fitzmaurice of Dublin, so it is possible that the house had been unoccupied for some time and that the better goods had already been removed. This is an important point that has to be borne in mind when looking at inventories.

Four

Public Rooms

From the second half of the seventeenth century and into the following one, the arrangement of the house into a 'formal plan' was based on French models. An example was Vaux-le-Vicomte, where the oval double-height salon, located in the centre, was flanked by *appartements* comprising *antechambre*, *chambre* and *cabinet*. In England and in Ireland these rooms became the drawing room, the bedroom and the closet. The dressing room, too, made its appearance in the second half of the seventeenth century, sometimes replacing, or in addition to, the closet. Isaac Ware recommended that in large houses where there was a garden to the rear, the rooms on the first floor that overlooked it should be disposed 'into a string or suit and that these should consist of a saloon, an anti-chamber, drawing room, bedchamber, and dressing-room'.[1] This was fairly typical of early to mid-eighteenth-century planning for houses in town, where the formal rooms were on the first floor. In country houses, on the other hand, the 'string' or suite was on the ground floor, with its hierarchy leading from the most public room, the saloon, through the drawing room and the bedroom, to the dressing room and/or the closet, the most private and intimate of the spaces. An enfilade close to the window walls provided a vista through the rooms. In England these suites were called 'state apartments', an old-fashioned term that dates back to when royalty spent much of the year travelling from one great house to another. In Ireland, with a couple of exceptions (Dublin Castle and Kilkenny Castle), the term is rarely to be found, so the bedroom suite attached to reception rooms (at ground level) in the earlier houses might be kept for important guests or used by the master of the house. The state bedroom and dressing room at Castle Coole are on the first floor and date from the early nineteenth century, when the notion of such a suite was quite outmoded. The lavish bed, said to have been made for the visit of George IV to Ireland in 1821, was in fact commissioned by Lord Belmore some years prior to that from the Dublin cabinet-makers John and Nathaniel Preston.[2]

The introduction of the formal plan to Ireland was probably due to the duke and duchess of Ormonde. Having lived for some time in France the couple were most likely to have encountered it there, but would certainly have enjoyed it at Clarendon House, London, where they lodged for a time. Roger Pratt, who designed the London house, had spent some years absorbing architecture in France and Italy, resulting in the innovative plans at both Coleshill, Berkshire and Clarendon. The Ormonde inventories reveal changes to the interior planning of their principal residences in Ireland following the duke's return as lord lieutenant in 1662, in particular the provision of apartments, reflecting their experience in England and France.[3] The first-floor state apartment at Kilkenny Castle (fig. 111) is contained in the range

111

View of Kilkenny Castle, Co. Kilkenny.

PICTURE GALLERY KILKENNY CASTLE. 3434 W.L.

2
cture gallery at Kilkenny Castle.

between the Duchess's Closet in the north-west tower and the Great Dining Room in the north-east tower. It extends across the dining room, a drawing room, 'the Alcove' (which was the State Bedroom, the bed being in a curtained alcove) and the closet, the most intimate of these hierarchical rooms.[4]

The sumptuous fabrics mentioned in the Ormonde inventories for their apartments in Kilkenny Castle, Dunmore House and Dublin Castle befitted a ducal and vice-regal family. It should be borne in mind that in the mid-seventeenth century more value was attached to textiles and tapestries than to 'built' furniture. Thus, the duchess of Ormonde's closet at Kilkenny in 1684 had blue damask wall hangings with fringes, fifteen cushions covered in the same fabric ('with blew Silke Tassells'), a counterpane for the couch bed, also of blue damask, and white Indian damask window curtains. In 1705 the duke's state bedchamber at Dublin Castle was hung with crimson damask trimmed with gold, with the same for the window curtains, the bed furniture, the firescreen and the chairs; the duchess had a similar matching arrangement in her bedchamber but the fabric was a flowered silk damask. Scarlet and white striped fabric was chosen for his grace's closet and for the duchess's dressing room, where one side of the room was hung with the fabric and it was also used for three door curtains and the seat covers. Two-thirds of the Ormonde picture collection at Kilkenny Castle were contained in just four rooms: the gallery (fig. 112), the supping room, the dressing

Newbridge House, Red Drawing Room.

room and the duchess's closet.[5] The last of these was 'extravagantly hung with paintings', so that the more important the visitor, the further they penetrated the formal rooms and the more the collection was revealed to them.[6]

In architectural plans, while many dining rooms were located on the opposite side of the house from the drawing room, there was, in most cases, an ease of access between these rooms, sometimes in the form of a circuit, sometimes in enfilade.[7] Ease of circulation was important, becoming more so as the century progressed and entertaining large numbers of guests occurred more frequently. After the middle of the eighteenth century the string of reception rooms that included bedrooms began to go out of fashion, and rooms that could be easily converted to different purposes heralded a new and less formal way of entertaining. In this way, a drawing room, dining room and library could be transformed into a ballroom, supper room and card room. Mrs Delany describes a ball she gave in her 'ballroom' at Mount Panther, Co. Down in 1758: 'my room is 32 feet long: at the upper end sat the fiddlers, and at the lower end next the little parlour the lookers-on'. Tea was served in the hall and a cold supper in the drawing room.[8] It is likely that the 'ballroom' would have been used for purposes other than dancing, particularly as it was, in this case, part of the dean of Down's residence, and her use of the word here indicates its temporary use.

This new way of entertaining and of room usage was evident in many Irish houses in the second half of the century. By removing a wall between two rooms in her house, Anne Cooke from Rahan in Co. Laois created a 'Long Room' in May 1771, where she and her husband gave a ball for their son's coming-of-age party, entertaining seventy guests to supper.[9] This 'long room' might equally have been called a 'great room', a gallery or even a saloon. It is notable that a number of 'great rooms', as distinct from saloons or drawing rooms and often built as additions to houses, appear from the mid-eighteenth century for the purpose of entertaining large numbers of guests. One example is the addition of the drawing room at Newbridge in *c*.1760 (fig. 113), intended both as a great room for company and for pictures, which both Thomas and Lady Betty Cobbe were collecting.[10] This shows an overlap with a gallery, a room designed for the display of pictures and sculpture. Another variation was seen at Shane's Castle, Co. Antrim, where, in 1787, Daniel Beaufort was impressed by the 'pretty and large theatre and magnificent ballroom', located to one side of the house. The ballroom measured 60 feet × 30 feet, 'all of wood and canvas painted and so sent ready made from London'.[11]

The difference between the saloon and the great room seems to have depended on the overall plan and how they were placed in relation to the hall.[12] Such matters were of concern to Robert Adam, who deemed them 'above all the others the most essential to the splendour and convenience of life'. He had an eye for the picturesque, the theatrical and, as Eileen Harris put it, 'For him, a "proper arrangement and relief" also depended upon an ascending gradation or progression of spaces which, in the words of his friend, Lord Kames, "gradually swells the mind" and culminates in a "climax".'[13] That climax was frequently the most important room of the house, the drawing room, often preceded by an ante-room. The significance of a dramatic progression from one space to another was similarly stressed by the Morrisons in their plans for Ballyfin (as has been seen in Chapter 2) and by John Nash at Rockingham. Rooms mentioned on the plans of these houses require further investigation as to their use and their relationship with each other.

The ante-room

The *OED* defines an antechamber as 'A chamber or room leading to the chief apartment; an ante-room, in which visitors wait' and 'any space forming an entrance to another'. In Johnson's Dictionary (1755), in addition to its definition, it is noted that 'It is generally written, improperly, antichamber'. The *Dictionnaire de l'Académie Française* expands its definition by recording that it is a room 'where the servants of those who come to visit must stop'.[14] It was used in France as a dining room, as has been seen (Chapter 3). In Paris, however, the ante-room moved from its aristocratic beginnings to the city's bourgeois apartments and the homes of merchants.[15] Roger North describes it as 'fitt for many uses, and need not have a chimny, because it is for passage, short attendance, or diversion. Musick is very popular in it . . . it must not be large, for that kills the rest of your rooms, and makes them seem less.'[16]

Of the thirty-three plans (for twenty-three houses) that include ante-rooms, only three – Lough Glynn and Castle Bernard (Co. Offaly) in the 1830s and Emo Court in the Encumbered Estates plan of 1852 – are spelt 'ante-room'.[17] In the first half of the eighteenth century Richard Castle was consistent in his use of the term 'anty chamber' and John Aheron preferred 'anti chamber'.[18] After that, 'room' was generally preferred to 'chamber', although Richard Morrison used both on different plans for Ballyfin (1821–2). All appear at ground-floor level, with the exception of two of the three Carton plans, Chearnley's plan, James Byres's plan for Charleville Forest and Aheron's plans for Dromoland, the last of which show ante-rooms on both ground and first floors.[19] The rooms are located almost equally between the front and rear of the house.

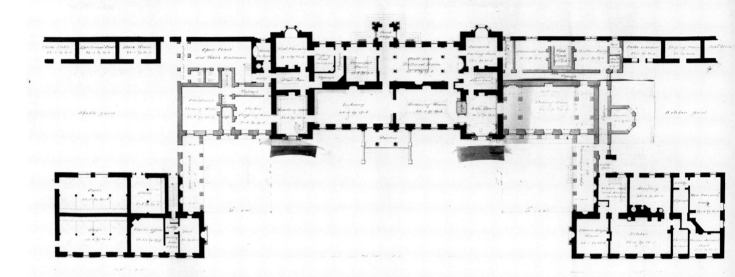

114

Carton, Co. Kildare, ground-floor plan showing
Richard Morrison's proposed alterations, 1815.

The ante-room was a space that was flexible in its usage, its main function being to serve
another room. Next to the hall, it was a waiting room; beside the dining room, it could be a
servery; and next to the library it might be a reading room. It could utilise redundant or awkward spaces on plans, or achieve a spatial effect of constriction between two larger areas, as
can be seen on Morrison's plan for Carton (1815; fig. 114). Newbridge House is another example where an ante-room with niches for sculpture leads to the new drawing room, through a
pedimented doorcase flanked by Corinthian columns (fig. 115). A room described by Arthur
Young as 'a pretty ante-room, with a fine copy of the Venus de Medicis' was part of the library
suite to the rear of Charlemont House, Dublin, designed by William Chambers for James
Caulfeild, the 1st earl of Charlemont in 1763.[20] At Lord Charlemont's house in Marino, Co.
Dublin the vicereine, the duchess of Northumberland, took breakfast in the ante-room to the
170-foot-long 'Hot House'.[21]

The rooms flanking Richard Morrison's tripartite hall at Mount Bellew were described
in 1820 as ante-rooms, leading to the dining room on the left and to the 'gallery' (probably
the 'library') on the right. These spaces, measuring 24 feet × 17 feet 8 inches, appear on a
Morrison plan (c.1819) as a breakfast room and a drawing room.[22] The countess of Shelburne
referred to the Green Drawing Room at Castletown ('furnished with pale green damask') as
an 'Antichamber'.[23] At Fota, where the Morrisons enlarged the hall (fig. 62), an ante-room
off it and to the right of the stair hall gives access to the bowed drawing room, but the small

ewbridge House, Co. Dublin, view from the stair-
ise hall across the ante-room to the Red Drawing
oom.

spaces to each end of the hall are interesting. They provide a vista or an enfilade terminating on each side with a niche. As they 'announce' the entry into two important rooms, the dining room to one side and the library to the other, they could be called ante-rooms. They bear a resemblance to the arrangement at Rockingham, where a vaulted ante-room links the rotunda drawing room with the rectangular dining room, providing a decorative architectural entrance from the 'Gallery of Communication' (fig. 56).

The absence of an ante-room in many houses was criticised by François de la Rochefoucauld when he visited England in 1784, 'since the dining-room door always leads . . . into the hall and the drawing-room door . . . onto the staircase, with the result that when they are opened one feels a considerable breeze around one's legs'.[24] This was a practical use for the room not specified by any of the architectural writers mentioned already, but was of some concern to Lady Emily Kildare in a letter to her husband in *c.*1762. In this she complains of the cold in Carton ('the stairs running with wet'): 'I feel the want of my winter rooms now sadly and shall set about finishing them directly. You'll say, was the Print Room cold? No, but the way to it from the apartments we are in at present perishingly so.' She 'lived' in the India-paper room chiefly, as ''tis near my own and that I have no passage or staircase to pass'.[25] This is an interesting comment on the reality of private lives in large houses, and it is the only reference to winter or summer apartments in Ireland that this study has produced, but it is unlikely to have been unique.

The plans confirm the multiple uses of the ante-room. Its location on ground-floor plans for Carton and Leinster House is similar: both serve the main reception rooms, and the doorways are on axis with the main entrance.[26] In both houses the rooms are flanked by a dining room to one side and a drawing room to the other, and have doors leading to the garden. At Carton (pre-Morrison) the ante-room leads into a drawing room, which in turn leads into a bedchamber and closet, creating a formal apartment. In the two first-floor plans for Carton it serves bedroom suites on each side on the garden front, and also the (first-floor) saloon to the front of the house. In the Morrison plan for Carton (1815) the room called the 'Billiard Room' on the south-east corner was transformed into a domed ante-room between the drawing room and the new dining room.

In other houses the ante-room served the library, where it might be used as a more private reading room or a sitting room, as at Slane Castle (1784), Ballyfin (1821), Farnham (1802) and Castle Bernard (1833).[27] Still other ante-rooms, located next to halls, seem to have been for waiting in, as at Ballycurry, Killeen Castle (where they are also located next to the chapel) and Mount Kennedy (where one plan (fig. 116) shows an ante-room next to the servants' staircase, where it could also be used to keep food warm for the adjoining dining room, and

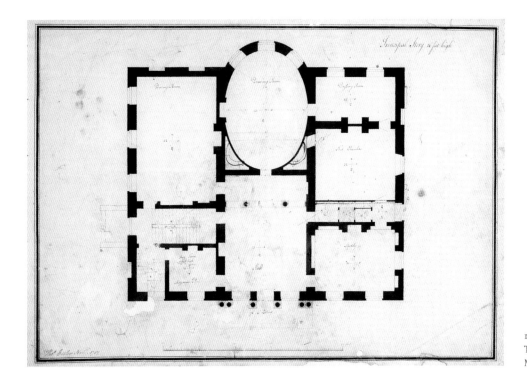

116
Thomas Cooley, *Plan of the Principal Story* of Mount Kennedy, 1781.

with a mezzanine overhead). The ante-room also occasionally functioned in relation to bed-chambers, though its precise purpose in this case is unclear.

At Shelton House (inv. 1816), where it is described as being 'off Drawing Room leading to Back Stairs', the ante-room contained just eight chairs, though this was six more than at Mount Stewart (inv. 1821), where the two chairs are described as of bamboo and painted. There are two ante-rooms listed in the inventory at Doneraile Court in the 1830s. One appears to have served two bedroom suites (the 'Blue' and 'Orange' bedrooms and dressing rooms) and contained a window curtain and drapery, a sofa with cushions, an armchair, four other chairs, a commode and two mirrors; there was also a wardrobe, an Indian chest and a trunk stand. The other ante-room was used for storage. Perhaps, in some cases, ante-rooms were rooms used to house objects that did not find a natural home elsewhere.

The saloon and its decoration

The Chambers *Cyclopaedia* (1728) defines the saloon as 'a very lofty spacious Hall, vaulted at Top, and sometimes comprehending two Stories, or Ranges of Windows . . . Embassadors, and other Great Visitors, are usually received in the Salon', a definition that Isaac Ware concurred with in 1756.[28] According to William Chambers (as noted in Chapter 2), 'The usual method, in buildings where beauty and magnificence are preferred to oeconomy [*sic*], is to raise the Hall and Salon higher than the other rooms, and make them occupy two Stories.'[29] The saloon derived originally from the great chamber of the medieval house and later from the Italian *salone* and the French *salon*, a room for the reception of guests. While the term 'salon' does not appear in a survey of houses in early modern Paris before 1720 or 1730, it was described in the *Dictionnaire de l'Académie Française* as early as 1694 as 'a large room, very high and vaulted, often with two stories or ranks of arches'.[30] The elliptical salon at Vaux-le-Vicomte (1657–61), located at the centre of the garden front and on axis with the vestibule, separates matching apartments. This was seen as a model of French planning (called a *salle à l'Italienne*, owing to its roots in Palladian symmetry and order) that was to exercise much influence on early eighteenth-century baroque architecture in England, and on Palladianism in both England and Ireland.

Throughout its history and despite its change of name, the saloon remained a room with certain definite characteristics, as Gervase Jackson-Stops explains: 'highly architectural in treatment, a magnificent setting for great gatherings rather than for everyday life, and essentially masculine in feeling, as opposed to the feminine attributes of the withdrawing room beyond'. He points out that saloons, 'with their great coved ceilings, massive doorcases and vast pictures, were always arranged formally as befitted their position on axis with the hall, as part of the "state centre" of the house'.[31] They are seldom found in late seventeenth-century houses because formal rooms were often located at first-floor level and opened off the great staircase. By the mid-eighteenth century, however, the saloon (variously written as 'sallon', 'salloon' and 'salon') usually appears centrally, on axis with the entrance hall or, infrequently, over the hall, as will be seen. The Green Drawing Room at Castletown (on axis with the hall) was described by a visitor in 1797 as 'the great saloon very superb, and containing many fine paintings, with some excellent sculpture' (figs 117, 118).[32] It has been said that few mansions in Scotland would have been considered grand enough to have a saloon, but such modesty did not daunt many Irish and Anglo-Irish families, who liked to feel that they were just as fashionable as their counterparts in England.[33]

While the saloon may have retained its physically central position in the house, by the 1730s its importance was on the wane in England, as were the reasons for putting it at the

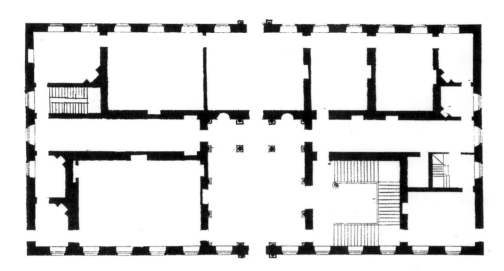

117
Ground-floor plan of Castletown, drawn by David Griffin.

118
Green Drawing Room at Castletown.

centre of the house with a great portico in front of it.[34] Neither point was true for Ireland: the portico was never popular here (see Chapter 1) and, as the earliest mention of a saloon among the plans under consideration is at Carton (1739), it went out of fashion with the formal plan only after the middle of the century, when larger dining and drawing rooms of a similar size were being created to facilitate a different way of entertaining. It did not, however, disappear, but it is notable that a saloon was not considered essential in plans dating to 1745 for Leinster House in Dublin.

It is often difficult to differentiate between a saloon and a drawing room, to ascertain exactly how architects and owners intended them to be used. At Carton, for example, what was originally the Saloon became a dining room by the second half of the eighteenth century, and by *c.*1815 it appears as a drawing room on Morrison's drawing.[35] The original oval hall at Castlegar was called a saloon when the house was turned back to front by 1820, and the room where Lord Coolooney's body lay in state in 1786 at Bellamont Forest was described in a newspaper report as the saloon, but was in fact that particularly Irish space, the upstairs lobby (off which were eight bedrooms), lit by the cupola.[36]

As mentioned, the earliest contemporary reference to a saloon is at Carton, though Craig mentions the elliptical saloon at Ballyhaise, Co. Cavan, dating to *c.*1733. In the period 1700 to 1750 a saloon appears in eleven plans for four houses: six plans locate it at the centre of the garden front, on axis with the hall.[37] Two plans for Carton locate it at the front of the house at first-floor level (over the hall), another places it to the right of the hall, another to the rear, with the door on axis with the main entrance. Finally, the 'Sallon' at Dromoland is located on the west of the house, between the Great Parlour to the front and the drawing room to the rear.

Between 1750 and 1800 a saloon appears on only eight plans, relating to five houses: three for Ardbraccan, two for Castle Coole, one each for Headfort and Carton, and in one of Richard Morrison's published drawings.[38] Six are located at the centre of the garden front and on axis with the hall; an Ardbraccan plan shows the saloon spanning the depth of the house to the east; and in Morrison's drawing it is in the form of a rotunda placed at the centre of the house, on axis with the hall and the drawing room to the rear.[39] In the third period, 1800 to 1850, the popularity of the saloon seems to have been on the wane. Out of thirty-one houses it appears in nine plans, which relate to only six houses.[40] In Limerick, at both the earl of Dunraven's Old Adare House and his newly built Tudor-Revival Adare Manor (from 1832; fig. 119), it is located at the centre of the garden front, as it is at Castle Dillon, Co. Armagh and on two plans for Emo Court. At Powerscourt, Co. Wicklow it is on the first floor, over the Great Hall to the front. In Ballyfin the circular top-lit 'Saloon' is part of a sequence of rooms at the centre of the house leading to the library to the west (fig. 46); in a plan closest to what was built, the room is called a 'Gallery or Saloon', a large rectangular top-lit space on axis with the hall.

The drawings on which the saloon appears have two things in common: the room is almost always located on axis with the hall, to the rear of the house, and it is flanked by reception rooms. In contrast, two saloons in Dublin for which original plans do not exist – in the Provost's House at Trinity College and at No. 85 St Stephen's Green – each take up the full breadth of the house to the front and are located on the first floor. In the case of the Provost's House, this room was referred to in 1790 as a 'ballroom', in 1820 as a 'Great Drawing Room' and in 1852 as a 'drawing room'.[41] It is therefore not clear at what stage it was called a 'saloon', but its decoration, as will be seen, concurs with Jackson-Stops's definition mentioned earlier. The 'very ornate' saloon at Rossanagh, Co. Wicklow (fig. 120) was located, uniquely it seems, in the east wing.[42] It should also be noted that a rear first-floor room at Leinster House,

119
Adare Manor, Co. Limerick.

called a dining room on Richard Castle's plans (1745), was later finished to designs by Isaac Ware in *c.*1759 and by 1775 had been renamed the saloon.[43]

Up to 1760 saloons were rectangular in shape but, with the advent of the neo-classical style, other room shapes were introduced: a rotunda appears in a plan possibly dated to the 1770s for Ardbraccan, a shape used later at Emo Court and at Ballyfin.[44] The circular rotunda in Morrison's drawing has already been noted, and oval saloons can be seen on the Castle Coole plans by both Johnston and Wyatt.[45] Early saloons were often larger than other rooms in the house, as in two of three plans by Castle for Headfort, and in two plans by him for Carton and also at Powerscourt, Co. Wicklow.[46] In view of the general acceptance by writers mentioned above that the saloon would normally be of two storeys, it is perhaps significant that the only examples of that appear at Powerscourt, Co. Wicklow (on the first floor), at Carton and at Emo Court.

By the 1820s the saloon had begun to lose its special place on axis with the hall, becoming smaller and just another reception room, if required at all.[47] While it is described by writers

on architecture as a particularly architectonic space, a formal waiting and reception room, more luxurious than a hall but just as lacking in comfort, it was in practice, as has been seen, referred to frequently as a ballroom or a drawing room.[48] Perhaps that was because it often contained comfortable furniture that was better suited to a drawing room.

The highly decorative architectural embellishment of some of these saloons would often have been associated with halls (as we saw in Chapter 2), and applies to a greater extent in some of the great houses in England. Christopher Hussey says that the baroque characteristics of the period 1715–30 'are most fully expressed in the decoration of the hall, saloon, and staircase, in which modelled stucco became almost universal', the orders usually progressing from Doric in the hall and/or staircase to a 'superior' order in the saloon.[49] Dining room walls, too, were frequently panelled with stucco rather than tapestry or fabric. In a description of Ragley Hall, Warwickshire in 1758, Horace Walpole wrote 'I have seen a plan of their Hall . . . and <u>both</u> their eating-room and Salon are to be Stucco, with pictures'.[50]

The saloon of Powerscourt, Co. Wicklow (also known as the Egyptian Hall, modelled on Palladio's version of Vitruvius's Egyptian Hall) was an example of an early Georgian baroque style, described as 'architecturally, the most dramatic saloon of the 1720s'.[51] Nine bays wide, it measured 55 × 41 feet; the lower level had screens of Ionic columns, with arches in the centre bays on each side and pilasters on the end walls (fig. 121). Above the entablature were Corinthian pilasters and pedimented aedicules on the end walls and at the centre of the long walls, where arcades opened into galleries. The 'Curious Stucco Work' in the 'Salloon' at Hazelwood, Co. Sligo shone 'like polished marble' in a description dated to the 1730s.[52] Rossanagh's decoration appears to date to the 1740s: the room is panelled and has a coved ceiling with a deep cornice and entablature supported by Corinthian pilasters. Its elaborate chimneypiece incorporates female herms, a convex mirror to the centre of the frieze, and an overmantel framed by drops and swags of flowers held by an eagle.[53]

The saloon at Carton (originally the dining room) has survived, facing the garden since the main entrance was moved to the other side of the house *c.*1815 (fig. 122). Of two storeys, the room has a deeply coved ceiling of sumptuous baroque plasterwork by Paolo and Filippo Lafranchini (1739), representing the 'Courtship of the Gods' (fig. 92). Like the decoration on the walls, the stuccowork was picked out in gilt. In the 1740s the Lafranchinis also executed the coved ceiling of the single-storey saloon at Russborough (fig. 123). A section by Aheron showing the interior decoration at the 'Sallon' at Dromoland indicates panelled walls with Ionic pilasters and 'shouldered' doorcases flanking the chimneypiece. At Emo Court, the saloon or rotunda (planned by James Gandon in 1790), measuring 26 feet in diameter and 50 feet to the top of the dome, with its giant Corinthian pilasters and coffered top-lit dome,

123
Saloon at Russborough.

124
Saloon at Castle Coole.

was completed in 1860 by the architect William Caldbeck. More architectural decoration, in the form of grey and black scagliola Corinthian pilasters, surrounds the walls of the oval saloon at Castle Coole (fig. 124), where the plasterwork (by Joseph Rose) and the joinery are of the highest quality: even the inlaid mahogany doors are curved.

The decoration of saloons in two Dublin houses is worth mentioning. No. 85 St Stephen's Green was built from 1738 to designs by Richard Castle, where the Great Room or Saloon on the first floor is lit by a Venetian window flanked by two others, all framed by Corinthian columns, repeated on the doorcases. The plasterwork of the coved ceiling is second only to that in Carton's saloon and was once again executed by the Lafranchinis. The saloon at the Provost's House (begun 1759; fig. 125) is a highly architectural space containing three Corinthian orders – at the doorway, at the windows and as columnar screens to each end of the room. The plasterwork in the coved ceiling, executed by the Dublin stuccadores Patrick and John Wall, has a light touch that can be seen in the frieze and on the walls, where birds (a motif much used in Dublin stuccowork) look as if they are about to take flight.

Unfortunately, few inventories mention saloons. That at Stackallen, taken in 1757, is disappointingly brief (perhaps for reasons suggested earlier), mentioning only the marble chimneypiece, a large lock 'to the Street door', a brass lock to the door leading to the 'Great

Stairs' and ten large walnut armchairs 'of Antient make'. Much later, the 1848 inventory for Brownlow House, Co. Armagh noted the saloon as having curtains of scarlet and gold damask and '5 Spring blinds'. Whether or not the seat furniture – two long ottomans and '1 Centre do.' with accompanying cushions – matched is not specified. However, a 'tete-a-tete chair oak frame' was upholstered in crimson damask with a cover of chintz. Other items of interest were two carved chairs, painted, with shell seats, an oak table with an inlaid 'Diamonded Top' and 'richly carved truss legs', a 'magnificent chandelier with 18 branches' and four portraits.

Other lists show the different versions of neo-classical styles that were available in early nineteenth-century furniture and furnishings. For the 'ballroom' at Brook Lodge, Co. Galway in 1808, furniture in the Empire style was supplied by Eggleso's of Abbey Street, Dublin.[54] The overall colour scheme seems to have been white and pink, with lots of burnished gold in the furniture. The '3 rich window curtains and suitable draperies' comprised 280 yards of white calico, almost the same of pink lining and 116 yards of a very expensive 'rich light ground English Ellwide Chintz Callico'. Also included were a rich Parisian silk and worsted fringe, twelve rich tassels, 60 yards of plaited rope and 'rich painted transparent window blinds'. Above the draperies were '3 rich bow cornices highly ornamented in burnished gold, eagles rings . . . faulse acretives [architraves]'; beneath the windows were stools 'with carved lions claws'. Against the piers, commodes with inlaid marble tops and decorated with bronzed figures had doors wired and lined with pink silk; above them were large mirrors framed with a rope motif and 'burnished gold and bronze'. The seat furniture comprised a 'Grecian lounger with cushions and bolsters', '18 Drawing room Grecian cane chairs, 6 arm chairs to match with bordered cushions'. The list also mentions a 'set of rich Dunstable sliding sattinwood tables highly ornamented 4 in number'. Some light was provided by '2 rich pedestals in burnished gold and bronzed ornaments with bronzed figures and lights'. The 'Room next Ball Room' was probably an ante-room, in which were twelve ornamented cane-seated chairs, a similar pedestal with lights, and smaller versions for the mantelpiece. A set of four elegant gilded lampstands in the Greek style to be found in the beautiful oval saloon at Castle Coole, supplied by John and Nathaniel Preston, cost the huge sum of £944 in the early decades of the nineteenth century.[55]

While the cost of the elaborate draperies at Brook Lodge was in the region of £165, it was modest compared to that for the drapes at the Provost's House, Dublin in 1820, where, for the 'Ballroom', a Regency flourish was achieved with '5 Parisian Window Curtains with crimson cloth draperies fringed & rich burnished gold ornaments', valued at the enormous sum of £250. Seat furniture – consisting of eight large easy chairs, two couches and five window seats – was covered in 'Pearl colour embossed moreen with crimson border and lace'. A large 'Brussells' carpet covered the centre of the room, with '2 grey cloth carpets for Recess' (presumably the areas behind the screens) and two hearth rugs. Two 'Grecian lamps' with three burners are also mentioned.[56] The following year Lewis and Anthony Morgan, cabinet-makers of Henry Street, Dublin, provided '12 rosewood drawing room chairs, with carved legs and top rails, ornamented with brass inlaying and moulding and having upholstered seats in linen', for which tabouret covers were included, for £27 6s. 0d. This bill also encompassed the making up of grey Holland covers for the new chairs, the armchairs and the window seats.[57]

In 1838 Venetian blinds of white linen were provided by Jones & Sons, of No. 134 Stephen's Green, for all seven windows, finished with a 'crimson line and tassels'.[58] Despite the fact that the original curtains had been taken down and cleaned on at least two occasions, by 1842 they needed to be replaced.[59] The Dublin cabinet-makers Williams & Gibton made up new curtains for the room of crimson silk damask, 'lined with fine tammy bound with silk lace, decorated with fringe tassels & rope and suspended from rich gilt cornices and to run on pully rods with trap hooks to preserve the architectural appearance of the windows'. The cost of these was £200.[60] They must be the curtains listed in the 1852 inventory, which also includes the blinds and, in addition to the other items of furniture already mentioned, a square ottoman, two glass chandeliers and a mahogany circular table.

Many members of the upper classes bought their furniture from Irish cabinet-makers, especially in the nineteenth century, by which time it had become difficult to differentiate between Irish- and English-made pieces. In the first half of the eighteenth century, furniture described as 'English' or 'from London' was advertised in Irish newspapers, the implication being that it was more desirable than its Irish counterparts. At that time, Irish furniture lagged a little behind fashions in London. There was a trend to purchase the most fashionable furniture in London; however, as soon as English cabinet-makers realised that there was a fertile market in Ireland for their work, they came regularly to Dublin, where they advertised their wares and took orders.[61]

The drawing room and its decoration

According to Girouard, a 'withdrawing chamber' was known in England before the end of the fifteenth century, when it was mentioned at Charlecote, Warwickshire, where it contained not much more than a bed and was probably used by the servant of whoever slept in the adjoining bedchamber. Located between the great chamber (later the saloon) and the ('state' or best) bedchamber, it gradually became 'the private sitting, eating and reception room of the occupant of the chamber' to which it was attached, and was slept in by servants until the end of the sixteenth century 'at least'.[62] As indicated by its name, it was a room to withdraw to, from the great chamber or, later, from the dining room. Therefore it has always had a relationship with another room or been part of a bedroom suite. In an early inventory of Geashill, Co. Offaly, dated 1628, the contents of the 'Drawing Chamber' are listed directly after those of the 'Great Chamber', indicating their physical proximity.[63] It is notable, however, that by the mid-eighteenth century the drawing room no longer related to the bedroom but to the dining room.[64]

It has been seen in Chapter 3 that parlours were frequently used as drawing rooms in the country but particularly so in town. In this chapter, however, we are looking at the drawing room as part of the formal suite of rooms. It tended to be a rather formal space, in which the most expensive fabrics (such as silk damask and velvet) were to be found. In some cases it is difficult to work out differences between the drawing room and the saloon, particularly when the saloon was also hung with fabric rather than architecturally articulated, and the term can be interchangeable, as has been seen. However, while the vast majority of the house plans here do not include a saloon, they all have a drawing room. Indeed, some houses had more than one drawing room, but there was never more than one saloon.

Drawing rooms are found in fifteen plans dating to the first half of the eighteenth century, fourteen being located at the rear of the house.[65] In all cases the drawing room relates to at least one other room: nine are part of an enfilade along the garden front (often including a saloon at the centre), and seven are part of a circuit through which people moved between the front and rear of the houses. The smallest in size is also the oldest – Curle's drawing for Castle Coole (1709) – in which the 'Withdrawing room' (the only example of this term in the plans of this period) measures 17 feet square. The largest is in the Charleville Forest drawing, at 36 feet × 24 feet, but it is interesting to note that in all four of the Carton drawings the size remains the same: 19 feet 10 inches × 17 feet 8 inches. At Leinster House the difference between the drawing room on the ground floor and that on the first floor is minimal – 23 feet 9 inches × 22 feet and 24 feet × 23 feet respectively.[66] The shapes are all square or rectangular.

As with the saloon there is some variety in the shapes of the drawing room in the period 1750 to 1800, for which there are twenty-eight plans.[67] Twenty-one show the room to the rear of the house: of these, three are oval and located in the centre, while one of Morrison's shows a bow and the other a canted bay, both similarly placed.[68] Also in this location are the drawing rooms at Woodville, with a canted bay, curved within (fig. 85), and at Mount Kennedy, where a drawing shows an octagonal room. The largest in this period is at Headfort (measuring 25 feet × 36 feet), the smallest at Prospect and in a Mount Kennedy drawing (both 20 feet × 28 feet). Enfilades appear in eleven plans, but in all cases there is easy access from one reception space to another. There are no original plans for Castle Martyr, Co. Cork, seat of Henry Boyle, the Speaker of the Irish House of Commons and later 1st earl of Shannon, which was singled out by Arthur Young (who visited it in the 1770s) as having the best room he had seen in Ireland. It is one of those rooms already mentioned that, like the Provost's House, are called variously saloon, ballroom and drawing room.[69] Young called it a drawing room, and it may have been the largest in Ireland at the time: a double cube of 50 feet in length.[70]

In forty-two plans dated between 1800 and 1850, twenty-two drawing rooms are located at the rear of the house and fifteen at the front (of these ten are placed next to the hall).[71] Those at Dromoland Castle, Old Adare House and Lissadell are on the garden front, where the entrance is on the short axis. Enfilades of reception rooms are to be found on twenty-six plans, with ease of circulation evident in eight others. Regarding size, drawing rooms in this period are generally larger than in the other periods, examples being Adare Manor (40 × 24 feet), Howth Castle (42 × 17 feet), Ballyfin (36 × 24 feet) and Carton (36 feet 6 inches × 19 feet 5 inches).[72] Another sizeable room was Rockingham's rotunda, at 35 feet in diameter. The majority of the room shapes are rectangular; a bow window appears only at Old Adare House, an elliptical bay at Ballycurry and a canted bay at Lough Glynn.[73] In one plan for Ballyfin, the Large Drawing Room has apsed ends and the Small Drawing Room an arched recess (fig. 46).

The view from the drawing room windows was important to show the gardens or the extent of the demesne or a landmark, and bay or bow windows helped to extend it. As we have seen, in 1769 the countess of Shelburne described the drawing room and dining room at Dawson Court as being of similar size, one with a bow the other with a canted bay; her description suggests that it was the drawing room that had the bow.[74] A columnar screen frames the view of Ben Bulben from Lissadell's drawing room. Richard Morrison remodelled Castle Howard, which overlooks the picturesque Vale of Avoca in Wicklow, in the Gothic style (c.1811; fig. 126), with views from the windows of the new ground-floor drawing room (which opens into two turrets, from the top of which are spectacular views). Later, Dominick Madden proposed a boudoir in a turret off the drawing room at Brook Lodge.[75] Daniel Beaufort, on his visit to Dromana, Co. Waterford, remarked that all of the principal rooms enjoyed a view of the River Blackwater, and he particularly admired the large oval drawing room.[76] The following year (1807) his daughter Louisa described as a 'square octagon 26 feet each way' the drawing room at Lisanour Castle, Co. Antrim, while that at Killymoon, Co. Tyrone had two views from 'a round-topped gothick [window?]' at the end and a large window in the side.[77]

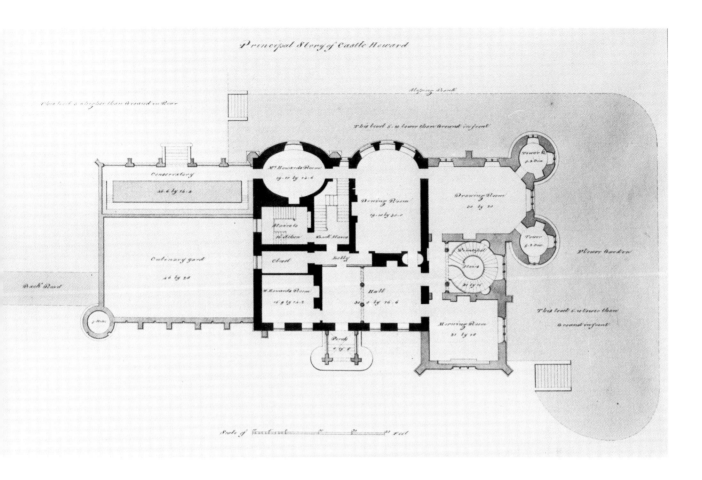

Principal Story of Castle Howard

6

stle Howard, Co. Wicklow, an existing house
ered and enlarged by Richard Morrison *c.*1811;
ound-floor plan drawn by Owen Fahy.

By the beginning of the nineteenth century the provision of double or folding doors between rooms had added drama and grandeur to country houses.[78] An observer at Bellinter noted that 'large folding doors have been added uniting the two back drawing rooms into one spacious apartment . . . overlooking a Flower Garden'.[79] They are marked on a plan for Durrow Abbey, where they separate the dining room from the rear drawing room, and the wide doorways on a Straffan House plan suggest their use there too, but they do raise the question of quite how safely 'withdrawn' the ladies were after dinner, in one of a pair of interconnecting rooms. Other possible retreats for them in both houses were libraries and, at Straffan, an ante-room beyond the drawing room.

We have seen the architectural articulation of halls, dining rooms and saloons; drawing rooms are quite different in that the decoration depends more on fabric, colour, upholstery and pictures.[80] However, there are some architectural details in drawing rooms that are worth mentioning, such as the shallow dome at Somerville, Co. Meath, the curved corners behind the screens of grey-black scagliola Ionic columns in the Large Drawing Room at Kilruddery and at the windows in the drawing room at Castle Coole, which were set with false arched heads designed to be equipped 'with French style curtains' that fitted over the space (fig. 127).[81] At Baronscourt the 88-feet-long principal drawing room on the garden front, created by Sir John Soane in the 1790s from three rooms, is divided by screens of Corinthian columns that 'replaced the existing Ionic ones in order to complete the development of the

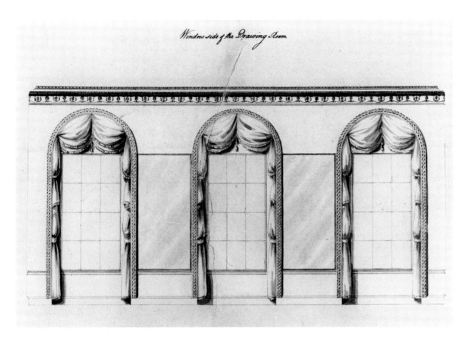

Windows side of the Drawing Room

127
Drawing for window and curtain arrangement
at Castle Coole.

orders along this axis'.[82] It might also be mentioned that in another room at Baronscourt, the marchioness's drawing room, the motifs used in the 'star-spangled, Empire-inspired ceiling', designed by Richard Morrison in the 1830s in the style of the French architects Percier and Fontaine, appeared originally in his design for the drawing room at Ballyfin (1822).[83] A survivor from the late eighteenth century is the ceiling painting by Nathaniel Grogan (*c*.1740–1807) in the drawing room at Vernon Mount, Co. Cork.[84]

Lady Sarah Bunbury was extraordinarily detailed in her letters of 1775 about the planning, decoration and furnishing of Frescati, the seaside home of her sister the duchess of Leinster in Blackrock, Co. Dublin (fig. 128). The drawing room there, she wrote, 'will gather the whole expense' and went on to suggest how that could be minimised by shopping in France (where the duchess was living). Apart from fabrics and colours she advised Emily that a gilded oak-leaf border for the ceiling, 'as French gold is both better and cheaper', can be 'smuggled over by Mr Power from Bourdeaux'. She explained that the 'idea of so showy a border is stolen from a drawing of Mr Gardiner's for a room he means to fit up in Dublin'. For the ceiling itself, Sarah suggested compartments 'filled with light Herculean figures, and the four corners with pretty ornaments', and recommended that the door opposite the window ('I beg [it] may be French') be 'made of looking glass' to reflect the garden opposite.[85] As regular visitors to family and homes in France, the Lennox sisters absorbed a great deal of French taste, as Thomas Creevey observed in 1828, after sleeping in the Chinese bedroom at Carton, which he described as 'French to the backbone in its furniture, gilt on the roof, gilded looking-glasses in all directions, fancy landscapes, and figures in panels' (fig. 129).[86] Apart from this, however, French taste did not manifest itself to any great extent in Ireland until the early nineteenth century.

Cornforth's claim for England that, from about 1740, many drawing rooms acquired a 'French character' is not immediately obvious in Ireland, apart from the rococo plasterwork of the 1760s; the white and gold walls with enormous mirrors that were so prevalent in France at the time gained little currency here.[87] The 'character' he mentions applies mostly

128
Frescati, Co. Dublin, the summer residence of the
duke and duchess of Leinster and their family.

129
Chinese bedroom at Carton.

to hangings, furniture and furnishings. French decoration appears in some houses, but a drawing room is not included among the rooms mentioned.[88] One visitor remarked on Rockingham as being (generally) 'fitted up in the French style, with a good deal of arabesque painting, gilding etc'.[89] The aforementioned Large Drawing Room at Kilruddery has Louis XV revival wall panels and pelmet cornices.[90] Another writer was impressed with the drawing room at Ballyfin, 'said to be one of the finest apartments in Ireland . . . decorated in the French style, the . . . prevailing tone being grey and gold; the walls are hung with pale grey satin brocade; exquisite old French brocade covers the white and gold furniture'.[91] As has been seen, the Morrison plasterwork in Kilruddery, Ballyfin and Baronscourt was greatly influenced by Percier and Fontaine, who were the leading architects of the Napoleonic period.

Wall coverings

The description of Ballyfin's drawing room brings up the subject of wall coverings. Surprisingly, the only references to them among the inventories are at Dromana (1755) and Stackallen (1757). The Dromana inventory is interesting as it suggests a very grand principal apartment, comprising (in order of listing) Lady Grandison's dressing room, Lord Grandison's bedchamber, the 'Anntie Chamber or Drawing room, commonly called the Picture Room' and Lord Grandison's dressing room. All were hung with 'crimson silk stuff damask', lined with linen; curtains and upholstery in the four rooms matched the wall covering.[92] Other rooms at the same house were the Blue Damask Room (a bedchamber) and its dressing room, both hung with 'rich blue damask silk'. At Stackallen, two walls of the drawing room were hung with gilt leather, 'the one with the heads of King William and Queen Mary and the other Queen Ann's'.

Despite the dearth of information on hangings in inventories, the subject is worth examining because of the references to them found elsewhere. Late seventeenth-century drawing rooms were often hung with tapestry, as at Dublin Castle (1678) and Kilkenny Castle (1684), and it has been seen (in Chapter 3) that tapestry and gilt leather wall hangings were in use in rooms other than drawing rooms in the early eighteenth century: for example, Rathfarnham House, Co. Dublin has gilt embossed leather wall hangings in its saloon.[93] It is not unusual to find, however, that fabric other than tapestry, leather or needlework panels was hung in various rooms in the 1680s. It is unclear whether the decor at Rathcline, Co. Longford in 1688 displayed a lack of imagination on the part of the owner or an effort at colour co-ordination.[94] The room over the 'Damask room' was hung with striped grey serge, while Lord Lanesborough's closet, his dressing room and the 'closet within dressing room' were hung with grey fabric, the latter two spaces containing matching chairs ('6 grey broadcloth chairs' and ' 3 grey chairs' respectively).[95] In 'Drumcondrah', Co. Dublin (1689), where the Parlour and the Best Chamber were hung with tapestry, other rooms were hung with 'Druggett' and with 'Brown Bays'. In Sheridan Le Fanu's novel *The Cock and Anchor* (Dublin, 1845), set in the early part of the eighteenth century, two young women were described as sitting 'in a large old-fashioned drawing-room; the walls were covered with elaborately-wrought tapestry, representing, in a manner sufficiently grim and alarming, certain scenes from Ovid's Metamorphoses'.[96] Mrs Delany's drawing room at Delville was hung with tapestry as late as 1744.[97]

While tapestry continued to appear on walls well into the eighteenth century, it was largely replaced in the early 1700s by other fabrics such as damask, caffoy and mohair, and from the 1730s by wallpaper.[98] While this last wall covering was being manufactured from the latter part of the seventeenth century, it was only in the 1740s that it was advertised in Irish newspapers.[99] One such advertisement was placed by Bernard and James Messink, who styled themselves 'original Paper-Painters opposite the great Mahogany Shop on the Blind Quay, <u>do make and sell</u> superfine Imbost shaded Paper Work, in imitation of Tapestry or Needlework, fit for hangings of Rooms, Skreens, Fire Skreens, Chimney Pieces and Door Pieces: and <u>make</u> all sorts of common Imbost paper Work in imitation of Coffoy, or Green Damask; as also all other sorts of painted paper with variety of colours, and patterns from London'. The final comment was intended to reassure prospective purchasers in Ireland that the Messinks were up-to-the-minute fashion-wise.[100] The Edgeworths purchased stamped flocked paper for their drawing room in 1749.[101] The duke and duchess of Bedford, when taking up their positions as viceroy and vicereine at Dublin Castle in 1759, were asked whether they would prefer paper or silk hangings in their apartments; if their preference was for paper they had a choice between flock or a chintz pattern; whichever they chose had to match the curtains.[102]

Hangings did not go entirely out of favour for some rooms but the fabric became lighter, as has been seen in the drawing room at Ballyfin (above). Lady Caroline Fox, after visiting Paris in 1764, wrote to her sister in Ireland, 'I am out of conceit with India paper, and am all for the magnificent style of single velvet damask. I have three immense looking glasses to put in my drawing room and propose hanging it with a damask or brocatelle of two or three colours. I am rather changeable to be sure in these things; but though whims and fripperies may have a run, one always returns to what is really handsome and noble and plain.'[103] For the drawing room walls at Frescati, Lady Sarah Bunbury recommended grey, green or white in damask, satin, India taffeta, lutestring or velvet.[104] Lady Shelburne remarked in 1769 upon the drawing room at Castletown being 'furnished with a damask of four colours'.[105] The fact that she does not specify a colour, when she has described the 'Antichamber' (saloon) as hung with pale green damask, means that it is probably safe to assume that the drawing room was hung with a variant of red, a colour associated with the room in England. Because fabric as a wall covering could be very expensive (it has been estimated that the price of one yard of damask would purchase eleven yards of paper[106]), it was sometimes omitted behind mirrors or pictures: Mrs Delany felt that 'it would have been ridiculous' to hang her room with mohair rather than paper 'when I desire to cover it with pictures'.[107]

○
ne gallery at Carton, early nineteenth-century
resent drawing room).

Before turning to the inventories, a few words should be said about the walls of the room as a background for paintings. Much consideration was given to this subject: crimson was considered the most suitable background, be it velvet, damask or flock paper, and it complemented the gilded frames.[108] Crimson flock paper can be seen at Newbridge, where there were thirty-one paintings in the drawing room in 1821. Crimson cut-velvet hung in the drawing room at Holkham, Norfolk, where a plan of the picture-hanging was painted in watercolour on a hand firescreen: dated to 1853, it was to help visitors identify the paintings and their artists.[109] At Dromana, since the other rooms of the suite were hung with crimson silk damask, as has been seen, this fabric must have provided the background for the drawing room's substantial number of portraits.[110] An early nineteenth-century watercolour shows the arrangement of pictures on the chimneypiece wall in Carton's drawing room against a lighter background, however (fig. 130).[111] At Russborough, it is the saloon that has crimson cut-velvet hangings as a background, while the drawing room has rather heavy stucco frames on the walls that were made especially to contain four oval *Times of the Day* by Joseph Vernet (fig. 131), commissioned by Lord Milltown in 1749. Panelling, used by Sir Edward Lovett Pearce and Richard Castle, and as portrayed in Maria Spilsbury Taylor's watercolour of the saloon/drawing room at Rossanagh (fig. 120), began to go out of fashion as paintings

131
The drawing room at Russborough, showing the stucco frames for the oval Vernet paintings.

trickland Lowry (1737–*c*.1785), *The Family of Thomas
ateson Esq.*, 1762; oil on canvas, Ulster Museum.

were acquired. At Russborough, where the plaster frames in the dining and drawing rooms
were created around the pictures, the panelling worked well, but problems arose when paintings did not fit. A painting in the Ulster Museum attributed to Strickland Lowry, *The Family
of Thomas Bateson Esq.* (1762; fig. 132), illustrates this.[112]

With the advent of neo-classical taste, colours and fabrics became progressively lighter
from about the 1760s, as houses – and, at the same time, gardens – became liberated from
the rigid formality that had been adhered to until then. Glass technology introduced larger
panes that provided rooms with more light, and the light that had previously been absorbed
by rich fabrics was now reflected on wallpaper, particularly plainer wallpaper. Isaac Ware
made some interesting comments on lighting : 'a wainscoted room painted in the usual way,
is the lightest of all; the stucco is the next in this consideration, and the hung room is the
darkest'.[113] The reason for the lightness of wainscoting was that it was usually painted white
or off-white in the 1750s. Therefore, a wainscoted room required only six candles to light it; a
stucco room required eight, but ten were required for the hung room – an important consideration, bearing in mind the high cost of wax candles.[114]

The inventories are surprisingly lacking in information on both colours and fabrics used
in drawing rooms. In most there is no information at all about curtains (perhaps there was
no need for them if the room was on the garden front); where they *are* listed, in many cases
only the fabric is specified. In the case of the 'Scarlet Room' in Killeen Castle, which is likely
to have been a drawing room, the bed and window curtains are of scarlet paragon and the
eight chairs are covered with green and white satin and have calico covers.[115] The curtains
and chair covers at Delville were of crimson mohair. At Dromana, where the curtains are
of crimson silk damask, the eleven chairs are covered with a tapestry flower pattern and the
loose covers are of 'scarlet stuff'. The invoice from Mayhew & Ince for the 'Oval Drawing
Room' at Caledon, Co. Tyrone in 1785 lists 'rich dove colour'd water'd Tabby, used for the festoon window curtains, chairs, sofa's & screens'.[116] The wood pelmets above the curtains were
richly carved, and painted dove and white. A 'fine Tabby' was used for the backs of the seat
furniture.

Again, the Killadoon inventories show how, over time, fashions changed and rooms were given a more up-to-date look. In 1807 the drawing room walls were probably covered in a flock wallpaper that dates from the 1770s (a fragment of which can still be seen between the bases of the pier mirrors and the dado rail).[117] The three 'green clouded silk curtains' with the gilt pelmet cornices mentioned in the 1807 inventory probably date from the same time. The cushions on eight green-painted chairs and the upholstery on four gilt chairs were also covered in 'clouded green'. Other seat furniture – which included a sofa with four cushions, a couple of 'Grecian' armchairs, two hunting chairs and three gilt chairs covered in tapestry – had chintz covers. In keeping with the colour scheme the firescreens were mahogany with green silk, and the handscreens and two footstools were also green. By 1833 six muslin curtains had been added to the existing window curtains; three years later, the 'mahogany leg sofa' was covered with crimson cotton velvet in a damask pattern, as were the four gilt chairs, and the eight green chairs and two armchairs had green and white striped calico cases.[118] By now the original flock wallpaper had been replaced with a running spray pattern and elaborate gold border which dates to the 1820s. Each wall is 'panelled' in a wide border with a white ground, with the border scroll along its inner edge running all around the 'panel'.[119] It seems that shortly after the 1836 inventory the drawing room was refurbished rather dramatically, the rest of the upholstery being redone with crimson printed cotton velvet, with curtains and draped valances in red and gold damask that had a small, dense pattern. By 1844 the bell pulls were of red and yellow silk with rich tassels, and a new Axminster carpet, with crossed Ls in the corners, had been acquired (made for the 2nd earl of Leitrim).

In his Co. Dublin home, Neptune (later Temple Hill House), Blackrock, the earl of Clonmell's colour scheme in the drawing room in 1789 was blue and silver. The five curtains were of blue damask hung on silvered brackets, chairs with silvered frames were covered in the same, and the two sets of covers for the chairs were of white linen and blue and white cotton. Two mirrors in the piers had silvered frames, as had the two marble inlaid tables beneath them. Both the grate and the fire-irons were plated, the glass sconces were set in silver and the '2 silver handled Locks' had silver moulding. An item of note was the oil-cloth cover on the hearth stone, a fairly common protective feature.

Not all of the inventories are as informative. At Powerscourt House, Dublin in 1728 the curtains of the drawing room were of white silk and the couch was green 'with fine Needlework Cover', but no colour is listed for the eight armchairs. Crimson damask and green (damask?) were also to be found in the Drawing (or Tapestry) Room at Drumcondra House (1773). The Great Red Drawing Room at Newbridge, 'the glory of the house' according to Frances Power Cobbe, retains the red flock wallpaper hung there possibly in the 1790s and the crimson silk damask curtains paid for in 1828.[120] Cotton was also used at Mount Stewart (1821), where the curtains were lined with orange cotton, with printed drapery of the same fabric, and had a white fringe with tassels.

Looking at fabrics and colours for wall hangings, curtains and upholstery among the inventories, and from other sources, with reference to drawing rooms from the beginning of the eighteenth century, we find that, in sixteen out of twenty-seven cases, damask was the principal fabric used, of which eight rooms were in red, three each in blue and in yellow, with two unspecified. (Overall, red (including scarlet, crimson and 'red') was the predominant colour (eleven), followed by yellow (five) and blue (three).) That damask was a desirable commodity from the early part of the century is underlined by a robbery that occurred in Dublin in 1736, in which 'three new pairs of crimson silk damask window curtains . . . lined with crimson serge' were stolen from William Handcock's house in King Street.[121]

Furniture arrangements and pictures in the drawing room

In a letter to Lord Lorton of Rockingham from the London firm of Morgan & Sanders, dated 9 September 1815, advice is offered about colour: 'respecting the two colours of the Damask for the Drawing Room Curtains, we feel inclined to recommend the Tea colour as being the most <u>Elegant</u> and <u>genteel</u>, in unison with the Blue, the Fawn is more showey, but in our opinion not so Genteel'.[122] An estimate for furniture, including '4 Elegant French Window Curtains etc.', two sofas and eight armchairs covered with the chosen fabric, amounting to 360 guineas, had been sent four days earlier, accompanied by a note in which the firm anticipated that Lorton would require more items for his room: 'an Ottoman is now a very handsome article for the centre of the Room, also sofa tables, card tables and round Loo tables with Glasses, Pier Tables and Commodes'.[123] They sent him drawings of their furniture to aid his selection, which was the usual practice.

In *c.*1807 Lewis & Anthony Morgan sent Ross Mahon of Castlegar plans for rooms in his house that demonstrate how furniture was arranged at the time. These have disappeared from the Mahon Papers in the National Library of Ireland but Edward McParland, who discovered them in the 1970s, made rough sketches, here redrawn, which are of interest (figs 133, 134).[124] The plan for the Oval Room (or saloon, formerly the entrance hall) showed chairs and sofas dispersed around the walls of the room with a central circular table measuring less than 5 feet in diameter. One plan for the drawing room shows a circular table to the centre of the room flanked by 'Grecian couches', three chairs to each side of the fireplace and six lined up against the wall opposite the tripartite window to the front of the house. This window, flanked by commodes, and the two smaller ones all contain window seats. The other plan by the Morgans is more interesting: Grecian sofas with sofa tables in front of them flank the fireplace, in front of which is a semicircle of five chairs. In the centre of the room are a grand piano with stool and a rectangular table with pillar and claw feet; the main window is flanked by card tables and has six chairs lined up along it. The six chairs along the wall opposite are broken up by a commode in the centre, while a 'Maltese' couch, flanked by a chair to each side and with a sofa table in front of it, is located between the east windows. Within these two windows are 'Grecian stools'.

Important items of furniture in a drawing room would be fairly similar to those used today – upholstered seat furniture, mirrors and tables. Pier tables, sometimes gilded and marble-topped, were placed between windows, often beneath a rectangular or oval mirror. According to the inventories there were, on average, about ten chairs (including all seat furniture) in drawing rooms up to the last decades of the eighteenth century, after which there was a notable increase in number. This may have been due to larger rooms, extended or as built. Drawing rooms in the following houses contain twenty or more chairs: Woodville (1797) has thirty-two, Killadoon (1807) twenty, Ashfield House (1808) twenty-two, Mount Stewart (1821) twenty, Newbridge (1821) twenty-four and Doneraile Court (1830s) twenty-six. Fire grates, which were moveable and which people tended to take with them when they moved house, are listed consistently. Most of the floors had carpets (Turkey, Wilton, Brussels), though none of the inventories mention whether or not these covered the entire floor, and hearth rugs appear more frequently from the beginning of the nineteenth century.

Only twelve inventories dating to between 1700 and 1850 list pictures in the drawing room.[125] Of these, nine mention portraits, mostly of family, but the subjects are usually not specified. The location of portraits in drawing rooms would appear to be at odds with English practice, as John Cornforth describes of an eighteenth-century owner: 'He would have tended to concentrate his Italian history pictures, classical landscapes and Dutch cabinet pictures

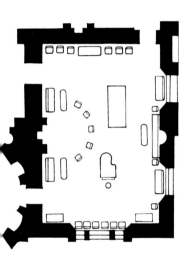

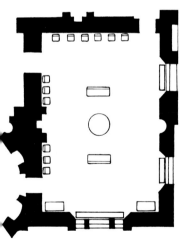

3 and 134
astlegar, Co. Galway, *c.*1807, furniture youts redrawn by Livia Hurley from original ketches by Edward McParland, gleaned from nanuscripts at Castlegar in the 1970s.

in a saloon or drawing-room, whose walls would have been hung with damask . . . and he would have grouped portraits, sporting pictures or still lifes in a dining room, which would definitely not have been hung with material and might have been panelled until about 1740 and then plastered.'[126]

On the other hand, Dromana's inventory (1755) names the subjects of the portraits (mostly family) hanging in the drawing room, all in gilt frames. In 1758 a portrait of 'Mr Pitt' was added. At Mount Stewart (1821) a portrait of Lord Stewart was over the chimneypiece, 'a Head of the Honble Wm. Pitt framed and Glazed', and '37 prints Various Framed'. Killadoon's 1836 inventory lists portraits of the duchesse de Clermont, of the countess of Leitrim by Lawrence, of Lady Clements and one 'after Rembrandt'. By 1844 another two portraits in gilt frames had been moved into the drawing room from the dining room. In many cases the frame and the size seem to have been of more interest than the picture itself to the person making the inventory: Barbavilla (1742) had a total of seventy-three pictures in the drawing room, listed as '26 Picturs Gilt, 20 with Black frames, 6 Pictures with Brass frames, 12 Large Picturs with Black frames, 9 More small Picturs with Black frames'. Baronscourt (1782) had '16 pictures'; at Doneraile Court (1830s) the Middle Drawing Room had eleven engravings and the Small Drawing Room had thirty-three, 'framed and glazed'. Finally, at Gaulston (1787), two flower pieces are listed as being over the doors in the drawing room, as was a watercolour of Lucca at Killadoon in 1844.

The reason for the drawing room being an important space for displaying pictures was that country houses with picture galleries were rare, probably because there were few collectors with a sufficient number of paintings or sculpture with which to furnish such a space as well as other rooms in their house or houses. One, containing a 'vast number of paintings', was at Woodhill, Tivoli, Co. Cork, home of the merchant Cooper Penrose, and was described by the artist Daniel Maclise as 'a very remarkable picture gallery, one of the chief in the South

135
Anne Maria La Touche, *The Drawing Room of Bellevu Co. Wicklow*, 1841; drawing.

of Ireland'. Consisting of three rooms, the galleries, one of which had niches in the walls for statuary, were contained within wings added in 1802 to the original Palladian-style house.[127] The artist and collector Hugh Howard approved of his brother William's decision to have a gallery in his Dublin house in 1726, and offered hints for its use: '[it] will be a great Addition to the House . . . we generally use them here [in London] as places only to walk in, the walls covered with a few pictures, & the most neglected part of the House; I think they are the fittest places for Studys & librarys, & as such they are us'd abroad, & by some of the best tast here'.[128]

Paintings and drawings of interiors in Ireland sometimes show a piano in the drawing room, such as in Spilsbury Taylor's image of that at Rossanagh (fig. 120) and in Anne Maria La Touche's of Bellevue, both of Co. Wicklow (fig. 135), but they appear in only five inventories.[129] Surprisingly, perhaps, for a room that is associated with the taking of tea, only eleven mention tea tables and/or items connected with tea. It should be noted, however, that many of the parlours discussed in the previous chapter contained similar items. The tea tables came in a great variety of woods and finishes: Powerscourt House, Dublin (1728) had an 'India' tea table, while that at Killeen Castle (1735/6) was of walnut; Barbavilla (1742) had a 'jepan' table and tea board, in addition to a table of 'oack'; Dromana (1755) had a round mahogany table with claw feet; at Stackallen (1757) the small table was described as old-fashioned, 'painted black much worm eaten'. Both Barbavilla and Dromana list china tea and coffee cups and small trays, that at Barbavilla of china, the other, at Dromana, 'Indian, with 11 handled chocolate cups, a milk jugg with a silver spout and a sugar dish', all in blue and white china. Significantly perhaps, much china for tea and coffee was kept in the 'passage next the door leading to Lady Grandison's dressing room', including 'enamelled china' bearing Lord Grandison's crest.

Tea chests or (lockable) tea stores (fig. 136) were also to be found, bringing to mind Jonathan Swift's satirical *Directions for Servants* (1745), in which he sympathised with the 'waiting maid' for one of the 'accidents' that had happened to lessen the profit of her employment: 'The Second [accident] is, the Invention of small Chests and Trunks, with Lock and Key, wherein they keep the Tea and Sugar, without which it is impossible for a Waiting maid to live: For, by this means, you are forced to buy brown Sugar, and pour Water upon the Leaves, when they have lost all their Spirit and Taste . . . Therefore, I fear you must be forced, like the rest of your Sisters . . . [to] pay for it out of your Wages'.[130] The serving of tea

136
George III rectangular yew wood tea caddy with lock.

could be quite a performance. In Lady Morgan's *Dramatic Scenes from Real Life* (1833) she tells how one of the upper servants enters: 'while other servants, in long file, bring the tea equipage. A table-cloth is laid on a distant table; and two French maids, elegantly dressed, with white gloves, &c., commence the elaborate process of tea-making, assisted by the page, and a groom of the chambers.'[131]

In addition to the tea table in the 'Scarlet' (or Drawing) Room at Killeen Castle, the bed (already mentioned) was of 'scarlet parragon' with matching curtains, and there were '7 Oacke chairs fineer'd with walnut with green & white sattin seats' and two stools similarly covered. These matched the decor in the adjoining Tea Room, where the curtains were of green and white calico and the walls covered with 'green paper Hangings'.[132] The Tea Room contained five cane chairs with silk cushions, three stools, a dressing mirror and two square tables – one a tea table of oak, the other described as a Japan table – but, curiously, china is not listed, nor is the equipage that accompanied the serving of tea.[133] However, a list of items brought to the house from Dublin included sets of blue and white china.[134] Such a room must have been remarkable in a private house before 1735 (a 'Small Tea room' is located off the Parlour in a design for the Hon. Mr Barnet dating to *c*.1740), but perhaps it was a small space off the main reception room used by the lady of the house, rather like a closet, for the entertainment of her friends.[135] Several decades later, in 1787, Daniel Beaufort found a coffee room at Shane's Castle, Co. Antrim: 'off the breakfast room is rotunda coffee room where in recesses are great quantities of china, a cistern with a cock and water, a boiler with another, all apparently for making breakfast; a letter box and a round table with four sets of pen and ink let in, for everybody to write'.[136]

Public reception

The entertainment of guests in the house took on various forms: it could be informal when a number of close friends or acquaintances came to dinner; or formal when important guests were invited. From the middle of the eighteenth century, people were extending or adding on a large room or two to the house, larger parties could be facilitated and all of the formal rooms were thrown open to the guests, allowing them to wander at will. Usually food was served in one room, another was for cards, one for dancing and one a space in which to sit. This made possible different types of parties – routs, drums, masquerades, musical gatherings – and, in many cases, amateur theatricals were performed. The house party in the country that extended over a number of days (and sometimes weeks) became popular, and many types of entertainment were provided, including field sports – hunting, shooting, racing – and, if there was a lake or river nearby, boating. It is, however, indoor entertaining that is of interest here and how the formal rooms were used in the course of these occasions.

As guests arrived at the house for dinner, they were ushered by a servant into a reception room, usually the drawing room. Robert Adam, on one of his plans, called such a space 'the Room for Company before dinner'.[137] It was not the custom to serve drinks prior to dinner, making it a potentially awkward period for a group of people who may never have met. In a novel of the time, a male protagonist called the half-hour 'that purgatorial period of suspense that one undergoes in the drawing-room', while another writer called it 'the melancholy twilight half-hour preceding dinner'.[138] A young American woman, accompanied by two relatives, was invited to dine at an English country house in 1852, writing later that, when they were shown into the library on arrival, 'an elegant circle of ladies and gentlemen rose to meet us' but no one was introduced.[139] A novel way of passing the time was found by Lord Blessington at his house in Mountjoy Forest, Co. Tyrone in the early nineteenth cen-

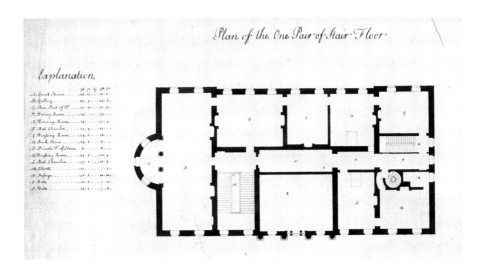

7
inster House, plan of first floor (not as executed).

tury, where John Ynyr Burges and two companions were invited to dine. In Burges's opinion, Blessington was a very fine gentleman but 'his conversation did not suit his company, who were all country neighbours'. Their host recited Thomas Moore's poetry, 'thinking to please us, but he was just as much at sea as ever' and, until dinner was announced, he 'began to act for us'.[140]

Once the serving of dinner was announced, the 'procession' of guests with their hosts to the dining room offered an opportunity to show off the decor, paintings, furniture and furnishings in other rooms en route. It is obvious from some of the plans that there could be variations in the route, but display was the object of the exercise. Plans for Leinster House, Headfort, Townley Hall and Lissadell help to illustrate how circulation for guests might be managed through the formal rooms of a house.

At both of the FitzGerald residences, Carton and Leinster House, there was an enfilade of reception rooms (including the dining room) along the garden front. Leinster House (figs 82, 137) was ideally suited to entertaining great numbers of guests by utilising both the ground and first floors, with formal rooms at both levels. At ground-floor level guests could pass from the hall, through the ante-room and into the drawing room; after dinner (in the dining room, to the left of the ante-room) the ladies could retrace their steps to the drawing room or pass through the parlour to the bow-ended dressing room.[141] When the first floor was used, guests arrived at the top of the stairs, from where they passed into the gallery which spans the depth of the house. The actor John O'Keefe was received there by the 2nd duke of Leinster when he attended a masquerade in 1775, the year the gallery was finally completed.[142] From the gallery an enfilade extends through the dining room, drawing room, Lady Kildare's bedroom and her dressing room.[143]

At Leinster House the dining rooms were part of the enfilades on both floors, but that was not the case in Chambers's plan for Headfort of 1765 (fig. 28), in which there is little processional sense. Chambers located the dining room at the front, off the hall, with a corridor between it and the drawing room behind. On arrival, guests could assemble in the saloon or drawing room – or, indeed, the library – and, when dinner was announced, move from the drawing room across to the dining room.[144] The ladies had a choice of rooms to which they could withdraw – the drawing room or the dressing room next to the saloon. In contrast, in a compact plan (unexecuted) for Townley Hall, Co. Louth (*c.*1790; fig. 138) there is a good flow of circulation. Guests could be led through the hall to a semicircular staircase hall at the centre of the house: from here they could enter the drawing room to the left, which had a door into the library. Access to the dining room could be gained from either of these rooms, as can be seen on the plan. In another plan for the same house the semicircular shape of the staircase hall became a rotunda, and there can be little doubt that the Balfour family guests were treated to the drama of this space as they left the drawing room on their way to dine. Drama was also to be found at Lissadell (1833; fig. 139). As was seen in Chapter 1, guests arrived under the protection of the porte-cochère. From the hall they could hardly fail to be impressed by the vista (and the parade) through the long 'Gallery and Music Room' to the bow-ended library and the drawing room, from which they could enjoy a view of Ben Bulben.[145] From there they approached the dining room via the ante-room. Another route allowed them to assemble in the gallery and move from there through the ante-room to dine.

In Lady Morgan's *The Wild Irish Girl* (1806), the protagonist is warmly welcomed when he arrives at a house unexpectedly. Interestingly, he is ushered into 'the refreshing comforts of a dressing-room', where the hosts dispensed with the servants and looked after him themselves. The dinner, served with much elegance and 'composed of every luxury the season afforded: though only supplied by the demesne of our host and the neighbouring sea-coast', was excessive 'compared to the compact neatness and simple sufficiency of English fare in the same rank of life'.[146] Such dinners might be presented to either large or small gatherings. Sir Jonah Barrington, the judge and politician, hosted many large dinners, 'according to the habit invariably adopted in those times, by persons circumstanced like myself', including one for over twenty guests, for which Lord Clonmell sent his two cooks to help.[147] In contrast, an elegant and very formal dinner took place in Co. Westmeath in 1773 when Lord Belfield invited just three guests – men who were known to each other – to Belvedere, his beautiful lodge on the banks of Lough Ennell. One of them, Sir James Caldwell, gave the following account of the occasion: 'Only think . . . a complete service of plate, covers and all, two soups, two removes, nine and nine, a dessert in the highest taste, all sorts of wine, burgundy and champagne, a load of meat on the side-table, four valets-de-chambre in laced clothes, and seven or eight footmen. If the Lord Lieutenant had dined there, there could not have been a more elegant entertainment.'[148]

For dinner parties, plans of the table were drawn up by the hostess. A number of these are to be found among the Maunsell Papers, where the rectangular table seated between sixteen and eighteen diners (two on each of the short sides), with their names noted and plans of the dishes annotated.[149] In one, dishes bearing rabbit, fish, ham and onions were laid along one side, while on the other were French peas, turkey and trout; calf's head was at one end of the table, venison and oyster soup at the other. Four dishes of butter were laid symmetrically, and hock and Burgundy flanked the centrepiece.

Mrs Delany believed that a long table was easier to set than a round or oval one.[150] Often diners could sit where they chose, but the host and hostess sat at the head and foot of the table, with principal guests on either side. The table was generally covered with a white cloth that extended to the floor, protecting the wood and covering any joins in the table. It also had two other roles: one was that it was used like a napkin, people wiping their mouths with it; the other was that 'its removal at the end of the main courses signalled a change in the nature of the dinner: before, the business was eating; after, it was drinking'.[151] The job of the servants was to ensure that guests' plates were never empty, so that asking for or reaching too far for a dish (signs of ill-breeding) were unnecessary.

One of the customs at dinner was the proposing of toasts, which prolonged the meal to the irritation of some. Elizabeth Ham wrote of her visit to a house in Kildare where she 'had

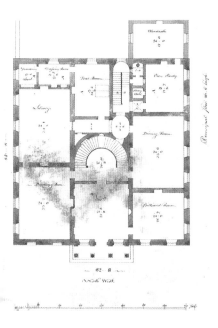

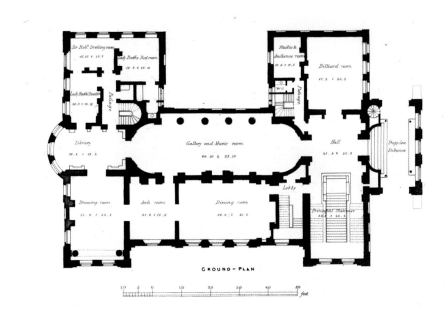

GROUND-PLAN

8
ancis Johnston, proposed ground-floor plan (not
ecuted) for Townley Hall, *c.*1790.

9
ancis Goodwin, ground-floor plan for Lissadell,
33. Francis Goodwin, *Rural Architecture* (2nd edn,
ndon, 1835), pl. 34.

to take Wine with every gentleman present'. After the cloth was removed, her host proposed a toast to her health and continued to each individual around the table; 'this was followed by all the company in the same rotation. The solemnity of the rite was quite ludicrous.'[152] One of the natural results of all this drinking was, as a French visitor to England found to his horror, that one of the cupboards of the sideboard was 'furnished with a number of chamber pots and it is a common practice to relieve oneself while the rest are drinking; one has no kind of concealment and the practice strikes me as most indecent'.[153] Another visitor to England, Prince Pückler-Muskau (who also visited Ireland), was of a similar opinion in 1826. He wrote to his wife that 'immediately after the departure of the ladies and immediately beside the table, free rein is given: a relic of barbarism which is extremely repugnant to our notions of propriety'. He told her of 'an old admiral who, clad in his dress uniform . . . made much use of this facility for a good ten minutes, during which period we felt as if we were listening to the last drops from a roof gutter after a long past thunderstorm'.[154] The custom was common practice in Ireland, too. At Newbridge House, a small cupboard in the Dining Room contains a chamber pot; in Strokestown Park, one was kept in a 'secret' compartment outside the Dining Room door, to be brought in by a servant as required. For the ladies, a chamber pot was concealed in the panelling of a turret off the drawing room in Malahide Castle.

An interesting series of changes evolved in the dining room in the course of the eighteenth century that affected furniture, furnishings, silver and china and, indeed, a way of life. To begin with, the hour for serving dinner became gradually later, moving from 1 pm to about 4 pm by 1780: by the end of the century it had reached 6 pm, but there was a great deal of flexibility. Mrs Conolly of Castletown, according to Mrs Delany in 1752, always dined at 3 pm (a very substantial meal), and had tea and coffee at 5.30 pm. At Hillsborough in 1758 Mrs Delany dined at 3.30 pm, had supper at 10 pm and retired to bed at 11 pm.[155] Many decades later, in the 1830s, Frances Power Cobbe wrote that they dined at Newbridge, Co. Dublin at 6 pm or 6.30 pm 'at the latest', and after that 'Tea, made in an urn, was a regular meal taken in the drawing-room about nine o'clock; <u>never</u> before dinner.'[156] The later hour for dinner meant that for much of the year it would be dark by the time it was served. In the country, to facilitate guests' safe return home, invitations were often issued to coincide with a full moon.[157] Mrs Delany intended 'to breakfast and dine at Lucan [House] this day, and to come home by moonshine', and Lady Leitrim returned home from a visit to Kilruddery in October 1823 'without accident or adventure, although we had no moon'.[158]

As Cornforth has pointed out, it cannot have been just a coincidence that dining late influenced 'the ordering of silver and the laying of the table, because few candlesticks were provided as part of early silver dinner services'; 'taller' candlesticks were now in demand, and the silver that was previously displayed on the sideboard or buffet was now being used on the table.[159] From the early eighteenth century in Ireland silver began to replace pewter and brass in reception rooms, though pewter remained popular. The 19th and 20th earls of Kildare were renowned for the extravagance of their silver services: the latter commissioned a silver-gilt dinner service and a pair of candelabra in London with which to decorate his table (fig. 140).[160] The earl of Orrery observed rather cattily in 1736 that the 19th earl 'makes a much greater show of his plate than of his virtues'.[161] Another silver collector was Sir Thomas Taylor, who had houses in Smithfield, Dublin and at Kells, Co. Meath: by 1728 his silver weighed 2,529 ounces and was valued at almost £620.[162] Joseph Leeson purchased a suite of plate in 1742 to be displayed in Russborough on its completion.[163] In the Nugent family's Dublin house, the 'sideboard of plate' in the back parlour, worth £60, made up about 30 per cent of the total worth of the family's effects,[164] and the silver displayed in the 'Buffett' in Laurence Delamain's house in Cork City was valued at £33 16s. 0d. in 1763, almost as much as the other contents of his house.

Much of this early silver, sometimes of a quite baroque design, might have been too old-fashioned and unsuitable for table use in the later decades of the century. However, one of the advantages of silver is that it can be melted down and re-designed. Cutlery sets with family crests were ordered, and some acquired perhaps by those with pretensions, such as Robert Smith's purchase at the Dawson Grove sale of much of the cutlery on which Viscount Cremorne's coronet was engraved. Sir Edward O'Brien expressed his desire to purchase items for his dining room at the newly built Dromoland Castle in 1825: 'I propose buying Silver and dishes, Candlesticks, Linen, everything wanted for a Table of 18 persons to dine: I saw yesterday several very Handsome sets of Coalbroke Dale China at £40, 6 dozen Plates—& what they call a full service . . . I wish my Parlour to be finished this Spring and should much wish to be able to give some Parties about the Summer Assizes—or Races—& I am inclined to get about a thousand Pounds worth of goods.'[165] One item with which to dress a dinner table was the Irish silver dish ring (fig. 141), four or five of which might be on the dining table, used to protect it from hot dishes. Made in Ireland from the mid-eighteenth century these highly decorated rings, precursors of the table mat, varied in height up to five and a half inches and could be up to ten inches in diameter.

Along with the silver, there was Chinese porcelain, which cost about ten times more than everyday ware, and much of which bore families' coats of arms. One such family was that of Lord Grandison, whose porcelain was recorded in the Dromana inventory of 1755. Among the items advertised for sale at Lord Donegall's house in Belfast in 1803 were a Wedgwood dinner service and a Colebrookdale dinner and dessert service in gold and scarlet.[166] Frances Power Cobbe described as 'exceedingly beautiful' the Indian (probably Chinese) and Worcester china that belonged to Thomas Cobbe at Newbridge House: one dessert service for thirty-six people 'was magnificent'.[167]

A profusion of wax candles lit dining rooms from torchères, candlesticks, candelabra and sconces, the last often fitted with a mirror to reflect light. Together with the mirrors on the

The Leinster dining service, a George II silver service with the mark of George Wickes, London 1745–56, reputed to be the most complete surviving aristocratic dinner service.

piers between windows and over the chimneypieces in many dining rooms, the effect of the reflections and the flickering light on the silver, porcelain and glassware on the table and, indeed, upon the clothes worn by those assembled, must have been striking.

After the meal, ladies generally withdrew to the drawing room for tea, coffee and conversation, or, as the playwright William Congreve put it, 'they retired to their tea and scandal after dinner'.[168] After a dinner at Dawson Court in 1778, the young and newly married Lady Caroline Dawson chose a different location for the ladies: 'to make it as pleasant as I could, I carried them into the little study, instead of the great drawing-room, and as soon as the men came out I sat the old lady down to cards with three of them and I remained chatting with the girls'.[169] In England, a visitor described the retirement of the ladies ('and servants') after dinner as 'the signal for alarming drinking', when the 'real enjoyment begins – there is not an Englishman who is not supremely happy at this . . . moment'. Endless toasts ensued, and the conversation was 'sometimes in gross bad taste by French standards'.[170] Lord Blayney of Castle Blayney, Co. Monaghan, as soon as the ladies had withdrawn, started off 'with all his merry men to a little adjoining room, which was called his own glory hole, and there we had such fun, such jolly stories, that it was difficult to leave our seats'.[171]

But such was not the custom in all houses in Ireland: a young woman writing in the 1770s describes how her husband 'not approving the custom of ladies retiring after dinner, has laid his injunctions on me, and we have none but mixed societies at this house'.[172] According to Edward Wakefield, in the first decades of the nineteenth century, excessive drinking 'is now entirely out of fashion' and men were free to leave the table when they wished, and retire to the drawing room.[173] In his *Memoirs* (published in 1820), Richard L. Edgeworth states that 'The gentlemen and ladies are not separated from the time dinner ends, till the midnight hour, when the carriages came to the door to carry off the bodies of the dead; or, till just sense enough being left, to find their way straight to the tea-table, the gentlemen could only swallow a hasty cup of cold coffee or stewed tea, and be carried off by their sleepy wives, happy if the power of reproach were lost in fatigue.'[174]

The custom of ladies quitting the dining room after dinner was unknown in Continental Europe and appears to have travelled from England to Ireland. As has been seen on examination of the plans, it is rare to find the dining room and the drawing room next to each other: one reason might be that an intervening space, be it hall or saloon, put the women at a little distance 'from the noise and talk of the men when left to their bottle', as Lord Lyttelton delicately put it in 1752.[175] Lady Morgan provided her readers with an insight into how women felt about this habit in a conversation in which one woman said to the other 'they say you would rather stay with the men after dinner; and vote women a bore', to which the other replied:

> Don't believe more than half what is said of me, dearest Lady Elizabeth: so far from desiring to stay with the men, I think the foreign habit of men and women, rising from the table together, is <u>lèze coqueterie</u>. Besides, the half-hour's repose, for silence and digestion, is a great luxury. I hate talking between dinner and coffee . . . The men have the advantage of us, every way. Men have always the excitements of stirring subjects after dinner, – politics, – fun; – and then the exhilaration of wine and good fellowship: while we women rise from table upon clotted cream, iced; or on clammy compots . . . and then we come out to gossip with each other, about nothing at all, and when we are fit for nothing at all, but a lounge, a book, or a sleep.[176]

According to Mrs Delany, at Castletown when the ladies retired to the drawing room, Mrs Conolly would take a nap while the others chatted. At 5.30 pm precisely, when tea and coffee were served, she awoke, after which she and her guests played cards until 10 pm. To amuse herself at Hillsborough, Co. Down after a wish that the ladies 'command the house', Mrs Delany chose instead to investigate the garden: on her return, the candles were lit and 'tea-table and gentlemen come together'.[177] In 1805 Mrs Hamilton, whose daughter lived at Rossanagh, Co. Wicklow, wrote a poem on a country dinner party in which she describes the departure from the dining room:

> A wink makes the table with laughter resound
> While the Hock and the Claret go briskly around
> So Madam conceives it high time to retire
> And the ladies encircle the Drawingroom fire
> The dress of her neighbour each handles and praises
> Examines her trinkets, gown, ribbons and laces
> Then [buidling?] her chest looks exaltingly down
> Most perfectly now in conceit of her own
> At length all the toils of the tea-table over
> In silence each Miss sits expecting a lover
> Till weary with anxiously watching the door
> She frowns at her fidgeting Mother no more
> Who quite out of patience no longer delays
> To send for her husband and order her Chaise[178]

Richard Edgeworth applauded the passing of such interminable dinners 'where the gentlemen could talk only of claret, horses or dogs' and the women 'only of dress or scandal'. Nor was he sorry about the departure of the 'stupid circle', where chairs were arranged in that configuration to encourage conversation: 'the chairs, which formerly could only take that form, at which the firmest nerves must ever tremble, are allowed to stand, or turn in any way which may suit the . . . pleasure of conversation'.[179] Elizabeth Ham, having survived the numerous toasts over dinner, described the circle in the drawing room as 'still more awful than the Dinner had been'.[180] Maria Edgeworth referred to the circle in *Ormond* (1817), when Sir Ulick O'Shane walked into his drawing room, accompanied by what he called his 'rear-guard, veterans of the old school of good fellows, who at those times in Ireland, times long since past, deemed it essential to health, happiness, and manly character, to swallow, and show themselves able to stand after swallowing, a certain number of bottles of claret per day or night', and exclaimed, 'What! no music, no dancing at Castle Hermitage tonight; and all the ladies sitting in a formal circle, petrifying into perfect statues, of all the figures in nature or art, the formal circle is universally the most obnoxious to conversation, and, to me, the most formidable.'[181]

As was usual practice at such an event, a room would be set aside for the playing of cards, an almost essential ingredient in an evening's entertainment (fig. 142). The duchess of Northumberland was a prolific card-player. She and her husband (as viceroy) landed in Dublin on 22 September 1763 and four days later she lost 48 guineas playing loo at the Clements' house in Phoenix Park. Her diary records card games four times or more per week.[182] This was not unusual: according to Lord Chief Baron Willes, 'there is scarce a gent or lady who has not one or more cards for a rout every night in the week' in Dublin.[183] And Frances Power Cobbe described 'incessant' card-playing at Newbridge House: 'Tradition says that the tables were laid for it on rainy days at 10 o'clock in the morning in Newbridge drawing-room; and on every day in the interminable evenings which followed the then fashionable four o'clock dinner. My grandmother was so excellent a whist-player that to extreme old age in Bath she habitually made a small, but appreciable addition to her income out of her "card purse", an ornamental appendage of the toilet then, and even in my time, in universal use.'[184] At Woodstock, Co. Kilkenny, Lady Betty Fownes enjoyed playing cards so much that in summer she would have the card table set up under the oak tree in the garden, 'when dinner was to be, as it frequently was, on the grass', much to the chagrin of her husband, who would beg her to allow them dine in the parlour 'for variety'.[185]

In the early 1730s Mrs Conolly (fig. 88), widow of Speaker Conolly, had a thriving 'basset bank', playing cards at Castletown. Her sister, Mary Jones, feared for her moral well-being, as 'her crowds of young Gaye compeney may dow her harm . . . Mr Burton [a member of Parliament and a nephew by marriage] keeps a basset bank at her house, she goes a third with him, he has had it but one night and she and he lost 100 pound . . . I am sorry she duse it, its what the Duke [of Dorset, Lord Lieutenant] does not alow at the Castell'.[186] They lost £131 on another night.[187] Jones worried that 'my sisters house is grown a gaiming house for ther is sometimes 40 or 50 pound lost of a night, all to Devart [divert?] Lady Ann [her daughter-in-law, Lady Anne Conolly]'.[188] As noted above, however, according to Mrs Delany, the usual routine at Mrs Conolly's house was that at 5.30 pm, when tea and coffee had been served, 'a party of whist was made for her till ten, then everybody retired', a pattern that does not quite fit in with Mrs Jones's account.[189] Cards continued to be played at Castletown after Mrs Conolly's death, as a letter from Lady Caroline Fox from England to her sister Emily makes clear when she asks her (perhaps enviously) if it is true that 'you have four or five loo tables at an assembly? One is the most can be pick'd up here.'[190]

At Carton in 1778, as Lady Caroline Dawson explained in a letter to her sister, 'it is not the fashion . . . to play at cards', but it was something that would be arranged, if a guest requested it.[191] Maria Edgeworth's eponymous hero, Ormond, prudently decided in advance to lose a sum of perhaps 500 guineas on gambling. Upon reaching that sum, he would stop short; 'By this means I have acquired all the advantages of yielding to the fashionable madness, without risking my future happiness.'[192] However, the numbers of card tables listed in inventories in drawing rooms and in parlours throughout the period under consideration show that many did indeed yield to the fashion.

On a rather dramatic note, it was said that the earl of Barrymore, having lost a great deal of money at cards on a visit to Dromana, shot himself in a room in the old tower. For the mistress of Dromana, the Countess Grandison, cards were a comfort to her after the death of her husband in 1759. Mrs Delany, a cousin of the countess, paid a visit a month after his death, expecting it to be a 'melancholy' occasion; instead, she found the countess sitting at a card table playing cribbage, 'but she looked melancholy and I believe is sorry', though she added, 'cards are now the nostrum to drive away all sorrow'. The countess's son and his wife, Lady Gertrude Seymour, third daughter of the marquis of Hertford, were addicted to the gaming table. Lady Gertrude was known as 'the toast of the town' in Dublin, gambling all night until dawn, when she regularly pelted the crowd who had gathered under the windows with (empty) wine bottles. It was also said that she disguised herself as a man to gamble in taverns.[193]

Playing cards was one thing; people arriving and expecting to be entertained if only to a 'dish' of tea or coffee was another. Many resented the dullness of entertaining in the country. The essayist Joseph Addison said: 'Giving and receiving visitors in the country from a circle of neighbours who . . . can be neither entertaining or serviceable to us, is a vile waste of time and a slavery from which a man should deliver himself if possible.'[194] The eccentric 11th

Baron Blayney had a way of dealing with unwanted guests: he sent his servant to say that he was gone to Belfast. 'Belfast' was what he called his cottage on the banks of the lake to which he would invite the more interesting of his guests. His *maître d'hotel* would arrive at the cottage by boat with the dinner, which he would serve.[195] But being entertained was not all fun for one visitor in the 1820s, who considered country life 'too social' for his tastes: he was seldom alone in the library when he wanted to read. Writing letters in one's own room 'is not usual, and therefore surprises and annoys people'; so 'you sit at a great common writing table, and they [the letters] are then put in a box with holes and taken to post by a servant'.[196]

How to pass the time in a country house must have presented some challenges. The duke of Abercorn's agent gave some thought to it in 1793 when the building of Baronscourt was almost complete. In a letter to the duke he suggested acquiring some cricket bats and balls, 'and what think you, as archery is in fashion, about bows and arrows? I think the latter would be a favourite amusement. For the ladies in wet weather, send some battledores and plenty of shuttlecocks.'[197] But by November many country houses were abandoned as families made their annual pilgrimage to Dublin, where they revived their spirits with the social events of the winter season, whether or not Parliament met.[198] There, in the town houses that they owned or rented, they could enjoy a dizzy round of dinners, parties, balls, suppers, concerts and the theatre.

Private theatricals

One pastime that was as popular in town as it was in the country was the staging of amateur theatricals: 'It is impossible to peep into a social corner of Irish life without getting a glimpse of the amateur stage with lamps lit and noble ladies and noble gentlemen in rich dresses playing their parts.'[199] It was probably at Dublin Castle in the early eighteenth century that the enthusiasm for amateur theatrical presentations was first encountered in Ireland. As the century progressed, the Castle became the scene of many a theatrical performance, including, in 1709 at the instigation of the lord lieutenant, the 1st earl of Wharton, Joseph Addison's musical play *Rosamund* (1707).[200] The earliest play in the Castle for which details of the cast and the setting exist was Ambrose Philips's *The Distressed Mother* (1712), acted by amateurs in January 1732/3 under the patronage of the lord lieutenant, Lionel Sackville, 1st duke of Dorset, himself an active supporter of the theatre in Dublin.[201] The performance took place in the council chamber. William Stewart, Viscount Mountjoy, who played the part of Pyrrhus, invited Mrs Delany to join his party of twelve, the number of tickets each performer had to dispose of. In a letter she wrote that 'all the Bishops, Judges and Privy Counsellors [were] to be there'. Meanwhile, regular theatregoers such as the FitzGerald and Conolly families from Carton and Castletown frequently exchanged details of plays and actors with each other and with their relatives in London. Almost all of the London successes came to Dublin, although the Dublin theatre managers did not slavishly follow that lead; while they shared London tastes, they were quite selective.[202]

But in the last quarter of the eighteenth century the upper classes in Dublin began to desert the theatre, finding the prospect of putting on a play in the privacy of their own homes more appealing. One reason for this may have been a reaction to the rowdiness of the audiences, sections of which were not slow about voicing their opinions of the actors during the performances. Further, the lords lieutenant had largely ceased attending by this time.[203] Finally, only in 1762 were spectators removed from the stage (where they had up to this point been allowed to stand), and it and the orchestra were railed off. Among the upper classes it was felt that more enjoyment could be had in the preparation and production of a play during the long winter evenings in the country, a play that would be performed to a more appreciative audience – families, friends, tenants and servants. In England there was a similar pattern but the catalyst there, according to one newspaper in 1776, was the resignation from the theatre of the actor David Garrick, after which 'the rage for dramatic entertainments in private families has increased astonishingly; scarce a man of rank but either has or pretends to have his petit théâtre, in the decoration of which the utmost taste and expense are lavished'.[204] The rage for theatricals in England coincided with that in Ireland but the period leading up to the 1798 Rebellion and following the Union with Great Britain in 1800 was a rather fallow one for Ireland in this context. The fashion was revived somewhat from about 1805, but not with the same enthusiasm.

The fashionable elite's partial abandonment of the Dublin theatre was only a shift in the *locus operandi*. Performances of plays might now take place in a house or garden, in a specially built theatre adjacent to or adjoining the house, in a barn or sometimes in a theatre, rented for the occasion, to which friends were invited. They occurred on a fairly regular basis from the middle of the century, reaching their height of popularity in the 1770s and 1780s. The print media were a valuable tool, and newspapers and periodicals of the time frequently reported on private performances and the accompanying festivities at various houses. It may be deduced from the amount of reportage that the newspaper-reading public avidly followed details of the plays, the performers, the dresses, the houses and the food.

The earliest reference to private theatricals in Ireland – that is, those held on private estates or in private houses – date to the 1740s and the early 1750s at Quilca, Co. Cavan, where Richard Brinsley Sheridan's father, Thomas, boarded over the top of a grassy mound in his garden to provide a *mise en scène* for his productions with family and friends.[205] Also out of doors, where 'the stage was the green sward, the scenery the leafy woods', John Milton's *The Masque of Comus* (1634) was performed at Rathfarnham Castle before the viceroy, Lord Townshend, while at Kilruddery the surviving Sylvan Theatre with its high hedge and grassy banks was the scene of private theatricals from the latter part of the eighteenth century.[206] At Lurgan, the seat of William Brownlow MP, *Midas* (by the Irish playwright Kane O'Hara) was performed in 1759: members of the Brownlow family played the parts, together with the author, who was one of the houseguests, and the performance took place in 'the private theatre attached to the [Brownlow] residence'.[207]

Despite the fact that the FitzGeralds and the Conollys were popular with Dublin theatre goers and continued to attend a number of performances, from at least 1760 plays were being produced in their homes in which family, friends (among them many members of Parliament) and even servants took part. As arguably the two 'first' families in the land, it is not surprising that their theatricals began a trend that gathered momentum into the mid-1770s, by which time it had spread to other parts of Ireland. At Carton in December 1760 *The Devil to Pay* was performed, the cast consisting of houseguests, 'none of us knowing any of our parts which we had been studying all morning', according to Lady Louisa Conolly.[208] The switching of social roles in performances, in which the upper classes played the parts of their inferiors, must have been half the 'fun' for all concerned.

The FitzGerald children put on plays on summer evenings for their own amusement at their Co. Dublin villa, Frescati (fig. 128), as did their Fox cousins at Holland House in London.[209] The duke of Leinster had some misgivings about the propriety of his children taking part in these events, and was anxious about 'the political judiciousness of Irish noble families indulging in such play-acting'.[210] In September 1771 Lady Louisa wrote to her sister Sarah that 'The Duke of Leinster . . . does not approve of his Children's acting therefore only indulged my sister with these plays for her own amusement provided there was to be [no] company therefore the audience consisted only of the Servants, and ourselves.'[211] As a ten-year-old that year, Lord Henry FitzGerald (later recognised as a fine actor) had played Lucia in *Cato* at Carton, and William Ogilvie, the children's tutor and future husband of the duchess, played Portius. The minor parts were 'done by the Servants among whom we have some good ones'. A month earlier, the footmen and postilions at Carton had acted in a performance of George Farquhar's *The Beaux' Stratagem* (1707) and the servants' play appears to have been an annual event, as, according to Lady Louisa, 'they acted last year very tolerably and are improved this year'.[212]

Late evidence of theatricals among the FitzGeralds and Conollys comes from 1775, when Louisa referred in a letter to plays put on that January by members of the large party she had entertained at Castletown over Christmas as 'the prettiest things I ever saw, and incomparably well acted'. Her guests included Luke Gardiner, his wife and family, Edmund Malone and Robert Jephson: 'Mr Jephson and Mrs Gardiner . . . are equal to any actors (Garrick excepted) I ever saw'.[213] Praise indeed for the actors, and so perhaps it is not surprising to learn that in 1778 the Gardiners built a theatre at their home, the Ranger's House in Phoenix Park, Dublin, where they, together with their friends, performed a double bill of *Macbeth* and *The Citizen* in the presence of the vice-regal couple (figs 143, 144). No fewer than four different dresses were worn by Mrs Gardiner as Lady Macbeth, described as 'dreams of beauty' and worn with diamonds 'to the amount of £100,000'![214] Praise for her performance was lavish in the Hibernian Magazine, as it was for the location: 'the beauty of the theatre, its superb decorations, and the inimitable taste displayed therein by the elegant master of the whole, rendered the entertainment one continued scene of delight'.[215]

In the early 1770s in Co. Kilkenny, a group of gentlemen – Sir Hercules Langrishe, MP for Knocktopher, Gervais Parker Bushe of Kilfane, Francis Flood of Flood Hall and Henry Flood, MP for Farmley – got together to put on plays in their houses. They were joined in this endeavour by Bushe's brother-in-law Henry Grattan, who took a seat in Parliament in 1775. Henry Flood's biographer states that the plays performed 'ranged from quality Shakespearean drama, through Goldsmith and Gay to ephemeral pieces of little substance'.[216] The group resembled a company of strolling players going from house to house to perform. Unfortunately, no indication is given as to what space in any house was used for these events. However, we do know that Marlay, the home of David La Touche MP at Rathfarnham, Co. Dublin, had its own theatre, 'The Mignonette Theatre, Fairyland', where adults and the many La Touche children performed.

An impressive theatre-cum-ballroom was built in 1779 by John O'Neill MP, later 1st Viscount O'Neill, at Shane's Castle, Co. Antrim, described by Daniel Beaufort (who saw it in 1787) as 'very pretty and large'.[217] O'Neill and his wife, the former Henrietta Frances Boyle, daughter of Lord Orrery, loved the theatre and had regularly invited players to act at their house, which encouraged them to build their own theatre and to act themselves. Mrs O'Neill was a patron and friend of the actress Mrs Siddons, who performed and was a guest at Shane's Castle in 1784.[218] In January 1780 they opened their theatre with a double bill of Shakespearean plays, after which a magnificent supper was provided for all.[219]

In August 1787, the *Dublin Evening Post* reported that 'a very beautiful theatre is now erecting' at Dromana, the earl of Grandison's seat in Co. Waterford. Another built theatre, that at Aldborough House, Dublin (begun 1793), is of interest because an architectural sketch for it drawn by the earl of Aldborough is the only drawing for a domestic theatre in Ireland (fig. 145).[220] While only a simple sketch, it gives a great deal of detail, showing five boxes, a refreshment room, the pit, orchestra, proscenium and backstage area, a green room and two dressing rooms with water closets.[221] As built, the theatre was a scaled-down version of this drawing. It was contained in one of the two pavilions linked to the house by curved quadrants in the Palladian style (the other held the chapel). Approached by steps, the entrance to the pavilion was located in the centre of the three-bay elevation facing into the courtyard. On the street sides the pavilions had blind arches and Coade stone panels, and were surmounted by lions and sphinxes in the same material. A diary entry for 6 July 1798 records the 'cornice to theatre columns done'.[222] Apparently just one large reception was held in the house, as it was finished only in 1799 and Aldborough died in January 1801 at his seat, Belan, Co. Kildare (fig. 33), where he had also built a theatre.[223] That in Dublin still stands, though devoid of its interior decoration.

As well as those mentioned above, plays were performed in houses large and small around the country. In all cases they were for entertainment, but they did vary in degree of sophistication (fig. 146). Dorothea Herbert describes the 'fun and merry house' at Castle Blunden in Kilkenny in the 1780s, where the young people put on 'small plays' in the evenings.[224] She, with her family and friends also used 'Mrs Jephson's large parlour' as a makeshift theatre for *The Padlock*: 'we made a real farce of it – we had only some old Bed Curtains for scenery and everything else suitable to them'.

A less primitive production was called for to celebrate the completion of work by the architect James Wyatt at Westport House, Co. Mayo in 1783, when John Denis Browne, 3rd earl of Altamont, invited guests to take part in a round of festivities, among them a play.[225]

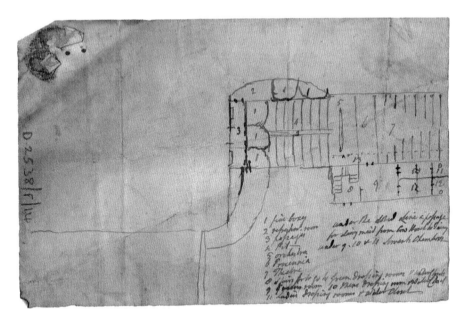

A large room was converted into a theatre, with 'a raised stage, gallery, scenery and magnificent chandeliers', where *Douglas* was performed. At Roebuck Castle, Lord Trimleston's seat in Co. Dublin, in 1795, a play in French took place in a room where 'a neat and commodious theatre was fitted up . . . for the reception of about a hundred friends'.[226] In November 1798 at Edgeworthstown, Maria Edgeworth wrote to her cousin that she and her father were

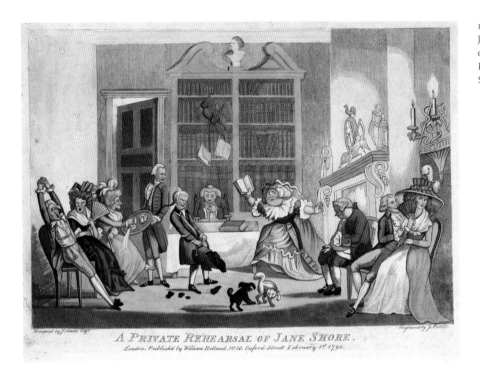

A PRIVATE REHEARSAL OF JANE SHORE.
London, Published by William Holland, N.o 50. Oxford Street February 1.st 1790.

146
John Pettit, *A Private Rehearsal of Jane Shore*;
engraving after painting by John Nixon.
Published by William Holland, No. 50 Oxford
Street, 1 February 1790.

writing a comedy, called *Whim for Whim*, and that her father 'is making a charming theatre in the room over his study'. The play was acted twice in January 1799 to an appreciative audience. Her stepmother painted the scenery and her father's mechanism for it was described as 'most ingenious'.[227]

There was advice available in books on how to transform a hall or saloon into a theatre: 'flanked with interior columns and surrounded by galleries [they] would with the aid of proper draperies or scenery in the inter-columniations make a rich and elegant appearance, and at the same time the music might be so disposed in the gallery, as to produce a most animating effect'.[228] For those not quite so rich, there were guidelines on transforming a drawing room or library to the same purpose.[229] Undoubtedly there must have been a degree of competitiveness among these builders of theatres: in Lady Morgan's *O'Donnel*, Lady Lorton is planning theatricals, but 'she had, however a theatre to build, and Lady Llanberis was determined to outdo her and has almost finished her own'.[230]

For Lord Mountjoy in Tyrone it was not just about the building: it was about lavish display, theatricals forming part of a series of entertainments laid on for his friends just once a year. The townland of Rash was part of the Mountjoy Estate, owned by Charles John Gardiner, Lord Mountjoy (created 1st earl of Blessington in 1816), son of Luke Gardiner.[231] In the early nineteenth century his annual income was said to be £30,000.[232] Mountjoy spent a great deal of money at Rash *c.*1807 when he extended his kitchen and wine cellars and erected a 'spacious and elegantly decorated theatre', for which he provided props and a wardrobe of magnificent costumes, which were described by his tenants in 1855 as 'a terrible waste of money'. The entertainment was held during the shooting season, lasting for three or four weeks, during which time no expense was spared with field sports, parties and theatricals. The productions were sometimes professional, with actors and actresses brought from Dublin and London, but frequently they were amateur – or rather, the gentlemen were, while the ladies were always professional actresses. These women were apparently lodged at the house of the schoolmistress, close to the avenue leading to the house. No details of the plays acted or the players have come to hand except that Lord Mountjoy enjoyed taking part, and another who might have done so was his friend and neighbour in Co. Tyrone, John James Hamilton, 1st marquess of Abercorn, who had acted in at least one play at his seat, Baronscourt, in 1793.[233] From their correspondence it is evident that they shared this interest.[234] Occasionally the gentlemen brought their wives to Rash, and for his guests Mountjoy fitted up and furnished temporary accommodation. For the rest of the year, Rash was, as the countess of Blessington's biographer describes it, 'a dull, solitary lifeless locality, in the midst of a forest and some fourscore miles from the metropolis'. Ultimately, the joys and excitement of the season at Rash soon bored Mountjoy, who returned to live in England.[235]

It is difficult to get an even-handed view of how good the productions were in general. With a few exceptions one can assume that the acting was not good. It would be fair to say that the main faults would have been 'inaudibility, rapidity of speech, self-consciousness and awkwardness'.[236] As a spectacle they must have been worth seeing, as no expense was spared regarding the accoutrements; the actors had the advantage of a respectful audience and, unlike the actors in public theatres, did not have to almost shout to make themselves heard above a din. In Joseph Farington's diary, a comment on Lady Caher's performance at Lord Abercorn's in 1806, might sum up the attitude of these amateurs: she was 'very imperfect in her part . . . Her Ladyship, however, did not seem embarrassed by her difficulties, but went on with perfect self possession.'[237]

This Bedchamber floor contains 9 Bedchambers, 6 of which have Dres
independant of Lady Cootes apartment and 3 Bedchambers without
Rooms,— there is to be a third story over Lady Cootes apartment &c w
contain 4 additional Bed Rooms, two of which will serve for Dressing R
making in all, 13 Bed rooms & 8 Dressing rooms. The Maid Servan
are tto be over the Nursery.

The Gallery is lighted by Oval windows on the flat Roof.

W.C.
Nursery 22. by 16.-0.
16. ft. high
Nursery
School room
20. by 24.-0
Maids Stairs
Nursery &c
Lady Cootes Maid 16. by 10.
Governess 16. by 10.
Upper part of Kitchen
This part only 2 stories high.
This part will have 3. stories
Bed chamb. 16. by 22.-0.
Dresg. room 16. by 8.-0
Bed Chamber 24. by 16.-6.
Dresg. room 12. by 16.-6.
Stairs
Lady Cootes Boudoir 10. by 16.
Lady Cootes Bed chamb. 18. by 22.-0.
Dresg. room 14. by 10.
Bath
W.C.
Passage
W.C.
The floor her
with Lady
and 6. fa
the other
Gallery
Closet
Bed chamb. 22. by 24.-0.
Closet
Gallery
Flat roof over Hall & Vestibule
Grand Stairs 24. by 24
Back Stairs
Passage
Bed chamb. 14. by 17.-0.
Gallery
Passage
3 Stories
Bed chamb. 16. by 22.-0
Dresg. room 16. by 8.-0.
Bed chamb. 14. by 17.
Dresg. room 17. by 11.-0.
Bed chamb. 18.-6 by 17
Bed chamber 25. by 17.-0.
Dresg. room 11. by 17.
Bed chamb. 14. by 17.-0
Portico
Scale 5 10 20 30 40 50 150 feet

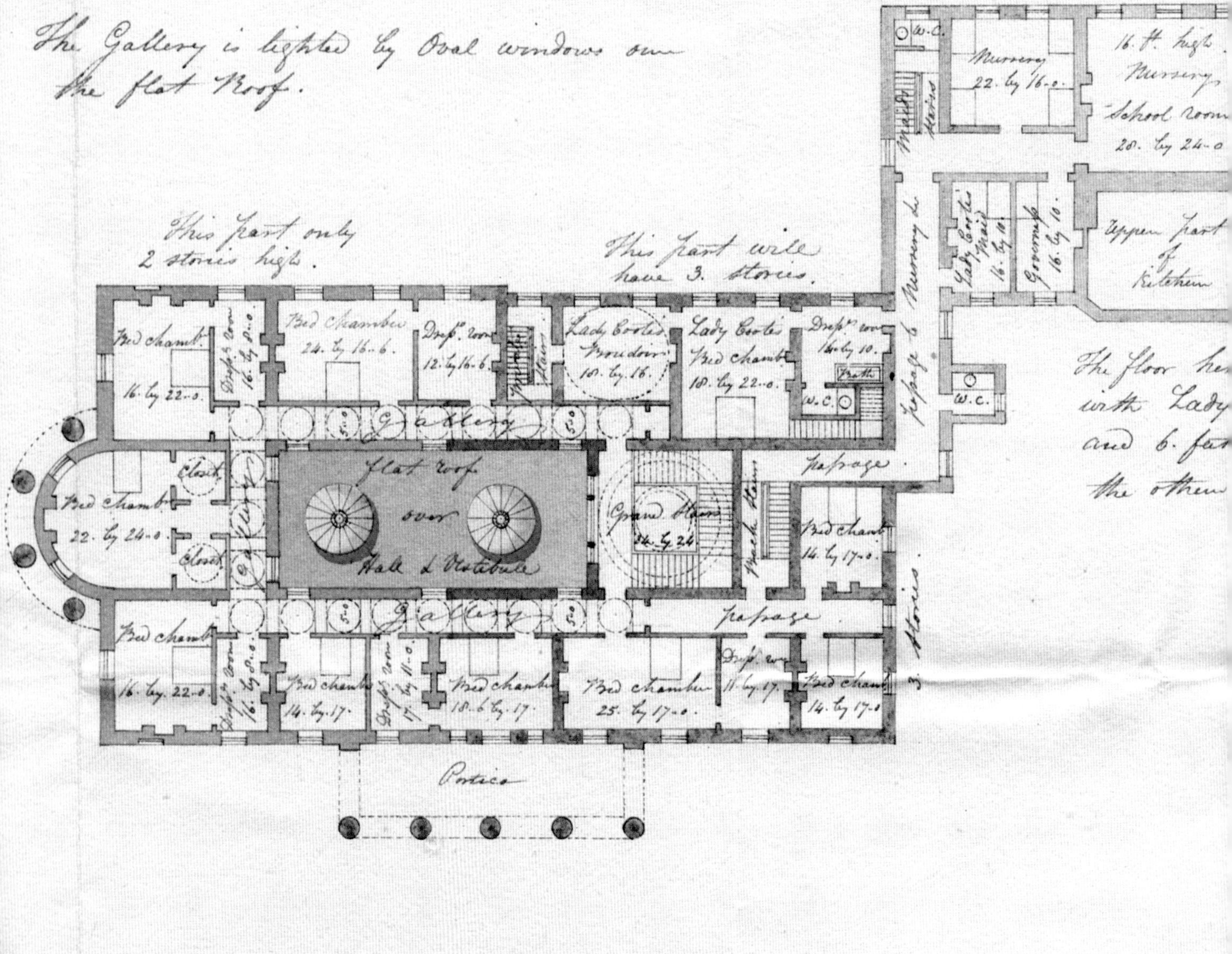

Five

Family Spaces

Before looking at libraries in country houses, it might be useful to consider briefly the publishing of books in Ireland. Prior to 1800, no copyright law pertained in the country and the Dublin printing trade flourished mostly, it has to be said, as a reprint business. Books published in London were reprinted in Ireland and a large export business was built up with North America. Within this aspect of publishing, the Irish trade chose 'the most readable and popular material from London publications and offered it to a wider readership than the expensive London book could command', at a low price.[1] The British could do nothing about this as Ireland was not covered by the Copyright Act enacted in 1710. This meant that ownership of a literary work was not acknowledged, and a writer publishing in Ireland was aware that his or her work was not protected from piracy.[2] Therefore, authors who had manuscripts to sell went to London.

As the novelist William Carleton wrote in 1842:

In truth until within the last ten or twelve years an Irish author never thought of publishing in his own country, and the consequence was that our literary men followed the example of our great landlords; they became absentees, and drained the country of its intellectual wealth precisely as the others exhausted it of its rents. Thus did Ireland stand in the singular anomaly of adding some of the most distinguished names to the literature of Great Britain, whilst she herself remained incapable of presenting anything to the world beyond a school-book or pamphlet.[3]

opposite
Richard and William Morrison, *Chamber Plan No. 1* for Ballyfin, *c.*1822, detail. Private collection (*see* fig. 163).

The population of Ireland in 1600 was reckoned at 1.4 million; by the end of the eighteenth century it was between 4.5 and 5 million. However, this is no indicator of a reading public: it is not known how many English speakers could read nor how many Irish speakers could understand English, let alone read it, and there was virtually no printed literature in the Irish language.[4]

It is obvious that a room for a library was a desirable space in a country house and a mark of an educated owner, as they appear on the majority of house plans, where they are also called 'book rooms', particularly in those dating to the first half of the nineteenth century. One of the earliest designs for a library in a great house in England was that for Wanstead in Vitruvius Britannicus, published in 1715. However, neither Blenheim nor Castle Howard was planned with a library.[5] In earlier periods, closets or studies may have functioned as 'libraries': the earl of Kildare kept a 'standard [a great chest] for Bookes' in the study of his Dublin house in 1656; at Kilkenny Castle the duke of Ormonde kept books in his closet, according to an inventory taken in the 1680s, which mentions, after listing the furniture, 'Besides the Shelves & books which his Grace hath an account of'.[6]

For the period 1700 to 1750 there is a small number of architectural drawings pertaining to libraries in Irish houses: a proposal for Stillorgan House, the Barnet house in the Dromoland Album, a design by Samuel Chearnley, one from the Charleville Forest Collection, one for Dromoland and plans for Leinster House. In 1729 Robert Howard, bishop of Killala, despite being a cultured cleric himself, wrote that 'books go off very heavily, in this Country, where there is little Money, and too little Inclination to read'.[7] Nevertheless, there is evidence that other members of the clergy possessed libraries during this period – for example, Bishop Thomas Rundle at his Dublin house in St Stephen's Green, and Dean and Mrs Delany at Delville. By 1739 Rundle had created a library with a coved ceiling, 64 feet long, 20 feet wide and 16 feet high, with a bow window to the rear which he described as 'exactly half a circle', stating that 'the glass is bent to answer the curvature of the building'. He wrote that his 'lesser' books were arranged uniformly on shelves between thirty-two three-quarter Ionic columns supported on a pedestal 'that goes round the room the height of window to floor. In this pedestal are my largest books.' Here he created a salon, where 'gentlemen and ladies, old and young, rich and poor, soldiers and bishops' brought 'learning into chit-chat'.[8] This was an interesting, and early, development that will be considered in more depth below. In 1744 Mrs Delany described the couple's library at Delville as 'most plentifully filled', though half the length of Rundle's at 32 feet, and only 11 feet wide. Three years later the Delanys extended it, creating 'a sort of closet to which you ascend by one step . . . adorned with pilasters', 12 feet square with a window at the far end and, to one side, a 'looking glass representing a sash window, which will reflect the prospect'. There Mrs Delany intended to have a table in the middle 'for writing and holding papers', with chairs around it.[9]

The earliest appearance of a library among plans is a section showing four bays of a double-height library with a gallery, among proposals for the refurbishment of Stillorgan House, Co. Dublin by Edward Lovett Pearce, dating to the late 1720s (fig. 147).[10] This shows three bays of bookshelves with double columns between each bay (Ionic order at ground level, Corinthian in the gallery); behind a columnar screen, the fourth bay has round-headed niches on each level. The section coincides with a plan for the house (not annotated) where the library projects forward from the main body of the house. With no windows at ground-floor level, light is provided by three overlooking the forecourt and two to the front. Meanwhile, for Leinster House Richard Castle executed three drawings: one is a plan indicating the library's location on the ground floor; the other two are proposals for the room itself with its fittings, both showing recessed, glazed bookcases decorated with Ionic pilasters (fig. 148).[11]

147
Edward Lovett Pearce, Stillorgan House, Co. Dublin, section, late 1720s.

8
chard Castle, design for the earl of Kildare's library,
inster House, *c.*1745.

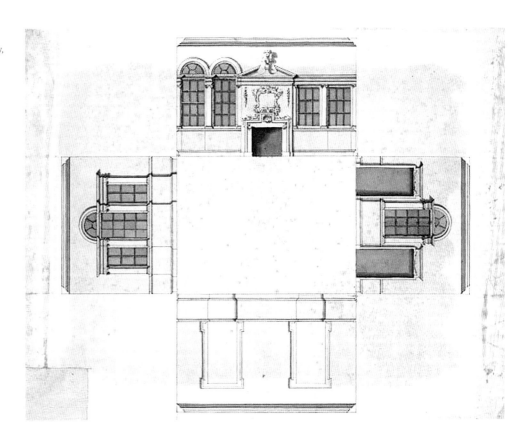

In Scotland there was an early tradition of book rooms on upper floors, but not so in Ireland although there are a couple of plans showing them, such as one by Castle where the room spans the depth of the house, is two storeys high and measures 61 × 24 feet.[12] A 'Library museum' appears on a plan drawn up by Samuel Chearnley in the 1740s of the upper storey of a pavilion attached to a house.[13] Finally, the proposed library at Portumna Castle, Co. Galway, mentioned by two separate visitors in the early nineteenth century, was planned for 'the highest storey', with reading closets in the turrets.[14]

Libraries appear on sixteen plans for the second half of the eighteenth century, and on twenty-seven between 1800 and 1850. There is no pattern to the location of the room within the house, but a large number are off the hall, to the front. Most are rectangular in shape, exceptions being the 'Round Room' at Slane Castle, where, prior to 1810, the alcoves were used to accommodate Burton Conyngham's valuable collection of books, and the circular library in the turret at Castle Bernard (1833). It appears that *c.*1775 Robert, 2nd Viscount Kingsborough, converted a tower that had been part of the former outworks of Mitchelstown Castle, Co. Cork into a library 'beautified with busts and paintings' and employed a librarian; at Clonbrock, Co. Galway, the Dillons' library was located in a turret in the bawn (fig. 149).[15] Richard Morrison proposed an intriguing design for a 'Book Room' at Mount Bellew: octagonal in shape, with its own entrance from the garden through an oval vestibule, off which was the staircase to the gallery.[16] Another octagonal library is on Daniel Robertson's plan of Powerscourt, Co. Wicklow (1843) on the garden front.

The importance of light for reading possibly accounts for bow and canted bay windows in libraries. At Emo Court and Ballyfin the libraries are tripartite in plan, the full depth of the

house, and with columnar screens. That at Rockingham (1809; fig. 56) had a space behind a
screen leading into the circular drawing room, called a 'Logia', with bookshelves. A plan for
Howth Castle (1824) shows a long 'Book room' leading into a small 'Reading room', and the
library at Carton, a section of which was part of the original hall and staircase, leads into a
'Reading room' with a gallery, called the 'Small Library' in the 1818 inventory.

There are numerous examples from the later eighteenth century of books and bookshelves in grottoes and other garden buildings in the demesne. The owner of Hazelwood,
Co. Sligo opened the library in a shell-house in his garden to members of the public, a
privilege that was soon abused, forcing him to withdraw what remained of the books.[17] At
Downhill, Co. Derry, the Mussenden Temple – a domed rotunda perched on the edge of a
cliff about 200 feet above the Atlantic Ocean – was built as a summer library by the eccentric
earl-bishop of Derry, designed by the Cork architect Michael Shanahan in the 1780s.

Possibly the most extraordinary library in Ireland (for which no original plan has yet
come to light, and which sadly no longer exists) was that built at Charlemont House in
Dublin (now Dublin City Gallery, The Hugh Lane), designed by Sir William Chambers (figs
150, 151). It comprised a number of rooms in the rear garden linked to the house by a long
corridor, in which were windows to the garden on the right, and niches filled with statues
on the left. Halfway down the corridor was a lobby, at the centre of which was Giovanni da
Bologna's *Mercury*, and a short flight of steps to accommodate the rising level of the ground
to the rear. At the end of the corridor was the Venus library (named after the copy of the
Medici Venus placed in a large arched alcove), top-lit, with an ornamental ceiling and the
bookcases framed by the Ionic order. Underlining its importance, the main library had
Corinthian pilasters and was a double-height room with light coming in from the coved ceiling.[18] Two smaller rooms lay beyond it, one for Lord Charlemont's collection of medals, the
other for part of his collection of pictures and antiques.[19] But Charlemont did not stop there:
in about 1788, he built the Rockingham Library, designed by James Gandon, which was at
the centre and to the west of the corridor, in the space behind the sweep wall of the house.
This room, with its curved end walls, had a columnar screen to each end.[20]

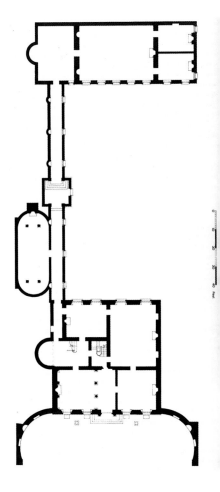

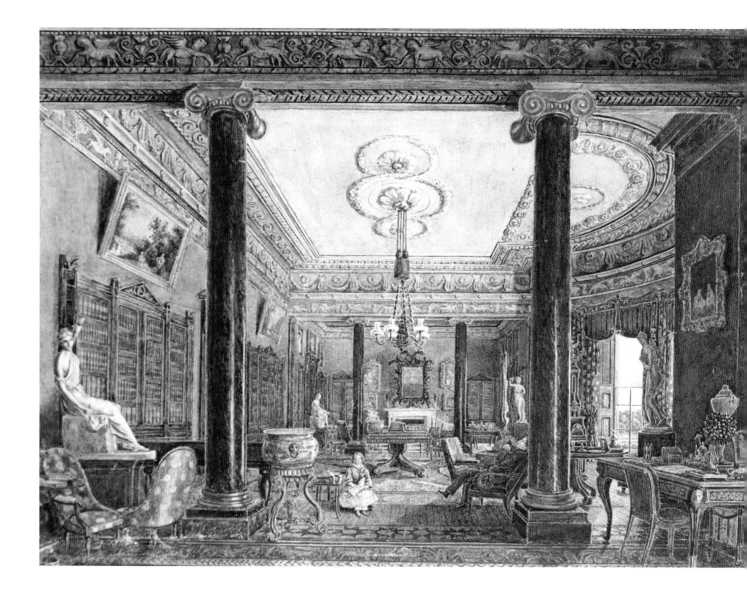

The furnishings and fittings for Charlemont's library occupied his thoughts in letters not just to Chambers but to others. To his friend Andrew Caldwell, to whom he entrusted its guardianship when he was out of the country, he referred to it as 'my favourite Mistress' and 'an object so highly interesting to me as my Library'. In the same letter he expressed the opinion that 'marble pilasters would be improper and cold . . . I am preparing colours here, under Chambers' directions, to paint the whole body of the library.'[21] In a letter to Chambers, Caldwell suggests the best way to light it: 'the Great Room, will . . . be sufficiently illuminated by the Lights which are to stand on the Chimneypiece and by candles placed on the Tables, but with regard to the Ante Chamber [Venus library] . . . nothing could be more proper than girandoles of two candles each fix'd in the centre of the two long panels at each side of the room'. He goes on to describe a suitable ornament on the girandoles, 'an Amazonian shield, cross'd by branches of Laurel and Palm', and he looks forward to the delivery of the purple carpeting from Moorfields in London.[22]

152
Marquis de Massigny de la Pierre, *The library at Ballyfin*, c.1855; watercolour.

It is interesting that as early as 1739 Bishop Rundle created in his library a room for social intercourse, with most probably a number of comfortable chairs for his guests. While those interested in books might have spent a part of their day enjoying their libraries (or studies/closets) from the seventeenth century, it was not until after the middle of the eighteenth century that they became, in addition, 'living rooms' where people gathered to pursue their various interests.[23] These bear no relation to the 'gloomy' library at Cullenaghmore, Co. Laois, remembered by the owner's grandson Jonah Barrington, who described it as 'rather scantily furnished with everything but dust and cobwebs: there were neither chairs or tables' in it.[24]

Thus, despite Humphry Repton's claim in 1816 that it was only then becoming the custom to use the library as a general living room, it seems that such usage was well established not only in Ireland but also in England, where Lady de Grey wrote from Wrest Park in 1744: 'Our Residence is fixed in the library, & you may imagine us if you please, for Tea . . . till Supper, sitting on each side of the great Table with a Competent quantity of candles, Books & Papers upon it & looking most profoundly Wise.'[25] It is interesting to note that on an early Morrison drawing for Ballyfin (1822) 'Library and Living room' appears. The painting of the library there by the Marquis de Massigny de la Pierre (*c*.1855; fig. 152) is an illustration of this relaxed approach to the room, used by all the family. According to a source in 1864 the Edgeworths never had a drawing room: 'the family room was the library, where all the family read and drew and worked together around the long centre table, with Maria's small desk-table in the corner' (fig. 153).[26]

A visitor to Berrington Castle in Wales lamented the absence of a good library, 'that first of all luxuries'.[27] In Lady Morgan's *O'Donnel* (1814), Lady Llanberis avoided this difficulty by tending to purchase two to three copies of 'amusing' books, which she liked to have 'lying about' in different rooms.[28] But the luxury of choosing a book and taking it to one's room was not allowed at the fictitious Brandon-Castle in 1771, as 'Lady P—', conscious of the valuable volumes that were located in the library, forbade reading in any other part of the house.[29]

That would not have bothered Richard Lovell Edgeworth, who, when entrusted with the key of the library at Pakenham Hall (Tullynally) by its chatelaine, 'passed whole days devouring the contents'.[30] His daughter, Maria, wrote descriptions of numerous libraries that she visited, describing one 'with nice books, small tables upon castors, low sofas, and all the other things which make rooms comfortable'.[31] She admired the earl of Moira's library in Castle Donnington, Leicestershire, which was 'fitted up entirely with books in plain handsome mahogany bookcases, not a frippery ornament, everything grand, but not gaudy, marble tables, books upon tables, nothing littered, but sufficient signs of living and occupied beings. At the upper end of the room sat two ladies copying music: a gentleman walking about with a book in his hand.'[32] Mrs Delany found the Moira library in Co. Down just as compelling in 1758, admiring 'recesses where you may sit and read books of all kinds, to amuse the fancy as well as improve the mind – telescopes, microscopes and all the scientific apparatus. Everyone chooses their employment; it is the land of liberty, yet of regularity.'[33] The 'excellent' library at Castle Saunderson near Cavan had a fire burning in it from early morning, as a guest mentioned in 1822; here he 'luxuriated, often wishing for a Briarean power of eye and intellect to read fifty books at one; then all the periodicals of note'.[34]

Care has to be taken, however, not to equate the existence of libraries with learning, particularly in view of comments made by visitors. Edward Wakefield, for example, in his book published in 1812, remarked that libraries were not common in Ireland, although some families acquired them almost as part of the furniture, the choice of the books depending largely on the elegance of the binding.[35] This might be borne out by Mary Beaufort's comment on the collection of elegantly bound books that she found in a bookshop in Sligo in 1808: the bookseller told her that nobody would buy them if they were not 'handsomely bound'.[36] Richard Cumberland's comment about Lord Eyre of Eyrecourt Castle, Co. Galway, who 'lived in the enviable independence as to reading, and of course had no books', also comes to mind.[37] George Hardinge, while very impressed with Lord Portarlington's library at Dawson Court in the early 1790s, whose 'books of drawings prints maps architecture &c. are perfect of their kind', observed that 'this in Ireland is a phenomenon as in the best House of the Island you can scarce find a common book for amusement – Learning is out of the case'.[38] Nevertheless, evidence shows that there were a number of libraries that were lovingly and carefully planned by their owners, from the architectural decoration (including the bookcases) through to the comfortable furniture and furnishings that made them such seductive spaces to 'live' in. Creating an attractive space was one thing; reading the books contained therein was another. But again, evidence gleaned from novels, diaries, letters and family papers indicates that family members and their guests were frequently found reading in their libraries or elsewhere in the house.

The use of libraries as family rooms, and their accommodation of musical instruments, might suggest conviviality rather than scholarly retirement. As can be seen, it was not just books that furnished a library but also curiosities, pieces of sculpture and *objets d'art* collected by the owners, many of whom had done the Grand Tour. So as time went by, the room became more and more a place where members of the family and their guests would assemble.

The inventories confirm in many cases how libraries were also used as sitting rooms. Not all mention bookcases or shelves, which might mean that they were built in or that it was just a room called a library. The books are rarely mentioned, but in some cases might have comprised a separate inventory. The earliest inventory is that for Dromana (1755), where bookcases *are* mentioned: '4 Large Wynscote book cases with glass sash doors, with locks/keys' and one similar bookcase in ebony. There were some walnut chairs covered with yellow flowered satin (and with covers of scarlet paragon), and three stools to match, as well as a high chair and a low chair for children. There was no desk, and the only tables were a 'mahogany tea table & frame with a tea chest fixt in the drawer' and a 'small one-leaved wynscote table and frame'. The only book mentioned sounds almost like a piece of furniture in its own right: 'Large book of maps with a marble cover in a dale [deal] case'. In a bequest of his books to a library in Kilkenny in 1756, the bishop of Ossory noted the ten double bookcases 'made of Danzig oak, now in my library at Dunmore' that were also to go to Kilkenny.[39] An estimate for library furniture for Caledon (1783) listed '4 mahogany cases for Books so contrived as to form the room into an Octagon (£210), a Large mahogany library table with drawers all round, the top covered with Leather' and six chairs covered with black leather. Also received were a mirror to be set over the chimneypiece and a 'carpet to cover the floor'.[40] At Gaulston in 1787 the library contained a mahogany writing table, a brazier and three rush-bottomed chairs painted green and white.

Killadoon's library was well furnished in 1807. In 1800 Lady Leitrim wrote: 'We live in a small Round Room [it has a bow window] at the end & have kept it very cool. We sit in this room all morning. We dine at six, walk from seven till ten & then drink tea.'[41] Again, the bookcases are not listed, but two Wedgwood sphinxes and twelve bronze figures and groups are noted over the bookcases. Otherwise there was a rosewood library table and two other tables, an 'Egyptian' sofa and footstool, various chairs including '2 cane chairs with 2 leather cushions & a mahogany reading desk & brass candlestick to each', a silver ink stand with a sand box and ink bottle, a paperweight and a 'mahogany railed stand for loose papers'. There were draped curtains of blue and orange calico around the bow, which had cushioned window seats. The contents of the room varied only slightly up to the 1836 inventory.

The 'book room' at the Rochfort house – Clogrenan, Co. Carlow – is interesting, mainly because, according to the inventory (*c.*1810), it contained an extraordinary 6,774 volumes in eleven recessed bookcases; this was in addition to 400 books on shelves that lined Mr Rochfort's dressing room. The book room was obviously large, with two fireplaces, '2 large bed settees with Posts', nineteen chairs, a 'very large' mahogany dining table and a mat that 'entirely covers the room'. It also had some curiosities: a 'prospect box', a 'standing tenniscope and a marine tenniscope [*sic*]', two globes (celestial and terrestrial) and '7 maps' (perhaps on the walls). A later painting (now in the National Gallery of Ireland) of the Irish poet and writer Thomas Moore (1779–1852; fig. 154) shows him in his study in his English home seated at a drum table surrounded by shelves of books and with his harp and piano to one side. Its modest chimneypiece and the shape of its elliptical ceiling indicate that it might be an attic room, while the framing archway suggests that it is annexed to another room, possibly a library.

Carton (1818) had two libraries, 'large' and 'small' – the latter with a gallery. As one would expect, they were well furnished (presumably with fitted bookcases, as none are mentioned). The five windows of the larger room and the single window of the smaller were fitted with green damask curtains lined with 'green silk persian with draperies, rich gilt cornices, silk fringe & bordering' with white roller blinds. As in Clogrenan there were curiosities, here in two cabinets in the larger room, where there were also numerous sofas, chairs and tables, many ornaments, pieces of sculpture and china, chess and card tables, and a grand piano. Among the furniture in the small library were two library tables (one circular in satinwood, 'lined with green cloth and a pair of plated branches in centre') and a reading chair covered with black leather 'and Mahogany Desk attached'.

Maria Edgeworth, while spending Christmas with the Pakenhams at Pakenham Hall in 1807, wrote of the library there as decorated in scarlet and black, with red morocco chairs and other, black chairs 'with white medusa heads on their backs', which had cost 9 guineas

154
English School, *Thomas Moore in his Study at
Sloperton Cottage*, nineteenth century; oil on panel.

each.[42] She mentions that the walls of the library at Moore Hall, Co. Mayo (seen on a visit in 1836) were 'papered with a sort of gothic paper representing a colonnade of pillars and fretwork arches above'.[43] Among the Mount Stewart accounts is an invoice 'for binding Mock Books for window shutters' in 1805, and the later inventory (1821) includes '6 mahogany Bookcases Inlayed and Full of Books', with busts and other ornaments on top of them, two writing tables and two desks, various other tables (including a 'square mahogany table Inlayed, game Box with 9 Holes and 9 Balls'), two sofas and fourteen chairs. The 'Anti Room' listed next to the library – which had cabinets of curiosities and ornaments of all types, as well as a mahogany 'swing Bookcase full of books', five tables and two backgammon boxes – appears to have been a room that was used in tandem with the library. Both rooms (together with the Music Room, where, incidentally, no musical instruments are listed) had printed blue cotton curtains with muslin drapery.

It is evident from an estimate dated 1811 for furnishing the library at Mount Bellew that Lewis & Anthony Morgan of Henry Street, Dublin provided drawings of the furniture for the owner, Christopher Dillon Bellew. They show a large mahogany table 'in the Gothic style', with an armchair to match, and six bergère chairs. A sofa for the window recess and three smaller sofas for the side windows were all to be covered in blue velvet (with blue calico covers), to match the window curtains. Instructions are given for the bookcase doors (all of mahogany) that include '404 ft of highly finished brass work for the pannells of the mahogany doors [and] 240 yds of blue sarsanet to make side curtains for the doors'. Also mentioned are two reading and book stands 'made as pidestals'. The following year, 'a very tall mahogany ladder' was required.[44] The library amassed by Bellew was recognised as one of the finest

Thomas Cooley, plan of the bedchamber floor at
Mount Kennedy, with a proposed billiard room at the
centre, 1781.

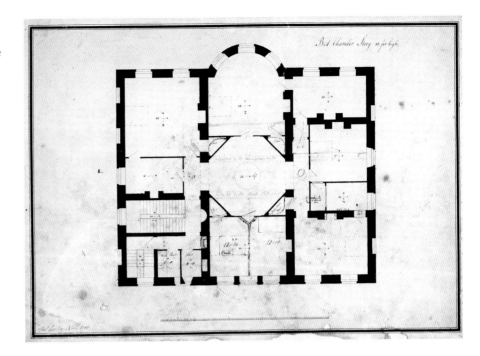

private collections in Ireland so it is not surprising that he took great care in the provision of
fittings for it.

A billiard room was sometimes attached to the library for the use of family and friends.
With few exceptions, such rooms were located next to either the hall or the library and they
seem to have become increasingly popular in the nineteenth century. One of the earliest references to billiards comes from 1587 when, shortly before her death, Mary Queen of Scots
complained that her *table de billard* had been taken from her by her captors. In the following
year it was noted that the duke of Norfolk owned a 'billyard bord covered with greene cloth . . .
three billyard sticks and 11 balls of yvery [ivory]'.[45] The duke of Ormonde had a billiard table
in Dunmore House, Co. Kilkenny in 1684.

However, while billiard tables were 'commonplace in aristocratic dwellings' at this time,
billiard *rooms* were less so.[46] The earliest plan in which such a room appears is one for Carton
(*c*.1739), where it is located off the saloon to the east of the house. A more unusual and out-
of-the-way location for a billiard room can be seen on Chearnley's drawing, where it is placed
on the upper storey of the south-west pavilion.[47] Among the Headfort drawings, Richard
Castle (prior to 1751) places it in the west pavilion at ground level and Chambers (1765) in
the east pavilion next to the stables. In both Francis Johnston's and James Wyatt's plans for
Castle Coole (1789 and 1790) it is tucked away discreetly in the west wing. The octagonal lobby on the first floor at Mount Kennedy was planned to function as a billiard room, at the centre of the house certainly, but on another level (figs 155, 156).[48] In 1833 the Bernards were un-
decided whether the room linking the hall with the drawing room at Castle Bernard should
be a gallery or a billiard room. The choice in room name has already been noted at Ballyfin
in the last chapter, where the ante-room next to the library on the garden front is annotated
'Anti Chamber & Billiards' on one plan and 'Billiards or Small Drawing Room' on another.
On John Nash's drawing for Rockingham the table can be seen at the far end of the house beyond the gallery, in a room with a canted bay, again next to the library (fig. 56).

From the inventories we learn that a billiard table was part of the furniture of the Long Gallery at Stackallan (1757), and at Newbridge (1821) there was one in the hall, but the only inventory that lists a specialised room (and that *has* a table) is at Mount Stewart (also 1821), where there were half a dozen mahogany chairs plus three chairs painted black with cane seats, a few prints on the walls, a bust of Napoleon on the marble chimneypiece and two busts (of the duke of Wellington and the Hon. F. Stewart) on pedestals. The curtains here were of printed cotton lined with white calico, with white muslin drapery lined in blue calico, a white fringe and tassels.

It is interesting to note that billiard rooms, or billiard tables, were accessible to all members of the family, at a time when playing billiards was just another occupation. In the Victorian age it was a different story: billiard rooms were considered a male preserve, at a remove from the other rooms and often adjoining a smoking room.

Bedrooms and dressing rooms

On plans up to the mid-eighteenth century, most country houses have bedrooms on the ground floor, as part of the formal rooms, and upstairs a mix that occurs frequently – a suite, some bedrooms with closets or dressing rooms, others with neither. Among Richard Castle's drawings for Carton, bedrooms, dressing rooms and closets abound on plans for both ground and first floors, and on the attic storey there are as many as fifteen bedrooms. In contrast, only one proposal among the drawings for Leinster House shows a bedroom on the ground floor, with a closet and a water closet. As built, Lord and Lady Kildare's bedrooms and dressing rooms were located opposite to each other on the first floor (fig. 137). Privacy

57
Richard Castle, plan of the first floor at Carton, 1739.

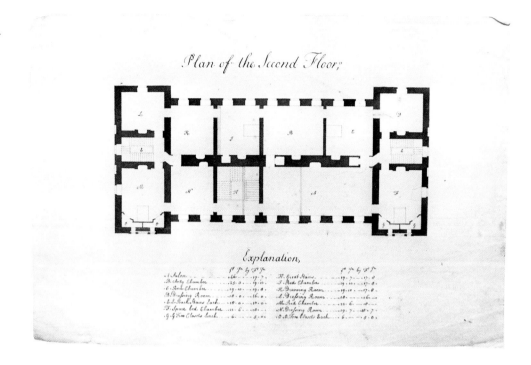

Plan of the Second Floor

Explanation,

was ensured with the location of a door to the right at the top of the main staircase, leading into the family quarters. Access for personal servants to those quarters was by way of a spiral staircase, the only stairs that went from the basement to the attic storey. In the attic was the nursery suite, which comprised a large room for the children (there were many in the family), a bedroom for their nurse(s) and a closet. At Carton, a second-floor plan (fig. 157) shows two bedrooms with alcoves, the small spaces lit by the window, creating closets similar to those on Castle's plan for Castle Coole.[49] It is noteworthy that the Castle Coole drawing shows no bedroom at ground-floor level, nor is there any evidence that there was ever one at that level at Russborough, another Castle building.[50]

From mid-century, while bedrooms continued to be on the ground floor, they were not part of the formal rooms but generally for the master (and mistress?) of the house. At Castle Coole, though, they were confined to the wings of the house in both Johnston's and Wyatt's plans, the latter managing the areas better, finding space for two bedrooms with dressing rooms in the west wing and three bedrooms with two dressing rooms between them in the east wing. By comparison, Johnston provided two bedrooms to each wing, with neither dressing room nor closet. The house was completed to Wyatt's plans and the private accommodation for the family was located in the west wing. Three plans for Mount Kennedy (1781) show General Cunningham's preference for a ground-floor bedroom with his study off the hall to the right. Two of these have a bedroom behind the study and to the rear is 'Mrs Cunningham's dressing room', off the drawing room.[51] Thus the private quarters are separate, with the option of using the dressing room with the formal rooms. The third plan has the bedroom off the hall to the left, with a closet behind it, and behind that is the dressing room, with a Wyatt window overlooking the garden (fig. 158). Here the family quarters take up the depth of the house, with no direct access to the formal rooms from the dressing room. At Townley Hall (1794) one of the proposals was for a bedroom, together with a dressing

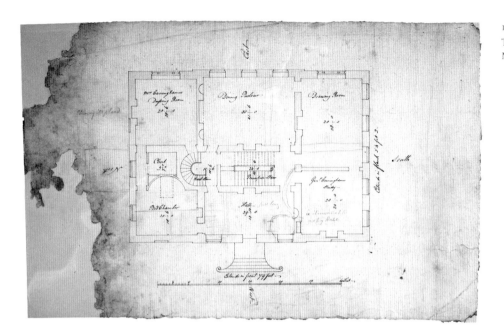

158
Thomas Cooley, proposed ground-floor plan for
Mount Kennedy, n.d., unexecuted.

room and powdering room for Mr Balfour, to the left rear of the house on the ground floor, with 'own study' to the right, but this was abandoned and, as built, the study remained, with a dressing room next to it and Balfour's bedroom upstairs (fig. 138).

In England at least, it was common by the 1820s for the 'family' bedroom and the wife's dressing room and boudoir to be on the first floor, with the husband's study and dressing room at ground level.[52] In Ireland in the same century bedrooms increasingly disappeared from the ground floor altogether in newly built or altered houses. There were exceptions, however. For example, at Dromoland Castle (fig. 159), in one of the drawings attributed to the Pain brothers (c.1826?; fig. 160), the private rooms are on the same level as the formal rooms, but at a distance from them along ranges that form a quadrangle to the rear of the house. The spaces for the family are located on one side of two corridors; beyond them are areas for servants and offices. The family spaces are worth a closer look. Access is gained to the family wing via a lobby off the (formal) gallery. This accommodation comprises 'Lady O'Brien's bedroom', off which is a dressing room at the top left of the quadrangle, while there are two rooms for her husband – 'Sir E O'Brien's room' and 'Sir E O'Brien's room of business' – which are almost diagonally opposite each other.

This introduces the interesting question of whether couples shared a bedroom. People of all classes thought nothing of sharing rooms even with perfect strangers when travelling or visiting. Dorothea Herbert, when staying at Castle Blunden in 1784, shared a room with her parents, who slept in one bed while she and her sister slept in another.[53] Lord Aldborough wrote that in 1792 he and his wife shared a room with their nieces when travelling, and that Lord Rochford and his man slept in a dining room.[54] Space was not a problem for a hostess in Co. Cork: she told one of her guests that 'Sammy [her husband] is very accommodating, he sleeps with the butler'.[55]

In France, the custom was normally for couples to have separate quarters.[56] In Maria Edgeworth's *Ormond* (1817), the hero was proudly shown 'the convenience, and entire liberty, that result from the complete separation of the apartments of the husband and wife' in

9

romoland Castle, Newmarket-on-Fergus, Co. Clare.

60

& G.R. Pain, ground-floor plan of Dromoland
astle, Co. Clare, *c*.1826, unexecuted.

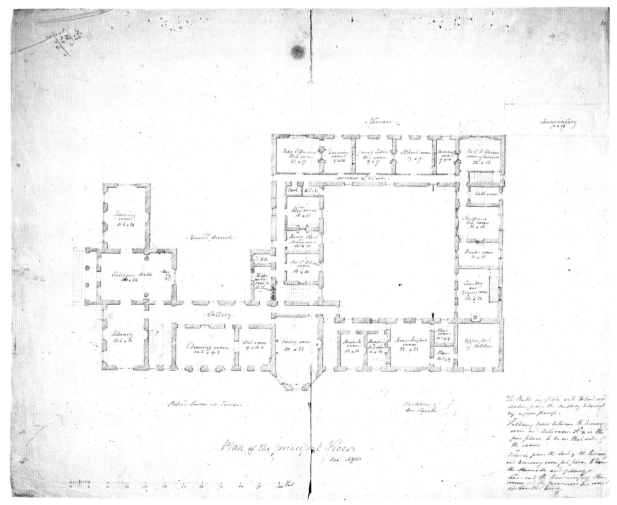

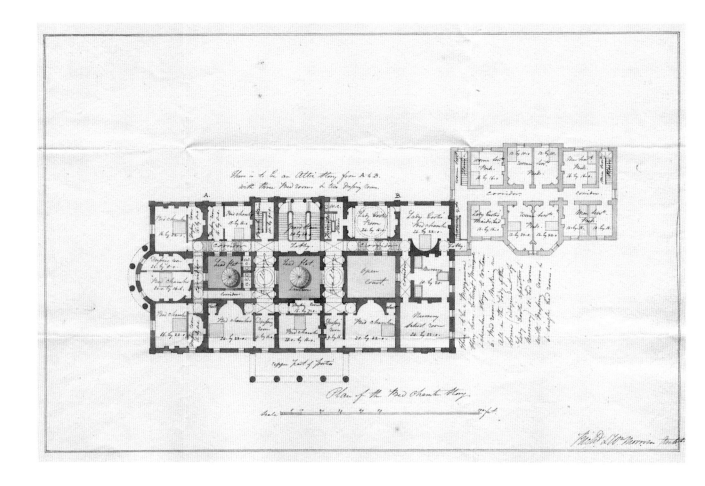

161

Richard and William Morrison, plan of the
bedchamber storey at Ballyfin, 1822, detail.

a Paris *hôtel* (town house), 'with their own staircases, their own passages, their own doors in
and out'.[57] In England, it seems to have been more often the case that couples shared a bedroom. To create sufficient personal space, Roger North recommended a dressing room each
for a husband and wife, saying that if there were a shortage of space, then the man should
have the dressing room 'who most needs it, because of the roughness of his service and
dressing, and the lady keeps possession of the bedchamber'.[58]

Returning to Dromoland, the second room for Sir Edward O'Brien is self-explanatory, but
was the other room a dressing room or a bedroom? Where did he sleep, or did the O'Briens
share a bedroom? An oddity about the plans is that the bedroom of the (male) owner is usually not specified, but there is little hesitation in calling a space a wife's bedroom, as here and
at Ballyfin (as will be seen below). Yet in the fairly detailed inventory for Dromana (1755), in
the red damask suite of rooms used by the Grandisons, a bedchamber is listed only for his
lordship, together with a dressing room each (beds in neither, though a 'large couch . . . with
a thick matterass' appears in his) and an 'anntie chamber or drawing room'. With lots of china listed in Lady Grandison's dressing room and in the bedroom, and little in her husband's
dressing room, it might be concluded that they slept in 'his' bedroom.

That bedrooms were at least sometimes shared is confirmed by Charles Manners, the 4th
duke of Rutland who, during his term as lord lieutenant, wrote to his wife on 12 May 1787,
'I have passed ye 2 last days at Castletown, & slept in ye same room when we did together at

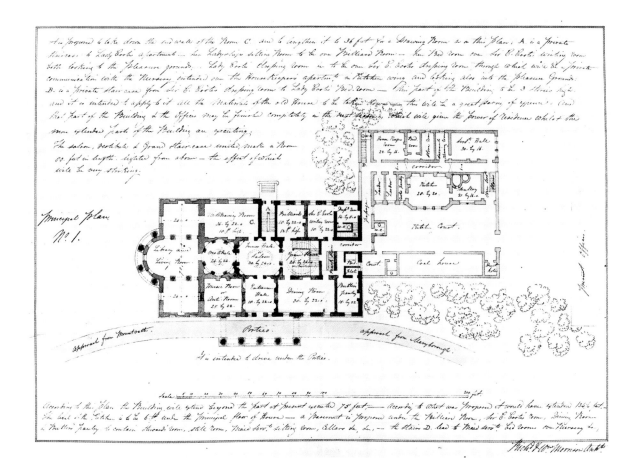

2

chard and William Morrison, ground-floor plan
Ballyfin, 1822, detail.

ye Ball', and a week later from Dublin Castle, 'Alas my dear it is very melancholy to go to Bed night after night without you. I lie on your side but I long to be turned over & sent to ye other side of the bed.'[59] There is little doubt that Lord and Lady Fingall shared the large circular bedroom at Killeen Castle, flanked as it is by the oddly shaped dressing rooms for each. The inventories, however, show that the Clements at Ashfield House (1808) and the Londonderrys at Mount Stewart (1821) had separate bedrooms and dressing rooms. Furthermore, beds were to be found in Mr Clements's dressing room and in both of the Londonderrys' dressing rooms. With regard to the O'Briens, it seems more likely that the bedroom was shared by the couple: the adjoining dressing room was either for Lady O'Brien or shared, and 'Sir Ed. O'Brien's room' was a dressing room or a private study for her husband.

The plans for Ballyfin show similar private accommodation. Lady Coote's first-floor apartment on the garden front in one of the Morrisons' early designs (1822) includes 'Lady Coote's Room' (a dressing room/boudoir), rectangular in shape with curved corners, and having a tripartite arrangement with a central domed area and arches (fig. 161). To the left the room opens to a private staircase, called on the plan 'a private Staircase to Lady Coote's apartment', and a water closet.[60] To the right, the dressing room is linked to 'Lady Coote's Bedchamber'. As at Dromoland, there is no mention of Sir Charles Coote's bedroom, unless it is the 'Bed chamber' across the open court to the front of the house, which would mean a fair distance between the two bedrooms. The ground-floor plan shows his 'Writing room'

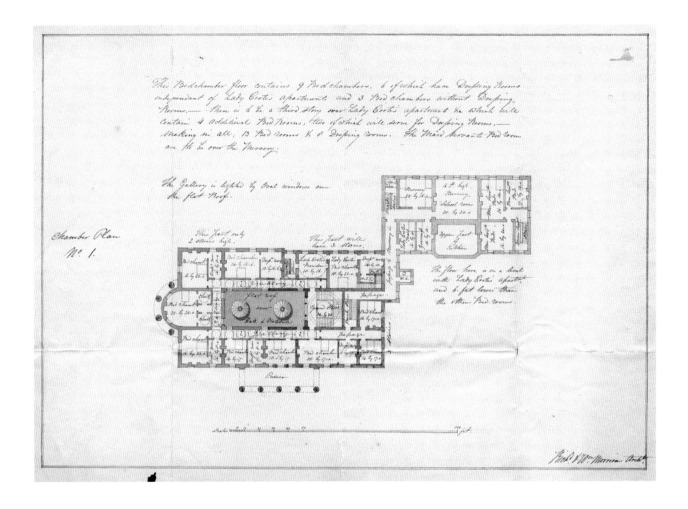

(fig. 162) with an accompanying dressing room below that of his wife, but no sign of his bedroom. Another plan of about the same date might throw some light on the subject. Here Lady Coote's suite consists of three interconnecting rooms on the garden front – boudoir, bedchamber and dressing room (fig. 163). Interestingly, the bedchamber has a private staircase that connects with Sir Charles's dressing room on the ground floor, at which level there were no bedrooms. It might be concluded, then, that they shared the bedroom.

As on the earlier plan (fig. 162), where a door from Lady Coote's bedchamber leads via a lobby to the nursery, and thence to the nursery schoolroom at the front of the house, the later one (fig. 163) shows a passage running from her dressing room to the nursery on the first floor of the service wing, where the schoolroom is also located, together with a room for Lady Coote's maid and one for the governess. In the main block a door in the gallery or corridor effectively cuts off the family apartments from the rest of the house, as the arch at the top of the private staircase cut off half of the first floor for the use of the family. The Dromoland Castle plan shows a similar layout. Next to 'Lady O'Brien's bedroom' and the adjoining dressing room is a 'Young Ladies bed room', a 'School room' and a room for the governess (fig. 160). Beyond the business room is a bathroom, followed by the 'Childrens Bed room' adjoining a 'maids room', where the solid wall indicates the end of the family quarters.

163
Richard and William Morrison, *Chamber Plan No. 1 for Ballyfin, c.1822.*

It is interesting to see at Ballyfin the proximity of the nursery to the mother's or the parents' apartments, an emphasis that was more pronounced in nineteenth-century houses. Before then, children were generally accommodated on the top floor, fitted in wherever it was most convenient. It is not clear whether the Cootes were specific about this requirement, but the architects mention it in a hand-written note on the second set of plans. This coincided with the trend leading to the Victorians' sense of family values and the advent of the family apartment.[61] But in 1791 Lady Portarlington, after a visit to Abbeyleix, Co. Laois (seat of Viscount de Vesci), had some interesting remarks about Irish families:

> I must admire the Irish manner of bringing up children, for in all the families I have happened to know there seems the most perfect ease and confidence and except from their attention to each other, you would never find out which were fathers and mothers, sons and daughters, everyone amusing themselves in the manner they like best, and nobody expecting any particular attention or respect . . . Even at the Duke of Leinster's, where there is a great deal of state, I could not help admiring the great grown-up girls stealing an opportunity when they thought the company did not mind them to hug their father and mother with an appearance of affection that did one good.[62]

Like Ballyfin and Dromoland, a ground-floor plan of Powerscourt, Co. Wicklow (1843) shows the proximity of the children's rooms to those of their parents. Here an interconnecting sequence from the centre of the garden front, comprising Lord Powerscourt's study, the breakfast room, the boudoir, the main bedroom and a dressing room, leads into the nursery rooms in the wing. As the formal rooms were on the first floor, this was obviously the family area, where Lord and Lady Powerscourt shared a bedroom, she had her boudoir and he had his study. At Castle Bernard, Co. Offaly, Mr and Mrs Bernard each had a study (1833; fig. 65). Doors from both studies lead across a passage to the 'Childrens Room' at the return. On the first floor are two bedrooms directly over the studies, with a dressing room (shared?) over the children's room. It is also worth noting that a back staircase in the return adjoins these rooms, and that access to the ground-floor suite is under the main staircase. This kept the family quite private and at a remove from the formal spaces.

While children took their meals in the nursery, where adult members of the family dined is not quite so clear-cut. Breakfast could be taken in one's bedroom, dressing room or boudoir, or in the breakfast or morning rooms, but whether the dining room was used every day or only when there were guests is a moot point. At Castle Coole the family lived in the wings, as was generally the case in Britain, with their own entrances from the colonnades, but this was probably unique in Ireland. In a letter to her sister in 1778, Lady Caroline Dawson wrote of the gallery at Castletown, 'they tell me they live in it quite in the winter, for the servants can bring in dinner or supper at one end, without anyone hearing it at the other'.[63] Lady Leitrim's description in 1800 of how she and her husband 'lived' in the library at Killadoon might imply that they also dined there or simply that it was where they spent their leisure hours.[64]

The dressing room

A 1512 reference to the earl of Northumberland's 'chamber where he maketh him ready' indicates that he dressed in a separate room to that in which he slept. Girouard's assertion that
the term 'dressing room' first appeared in the second half of the seventeenth century places
the earl of Kildare (1611/12–1660) at the vanguard of fashion in his Dublin house, according
to a 1656 inventory which names such a room.[65] At the end of the seventeenth century it became fashionable for women to dress in their bedchambers, but in the course of the following century the dressing room as part of the bedroom suite (which also usually included a
closet) became an important space, particularly for women.[66] In seventeenth-century French
houses it was not unusual to have two or three closets adjoining a bedroom and their usage
varied: one was for the close-stool; another was a *garde-robe*, where clothes were stored and
a personal servant slept; a third might be for prayer, study or work. This last room was often
called a *cabinet*, where small, expensive works of art and sumptuous furnishings could be
privately enjoyed or shared with a few select friends.[67] Gradually one of the closets became a
dressing room, as furniture suitable to its new use was acquired: a table covered with a carpet, over which a *toilette* or piece of muslin was placed to protect it from stray hairs and cos-
metics; a mirror; and a pair of candlesticks, all of which evolved into an ensemble of furniture that showed off the silver dressing sets that were fashionable by the end of the century
(figs 164, 165, 166).[68] In inventories of the latter part of that century (such as those of the
Ormonde family), the terms 'dressing rooms' and 'closets' are used fairly continuously, both
separately and as adjuncts either to bedrooms or to each other.

In Sir Roger Pratt's plan for Coleshill (*c.*1660), which has already been mentioned, a co-
herent and compact form of interior planning was conceived that allowed a flexible system
of circulation within the house. Sets of three rooms – one large room (flexible in function,
as a bedchamber, parlour or withdrawing room) with two small rooms or closets off it – are

164
The silver-gilt Kildare toilet service by David
Willaume was commissioned by the 19th earl of
Kildare for his wife in 1720, and comprises twenty-
eight pieces.

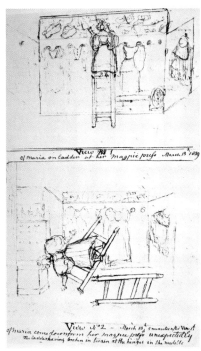

5
fashionable lady considers her make-up as she is
:ed into her stays by a maid.

6
:etch by Maria Edgeworth of herself as she attempts
retrieve something from her 'magpie press'. Note
w Maria's dresses were hung by the shoulders.

located at each corner of the house on both main floors. This layout placed the formal rooms –
the hall, the Great Parlour and, above it, the Great Dining Room – at the centre of the house.
The central or spinal corridor provided access to rooms and apartments and had back stairs
at each end. Pratt explained that the bedchambers 'must each of them have a closet, and a
servant's lodging with chimney both which will easily be made by dividing the breadth of
one end of the room into two such parts'; from the servant's room, 'a pair of backstairs ought
to be adjoining'.[69] One of the closets in each set opened onto the corridor, a system that had
two advantages. One was that the servant could carry the contents of the close-stool directly
down the back stairs, thus avoiding unsavoury odours throughout the house. The other was
that a mode of escape from unwanted visitors was created. Pratt's plan was an architectural
response to a demand for privacy and convenience that was not new but was articulated in
the seventeenth century, an important point that will be addressed later. It provided more
privacy than had heretofore been possible, and more comfort, with smaller rooms that were
easier to heat.

Not unlike the ante-room, a dressing room could be found on any floor in a house and
frequently assumed the role of a sitting room, particularly when it formed part of the rooms
of parade. A quote from William Wycherley's *The Country Wife*, 'I . . . was made free of their
society and dressing rooms for ever hereafter' in 1675, indicates the use of the room for
the entertainment of guests.[70] By the second half of the eighteenth century ladies' dressing
rooms, especially those in London, had become like jewel cabinets, sumptuously decorated
and furnished; they were on public display on grand occasions and at other times were for
the reception of close friends.[71] An auction advertisement in a Dublin newspaper in 1765
mentioned 'several Cabinets of Ebony, and other scarce Materials most pleasingly embel-
lished with inlay of Pearl, Turquoise-shell and Ivory; they are that desirable (Dressing Room)
Size, so deservedly seeked [*sic*] and esteemed by the Ladies, as being in the present Taste'.[72]

There appears to be no obvious reason why the dressing room was sometimes used as a well-furnished and decorated reception room. It may have had something to do with the fact that there was considerable flexibility in its usage, as at Holkham Hall in Norfolk, where reception rooms served the state bedrooms as dressing rooms when required.[73] The fact that dressing rooms appear on the *piano nobile*, unattached to bedchambers, indicates their separate function as sitting rooms. Robert Adam designed dressing rooms specifically for women: they were the most inventive spaces in his houses, sizeable rooms, designed to be seen and admired. One of them was at Wynnstay in Wales, where the dressing room was entered directly from the drawing room, to which it became an appendage, 'a coda to the parade of grand reception rooms, thrown open to the public at large assemblies and expected to be as glamorous as the rest, yet different'.[74]

For the dressing room as a public space, there were degrees of formality. Many that were located next to bedrooms on an upper floor seem to have been richly decorated, as demonstrated by Lady Coote's room at Ballyfin with its tripartite plan and domed ceiling, which was undoubtedly at least a semi-formal sitting room. The same might apply to Mrs Clements's octagonal room at Woodville, and to Lady Fingall's elliptical dressing room at Killeen Castle, which led into her spacious morning room (fig. 87).[75] But evidence for formal dressing rooms is scant and little information can be gleaned from the plans, apart from the fact that they sometimes existed alongside reception rooms. At Carton, in all of Richard Castle's drawings, main reception rooms are found on both ground and first floors. In his earliest ground-floor plan, a dressing room is located in the north-west corner on the garden front: it leads in an enfilade to a bedroom, drawing room, saloon and dining parlour. His other plans vary only slightly, with the same space becoming either a closet or a dressing room, with a bedroom, as part of the formal suite. A first-floor plan shows a dressing room at the same corner of the house, next to a drawing room, bedroom and 'anty chamber' (creating an apartment), with the saloon on the same floor at the front of the house.

Lord Kildare's 1762 sketch plan for Carton (fig. 25) locates a suite of dressing room–bedchamber–closet to the right of the saloon. At Leinster House the bow-windowed space that became part of the supper room by 1759, and which spanned the depth of the house, was originally planned (and built) as one of three rooms, the central one (with the bow) being a dressing room and part of the formal suite along the garden front.[76] In the family quarters, located on both floors on the south side of the house, are the dressing rooms of Lord and Lady Kildare (fig. 167). While her husband's rooms were private, the countess could open her bedroom and dressing room to extend the rooms of parade from the gallery, dining room and drawing room. At Westport House, Co. Mayo, which Daniel Beaufort visited in 1787, the view from the 'State' dressing room was enhanced by the mirrored panels in the window shutters, 'which has [*sic*] a good effect in reflecting the bay and the surrounding hills'.[77]

An Ardbraccan plan shows a dressing room off the library (fig. 29). The circulation here is not completely straightforward: the saloon is at the centre of the garden front, with the library to the left, while the drawing and dining rooms are at the front of the house. These latter two rooms are not interconnected and there are no doors from the hall/vestibule except into the saloon. While dressing rooms are sometimes related to libraries, the proximity of the one at Ardbraccan to the saloon indicates its public or semi-public role, acting as a reading room, a sitting room or both.[78] Plans by Thomas Cooley for Mount Kennedy (1781) show ground-floor dressing rooms (one called 'Mrs Cunningham's'), with doors leading to drawing rooms, oval on one plan, rectangular on the other. Both dressing rooms are attached to bedrooms, but they could be used as formal rooms (fig. 116). Inventories for other formal dressing rooms are scarce, but there is an early example at Barbavilla (1742–3), where the

ac Ware, design for Lady Kildare's dressing room
Leinster House, c.1759.

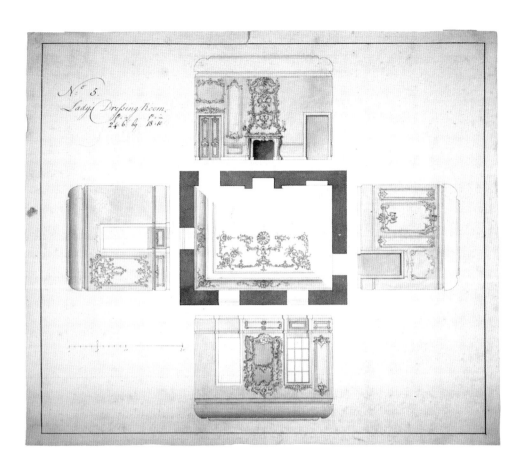

dressing room's location next to the drawing room, the absence of a bed, the presence of a card table and the crimson mohair covers on the stools and walnut armchair point to its being a room in which guests were entertained.

The fabrics listed in the inventory of the Grandisons' suite of rooms at Dromana (1755) – Lady Grandison's dressing room with a small ante-room to it, the earl's dressing room and their bedroom – where the furnishings and wall hangings were of crimson silk damask, are almost as luxurious as the Ormonde residences. While the dressing room of Lady Grandison was likely to have been semi-public, it appears that her husband's was private. In her dressing room she had a bookcase 'with desk & drawers', a dressing chair 'with redd Russia Leather' covering the seat, and seven mahogany carved chairs with quilted backs and seats covered with crimson silk damask, with loose covers of blue and white check linen.[79] Over the marble chimneypiece was a 'Picture of our Saviour, the virgin Mary & their shepherds, in a Gilt frame', and in the grate was an iron fireback 'with the Pope and Cardenials' on it. All of the doors mentioned in this suite had 'a brass lock with key & asscotchin [escutcheon]'. There was also equipment for making tea, with a teapot described as having 'a Silver spoute, the handle ebboney joyned on with silver & the cover with a silver chain', together with an amount of china.

By the mid-eighteenth century, 'china fever' – the collection of fine china or porcelain – was at its height and china became a commodity that was popular with rich and poor alike.[80] Unknown in 1675, it had become a normal part of household equipment by 1715.[81] An inven-

tory of the first duchess of Ormonde's closet at Kilkenny in 1684 listed 'fower small Pedistalls gilt for China'. The duchess enjoyed a collection of china that was dispersed around her closets in the fashion of the day, 'piled under and on top of the japanned cabinets, stacked up along the chimney piece and overmantel, standing grouped in the corners of the room, on the silver table and displayed on small pedestals around the walls'.[82] Much of the Chinese porcelain that arrived in Europe was imported by the Dutch and it was they who set the fashion for displaying it in this type of massing arrangement.[83] Though china was usually associated with women, men were not immune to the charms of this commodity.[84] Purchases of china, such as the set recorded in Dromana's inventory that bore Lord Grandison's crest, were frequently made by men. The wealthy Cork merchant Cooper Penrose acquired a large collection of Chinese porcelain, brought to that city by tea clippers from China.[85] In the years between 1720 and 1820 over one hundred porcelain dinner and tea services with family coats of arms were made in China for families in Ireland such as those of the duke of Leinster,

Castletown House, Lady Louisa Conolly's boudoir.

Pole Cosby of Stradbally, Co. Laois, Baron Kingsborough of Boyle Abbey, Co. Roscommon and the earl of Ely.[86]

The dressing room, the boudoir and the closet were rooms where women liked to display their china. Louisa Conolly wrote to her sister Sarah in 1760, describing her newly finished dressing room at Castletown: hung with green paper to match the green and white linen covers for her chairs, it had a number of tables, a bookcase, pictures and a display of china (fig. 168).[87] By the mid-1760s her collection had grown extensively.[88] Meanwhile, her sister Emily was particular about the placement of her husband's portrait in relation to the china in her dressing room at Leinster House in 1762: it was to hang over the chimneypiece 'upon the hangings, not to be made up as part of the chimney, for a lady's room that is not pretty. Besides I like the blue hanging should appear a little behind my fine china which is to stand on the white marble mantelpiece, then your picture above.'[89] Lady Shelburne described Castletown in 1769 as 'full of cabinet work of inlaid wood made in London and pieces of French and old China', which gave it great elegance.[90] Other references to china as ornaments include a 'press of china desert [*sic*] ornaments' in Mrs Rochfort's closet at Clogrenan, Co. Carlow, and pieces of Worcester, Wedgewood and Dresden on the mantelpieces in Lady Leitrim's bedroom and two dressing rooms at Killadoon in 1807, where, in the entrance hall and under the main staircase, were twenty large china items.

Female dressing rooms, boudoirs and closets

That women's closets, dressing rooms and boudoirs were perceived as essentially female spaces possibly owes much to the Enlightenment and its emphasis on the autonomy of the individual. From letters, journals, diaries and visitors' accounts, it is clear that these spaces held a fascination for women over the course of the eighteenth century. Details of furniture, decor and *objets d'art* were seized upon, eagerly discussed and imitated. It is evident from plans and inventories that there was often a blurring of distinction between these rooms: they could have similar furniture and be of a similar size, though the closet was usually smaller than the dressing room or boudoir. But in novels, correspondence and journals a difference is discernible: the closet was a small, intimate and secluded space in which to pursue one's personal interests, a room that furnished the need for privacy and relaxation.

In his essay in *A History of Private Life* (devoted mainly to France), Orest Ranum observes that, in the early modern era, architects created new private spaces in houses 'or, rather they increased the amount of private space by transforming into rooms what had previously been mere objects of furniture'. He concludes that 'a man who once kept a locked writing desk could now closet himself in his writing room and lock the door'.[91] Lord Chesterfield's comment in 1746 that 'the knowledge of the world is only to be acquired in the world, and not in the Closet' underlines its seclusion.[92] But it was precisely that quality of undisturbed privacy that appealed to women, in a space that was sometimes so small that ladies needed to remove their hoops (figs 169, 170). In a letter to her brother the duke of Richmond in 1769, Lady Louisa Conolly wrote from Castletown that she had locked herself up 'in my Closet and am sure of no interruption, for the very act of setting down to write to you'.[93] Lady Carlow wrote to her sister in 1782 that she was going 'to do up a small room above stairs for my sanctum sanctorum, in which I intend to have everything to myself, and retire to it to paint, read or write let who will be in the house'.[94] Similarly, Maria Edgeworth describes a visit to Trentham, Staffordshire in 1819 when she and her sister were taken to sit in Lady Elizabeth Gower's 'darling little room at the top of the house, where she has all her drawings, and writing, and books, and harp', at a distance from other spaces.[95]

Mary Ashwoode's room in Sheridan Le Fanu's *The Cock and Anchor* contains the same items except that a guitar and a spinet replace the harp. Throughout the book the space, which is next to her bedroom, is rather confusingly called by different names – 'room', 'study', 'little drawing-room', 'dressing-room' and 'boudoir' – but perhaps they all amount to something similar. (It should be borne in mind that, while the author set his story in the first decades of the eighteenth century, it was written a hundred years later.) Le Fanu describes the 'dressing room' as where Mary and her cousin sat, worked, read and sang together, and that it had become, 'by long established usage, the rightful and exclusive property of the ladies of the family, and had been surrendered up to their private occupation and absolute control'. This privacy is underlined by Mary's response to a suitor whose unwelcome attentions she spurns: 'I am sure you are not unaware, Mr Blarden, that this is my private apartment; no one visits me here uninvited, and at present I wish to be alone.'[96]

Those sentiments could also be applied to the boudoir, which, like the dressing room, could be a private or public room. It has always been perceived exclusively as a woman's space, but examples of the use of the word in the *OED* show otherwise, though it must be said that they are exceptions. The writer William Cowper is quoted in a letter dated 1785: 'I write in a nook that I call my boudoir'; the following year John Adams (later second president of the United States) referred to his boudoir as a little room between his library and drawing room. The dictionary defines the room as 'a small elegantly-furnished room, where a lady may retire to be alone, or to receive her intimate friends'. As implied, the boudoir is a room with an interesting and amusing history.

169
Townley Hall, boudoir.

170
Russborough, boudoir.

The etymology of the term is interesting. It comes from the French word *bouder* – to pout or sulk – and, according to a 1752 dictionary, was defined as a small closet or cabinet 'named because of the habit of retiring there, to sulk unseen, when one is in a bad mood'.[97] Apparently it came into being in the mid-eighteenth century in France, when women began to abandon their roles as courtiers and *salonnières* to take more seriously those of wife and mother: this gave them a more flattering image of themselves and more control over the domestic sphere.[98] It also coincided with a desire for privacy and intimacy that grew from the early part of the century, and that included the provision of smaller, more comfortable, rooms. Women were better educated, read books, wrote letters, kept journals and probably required a private space for themselves, just as their husbands had their study or cabinet.[99] The French were quite clear about the function of the boudoir. It was a private room for a woman, where she could relax, read, contemplate, pray or entertain her friends. It was decorated luxuriously: in the 1750s Madame de Pompadour had embroidered silk hangings and a blind of Italian painted taffeta with a 'silk and gold cord ending in an elaborate tassel' in her boudoir at Bellevue.[100]

The boudoir as a concept was not long in acquiring overtones of sexual intrigue: a private space, controlled by a woman, into which men might be specifically invited, could titillate the imagination. The architect Le Camus de Mezières set the scene: 'the boudoir is regarded as the abode of sensual delight, where plans may be meditated and natural inclinations followed. It is essential for everything to be treated in a style in which luxury, softness and good taste predominate.'[101] Peter Thornton describes a number of sumptuous boudoir interiors of *demi-mondaines* in France, one of which, in 1788, boasted a ceiling and walls of mirror.[102] Such an interior was known at least in satire in Dublin in the early 1730s. Adjoining her bedroom, Lady Newburgh's small room, 'where she was accustomed to lie with people', was hung with mirrors 'so that wherever [she] might look . . . the image of her pleasant work might be given back to her and so that by this ingenuity . . . her pleasures might be doubled'. She boasted that she was the first to design such a scheme but, while her room sounds every bit as intriguing as some of the French boudoirs of the latter half of the eighteenth century, no indication is given of its name, apart from the innocuous-sounding 'little room'.[103] Apart from the mirrors and, one assumes, a bed or cushions, we know nothing of furniture or furnishings in Lady Newburgh's room, nor is there any indication that she started a fashion in Ireland. Fifty years later the boudoir of Mlle Dervieux in Paris must have caused a ripple of excitement when it was described as having not only walls of mirror but the ceiling and the floor too, on which cushions were strewn about for 'amorous combats'.[104]

The boudoir was not a popular room name in Irish houses, where, if the name 'dressing room' did not quite fit, 'sitting room' or 'morning room' appear to have been the preferred alternatives. Nevertheless, there are a few notable occurrences. The earliest mention of such a room in the plans and inventories under discussion is among drawings for Townley Hall, by Blayney Townley Balfour and his sister Anne. It is dated to about 1794, well after the boudoir became popular in France, and appears just off the library.[105] It is part of an enfilade of rooms on one side of the house, comprising (from the front) a drawing room, a library and a boudoir to the rear: small in size (11 × 24 feet), it would have made an ideal sitting room, dressing room or closet.[106] In a plan of the tower house of Killeen Castle dated 1795, a boudoir is located off the drawing room, in one of the towers, and in 1808 Mary Beaufort described one of the towers at Portumna Castle off the 'Grand drawing room' as 'fitted up as a nice little boudoir'.[107] In both these cases the descriptions must refer to recent re-planning, as the original castles of Killeen and Portumna long pre-date the invention of the room name. It is noteworthy that, on Francis Johnston's plans for the enlargement of Killeen from 1802 (fig.

87), the name 'boudoir' is not used at all, but, while Lady Fingall may have lost a boudoir, she gained a 'Morning Room'.

At the Gothic Revival Charleville Forest a small boudoir is located in the north-east tower; it has a tent-like vault of plaster surmounted by an eight-pointed star.[108] The proposed boudoir in a turret off the drawing room at Brook Lodge (*c*.1826–9) has already been mentioned (see Chapter 4). Lady Booth's boudoir at Lissadell (1833) is located next to the bowed library, where a doorway links the two rooms; while the room also leads to her and her husband's private quarters, it would have been possible to use it as part of the circulation space (fig. 139). There is an intriguing suite of ground-floor rooms on the plan of Castle Bernard (fig. 65).[109] Mr and Mrs Bernard each have their own study, with Mrs Bernard's longer than her husband's by four feet and having a canted bay. A door connects her study to a boudoir with a quadripartite vaulted ceiling, this door being the only means of access to the room. References to a study for a woman are unusual, as is the allocation of two rooms for her use on the ground floor.

Lady Erne's boudoir at Crom Castle, Co. Fermanagh forms part of the enfilade after the library and drawing room.[110] Though an inventory for this room is beyond the Georgian era (it dates to the 1860s), as the only example of a public boudoir, it gives an idea of contents.[111] As well as a large collection of Dresden china and other porcelain and an amount of Bohemian glassware, items in the room included a mirror-backed cabinet, a bookcase, two whatnots, a writing table and a writing desk, three tables (two covered in velvet), a sofa and cushion, with other cushions, three easy chairs, two cane-bottomed chairs, a small chest of drawers, a screen and a folding chair. There is no mention of floor covering, light fittings, mirrors or pictures. The overall impression is one of a room of display, where Lady Erne could work at her desk surrounded by the objects that gave her pleasure, much as other women such as Louisa Conolly and her sisters did in their dressing rooms one hundred years earlier.

As we have seen, in Lady Morgan's book *O'Donnel* Lady Llanberis is in the habit of acquiring multiple copies of books she has enjoyed and leaving them in different rooms in the house. That this was part of Morgan's own experience in country house visiting is evident. In 1829 she published *The Book of the Boudoir*, a manual with essays on various topics, the result of nightly entries composed in private – in her own boudoir, one supposes. Of the title subject Lady Morgan writes:

> All who have the supreme felicity of haunting great houses, are aware, that those odd books, which are thrown on round tables, or in recesses of windows, to amuse the lounger of the moment, and are not in the catalogue of the library, are frequently stamped, in gold letters with the name of the room to which they are destined: as thus;— 'Elegant Extracts, Drawing-room'; 'Spirit of the Journals, Saloon', &c. &c. As my Book of the Boudoir kept its place in the little room which bore that title, and was never admitted into my bureau of official authorship, it took the name of its <u>locale</u>.[112]

A publication in a similar vein was *The Diadem: A Book for the Boudoir*, edited by Louisa Henrietta Sheridan, a descendant of the theatrical family originally from Quilca, Co. Cavan.

The possibilities of the boudoir had perhaps narrowed slightly as the nineteenth century progressed, if the locations of Lady Coote's and Lady Powerscourt's rooms as part of the family quarters, and close to their children, are taken into consideration. It is interesting to note that, among the drawings for the three houses Ballyfin, Adare Manor and Powerscourt, Co. Wicklow, no closet is to be found attached to bedrooms in the family quarters, perhaps because bathrooms were becoming popular. So was the boudoir sometimes seen as a re-

'I

and G.R. Pain, *Plan of the Principal Floor,*
dare Manor, 1834.

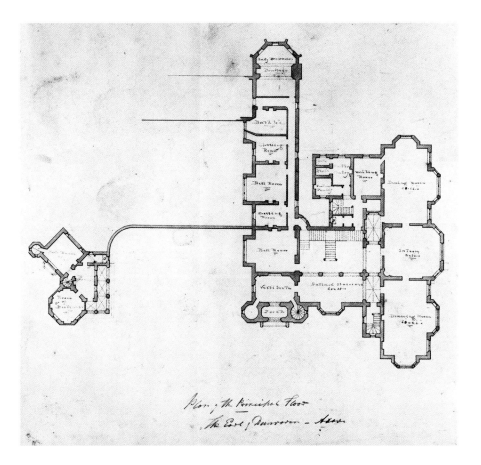

placement, a larger version of the closet, now that privacy for a woman was established and respected? Lady Coote had a four-room suite of boudoir, bedroom, dressing room and an unnamed room in which was a water closet and a bath. Morrison refers to the boudoir as a 'sitting room' in a note on the plan, and on another it is called 'Lady Coote's room', indicating again the fluidity of room names. At Adare Manor in the Pains' asymmetrical plan dated 1834, Lady Dunraven's boudoir terminates the family wing, which comprises a bedroom flanked by dressing rooms, followed by a bathroom (fig. 171). As with the family wing at Dromoland Castle, and that at Powerscourt, Co. Wicklow, it is apparent that picturesque planning was a matter of consideration.

Peter Thornton and John Cornforth have both pointed to the fact that the closet and the dressing room were spaces where women tended from an early date to experiment with decorative ideas that later became fashionable, often using less expensive materials that had a short life span. The Princess of Orange, in the first half of the seventeenth century, 'cannibalised' Oriental lacquer screens to insert them as panels in the walls of her closet. For her imitators, when the genuine article was unattainable, European painters could produce *chinoiseries* using ordinary paints and varnishes.[113] The result of such experimentation was the introduction of lighter fabrics, in both weight and colour, and a taste for *chinoiserie* that became associated with bedrooms (fig. 129) and dressing rooms, and also the later popularity of painted furniture.[114] Furthermore, as the seventeenth-century closet was a place of comfort and ease for one's temporary retirement, it was here that the comfortable seat furniture 'that was so striking a product of the late seventeenth-century upholsterer's skills' could be seen, such as cushioned couches and easy chairs.[115]

Details of schemes for these rooms were enthusiastically related in correspondence: women enjoyed designing decorative projects, exchanging ideas and selecting colours and fabrics. From a very young age, Louisa Conolly worked unceasingly on her home and gardens at Castletown. As a sixteen-year-old bride in 1759, she described her plans for the closet next to her bedroom at Stretton Hall, Staffordshire, the Conolly seat in England: 'I am now sitting in [the] small closet next to my bedchamber that is going to have a window down to the ground and hung with pretty paper and pictures, and my things for writing, and all litter in it. The closet is not larger than Mrs Vesey's little tidy one at Lucan.'[116] By April 1761 she had decorated two closets at Castletown with India paper, sent to her by her mother-in-law, Lady Anne Conolly, who was frequently commissioned by Louisa and her sister Emily (countess of Kildare) to purchase items in England that were either not available or more expensive in Ireland. In her attic storey Louisa created a 'delightful pretty room' out of a lumber room, 'with blue paper and white knotted furniture in it', and hung white satin in another.[117] In 1769 the countess of Shelburne admired Louisa's 'very pretty dressing room fitted up in ye French taste hung with white damask and ye portraits tied with knots of purple and silver ribbons'.[118] Caroline Fox, another of Louisa's sisters, had a white damask dressing room on the first floor at Holland House, London, where the hangings had gilt borders, and Emily had a similar colour scheme at Leinster House, Dublin.[119]

Lady Glandore's dressing room at Ardfert Abbey, Co. Kerry was on a fairly modest scale. The room was 'a sweet little place' according to Lady Carlow, who was less than complimentary about the house after her visit in 1785, when she described it as 'an old fashioned place in a very bleak country, with a bowling green surrounded with clipped hedges to look out upon . . . a dismal place' (fig. 5). Its chatelaine had 'been here these two years without stirring which . . . is doing penance for a young woman that likes diversion as much as she does'. The rooms were small, low and wainscoted. Lord Glandore, however, grudgingly allowed his wife to 'fit up a little dressing room belonging to the apartment I am in', and Lady Carlow describes it as

> hung with white paper, to which she has made a border of pink silk, with white and gold flowers stuck upon it, and hung the room with all Mr Bunbury's beautiful prints; the window curtains are pale pink linen with white silk fringe, the chairs pink linen with a border painted on paper, cut out and stuck on gauze and then tacked on the linen. It does not sound well but it has a very pretty effect, especially for a little room. The mouldings are gilt, and the windows down to the ground, the toilet gauze, with flowers of foil and straw, etc . . . two charming little screens done with prints from Lady Spencer's drawings.[120]

In 1747, Bishop Edward Synge of Elphin took pains to ensure that his young daughter's dressing room in their house on Kevin Street, Dublin was in tune with the latest trends. In letters to Alicia he encouraged her to have her 'whole dressing room painted', but was unsure whether or not to paint over the new carvings just put up by John Houghton (probably wainscoting). Two years later he suggested that she might want sprigged muslin for the room as it was so pretty, and he informed her that papering down to the floor (the skirting board) was now all the fashion.[121] Maria Edgeworth's father purchased blue and white paper for his wife's closet as early as 1742.[122] Mrs Delany was busy with her decorative ideas at this time too. She wrote to her brother that she had 'greatly improved' her dressing room by covering the painted olive walls with 'a dove-colour flock paper', and some years later informed her sister that she had hung her closet with crimson paper with 'a small pattern that looks like velvet'.[123]

Male dressing rooms and studies

The male dressing room served a number of purposes. It was the precursor of, and sometimes in addition to, the study or 'own room', and was often located on the ground floor. There, according to Isaac Ware, it was ideally next to a waiting room where business callers with a previous appointment, and 'of better rank than those who remain in the hall', waited to see the master. As the morning was the usual time for business, they were admitted to the dressing room while he was still *en déshabille*.[124] In a great number of the plans of Irish houses dressing rooms are located next to or close to the hall. Most of these do not name it as that of the owner of the house, but it was likely to be understood at the time that this was at once 'a place of dressing', a study and a room in which business was conducted. It was also, in houses built on the Palladian plan, conveniently close to, and sometimes attached to, the stables, an important space in every country house up to the advent of the motor car, and one that will be discussed below.

In 1759 Louisa Conolly described her husband's wainscoted dressing room as being to the right of the hall at Stretton.[125] Richard Castle was fairly consistent on this point in his plans. In all three ground-floor plans for Carton (*c*.1739) he placed a dressing room to the left of the main staircase, leading into a closet and a water closet in the south-west end bay. This suite was probably for Lord Kildare's business meetings and must have suited him because, in a proposed plan drawn by him in 1762, he retained these rooms but placed them to the right of the hall. In a design for Castle Coole (*c*.1741) the dressing room and closet are again located to the left of the hall, with two interconnecting bedrooms to the right, where it is likely that the earl of Belmore slept. In a plan for Leinster House, a parlour and a dressing room are to the right of the hall: the former as a waiting room, the latter in which to conduct business. Some dressing rooms or studies had a door leading to a courtyard either directly or via a back hall so that people coming to the house on business were not required to use the main entrance. This occurs at Headfort in two plans by Castle, at Lucan House, at Townley Hall (in plans by both Johnston and the Balfours), at Dromoland Castle (*c*.1826), at Pakenham Hall and at Killeen Castle.

It is interesting to note a new trend in room names on plans produced towards the end of the eighteenth century. 'Study' and 'own room' or 'Mr [owner's name]'s room' began to grow in popularity and were used at times in conjunction with a dressing room, but eventually replaced it at ground-floor level.[126] The study as a room name was known from the early seventeenth century. It had established itself in England by the end of the century, and is listed in three Irish inventories dating to 1645, 1656 and 1686.[127] The earliest study among plans examined here is much later, being included in the drawings by Thomas Cooley for Ardbraccan in 1773, where, to the right of the hall in one of them, there is a grouping of study, dressing room, powdering room and water closet. The earliest reference to the term 'own room' appears on a drawing by Johnston for Townley Hall in 1794, where a 'wardrobe' adjoins it; in another, undated and unsigned drawing at the same locations are 'Mr Balfour's own room' and 'Mr Balfour's dressing room'.[128] According to the plans, 'own room' was a name much favoured by Johnston and his clients, who were perhaps aware of a trend whereby the 'public toilette' was going out of fashion for men who now preferred to dress in an upstairs dressing room. 'Own rooms' and studies, such as that at Mount Kennedy, where business was contracted, were overtaking these dressing rooms for men (figs 172, 173).

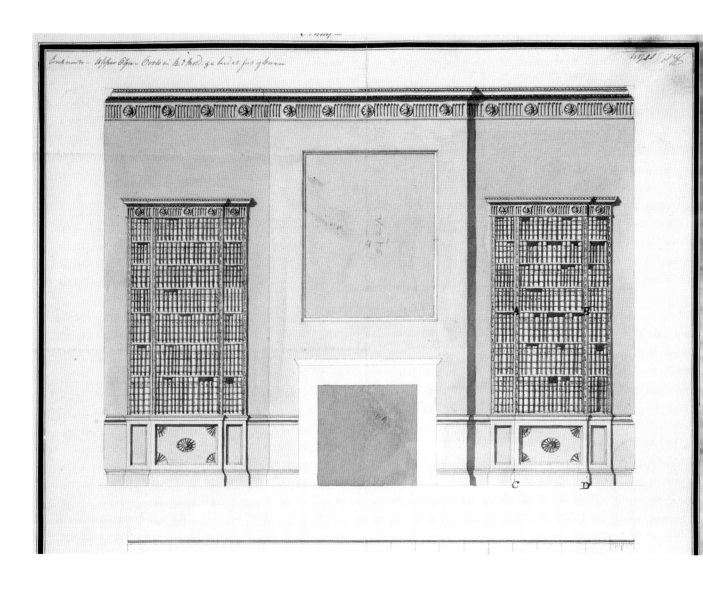

In *Vanity Fair*, Thackeray described how the master's study and its location enabled him to control his household:

172

Thomas Cooley, elevation of wall of study with bookcases at Mount Kennedy, n.d.

Behind Mr Osborne's dining room [at his house in Russell Square, London] was the usual apartment which went in his house by the name of the study; and was sacred to the master of the house. Hither Mr Osborne would retire of a Sunday forenoon when not minded to go to church; and here pass the morning in his crimson leather chair, reading the paper . . . No member of the household, child or domestic, ever entered that room without a certain terror. Here he checked the housekeeper's accounts and overhauled the butler's cellar-book. Hence he could command, across the clean gravel courtyard the back entrance of the stables with which one of his bells communicated, and into this yard the coachman issued from his premises as into a dock, and Osborne swore at him from the study window.[129]

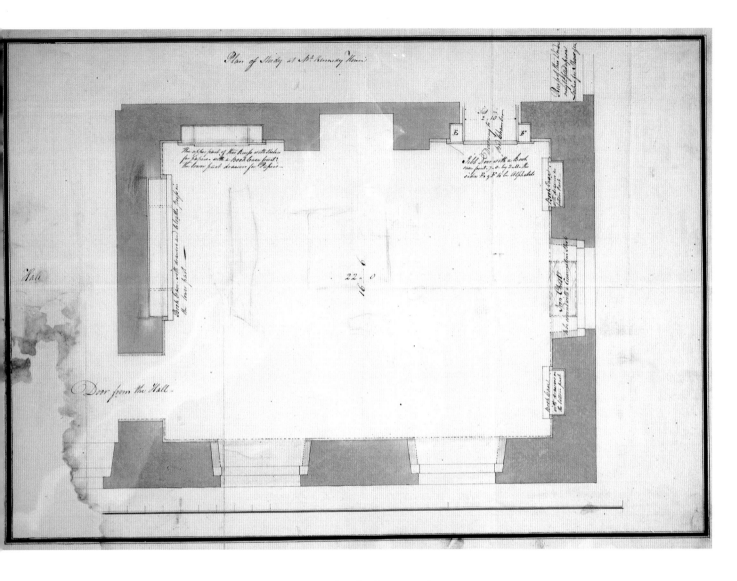

Plan of Study at Mr. Kennedy's House

Door from the Hall.

Dressing rooms in the inventories

The inventories are not informative about wall treatments. In 1728/9 tapestry and Kidderminster hung on the walls of Lord Powerscourt's closet at his Wicklow house, and there were gilt leather hangings in 'Mr Wingfield's Dressing room and Closet' in the Dublin house. At Dromana (1755) the dressing room belonging to the Blue Damask Room was similarly hung with blue Indian silk damask and matching curtains, while at Kilrush (c.1750) there were four panels of caffoy in a dressing room with a matching settee bed.[130] Beds were contained in many dressing rooms and closets (though not often in boudoirs), underlining the historical importance of the bed as the major piece of furniture in a house. Interestingly, the trend continued well into the nineteenth century, if the Crom Castle inventory of c.1860 is anything to go by, where almost every dressing room had one.[131] It also seems to be the case that, from the second half of the eighteenth century, dressing-room beds were often in the form of sofa, settee, or couch beds, though these did appear earlier. It is not quite clear how the beds in these rooms were used. In some cases earlier in the century they may have been for servants, but mostly they seem to have been for resting in during the day, if required, and perhaps as an occasional alternative to the marital bed.[132]

Looking at items of furniture in the inventories that were most frequently to be found in dressing rooms and closets, it is perhaps surprising that there is not a great deal of difference between those in women's and those in men's rooms. Leaving aside beds, furniture that was generally common to both was upholstered seat furniture and painted, rush-bottomed or cane chairs and covers. Dressing tables were often made of deal because they were covered – concealed by fabric – as at No. 10 Cavendish Row, Dublin (1763), where red tammy (a twilled worsted fabric) was used, over which was flowered muslin and a 'vail' (perhaps of muslin) which could be placed over the dressing table or the floor to protect it from stray hairs, pins, or hair or face powder. Mirrors of different sizes (usually in greater numbers in women's rooms), desks, writing tables, chests of drawers, shelves and various small tables made up most of the furniture, together with fire guards, fire irons, firescreens (sometimes with their own covers, as at the Ingoldsby house in Dublin (1731), which was of blue paragon), fenders and prints. It seems surprising that full-size screens (as opposed to firescreens) were not common items in these rooms, but perhaps the need for privacy when attending to one's ablutions was minimal.

There were also utilitarian items such as clothes airers, washstands, basins, ewers, tumblers and foot pans. 'Necessary' pieces, such as the close-stool or bidet – sometimes called 'deception commodes', as at Furry Park, Co. Dublin and Carton – were often found in dressing rooms, but perhaps more frequently in closets (fig. 174).[133] Lady Mary Wortley Montagu explained to a friend why her close-stool was painted with the spines of books by Pope, Swift and Bolingbroke: 'They were the greatest Rascals, but she had the satisfaction of shitting on them every day.'[134] In a similar vein, chamber pots were sold in Ireland with the face of Richard Twiss painted on the bottom, after some unflattering remarks by him in the account of his tour in Ireland.[135] Lady Clare, wife of the Lord Chancellor, is said to have composed a little ditty:

> Here you may behold a liar
> Well deserving of hell-fire
> Every one who likes may p—
> Upon the learned Doctor T—.[136]

There is neither close-stool nor chamber pot in the two boudoirs for which there are inventories. That at Mount Stewart (1821), on the first floor, appears to have been en suite with the 'Pink Bedroom' and dressing room. The window curtains were of pink cotton and white muslin trimmed with blue and black cotton that matched the drapery of the mahogany (day?) bed, held in place by an eagle and ring. Apart from the bed, two armchairs and a carpet, the only other item of furniture listed is a 'mahogany inlayed chamber bath with white lyner'. Lady Crichton's boudoir at Crom Castle (*c.*1860) was also on the first floor. Not quite as sophisticated as her mother-in-law Lady Erne's downstairs, there is nevertheless evidence of her ladyship's interest in music, as it contains a piano, a harp, a music stool and a music stand. There is also a sofa and pillow, three armchairs, nine other chairs with white satin covers, a number of tables including two for writing, four mirrors including one over the chimneypiece, ten pictures, a chandelier and a 'chimney board and curtains'.[137]

It is worth noting that, of the five men's dressing rooms in the inventories where fabric is specified, four – perhaps surprisingly – had chintz furnishings and date to the first half of the nineteenth century: they are Lord Leitrim's at Killadoon (1807), 'Mr Cobbe's dressing

174

A Regency mahogany commode, with fold-down top and faux drawers, fitted with a chamber pot.

5
…raham Tuppy, gentleman's travelling set, *c.*1786–7;
…ver and rosewood.

room' at Newbridge (1821), Judge Vandeleur's at Furry Park (1834) and Lord Lurgan's oriel window at Brownlow House, which was hung with chintz in 1848 (the other room was Lord Powerscourt's, discussed above). Lord Howth's dressing room at Howth Castle (inventories dated 1746–52) was quite austere, with six walnut chairs covered in Spanish leather (his wife also had walnut chairs, but with chintz covers, in her dressing room). He had a walnut escritoire, a 'delf fountain and basin', a pair of backgammon tables and a large cache of arms.[138] Lord Leitrim had fifteen oil paintings on his walls (many painted by his wife), eleven of them with gilt frames, and Lord Lurgan had an unspecified number of prints.

There are a few items of note in some of the men's rooms. Dressing boxes appear in Lord Powerscourt's closet in 1728/9 ('a set of fine India Japan'd Dressing boxes') and in Mr Cobbe's dressing room at Newbridge House (1821). A 'Morocco hair case for travelling' in Mr Clements's dressing room at Ashfield House (1808) might be another dressing box (though it may have been intended to hold his wigs) and, in a later (1843) inventory for the same house, two appear in another dressing room (fig. 175). Such boxes are also listed in the Best Bedchamber at Killeen Castle (1790) – 'sett of dressing boxes Indian and glass' – and in two bedrooms at Clogrenan (*c.*1800). Holding dressing and grooming accoutrements, such a container might seem to have been an essential item at a time when people moved from house to house, but it does not appear as frequently as one would expect, though it might be mentioned simply as a 'box' in inventories. Tool boxes are listed in the dressing rooms of Lord Fingall at Killeen Castle (1790) and of the duke of Leinster at Carton (1818), where he also kept a 'bench with vice and anvil'. While these might indicate an interest in DIY, another explanation might be that it was a safe place to keep some essential tools in case of emergency.

As well as over 6,000 volumes in his Book Room at Clogrenan, Mr Rochfort had 400 books on his dressing room shelves, while books to the value of £600 were in the study at Convoy, Co. Donegal (*c.*1844). Together with a 'gold-headed Kane', Mr Balfour kept '2 Small Silver-headed Swords and a Mourning sword in his closet (*c.*1741) at St Stephen's Green. Sir Edward O'Brien, in his will dated 1765, left to his son, Donough, all his pistols and guns 'kept in my little armory or guncase in my closett at Dromoland'.[139] At Carton (1818) the duke of Leinster kept a case of pistols, a sword and a sword blade in one of his dressing rooms (in addition, he had a tomahawk in his study, though his proficiency in using it remains undocumented); Lord Erne kept a sword and handcuffs in his room at Crom Castle (*c.*1860). A 'grater for tobacco', a 'Leather Case with four Tortois Shell Razors, 2 Small Daggers, one of them a Poison'd Blade, a Pair of Nail Nippers' and '2 Spy Glasses', together with '12 Chairs covered with Barbary Leather', seem to indicate that the Dressing Room at the Ingoldsby house in Mary Street, Dublin (1731) was a man's room. Similarly a 'bootjack' (a device for holding the boot by the heel to ease withdrawal of the foot) is mentioned occasionally; at Carton they seem to have been attached to mahogany clothes horses.[140] Items such as estate maps, topographical images and paintings of houses and demesnes were proudly displayed as reminders of the owner's wealth in studies and offices belonging to men. The horse-mad Sir Edward O'Brien had, appropriately, 'A Landscape of Newmarket' over the chimneypiece in his closet at Dromoland in 1753, and a 'Small Hunting Piece' among other paintings in his closet. Whether Newmarket landscape referred to Sir Edward's home village, Newmarket-on-Fergus, which he named after the English racecourse, we can only guess.[141]

From study to stable

On the subject of horses, it is worth noting the location of men's studies or dressing rooms on the ground floor, frequently with convenient access to a doorway or passage that led directly into the stable yard, particularly in houses built on the Palladian plan. Tom Conolly at Castletown, for example, had access to the stable yard from a doorway outside his study (fig. 176), or he could walk along the curved colonnade into the stables. The importance of horses and stables in Ireland can hardly be exaggerated, and time should be taken to consider both.

The vaulted stable, first used in designs by Edward Lovett Pearce at Castletown, became a particular Irish feature that was continued after Pearce's death by Richard Castle, and can be seen at Carton, Russborough, Ardbraccan and many other houses (fig. 177).[142] Though common in Ireland, it was exceptional even in aristocratic stables in Britain, where it was considered too expensive for most owners.[143] By the early eighteenth century in Ireland, however, stables were becoming important status symbols among the nobility and gentry – somewhere to take one's guests to view not just the building but the horses within it, which, like works of art, required a good deal of connoisseurship in order to appreciate them.[144] This was particularly evident in the differences in the quality of the stables provided for racehorses, hunters, riding and carriage horses on the one hand, and those for farm horses on the other. The convenience of the Palladian plan meant that the horses most used by the

176
Ardbraccan, mounting block at side entrance to the house from the stable yard.

177
Strokestown House, vaulted stable.

178
orge Nairn (1799–1850), *The Interior of the Stables*
Carton, County Kildare: a Liveried Groom, Lord
arles William FitzGerald, and His Sister, Lady Jane
ymour FitzGerald, c.1825; oil on canvas.

family – riding and carriage horses – were accommodated in stables attached to the house (fig. 178). However, the second half of the century saw the stable emerge as a building in its own right, often quadrangular in shape, built at a remove from the house and dressed in a variety of architectural styles.

While the stables were important to owners, the horses were their real concern and, indeed, passion – sometimes to the exclusion of all else, with the possible exception of drinking.[145] Edward Pakenham described his friend Lord Buttevant in 1737 as 'a man the world may call a good natured man but . . . his abilities range little further than a pack of hounds or horses'.[146] Similarly, the inventory of goods left by Sir Philip Perceval in 1680 was pathetically short but he had more than fifty horses in his stables, and work had begun on new kennels.[147] This passion had the potential to create tension in a family: Lady Broghill complained of being 'eaten out of house and home, for my lord's horses, dogs and strange company do devour most unconscionable'.[148] Reference to the 'strange company' may have had a resonance almost a hundred years later when the duchess of Northumberland wrote in her diary: 'Men that are fond of Horses generally prefer the Stable to good Company & occupied with the Conversation of Jockeys Coachmen Grooms & postillions they contract in such Company a rude coarse manner of speaking wch destroys that politeness so necessary in the Society of Ladys by wch means they come to neglect them & often become swearers & Brutes. And the Ladys in return always reckon them to have little wit & much ignorance.'[149] The O'Briens at Dromoland were as famous for their stable as they were for gambling. In response to his heir's plea to sell some of his horses to pay debts in 1758, Sir Edward wrote: 'Every man in the British Dominions, that knows me, knows as Well as I do, that my Sole Amusement is my Horses, and that I neither play Cards or Dice, keep neither Whores nor Hounds.'[150]

Carriages, too, were important for a family's standing in society, where one's place could be judged by one's equipage. Display extended even to funerals, when the attendance of a family's coach and horses, even with nobody inside, was considered a courtesy to the deceased: the crest and livery of the servants indicated ownership. Both coaches and coach horses were expensive. The horses had to be of the right size and appearance to reflect the standing and income of the owner: blacks and bays were the most desirable colours, and the minimum number for making an impact was six.[151] Fine horses were appreciated and attracted much attention. Among the instructions to his agent at Belan in 1788 for his homecoming with his new bride, the 2nd earl of Aldborough required 'two or four more black Coach horses to match those I have, and two or more horses for servants to ride, as we are to make the tour of Ireland'.[152]

Lord Doneraile paid over £150 for a coach bought in London and shipped to Ireland in 1775. The coach is described as:

> neatly run with raised Beads, painted Barrie Colour with Arms in handsome Ornaments, a handsome Border round the Pannells, the Beads Gilded, the Leather Japan'd & brass Beads all round it, lined with Spotted Manchester Velvet, the Seat Cloth with one row of fringe with Silk button hangers, Plate Glasses to slide in front, Glasses & Mahogany Shutters in the Doors, an Oval Glass & Cushion to the back, wainscott Trunks under the Seats, a carpet to the bottom, hung on a light strong Carriage with Iron Axletree screw'd at the Ends, wrought Boxes and patent Wheels with browhoops, upright Steel Springs, small hind Standards, Coachbox to take off, high Budget, the Carriage & Wheels painted the Colour of the Body & pick'd out green and white . . .[153]

In 1837 a Doneraile heir ordered ten harnesses (again in London) with 'silver embosd and chasd crests and coronets on do.'[154]

But handsome carriages with silver trimmings were not solely for the nobility and the rich. Dorothea Herbert vividly describes going to the Cashel Races in 1789 in the family's new coach, just arrived from Dublin, with 'four of the handsomest young Bay Horses in the Kingdom . . . really a Most beautiful Vehicle, Bottle Green adorned with a Quantity of Silver Plate, and the harnesses equally enrich'd with Silver . . . in short we were the Gaze and Astonishment of the Whole Race Course'.[155] Bishop Edward Synge's requirements for his new coach included some colour coordination in his equipage: 'Blue Cloath for the lining – a fuller blue than the Servants Big-Coats. Get also a very handsome fringe for the Hammer-Cloth and a leather one for journeys', and 'good clever large pockets at the Doors, well bound and secure'.[156]

The expense of owning a coach included the provision of livery for servants such as the coachman, postilion(s) and footmen. In 1767, the duke of Leinster upgraded his footmen in line with his newly acquired ducal status, providing them with 'a Pair of black Worsted Shag Breeches . . . a fine Felt Hat with a Silver Chain Loop and Buttons and a Horse Hair Cockade'.[157] The Rev. Robert King of Ballylin, Co. Offaly paid his coachman £12 per annum, 'with Hat, Coat, Breeches and Jackett & Trowsers & Waistcoat', in 1821.[158] Family papers give lists of liveries made for servants, the buttons of which were stamped with the family's crest.

Other expenses included a tax on carriages: Lord Shannon paid a total of £68 5s. 0d. in 1800 for two four-wheeled carriages in Dublin and three in Castlemartyr, Co. Cork.[159]

In considering the importance of horses and carriages to the country house, it is important not to overlook the practical and important role of the humble cart and carthorse in providing fresh produce from country estates to houses in Dublin. An example is the constant flow of food from Carton to Leinster House in Dublin.[160] A mule departed from Carton at 10 am each Monday, Wednesday and Friday, carrying 'Rowls, Butter, Eggs, Fowl, Game &c and Sallading' and returning the following day. On Tuesday and Saturday mornings a cart and two horses brought meat, garden produce, bread and anything else that was required. The mule was 'never to go faster than a Walk', the saddle was to be kept in good condition and 'great care to be taken of [the mule's] Feet, in the Shoeing, &c.'. Worrying that fruit might be damaged in the cart during transportation, the duke dispatched a note to the gardener that in future it should be sent either with 'Joe' (by mule or horseback) or by a man on foot (a footman) on Mondays, Wednesdays and Fridays.[161] In both directions the loads were weighed and an account sent to Lord Kildare and to the clerk of the kitchen. Detailed instructions about when and what harnesses and bridles were to be worn by the carthorses were laid down, as were orders regarding letters going to Dublin: only those 'directed by the [by then] Dutchess [sic] of Leinster, Or marked E:L by her Grace or directed or marked L by me shall be carried to Dublin by the Carters to the Porter at Leinster House'. If these orders were disobeyed, the duke imposed a fine on the farmer and the carter.

It would be unheard of in the Leinsters' well-staffed establishment in Dublin to have the coachman wait at the dinner table, but this did happen regularly in town houses, where use was made of a smaller number of staff than would be the case in the country. The coachman would be given an hour or so to wash down the carriage and tend the horses, which frequently left him little time to wash himself, with the result that all too often the gastronomic delights of the dinner might be accompanied by the odour of the stables.

Water closets and bathrooms

Turning back to the main block of the house, we find that, in all of the inventories throughout the period of this study, close-stools, 'necessaries', chamber pots, commodes and bidets are mentioned. Yet, according to Michel Gallet, in eighteenth-century Paris 'sanitary installations were already in wide use and greatly improved'.[162] In 1710 a French architect wrote about the closet in which the close-stool had previously stood, but which was now a water closet; he does not use that term, explaining that 'this sort of place is entirely new', but he mentions pipes, a tap and a valve.[163] Whether the 'delightfull Waterhouse' seen by Thomas Dineley in the 1670s at Kilkenny Castle, had anything to do with water closets is unclear. He described it as 'adjoining to the B[owling?] Green, which with an Engine of curious artifice by the help of one horse furnisheth all the offices of the Castle with the necessary Element'; it had apparently been in place ten years previously.[164] However, close-stools are to be found in the Ormonde inventories in the 1670s – the duke's covered in leather with pewter pans.

The box-like close-stool continued to be used throughout the eighteenth century, sometimes decorated with velvet or leather, sometimes later disguised as a 'deception commode'. It certainly deceived the duchess of Northumberland, who complained in her journal that at Hopetoun, in Scotland, 'the Housekeeper sent me into the Closet to look for a Chamber pot but it being in a Box I could not find it'. Meanwhile, during the 1780s cabinet-makers in England such as Hepplewhite and Sheraton were producing such commodes (or what they called 'harlequin' furniture, magic transformation being the business of the Harlequin in

a pantomime), with ingenious sliding and folding parts that disguised the real purpose of the piece, namely as a container for the bidet or chamber pot.[165] 'Mahogany and red leather bidets' appear in bedrooms in the 1807 inventory at Killadoon; and Eggleso provided '2 maho[gan]y Bedsteps with commodes covd. in Carpeting' at £5 13s. 9d. and a 'Mahoy night stool & pan' for Brook Lodge in 1808.[166] At Carton (1818) bedrooms and dressing rooms contained 'deception' and 'night' commodes, and frequently bidets with delph pans.[167]

According to the *OED* a water closet is 'a small room . . . furnished with water-supply to flush the pan and discharge its contents into a waste-pipe below'. Significantly, perhaps, the entry continues by noting that the term is 'sometimes applied . . . loosely, to any kind of privy'. So it was a space within which either built-in privies with hinged tops or close-stools could be located. It appears that the water closets of the late seventeenth century were not efficient and no patents for such a device were entered between 1617, when the Patent Office opened, and 1775, indicating that none of the varieties available were worth patenting. It is hardly surprising, therefore, that the duchess of Northumberland complained in 1771 that the water closet at Harewood House in England 'stinks all over the House'.[168] A 'water closet', drawn on the plan as a circle within a rectangle (the standard architectural illustration for the space), is annotated on all of Richard Castle's ground-floor plans for Carton (c.1739), and a similar configuration, though with three circles (a 'three-seater'), appears on one of

179
Anon. (sometimes attrib. to François Boucher), *La Toilette intime*, n.d.

his plans for Headfort. Was he indicating a water closet complete with valve, cistern and so forth? Such a mechanism was certainly known at the time, having appeared in a French architectural treatise of 1738, which described a ceramic pan with a valve and a cistern with a tap: a handle opened the valve, or it could be opened by lifting the flap-seat.[169]

Later eighteenth-century water closets may owe something to the patent taken out in 1775 by Alexander Cummings on his valve-closet and his invention of an early version of the S-bend in the waste pipe that remained filled with water, thereby preventing unsavoury smells rising from below. Joseph Bramah, a cabinet-maker, improved this valve in 1778.[170] In 1784–5 Archbishop Charles Agar built a study over offices to the rear of his palace at Cashel, equipped with a water closet.[171] Nevertheless, while water closets grew in popularity throughout the nineteenth century – and the plans demonstrate this – their provision seemed to be at the discretion of the owner.

It is notable that the term 'close-stool' had all but disappeared from inventories by the end of the eighteenth century. Servants used the outdoor 'bog houses', located at a safe distance from the house. At Ardbraccan, on a staircase landing on the attic floor, there is a lead-lined window-box with a drain and a lid, into which the contents of the chamber pots were conveniently dispensed by servants down a drain pipe. Other such conveniences of the period were 'bourdeloues' or chamber pots designed for women, with a shape similar to a sauce-boat, often with a lid (figs 179, 180). Apparently they were so called after a seventeenth-century French Jesuit priest, Louis Bourdaloue, whose sermons were so long that a lady's maid could slip the bourdeloue under the skirts of her mistress (who performed while standing) and then discreetly carry it away. They were also available in tin or leather for use while travelling.[172]

Washstands with ceramic bowls, jugs and soap dishes are frequently mentioned in dressing rooms and, as the eighteenth century progressed, attractive pieces of furniture were designed for that purpose. Some of the plans show baths. One of Castle's designs for Leinster House is interesting: to the right of the hall is a room in which a monumental walk-in bath is approached by steps and flanked by columns (fig. 181). It adjoins a bedroom and closet and is an early design for what looks like a plunge bath (which were more for therapy, as at a spa, than for cleanliness). A number of very elegant plunge baths were being installed in houses

...amber pot (bourdaloue), *c*.1740, from the ...antilly Porcelain Manufactory (active *c*.1725 *c*.1792). The J. Paul Getty Museum.

in England from about 1730, when 'any country house could in theory have running water on all floors'; they were generally located in the basement or on the ground floor, owing to the difficulty of getting running water above that level.[173] At Wimpole Hall, Cambridgeshire, a plunge bath designed by John Soane in *c*.1792 is located on the ground floor, on the servants' staircase, where a double staircase leads down into it and steps are built into its wall.[174] Thomas Coke, 1st earl of Leicester wrote to his architect in the 1730s about his proposed plunge bath: 'I would not have the floor in the bathing room done anything to, till I see you for we shall have a trap door in it into the cellar. Wt. I mean is I shall have a bath made in the cellar wch. will rise to that story & fit for me to jump into, besides the bath that stands on the floor for a hot bath.'[175]

The bath at Leinster House may have been was raised above the floor rather than sunk towards the basement, as it was in another unexecuted plan by Nash for Rockingham (1809), which shows a mezzanine floor containing five nurseries and a large bathroom within which is a 'large raised plunge bath and a smaller hot bath'.[176] Running water, and hot and cold baths with accompanying dressing rooms were provided for in plans by Playfair and Johnston in the basement at Townley Hall in 1792 and 1794. A bathroom appears on a first-floor plan by Benjamin Hallam for Straffan House (1808), and at Pakenham Hall (Tullynally) in a drawing by R. Richards (1820), where the 'countess of Longford's Bath' is in a room off the 'Earl of Longford's Bedroom' at the front of the house: it can probably be assumed that they shared the bedroom. Bathrooms and baths formed part of Lady Coote's suites in Ballyfin plans (*c*.1822) and part of the family wing at Adare Manor (1834). Lord Belmore installed a 'genuine ancient marble bath from his tour in Italy' and had it fitted into a small room in

181
Richard Castle, ground-floor plan for Leinster Hou detail showing the proposed bath in the room next the entrance hall, *c*.1745.

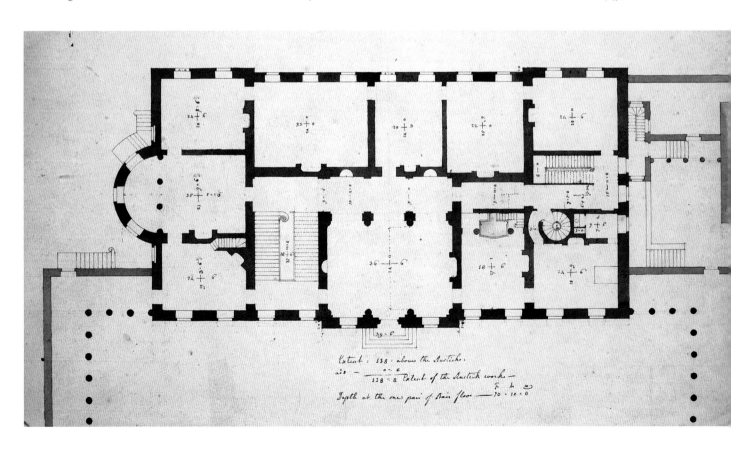

the basement in 1820 at Castle Coole.[177] Castletown, Lucan and Luttrellstown each had eighteenth-century bath-houses in their grounds, but by the 1820s the technology for plumbed-in bathrooms with hot and cold water was available.

While fixed baths were convenient, the portable bath, placed next to the fire in the bedroom, was more comfortable, an example being the mahogany 'Chamber Bath Tin Lyne' in the marchioness of Londonderry's bedroom in Mount Stewart in 1821. The downside of the portable bath was felt only by the servants, who had to fill it with sufficient water and had the prospect of later decanting it. Decanting the contents of his master's bath was no bother, however, to the servant of Lord Robert Tottenham, bishop of Clogher from 1822. The bishop, suffering from a skin disease, was recommended to bathe regularly in red wine; the contents of the bath were later sold by the enterprising servant in the local village.[178]

$\mathscr{S}ix$

Servants and Privacy

Servants

The Irish nobility and gentry were well known for the numbers of servants they kept throughout the eighteenth century and beyond. They were 'in the lower sort', according to Arthur Young in 1772, 'owing not only to the general laziness but also to the number of attendants everyone of a higher class will have'.[1] While the idea of living in such state had become unfashionable in England after the middle of the century, in Ireland the numbers pandered to the employers' desire for status. Samuel Madden wrote in 1738 that 'We keep many of them in our houses, as we do our plate on our sideboards, more for show than use, and rather to let people see that we have them than that we have any occasion for them.'[2] Lady Caroline Dawson remarked in 1778 on the 'servants without end' at Carton, and at a dinner in Kilkenny Castle about a decade later a servant was noted 'nearly behind every man'.[3] Servants also arrived with invited guests, as was the case for Mrs Delany and her husband. As we saw in Chapter 1, when travelling between their Dublin home and the dean's residence in Down, they were accompanied, in a separate coach, by their cook and two maids, and by a baggage car. With three men to drive the carriages, their entourage totalled eight people plus horses, all requiring food and a night's accommodation.[4]

The question of accommodation, not only for the servants of the house but also for visiting servants, is an interesting one. For servants generally, living space within a comfortable house was preferable to other options, but one writer criticised the many who 'squeeze into houses for an easy and indolent life where they may feed and lie well'.[5] Indeed 'squeeze' appears to be an apt description of the servants' accommodation in many houses. On paper, as in architectural drawings, it looks neat and ordered. But whether or not this reflects the numbers of staff in the house is questionable. The constant comings and goings of servants makes it difficult to calculate how many were living in a house at any particular time, as the numbers often do not differentiate between domestic and outdoor staff, the latter (usually in the majority) being accommodated elsewhere.[6] Annotated plans of houses show where they slept, but do not tell us whether they slept two or three to a bed, if any slept on the floor or if, indeed, they even slept in a bedroom. Isaac Ware in 1756 advised that if garrets proved too small, 'a bed for one man, or two maid-servants is contrived to let down in the kitchen'.[7] Some may have slept on straw, or upon rugs on the floor.

Lady Sarah Bunbury gave some thought to the matter when she advised her sister, the duchess of Leinster, on the layout of the servants' quarters at Frescati in 1775. However, the thought seems to have been directed more towards filling any gaps in the house with servants' quarters than to a consideration of their comfort. She recommended that the servants' hall be located under the dining room, where the smell of food and the 'riot that goes on at supper wouldn't disturb you there, as it would under your sitting room'. Two rooms could be made into one for the menservants and another room, which seems to have been a small space, could be used as a 'lock-up' plate room for the butler, 'or that space can be given to the footmen for another bedchamber'. She also suggested that the maids could be 'sent' to 'that long strip up at the top of the house over your bed', presumably an awkward space in the garret.[8]

The Stackallen inventory of 1757 indicates a similar pattern of accommodation as an afterthought for some servants. One of the maids shared her bedroom with the household brushes: 'Mary's apartment near the back door' had no bed frame but a 'feather bed boulster, a pair of blanketts' and a rug, as well as a broken deal press and '2 racks for cloaths', with other broken bits of furniture, in addition to the various brushes. Pole Cosby, in contrast, provided new rooms for maidservants and six rooms for menservants at Stradbally after his father's death, when his mother and sister came to live with him in 1729. Together with the furniture from her house, his mother brought a coach and six horses, a coachman, postilion, footman and maid, while his sister brought her maid and a manservant. Cosby was therefore obliged to provide more accommodation, building not just for the servants but for his extended family.[9]

Accommodation for servants was relatively straightforward in plans: bedrooms were to be found in the basement, in the attic storey, in garrets, in service blocks separate from the house or in the pavilions of Palladian-style houses. Sleeping accommodation for those servants connected with the stables – coachmen, grooms, postilions and stable hands – was provided in the stable block or in its proximity. In the Carton inventory (1818) some servants slept next to their place of work: for example, there is a bedroom next to the dairy, another next to the 'smoothing room' in the laundry, 'oak beds' in the 'Mangle Room' and a bedroom adjoining it. Other accommodation, such as servants' halls and sitting rooms, were generally located in the basement of the house or in the pavilions.

A more realistic picture emerges when one looks at the inventories. It is clear that many servants did not have bedrooms at all but slept in kitchens and elsewhere on palliasses (mattresses filled with straw) thrown on the floor.[10] References in early inventories to pallet beds in workrooms and in employers' bedrooms confirm that personal servants slept all over the place, in order to be on call quickly if they were needed, and personal maids sometimes slept in the same bed with their mistress, particularly when travelling.[11] In 1656 a settle bed was listed in the entrance hall of the 16th earl of Kildare's Dublin house, something that was not unusual throughout the eighteenth century in town houses, where 'servants . . . were stowed away anywhere, footmen constantly sleeping on trestle-beds in the front hall'.[12] A bed appeared in each of the 'Boarded' and 'Stone' halls at Powerscourt, Co. Wicklow (1728), in the 'little room under oak stairs in the hall' at Mary Street (1731) and in the hall at Antrim House, Dublin (1801), while at Cloncarneel, Co. Meath a plan of the old house reveals a tiny bedroom within the hall.[13] A bed is noted in the Boot Room at Kilrush (*c*.1750), and a palliasse in the Mangle Room at Woodville (*c*.1797), where there were also '2 stump beds' in the 'Dark room' (a room with no window). At Mount Stewart (1821), apart from bedding to be found in the dairy, there were four 'Cabin bedrooms' in the 'old house' but their use for servants is not specified, so the term may simply imply small bedrooms. Finally, various inventories mention field beds with foldable frames, which could be used when travelling or as an extra bed for servants or visitors.

Often mentioned in architectural plans, diaries and novels are barrack rooms, a name that is probably a throwback to fortified dwellings of the sixteenth and seventeenth centuries, when soldiers doubled as servants (fig. 182). But they were not exclusively for servants. Lady Morgan wrote in her memoirs of the earl of Rosse's description of one in a house in a remote part of Ireland: 'At festive seasons, when the country houses were thronged beyond even their expansive power of accommodation, the "Barrack-room", the room appropriated to all latecomers, had a hearth in the centre, and an opening in the roof for the emission of smoke, when they all lay down on the floor, with their feet to the fire, in a ring, and their heads on their portmanteaux.'[14] These rooms were also remarked upon by Prince Pückler Muskau in the 1820s on his visit to England, where he wrote 'To save space, visitors usually get only one large bedroom on the second floor, and the English rarely enter this apartment for any purpose other than to sleep and to perform their twice daily toilette.'[15]

This dormitory-type accommodation usually applied to surplus single male guests, but not exclusively, as is clear from Richard Johnston's plans for Castle Coole (1789), where it pertains equally to young lady guests. For the same house, James Wyatt's plan for the basement (1790) shows two rooms of similar size to those in the attic, each called 'servants bed room'. Instead of a number of rooms each accommodating two or three servants, it made more sense and was less expensive to provide a barrack room. At Townley Hall (1794) and at Farnham (1802) there were two in the attic storeys, but it is unclear if they were for servants. Similarly, it is more likely that the bed ordered for Brook Lodge, Co. Galway from Henry Eggleso, Dublin in 1808, and listed for the 'Barrack Room Below stairs', was for guests, given the details: a 'Waggon Roof bedstead' and the 'making up 2 suits bed curtains' in calico trimmed with lace.[16] Dorothea Herbert relates an amusing incident at Castle Blunden, Co. Kilkenny in 1780 where she and her sisters were lodged in

a small Closet in the upper Story – with a Window looking out on a Dark Lobby which parted it from the large Barrack Room where all the Gentlemen dress'd and lay . . . One Day in a Hurry we found ourselves without Pomatum and had a great battle for the Scrapings of the Pomatum Pot and the use of the Powder Puff – When we were startled by a loud Tittering at the Lobby Window – We found to our great Confusion that we forgot to draw the Window Curtain and the Whole Set of Gentlemen were stationed giggling at the Casement where they had heard our fracas and seen our Tears besides catching us En Chemise – With the assistance of Mammy Shortal [the family dry nurse] we routed them back to their Barrack but no sooner was this Victory gained

Townley Hall, barrack room in attic.

than another Disaster completely undid us – We in our Confusion overturned the Pot-de-Chambre and the two Doors being opposite the Whole Contents meander'd across the Lobby into their Barrack – Immediately the House rang with their laughter and left us au Desespoir.[17]

The inventory for Killeen Castle (1790) lists two beds, four chairs, two tables, a wash-stand and a mirror in the 'Nursery or Barrack Room' (possibly a room for children of varying ages). A 'Gents Barrack Room', together with a 'Strangers Servants Room', both notable by containing just one bed in each, were located in 'Stables to West'. Here, too, was a barrack room for the 'coachman', containing two beds and bedclothes. Our expectations of a barrack room are perhaps better met by that for servants at Prospect (Ardgillan), Co. Dublin (1795), where there were five deal bedsteads. At Doneraile Court, Co. Cork (*c*.1830) there was a 'Soldiers

183
ichard Castle, elevation and plan of the first floor
f the kitchen and laundry block at Leinster House,
1745.

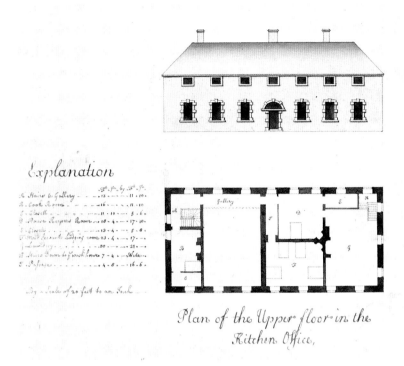

Explanation

Plan of the Upper floor in the
Kitchen Office.

room' with two bedsteads and hangings, and two tables: this might have had a specific meaning or it may have been similar to the barrack room. The Carton inventory (1818) contains
the heading 'Barrack', under which are listed 'Coachmans room[s] no. 1–4', 'Sportsmans
Room' and 'Post Boys Room', along with a list of equipment for the 'Barrack room maid' to
use in servicing these rooms.

It should be noted that accommodation in an attic storey was by no means reserved for
servants – many houses had guest bedrooms at this level.[18] In the eighteenth century, the
attic did not have the pejorative meaning attached to it today, and should be distinguished
from the garret, which *was* usually for the use of servants.[19] Nevertheless, on his visit to
Castle Coole, the French tourist the Chevalier de Latocnaye described the attic rooms 'intended for visitors' as 'like cellars'.[20]

Care was taken to keep the maidservants' sleeping quarters separate from those of the
men, as at Headfort (*c*.1750, by Richard Castle), where the women were accommodated on
the opposite side of the house from the menservants. At Lissadell (1833) the housekeeper's bedroom served as a barrier between maids' and menservants' quarters. It is difficult
to know how many servants slept in each room in practice. A first-floor plan for the kitchen
block at Leinster House (*c*.1745; fig. 183) shows four beds in a room for maids: two were larger than the others, indicating double beds, so at least six maids could sleep there. Similarly,
according to the inventory of the Provost's House at Trinity College (1852), the maidservants'
room in the basement contained two 'painted wood press bedsteads with double pallyasses
on each'.

While most servants seem to have slept in rooms – single, shared or barracks, depending
on their status – as has already been noted, the evidence in inventories shows that press beds
and portable beds were by no means unusual. No bed is indicated in the kitchen at Leinster

House but it was common practice, borne out by the inventories in this study, that kitchen maids or boys slept there: on the one hand, it was warm; on the other, they were prey to unwanted advances from other staff or from employers.[21] The servants' hall was another room in which servants slept; the inventories list 'a cubboard bed' at Killeen Castle, a 'tallboy bed' at Strokestown and a number of settle beds, press beds and deal beds. For servants with bedrooms the furniture was scant, particularly in the first half of the eighteenth century, when there was rarely more than a bed, bedclothes and sometimes a chair and/or a deal table. At that time their masters and mistresses may not have been accommodated in much better conditions, but such a state of affairs continued to be the case for servants in the majority of houses throughout the period of this book.

Servant hierarchy

On a plan for servants' quarters at Townley Hall by James Playfair (1792), four blocks of offices and accommodation range around a court. The second floor includes his accommodation for servants. One range of rooms is for women servants, another is for upper servants, a third for footmen and the fourth for 'strangers' servants'. Rooms for the steward, butler, housekeeper and 'strangers' upper servants' were located in the four projecting

184
John Nash, plan of the upper floor of the basement at Rockingham, 1809.

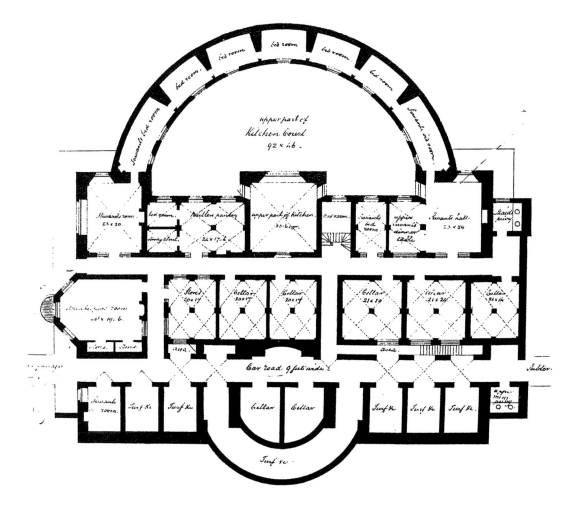

corners of the square.[22] Within the footmen's range is a 'hospital' or sickroom. This raises the question of the hierarchy of servants that existed. In a plan by the Balfours for the same house there are separate halls for upper and lower servants, while at Rockingham, John Nash provided the upper servants with a 'dinner table' in a small area separated from the bigger servants' hall by a screen of columns in the upper basement (1809; fig. 184). Not only that, but there is an 'Upper Mens Privy' and a 'Maids Privy' there too. At Castle Bernard (1833), Pain's plan shows a 'Servts Dining Room' in the basement, where there was also an 'Upper Servts Sitting Room'.[23]

Those holding positions in the upper echelons of the servant hierarchy – steward, butler, housekeeper, cook – generally occupied single rooms, which were sometimes quite well furnished. Besides a bedroom, most housekeepers had a sitting room and a closet in which china was kept. At Castle Bernard, the butler had his quarters located in the basement of the round tower, divided into his 'room' or pantry, a bedroom and a closet (fig. 185). Francis Johnston's plan for a large extension to Corbalton Hall, Co. Meath (1801) shows accommodation for a butler and a 'housekeeper or cook' fitted into spaces created by the acute angle of the old and new houses. In Wyatt's plan for Castle Coole (1790), and in one for Ballyfin (1822), the butler's bedroom is located between the pantry and the strong room. Butlers' pantries also frequently had beds in them for the use not of the butler but of a footman – as security.

Valets and ladies' maids slept either in designated servants' bedrooms or in dressing rooms attached to their masters' and mistresses' bedrooms, though this was a practice that all but disappeared in the course of the eighteenth century. 'The Duke's Own Man's Room' at Carton does not appear to be a bedroom (there is no bed listed) but a room in which he

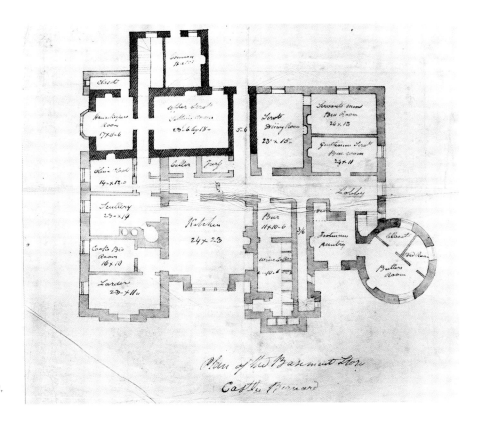

185
..R. Pain, plan of basement at Castle Bernard, with
e butler's rooms contained in the turret to the right,
.33.

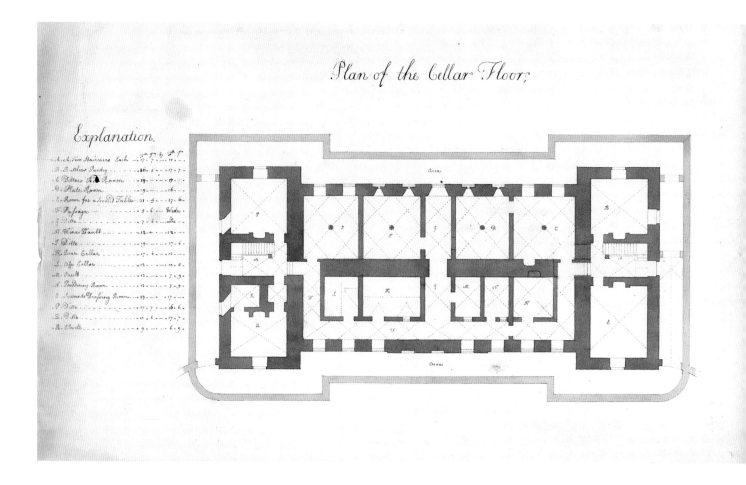

took care of the duke's clothes. As early as 1751 the furniture in the bedroom of Lady Howth's personal maid in their Dublin house at St Mary's Abbey comprised a yellow paragon four-poster bed with bedclothes, four black leather chairs, a dressing table and mirror; it also had a fireplace and a 'Pr of chamber bellows'. Lady Grandison's personal maid's room was similarly furnished (Dromana, 1755), but the furniture in ladies' maids' rooms at Clogrenan (c.1810) and Doneraile Court (c.1830s) was very sparse. While there is no named steward's bedroom in the Baronscourt inventory, his 'Parlour' is listed with much furniture, including two mahogany dining tables and twelve chairs covered in silk, perhaps indicating its use as an occasional dining room.[24] From the list of its contents it seems that the housekeeper's sitting room at Carton probably served a similar purpose. The housekeeper and the two ladies' maids (the latter shared a room) at Woodville (c.1797) even had their own 'oak close-stool chairs'.

'Powdering rooms', where servants could powder their or their masters' wigs (or hair), are to be found in many houses, such as Carton, Dromana, Ardbraccan, Castle Coole and Townley Hall. These rooms, also to be found 'above stairs', contained wig blocks and stands, powder troughs with lock and key, a chair, a table and often an oil-cloth on the floor.[25] In the Baronscourt inventory of 1782 the 'Room over Blue Morine dressing room' in the attic storey is annotated: 'This is a roome for all Gentlemen to Powder in, with a table and one chair and a sett grate'. By the end of the eighteenth century, however, hair powder had gone out of fashion and powdering rooms are absent from both the plans and the inventories under discussion after that.

In a plan for Carton, Richard Castle locates the butler's pantry and the housekeeper's room at ground-floor level at the east end of the main block.[26] The basement plan here is interesting as, apart from a powdering room and a 'room for a second table', it includes three servants' dressing rooms (fig. 186).[27] This appears excessive: while many of the male servants would be dressed in livery, women servants generally did not wear a uniform. At Townley Hall the basement plan attributed to the Balfours shows a dressing room for servants, and both Playfair's and Johnston's plans (1792 and 1794 respectively) locate 'dressing rooms' next to baths in the basement. Playfair's is a large bowed space where he has a 'cold bath' and a 'warm bath', while the rest of the basement – except for a space for coal – is given over to beer and wine cellars. The only entrance to Johnston's bathroom (9 feet × 8 feet) is through the dressing room to the rear of the house.[28] As neither of these plans is annotated for the use of servants, they could be bathrooms for the use of the gentlemen of the house and/or their guests, perhaps after hunting or riding, as, in Johnston's plan, the dressing room is next to a passage that leads to the yard.

By the 1850s Sir Charles Domville of Santry Court, Co. Dublin expected every man working for him to have a bath once a week. A fire would be lit for one hour for each bath 'and the person using [it] must empty it, mop the room and leave all tidy'. He further expected all of his servants to have clean hands 'even if they have to wash them 10 times daily'.[29] One wonders whether, if Sir William Ponsonby Barker of Kilcooley Abbey, Co. Tipperary had been stricter in the 1830s about the personal cleanliness of his servants, he would have had a less disturbed night's sleep. After evening prayers this aged evangelical, apparently inspired by the biblical example of King David, was in the habit of selecting one of his maids to act as a human hot water bottle in his bed. One night the odour from his chosen one was so strong that he got out of bed and grappled in the dark to find some eau de cologne to sprinkle over her, only to find the next morning that he had covered her with ink.[30]

Other, more specialised rooms should be mentioned: in the basement at Leinster House is one for the 'Groom of Chambers' (the man who not only kept all of the furniture in good order but had some duties similar to the butler) and the 'Confectioners Room', indicating the importance of table decorations and desserts, as has been seen in earlier chapters (fig. 187).[31] Another room in the same house is a 'servants waiting room' at the front of the house on the ground floor, which has a small staircase leading from it to the basement (fig. 82).[32] It was there that servants waited on call for any room on that floor (or elsewhere), and the two windows to the front court permitted them to see anyone approaching the house. A door leading into the colonnade allowed them to take care of visitors' horses and carriages or to direct their staff to the stable yard, without having to cross the staircase hall and use the front door.[33] Chambers's plan for Headfort (fig. 28) has one in a similar position; a plan of Powerscourt, Co. Wicklow dating to 1843 shows one next to the great hall to the east; and in Morrison's plan for Carton (1815) a large room with a canted bay to the west (of the new front) is for the same purpose.[34]

'Shoe Rooms' are noted at Townley Hall and at Ardbraccan; and in two of James Lewis's designs published in 1797 – Coole House, Galway, 'seat of Robert Gregory, esq', and the villa designed for Silver Oliver at Cork ('to be close to Cork city with a view of the Cove and the beautiful scenery near it') – are large rooms in the basement 'for brushing clothes'.[35] Specialised spaces such as these became more common in the course of the nineteenth century. One room, however, seems quite unique: a plan for Pakenham Hall shows a servants' library in the main block (presumably in the basement) in front of the strong room.[36]

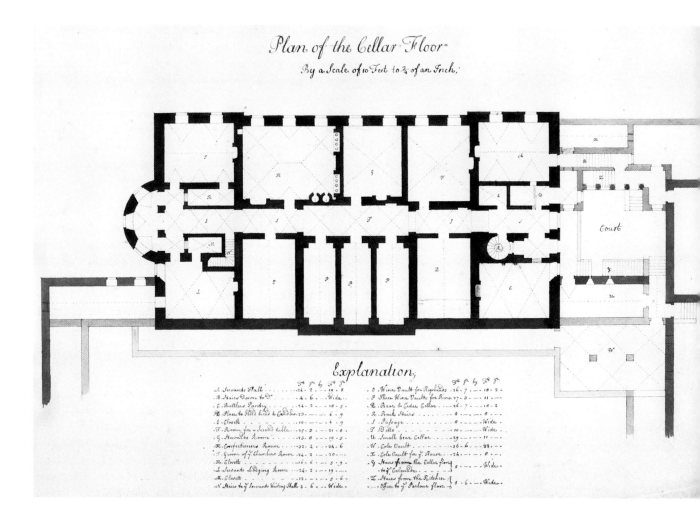

187
Richard Castle, plan of basement at Leinster House
*c.*1745.

Servants and their perks

Servants' wages in Ireland were low – on average 30 per cent lower than in England, according to Arthur Young in 1780 – which accounted for the large number of servants and retainers to be seen in houses. Frequently servants were not paid at all, having board and lodging in lieu; when they *were* paid, it was at the end of each year of service. The result of this was that the servant had to borrow on his or her wages, leaving little to collect at the end of the year. In his will made in 1765 Sir Edward O'Brien of Dromoland instructed his son to pay his debts 'in particular my poor servants wages to some of whom I stand indebted for many years'.[37] Similarly, in the 1790s, the agent of the 2nd marquis of Downshire wrote to his employer, then residing in his London home, to say that all the Hillsborough servants were due three years' wages: 'For God's sake, my Lord, have the goodness to direct Mr Lane to pay me something for the servants . . . some are really starving.'[38] Under such circumstances it is no wonder that servants found numerous ways to supplement their income (if they were lucky enough to have one), including board wages, cast-off clothes, bequests, card money and vails.

Board wages were cash payments to servants in lieu of meals and in addition to wages.[39] They were given when employers were away from home, or on occasions when servants travelled with the family and meals (and sometimes accommodation) were not provided for them. While their employers were at Leinster House, servants on board wages at Carton were allowed 'such Garden Stuff as they may want'. How this was to be measured by the gardener (to whom the instruction was addressed) is not disclosed. Married servants were not allowed to live in the house but were given board wages for living outside the estate. The steward was instructed that they were not to eat or drink in the house 'except now and then, they and their Wives may be asked to Dinner on Sunday to live in Harmony with them so far as to carry on their mutual Business to Lord Kildare's advantage'.[40] Occasionally, servants managed to find ways of saving board wages, one of which was to get themselves invited to eat in the servants' halls of houses where they had friends. This payment therefore gave the servants more independence than most employers desired.[41]

Cast-off clothes given to servants by the family could be sold off or, more often, worn by them. At the upper end of the scale, Mrs Clotworthy Upton (later Lady Templeton, when her husband was created Baron Templeton in 1776) of Castle Upton, Co. Antrim, who was Woman of the Bedchamber to Queen Charlotte from 1772 to 1778, made a considerable amount of money by selling her employer's cast-offs. Apart from dresses, items listed were 'dirty gloves' and three pairs of the queen's stays.[42] This arrangement was probably agreed in advance of employment. Female servants did not fare as well as their male counterparts, who frequently had clothes supplied in addition to their wages. This was because male servants were generally more visible than female, and it reflected well on the employer and the household to have them well dressed. In Chapter 5 we noted the largesse shown by the duke of Leinster and the Rev. Robert King to their menservants. At Strokestown Park, a bill from the 1840s shows clothing for nine male servants, down to the 'Pantry' and 'Kitchen' boys, each of whom received 'a suit of moleskin'.[43] Liveries were provided on loan to the servant, being left behind on departure to be worn by a successor, and replaced when needed. According to Bishop Edward Synge, his servants were 'so shabby they will not be fit to appear in town'; he therefore ordered frock coats and waistcoats in September 1747 for liveried servants at his palace at Elphin (where there were five) and his Dublin home at Kevin Street.[44]

Servants who had given years of service were often left bequests in their employers' wills. These varied from employer's clothes or linen to sums of money. The dowager Viscountess Powerscourt, who died in 1785, was generous to the female servants who were in her service at the time of her death. Those who had been with her one year were given one year's wages; those who had attended her less than a year received a half-year's wages. But to every manservant she left just one month's wages.[45] She also bequeathed to every servant the sum of five pounds, which 'will do them more good' than putting them all in mourning clothes, a custom of the time.[46] However, female servants were not so highly esteemed by Sir Edward O'Brien of Dromoland. He left one year's wages to male servants of five or more years' standing, but declared that he had 'met [with] not one woman servant worth salt to her pottage since Mrs Barnwell left me'.[47]

'If your Lady loves Play, your Fortune is fixed for ever: Moderate Gaming will be a Perquisite of ten Shillings a Week; and in such a Family I would rather choose to be Butler than Chaplain . . . It is all ready Money, and got without Labour.'[48] So said Jonathan Swift on a rather lucrative perk for the butler, or sometimes the footman, whose job it was to supply cards and candles whenever the lady of the house invited her friends to play cards. The system, whereby he 'sold' the cards to the guests, allowed for greater numbers at these parties than perhaps the hostess's own means would allow, and the guests were expected to leave on the table for the butler double or even treble the amount of the cards' purchase price.[49] The higher the stakes, the more new decks of cards were called for, and the more money the

butler made. As each new pack made its appearance, the money was placed under the candle-sticks on the tables.[50] The butler was then free to sell off the old cards to coffeehouses, or to poorer families who liked to play cards, while he could sell on the wax candle ends to gro-cers.[51]

For most of the servants, however, the potential benefit from visitors to the house came in the form of vails. These are defined by the *OED* as 'a gratuity given by a visitor on his de-parture to servants of the house'. The custom appears to have been well established by the eighteenth century. It is not clear how it came into being, but it obviously had the tacit agree-ment of employers for as long as it suited them. The customary scene in the hall, as their guests waited for their carriages or horses to be brought to the door, embarrassed many.[52] Hosts feigned ignorance of their guests' fumbling in their pockets to find shillings and half-crowns to distribute to servants, who had lined themselves up expectantly. Whether the mo-tive for allowing the practice was to salve the collective conscience of the employers at pay-ing such low wages is not clear.[53] It was not confined to great houses, but was also expected in more modest establishments, though the amounts given were less. It was also not only expected on departure from the house of a friend: vails were disbursed by 'house tourists' to whichever servant showed them around – in most cases an upper servant.[54]

For the servants the giving of vails was a well-established way of increasing their income (often by 50 per cent or more) and something to which they believed they were entitled. But it became a problem from the first half of the eighteenth century, when there was a feeling among employers that it had got out of hand. For potential guests it led to a situation where in many cases it became prohibitively expensive to accept invitations either to dine or to stay overnight. An army officer described how much his visit to the house of a friend would cost him:

> The moment your departure is known, all the domestics are on the qui vive; the house-maid hopes you have forgotten nothing in packing up, if so, she will take care of it till you come again; this piece of civility costs you three ten-pennies; the footman carries your portmanteau . . . to the hall, three more; the butler wishes you a pleasant journey—his great kindness in so doing of course extracts a crown-piece; the groom brings your horse, assuring you 'tis an ilegant baste, and has fed well'—three more ten-pennies go; the helper runs after you with the curb-chain, which he has 'till this moment carefully secreted—two more; making a total of seventeen, or, in English money, upwards of fourteen shillings. A heavy tax for visiting a friend![55]

Richard Griffith from Bennetsbridge, Co. Kilkenny, complained in *c*.1760 in a letter to his wife that

> an heavy and unprofitable Tax still subsists upon the Hospitality of this Neighbourhood . . . In short while this Perquisite continues, a Country Gentleman may be considered but as a generous Kind of Inn-holder, who keeps open House, at his own Expence, for the sole Emolument of his Servants . . . this Extravagance is not confined, at pres-ent, solely to the Country . . . ; for a Dinner in Dublin, and all the Towns in Ireland, is become . . . an expensive Ordinary. Nay, if you have any Sort of Business to transact, even in a Morning, with a Person who keeps his Port, you may levee him fifty Times, without being admitted by his Swiss Porter. So . . . I shall consider a great Man as a Monster, who may not be seen, 'till you have fee'd his Keepers.[56]

DIRECTIONS
TO
SERVANTS

In General;

And in particular to

The Butler,	Porter,
Cook,	Dairy-Maid,
Footman,	Chamber-Maid,
Coachman,	Nurse,
Groom,	Laundress,
House-Steward,	House-Keeper,
and	Tutoress, or
Land-Steward,	Governess.

By the Reverend Dr. Swift, D.S.P.D.

188

Jonathan Swift, *Directions to Servants* (London, 1745).

Griffith was by no means alone in believing that he was being 'punished' by the porter or butler for the paucity of his vails or perhaps his refusal to 'pay his way'. An unfortunate guest in England in 1754 found his punishment truly humiliating. 'I am a marked man,' he wrote, 'if I ask for beer I am presented with a piece of bread. If I am bold enough to call for wine, after a delay which would take its relish away were it good, I receive a mixture of the whole sideboard in a greasy glass. If I hold up my plate nobody sees me; so that I am forced to eat mutton with fish sauce, and pickles with my apple pie.'[57]

Perhaps the servants at that house had taken to heart the advice offered to them in Swift's ironic *Directions to Servants* (fig. 188). Swift suggests such methods, in the event of a gentleman who often dines with their master and gives no vails, 'to shew him some Marks of your Displeasure, & quicken his Memory', and he concludes 'By these, and the like Expedients, you may probably be a better Man by Half a Crown before he leaves the House.' He further urges those servants who expect vails 'always to stand Rank and File when a Stranger is taking his Leave; so that he must of Necessity pass between you; and he must have more Confidence or less Money than usual, if any of you let him escape, and according as he behaves himself, remember to treat him the next Time he comes'.[58]

It was probably the sum of these perquisites that brought about a shift in the perception and status of domestic servants by the end of the eighteenth century. Board wages could be pocketed and they provided the servant with time and money to spend on drink. Servants wearing the cast-off clothing of their employers and aping their manners were felt by many observers to encourage ideas above their station. Card money was particularly lucrative for butlers and footmen – so much so that, in London at least, such menservants refused service in houses where gaming parties were not held.[59] But it was vails that finally undermined the authority of the employers, who virtually allowed servants to dictate whom should be received, and then pretended not to notice when the servants extracted money from the departing guests.

The custom of vails-giving was the subject of much argument in the printed media in England.[60] The writer Daniel Defoe abhorred the idea and newspapers ran numerous articles and letters giving both sides of the argument.[61] In the *London Chronicle* a correspondent wrote in 1762 that 'Masters in England seldom pay their servants but in lieu of wages suffer them to prey upon their guests'.[62] George Mathew of Thomastown, Co. Tipperary, a man famous for his hospitality, was one of the first employers to ban that 'inhospitable custom' of giving vails to servants, and to compensate them by increasing their wages. This was apparently as early as the 1730s. His servants were warned that, if they disobeyed, they would be discharged. He also informed his guests that he would 'consider it as the highest affront if any offer of that sort were made'.[63] A crusade against the giving of vails began in 1760 in Scotland, where seventeen counties issued appeals to abolish them. Four years later the movement had spread to London, resulting in riots there by footmen, the servants who stood to lose most.[64] It was probably at about the same time that employers from a number of counties in Ireland agreed among themselves to abolish vails.[65] Like George Mathew before them, they decided to increase staff wages in an effort to compensate them for loss of earnings. One of them was Lord Kildare: in March 1765 he issued a directive from Carton to members of his household, stating that 'In Consideration of Vails &c, which I will not permit for the future to be received in any of my Houses upon any Account whatsoever from Company lying there or otherwise I shall give in lieu thereof . . . five pounds per annum each to the housekeeper, Maitre D'Hotel, cook and confectioner; three pounds per annum each to the steward at Carton, the butler, valet de chambre and groom of the chambers, and two pounds to the Gentleman of Horse.'[66]

Privacy and the changing role of service

Visitors to a house understood that the family apartments were private, and therefore out of bounds, leaving them to the family and their servants. This separation of private from public spaces is something that is visible in the plans. It facilitated comfort in the use of smaller rooms and more intimate spaces. During the eighteenth century, according to Philippe Ariès, 'the family began to hold society at a distance, to push it back beyond a steadily extending zone of private life', with, for example, beds becoming confined to bedrooms (increasingly upstairs) and corridors providing a more direct way from one space to another without having to pass through rooms. Some specialisation of rooms became apparent, bells could summon servants from a distance, and people were visited by their friends on a specified 'at home' day, emphasising a new respect for privacy. Ariès also mentions that people became more health- and hygiene-conscious, something that can be seen in inventories for dressing rooms, closets and, later, bathrooms.[67]

Solitude was sought for activities such as reading and the pursuit of one's own interests; keeping a diary and writing memoirs and correspondence point to an increasing desire for self-knowledge. This coincided with a new emphasis on family life, and on children in particular, a quality noted and commented upon in Irish houses. Ariès was of the opinion that 'Ultimately the family became the focus of private life . . . It became something it had never been: a refuge, to which people fled in order to escape the scrutiny of outsiders; an emotional center; and a place where, for better or worse, children were the focus of attention.'[68] This was therefore privacy for the family from society. But two questions can be asked: first, how private were the private apartments from servants, and secondly, was there a desire among Irish families for privacy from servants?

With regard to the architectural plan, quite how segregated the servants were from the family is difficult to quantify in practice. Plans probably showed the 'ideal' way of accommodating servants, as has been seen. Personal servants – ladies' maids, valets or 'own men', nurses and governesses – obviously had their sleeping quarters close to or in the family area, and there was probably little they did not know about those whom they were serving. Employers were aware of this and some measures were taken to enable private conversations, one being the dumb waiter, which, when set up in the dining room, dispensed with the presence of servants. In at least one case in England, the owners spoke to each other in French.[69] It was sometimes considered an advantage if a servant was illiterate, so that letters could not be read. But it must be stressed, from looking at plans, that there were places such as the closet in which one could isolate oneself. The design of a town house, however, was not conducive to privacy, not least because back stairs were frequently used by the employers to get to their bedrooms, as the main staircase rarely went beyond the first floor and space was at a premium. But there is little evidence that such proximity to the servants distressed many families.

As to the question of whether there was a desire for privacy from servants, Tim Meldrum makes the pertinent point that the 'quality of the interaction between household members was more important in determining the degree of "privacy" available than bricks, mortar, wainscot or separate accommodations'.[70] Well into the eighteenth century the 'family' not only referred to blood relations but also included the servants: both Bishop Synge in the 1740s and Lord Kildare in the 1760s indicated as much.[71] The employers' role was paternalistic: they ensured that their servants were warmly dressed, well fed and taken care of when ill. Irish houses were remarkable for the numbers of servants and various hangers-on, some of whom were given odd jobs for payment in kind. Punishments for misdemeanours were handed out as one would treat an unruly child. Bishop Synge wrote to his daughter, 'you know me to be strict and Severe with regard to the Conduct of my Servants: This is not the effect of temper, but of prudence. Harshness, irksome to myself, I find necessary to keep them in order.'[72] In an effort to curb any excess among his staff, the duke of Leinster ruled in 1769 that he would not for the future 'permit any dancing to be in any part of my House without my leave or the Dutchess [*sic*] of Leinster's, which Occasions Neglect, Idleness and Drinking and makes the Family Irregular'.[73] A letter that appeared in the *Hibernian Magazine* in November 1781 indicates what could happen if discipline was not imposed:

> On Thursday evening last, or rather Friday morning, a scene of 'High life below stairs' was exhibited in the house of a person of distinction near Stephen's-Green. Mrs Margery the cook gave a grand route to several ladies and gentlemen of her acquaintance. But they were all routed about 4 in the morning by the unexpected appearance of the house steward, who had come from his master's country seat on particular business. The butler was instantly discharged, just after having amused the company with the finest exertions of theatric excellence in the soliloquy of Hamlet.

In many cases, there was a fairly good relationship between servants and their employers in Ireland: depictions of them in novels such as Maria Edgeworth's *Castle Rackrent* convey an amount of intimacy between the two groups. Employers sometimes gave servants tickets to the theatre and time off for the races, and even included them in their amateur theatricals. Mrs Delany (as Mrs Pendarves, in January 1732/3) attended 'a masquerade among the servants at Plattin [Platten Hall, Co. Meath] that entertained mightily. Lord George Sackville dressed himself up in women's clothes, and played his part archly; he is a comical spark.'[74] The household servants at Carton attended performances of plays put on by the FitzGerald children in 1771, and, as was seen in Chapter 4, they too acted in plays with the family. The play mentioned above, *High Life Below Stairs*, caused riots by the servant class in England, led by footmen who regarded the farce as an insult to the 'fraternity'. This was one of the reasons why private theatricals in houses became popular there, and quickly extended to Ireland, where the 'elite were able to savour fully the pleasure of aping the lower orders', as well as the questionable pleasure of seeing the lower orders aping them.[75] At Shane's Castle, Co. Antrim it was a *sine qua non* in the engaging of a servant that he should play an instrument, as part of a band 'which was always ready either for orchestra or pleasure-boat' or to accompany the many private theatrical performances put on there by the O'Neills.[76]

Nevertheless, towards the end of the eighteenth century the relationship between employer and servant began to change. It is evident that most Irish employers at best tolerated the presence of numerous servants, as Samuel Madden noted. Their presence certainly proclaimed the social standing of the employer, particularly if they were in livery.[77] But as the numbers of servants in a house seldom distinguished between those working indoors and outdoors it is entirely possible that both types of servants might be found rambling about the house and its immediate environs. On his visit to Ireland in 1842, William Thackeray noted the 'numerous people loitering about the stables and outhouses', the 'immense following of the Irish house, such as would make an English housekeeper crazy'.[78] Yet for all this apparent camaraderie and inclusiveness, there was another side to the situation, outlined as early as 1738 by Madden. Addressing the 'Gentlemen of Ireland', he deplored the insolence, greed and idleness of the Irish servant, and warned that 'if we do not resolve to remedy matters in time, and reform [the servants] by proper laws, we shall find ourselves very soon in as uneasy a situation . . . as they are in England'.[79] Later in the century, when perhaps an 'uneasy situation' had arisen, the earl of Clonmell gave vent to his frustration in a tirade of abuse about servants, calling them 'an absolute band of robbers'.[80]

There are other points to be made about Irish servants. The preferred servants from the early eighteenth century were English and Protestant, as these were considered cleaner in their habits and dress. Lady Portarlington wrote to her sister from Dublin in 1781, 'I am out of all patience with the slovenliness and dirt of the people in Ireland, and I have just been hiring a housemaid who is an Englishwoman in hopes of getting my house kept clean.'[81] As the century progressed it became more difficult to find Protestants, some of whom had an aversion to being dressed in livery, which they considered to be a badge of servitude or of bondage; thus Protestant employers, while 'uneasy about entrusting the impressionable young to those of another confession, resigned themselves to being served by Catholics'.[82] Added to this were the political tensions of the latter part of the century, leading to the 1798 Rising, which must have in themselves caused a degree of unease in the 'family'.

It should be stated that comments from families and correspondence regarding problems with servants are limited, and that what attitudes prevailed in houses such as those of the FitzGeralds, Conollys and Delanys were not necessarily echoed in other houses where the domestic life of their owners is undocumented. The majority of houses were smaller than Castletown or Carton, and so family and servants lived in close proximity to each other. Bearing these points in mind, the servants of both Lady Emily Kildare and her sister Lady Louisa Conolly are referred to throughout their correspondence in a way that is far from abstract: servants are individuals, often mentioned by name. However, how particular servants were about the conditions of their employment, and how anxious an employer was to get a suitable servant can be gleaned from a letter written by Louisa on behalf of Emily, who required a maid for Carton: 'She [Emily] begs that you will make her understand that the not dining at the Stewards table in this house is different from what it is in others for the maids Table is a more orderly creditable thing than in other Familys as they all dine by themselves in the Still Room and of course do not mix with the grooms, postillions &c. There is a better sort of Servant belonging to the Nursury here at present upon the footing that the other would be upon, who dines with the maids, and has very good wages, the Wet Nurse also dines there.'[83]

On the occasion mentioned above when the servants went to the horse races, Lady Kildare wrote to her husband: 'All our servants ask'd leave to go; Sarah [her sister] and I stay'd at home to take care of Charles and Charlotte, who the women wanted to carry with them, but I wou'd not consent, as you may imagine.' Three years later, in 1762, she remarked that the two nurses at Carton 'are the best play-fellows for children I ever saw; they invent some new diversion every night, they play and romp in Lady Kildare's dressing-room, and I sit in the India paper drawing-room, so I have them or not just as I like'.[84] But revealingly, in an (unfortunately) undated letter from Castletown, Lady Louisa observed, 'As to Servants, I think we treat them too much as if they were dependants, whereas I cannot think them so much so, for I am sure they give us a great deal more than we give them, and realy, if we consider it, 'tis no more than a contract we make with them.'[85] This opinion, undoubtedly shared by others, indicates a major shift in the way servants were considered. Their membership of a 'family' was beginning to be a thing of the past, their employment now on a business-like or 'contractual' basis.

Notes

Details of inventory locations do not appear in the notes but are supplied in the separate List of Inventories, which also includes several invoices and estimates that have been treated as inventories.

Introduction

1   Edward McParland, 'Eclecticism: The Provincial's Advantage', *Irish Arts Review Yearbook 1991–92* (1991), 210–13.

2   Toby Barnard, *Making the Grand Figure: Lives and Possessions in Ireland, 1641–1770* (New Haven and London, 2004), 22.

3   Finola O'Kane, 'Leamaneh and Dromoland: The O'Brien Ambition, Part I', *Irish Architectural & Decorative Studies*, 7 (2004), 64–79.

4   David Dickson, *Old World Colony: Cork and South Munster 1630–1830* (Cork, 2005), 97.

5   Terence Dooley, *The Decline of the Big House in Ireland: A Study of Irish Landed Families 1860–1960* (Dublin, 2001), 28, 29.

6   Mark Bence-Jones, *A Guide to Irish Country Houses* (rev. edn, London, 1988), xiii.

7   John Bateman, *The Great Landowners of Great Britain and Ireland* (4th edn, London, 1883); U.H. Hussey de Burgh, The Landowners of Ireland (Dublin, 1878).

8   Patricia McCarthy, 'From Parlours to Pantries: Inventories and the Eighteenth-century Dublin Interior', in Christine Casey (ed.), *The Eighteenth-century Dublin Town House* (Dublin, 2010), 110–19.

9   While it is important to note that the destruction of the Public Record Office in Dublin in 1922, together with most of the records that had been held there, has significantly affected the accessibility of primary sources for historians, it does not appear that a great deal of material relevant to this study – for example, on family histories and their estates – was lodged there at the time. This is evident from a book published in 1919, *A Guide to the Records Deposited in the Public Record Office of Ireland*, compiled by Herbert Wood, Assistant Deputy Keeper of the Public Records Office.

1   Approaching and Arriving

1   Finola O'Kane, *Landscape Design in Eighteenth-century Ireland* (Cork, 2004), 1.

2   R.F. Foster, 'Ascendancy and Union', in R.F. Foster (ed.), *The Oxford Illustrated History of Ireland* (Oxford, 1989), 172.

3   Quoted in James Howley, *The Follies and Garden Buildings of Ireland* (New Haven and London, 1993), 70.

4   Letter from Robert Molesworth to his wife dated 13 October 1716, quoted in O'Kane, *Landscape Design*, 12. The fact that he was granted the title 'Viscount Molesworth of Swords' in the same year is perhaps significant.

5   Trinity College Dublin (TCD), MS 4030, Daniel Augustus Beaufort, 'Journal of a Tour 3 July–17 September 1788', ff. 87–8. On a return visit to Castle Martyr in 1806 Beaufort reiterated his dislike of the house and its 'tasteless imitation of Gothic' gateway: Representative Church Body Library, Dublin, MS 49/3–4, 'Beaufort's Journal of Irish Travels 1806', vol. 4, f. 73.

6   Irish Architectural Archive, Photograph collection, 'Emo Court: Design by James Gandon 1780, for entrance gates'; 'Carton: South Front and Plan for a Lodge and Entrance to the Cottage and Plantations at Waterstone'. Gandon's triumphal arched gateway to Carriglas, Co. Longford is also flanked by matching lodges: see Jane Fenlon, 'Portumna Restored', *Irish Arts Review*, Autumn 2003, 110–17; Anne Crookshank and the Knight of Glin, *Ireland's Painters 1600–1940* (New Haven and London, 2002), 168, pl. 213. Maurice Craig, *Classic Irish Houses of the Middle Size* (London, 1976), 28, mentions 'ink-pot' wings at Belline, one of which 'was designed as a dovecote'. See also J.A.K. Dean, *The Gate Lodges of Ulster* (Belfast, 1994), 62, 65.

7   TCD, MS 4028, D.A. Beaufort, 'Journal of a Tour Through Part of Ireland Begun August 26, 1787', f. 30; Howley, *The Follies*, plates 108, 125, 146; TCD, MS 4034, Louisa Beaufort, 'Journal of a Tour to the North, 1807', f. 23. This must have been the Bishop's Gate and lodge.

8   My thanks to Professor Rolf Loeber for this information.

9   Finola O'Kane, 'Leamaneh and Dromoland: The O'Brien Ambition, Part II', *Irish Architectural and Decorative Studies*, 7 (2004), 88–105.

10   Fenlon, 'Portumna Restored', 110–17.

11   O'Kane, *Landscape Design*, 10, 12, fig. 5.

12   Ibid., 101.

13   That at Castletown can be seen on maps by Noble & Keenan of 1752 and John Rocque of 1760; Carton's axial avenue can be seen in William van der Hagen's *A View of Carton House*, c.1738; it took 1,100 sheep to crop the lawns at Carton, according to Arthur Young, *A Tour in Ireland with General Observations on the Present State of That Kingdom Made in the Years 1776, 1777 and 1778*, 2 vols (Dublin, 1780), I, 32.

14   Canon C.C. Ellison, 'Remembering Dr. Beaufort', *Quarterly Bulletin of the Irish Georgian Society*, 18, no. 1 (January–March 1975), 1–36.

15   James Kelly (ed.), *The Letters of Lord Chief Baron Edward Willes to the Earl of Warwick 1757–62* (Aberystwyth, 1990), 101; John Barrow, *A Tour around Ireland, through the Sea-Coast Counties, in the Autumn of 1835* (London, 1836), 217; J.S. Dodd, *The Traveller's Director through Ireland* (Dublin, 1801), 51.

16   'Two Tours in Ireland, in the Years 1792 and 1793 . . . By George Hardinge, Esq MA. FRS FSA. Chief Justice of the Counties of Brecon Glamorgan and Radnor'. Original in the possession of the Shirley family of Lough Fea. Notes kindly supplied by Edward McParland.

17   Young, *Tour in Ireland*, 70.

18   Chevalier de Latocnaye (trans. J. Stevenson), *A Frenchman's Walk Through Ireland, 1796–7* (facsimile edn, Belfast, 1984), 79. Representative Church Body Library, Dublin, MS 49/3–4, 'Beaufort's Journal of Irish Travels, 1806', Part III, eastern Munster Circuit, f. 73.

19   TCD, MS 4035, Mary Beaufort, 'A Journal of Our Tour to the Westward to Inspect the Charter Schools 1808', ff. 113–17; TCD, MS 4034, Louisa Beaufort, 'Journal of a Tour to the North', f. 4.

20   Frances Power Cobbe, *Life of Frances Power Cobbe. By Herself*, 2 vols (Cambridge, 1894), I, 6.

21   Maurice Craig and the Knight of Glin, *Ireland Observed* (Cork, 1970), 37.

22   TCD, MS 4024, D.A. Beaufort, 'Tour of England and Wales (via Waterford), 9–30 August 1779', f. 46.

23   Mark Bence-Jones, *A Guide to Irish Country Houses* (rev. edn, London, 1988), 97.

24   Formerly Mrs Pendarves, she later married the Dean of Down, Patrick Delany DD.

25   Angélique Day (ed.), *Letters from Georgian Ireland: The Correspondence of Mary Delany, 1731–1768* (Belfast, 1991), 158.

26   Craig, *Classic Irish Houses*, 23.

27   Bence-Jones, *Guide to Irish Country Houses*, xiii.

28   Niall McCullough and Valerie Mulvin, *A Lost Tradition: The Nature of Architecture in Ireland* (Dublin, 1987), 61.

29   Bence-Jones, *Guide to Irish Country Houses*, xix.

30   Alistair Rowan, *The Buildings of Ireland: North-West Ulster* (Harmondsworth, 1979), 334.

31   TCD, MS 4033, D.A. Beaufort, 'Tour of North of Ireland 9 October–18 November 1807', f. 11; TCD, MS 4034, Louisa Beaufort, 'Journal of a Tour to the North', f. 9.

32   Edward McParland, 'Lissadell, Co. Sligo', *Country Life*, 6 October 1977, 914–17.

33   Henry Heaney (ed.), *A Scottish Whig in Ireland 1835–38: The Irish Journals of Robert Graham of Redgorton* (Dublin, 1999), 282.

34   Trinity College Irish Art Research Centre, TRIARC/1/22, Rolf Loeber and Magda Stouthamer-Loeber (eds), 'An Unknown Account of Georgian Architecture and the Arts in Dublin and its Vicinity in 1797', 47.

35   Constantia Maxwell, *The Stranger in Ireland from the Reign of Elizabeth to the Great Famine* (Dublin, 1979; first published 1954), 190. Umbrellas have a long history as parasols, sheltering women from the sun. An umbrella hoop is mentioned in the Killadoon inventory of 1829, where it is located in the hall.

36   John Cornforth, *Early Georgian Interiors* (New Haven and London, 2004), 19.

37   Howard Colvin and John Newman (eds), *Of Building: Roger North's Writings on Architecture* (Oxford, 1981), 127–8.

38   Isaac Ware encouraged his English readers to follow this example, as quoted in Craig, *Classic Irish Houses*, 27; Giles Worsley has pointed out that most iconic Palladian houses in England, such as Wanstead in Essex, appeared isolated in the landscape, with stables placed to one side. Giles Worsley, *The British Stable* (New Haven and London, 2004), 131–2.

39   Christopher Hussey, 'Castletown II', *Country Life*, 22 August 1936, 196–201.

40   TCD, MS 4028, D.A. Beaufort, 'Journal of a Tour . . . 1787', f. 33.

41   Palladio placed similar doorways at the same place at the Villa Piovene (1539–40) and the Villa Malcontenta (1559–60).

42   Isaac Ware, *A Complete Body of Architecture* (London, 1756), 322.

43   Craig, *Classic Irish Houses*, 19–20.

44   Heaney, *A Scottish Whig*, 290.

45   David J. Griffin, 'Richard Castle's Designs for Castle Coole, Co Fermanagh', in Terence Reeves-Smyth and Richard D. Oram (eds), *Avenues to the Past: Essays Presented to Sir Charles Brett on His 75th Year* (Belfast, 2003), 135–42.

46   Lord Walter FitzGerald, 'Carton', in *Journal of the County Kildare Archaeological Society*, no. 4 (1903–5), 3–34, illustration of 'The Proposed Restoration of the House at Carton by James, 20th Earl of Kildare in 1762'. The marquis of Kildare was created first duke of Leinster four years later, in 1766.

47   Constantia Maxwell, *Country and Town in Ireland under the Georges* (rev. edn, Dundalk, 1949), 59–60.

48   Day, *Letters from Georgian Ireland*, 203.

49   Lord Ernest Hamilton, *Old Days and New* (London, 1923), 35. No date is given for this event but it would appear to have occurred in the early decades of the nineteenth century.

50   Though he was an absentee, Abercorn's correspondence in the Public Record Office of Northern Ireland reveals him to have been a well-informed landlord with, as Anthony Malcolmson writes in his abstract of the Abercorn Papers, 'a sympathetic, practical

and flexible approach to the problem of estate management'.

51 John H. Gebbie (ed.), *An Introduction to the Abercorn Letters (as Relating to Ireland, 1736–1816)* (Omagh, 1972), 260, letter from eighth earl of Abercorn to his agent, 20 September 1745; 262, letter from earl to agent, 13 February 1945/6; 16, letters from agent to earl, 22 March 1845/6 and 12 May 1746; 263, letter from earl to agent, 1 April 1746; 16, letters from agent in Dublin to earl, 22 March 1745/6 and 12 May 1746; 269, letter from earl to agent, 22 April 1749; 379, letter from agent to earl, 26 April 1807.

52 John Andrews, Lord Londonderry's agent, assured his employer that 'there can be no doubt of the apartments destined for her Ladyship being perfectly dry, warm, and healthful' for the forthcoming arrival of both to Mount Stewart, then building in 1847, and that fires would have been burning for some time to ensure their comfort. Anne Casement, 'William Vitruvius Morrison's Scheme for Mount Stewart, Co. Down: Was It Ever Realised?', *Irish Architectural and Decorative Studies*, 7 (2004), 32–63.

53 Edward McParland, *Public Architecture in Ireland* (New Haven and London, 2001), 109–10.

54 Leinster House was built as Kildare House from 1745 by James FitzGerald (1722–73), 20th earl of Kildare to designs by Richard Castle; it was renamed Leinster House in 1766, when FitzGerald was created duke of Leinster. The term 'Leinster House' is used throughout this book.

55 Brian FitzGerald, *Correspondence of Emily, Duchess of Leinster 1731–1814*, 3 vols (Dublin, 1949–67), I, 234.

56 Memoir of Lady Isabella FitzGerald, wife of Vicomte Rohan Chabot, daughter of the 2nd duke of Leinster. My thanks to the Knight of Glin for notes on this.

57 Marie-Louise Legg (ed.), *The Synge Letters: Bishop Edward Synge to His Daughter Alicia Roscommon to Dublin 1746–1752* (Dublin, 1996), 248, Letter 117, 11 September 1750; 173, Letter 80, 29 September 1749; 265, Letter 128, 20 October 1750; 173, Letter 81, 3 October 1749; 92, Letter 43, 30 September 1747.

58 Maurice Craig, *The Architecture of Ireland: From the Earliest Times to 1880* (rev. edn, Dublin, 1997) 186n, 245.

59 Among other underground service tunnels in Ireland were those at Lucan House, Co. Dublin, Florence Court, Co. Fermanagh, Lissadell, Co. Sligo, Drumcree House, Co. Westmeath and Killua Castle, Co. Westmeath.

60 P. Somerville-Large, *The Irish Country House: A Social History* (London, 1995), 198.

61 Heaney, *A Scottish Whig*, 284.

62 Valerie Pakenham, *The Big House in Ireland* (London, 2000), 107.

63 Maria Edgeworth, *Ormond* (reprint of 1st edn, London, 1972), 388.

64 William Butler Yeats, 'In Memory of Eva Gore-Booth and Constance Markiewicz' (1933), in W.B. Yeats, *The Winding Stair and Other Poems* (London, 1933), 1.

65 It became quite common for soldiers in garrisons around the country to put on plays for their own amusement, as well as in local hospitals and in theatres, where they would perform in aid of a charity.

66 'T.U.S.' (T. U. Sadleir), 'Letter from Edward, 2nd Earl of Aldborough, to His Agent at Belan', *Journal of the Kildare Archaeological Society*, 7 (1912–14), 333–4.

67 David Large, 'The Wealth of the Greater Irish Landowners, 1750–1815', *Irish Historical Studies*, 15 (1966–7), 21–47.

68 Quoted in Lena Boylan, 'The Conollys of Castletown: A Family History', *Quarterly Bulletin of the Irish Georgian Society*, 11, no. 4 (October–December 1968), 1–46.

69 Brian FitzGerald, *Lady Louisa Conolly, 1743–1821* (London, 1950), 21–2.

70 Day, *Letters from Georgian Ireland*, 38–42, 51.

71 Joseph Robins, *Champagne and Silver Buckles: The Viceregal Court at Dublin Castle 1700–1922* (Dublin, 2001), 73.

72 *Ibid.*, 74.

73 University of Limerick, Dunraven Papers, MS D/3196/D/3/64, newspaper account from the *General Advertiser*, 10 October 1809.

74 R. Warwick Bond, *The Marlay Letters 1780–1820* (London, 1937), 128–9, letter from the countess of Charleville to her son, J.T.T. Tisdall, 7 October [1809].

75 Gervase Jackson-Stops, 'Temples of the Arts', in Gervase Jackson-Stops (ed.), *The Treasure Houses of Britain: Five Hundred Years of Private Patronage and Art Collecting* (New Haven and London, 1985), 14–21.

76 John Harris, 'English Country House Guides, 1740–1840', in John Summerson (ed.), *Concerning Architecture: Essays on Architectural Writers and Writing Presented to Nikolaus Pevsner* (London, 1968), 58–74.

77 *Ibid.*

78 Toby Barnard, *Making the Grand Figure: Lives and Possessions in Ireland, 1641–1770* (New Haven and London, 2004), 203.

79 Jackson-Stops, ' Temples of the Arts'.

80 D.M. Beaumont, 'An Irish Gentleman in England: The Travels of Pole Cosby c.1730–35', *Journal of the British Archaeological Association*, 149 (1996), 37–54. How detailed this guide was is unknown, but it is not mentioned among the early guides listed in Harris, 'English Country House Guides'.

81 Jackson-Stops, 'Temples of the Arts'.

82 FitzGerald, *Correspondence of Emily, Duchess of Leinster*, I, 59.

83 *Dublin Journal*, 17 August 1725.

84 Maxwell, *Stranger in Ireland*, 133.

85 John Loveday, *Diary of a Tour in 1732* (Edinburgh, 1890); George T. Stokes (ed.), *Pococke's Tour in Ireland in 1752* (Dublin, 1891); Kelly, *Letters of Edward Willes*; Richard Twiss, *A Tour in Ireland in 1775* (London, 1776).

86 Young, *Tour in Ireland*.

87 Quoted in Crookshank and Glin, *Ireland's Painters*, 52.

88 Heaney, *A Scottish Whig*, 37–8.

89 Crookshank and Glin, *Ireland's Painters*, 51.

90 Barrow, *Tour around Ireland*, 363.

91 Rolf Loeber and Magda Stouthamer-Loeber, 'Dublin and its Vicinity in 1797', *Irish Geography*, 35 (2002), 133–55; Judith Flannery, *Christ Church Delgany 1789–1990: Between the Mountains and the Sea: A Parish History* (Delgany, 1990), 62.

92 National Library of Ireland, Domville Papers, MS 9391.

93 Flannery, *Christ Church Delgany*, 51.

94 Heaney, *A Scottish Whig*, 51.

95 Alnwick Archives, Duke of Northumberland MS 670, 'Rules for the Government of the Marquis of Kildare's (Duke of Leinster's) Household 1763–1773', f. 83.

96 Loeber and Stouthamer-Loeber, 'Unknown Account of Georgian Architecture'.

97 Anthony Trollope, *The Kellys and the O'Kellys* (Oxford, 1978; first published 1848), 133.

98 TCD, MS 4030, D.A. Beaufort, 'Journal of a Tour . . . 1788', ff. 13v, 14.

99 Edward, Viscount Kingsborough, was the eldest son of the 3rd earl of Kingston and predeceased his father. He was an antiquarian and the author of *Antiquities of Mexico* (London, 1830–1, 1848).

100 Heaney, *A Scottish Whig*, 107, 46.

101 TCD, MS 4035, Mary Beaufort, 'A Journal of Our Tour', f. 118.

102 Quoted in Jackson-Stops, 'Temples of the Arts'.

103 John McVeagh (ed.), *Richard Pococke's Irish Tours* (Dublin, 1995), 101–2; Charles Topham Bowden, *A Tour Through Ireland* (Dublin, 1791), 70.

104 McVeagh, *Richard Pococke's Irish Tours*, 73; TCD, MS 4033, D.A. Beaufort, 'Tour of North of Ireland', f. 11.

105 Quoted in McParland, *Public Architecture in Ireland*, 19.

2 *Crossing the Threshold*

1 Quoted in Edward McParland, 'Lissadell, Co. Sligo', *Country Life*, 6 October 1977, 914–17.

Interestingly, a visitor to Lissadell in 1836 was critical of Goodwin's plan: after the grandeur of the 'splendid music gallery . . . the effect here is to kill the series of living rooms to which leads, an ante-room, the drawing room, a middle room, and a dining room, which are all nothing more than good, lodgeable and moderately sized apartments'. Henry Heaney (ed.), *A Scottish Whig in Ireland 1835–38: The Irish Journals of Robert Graham of Redgorton* (Dublin, 1999), 281.

2 Toby Barnard, *Making the Grand Figure: Lives and Possessions in Ireland, 1641–1770* (New Haven and London, 2004), 22, 23. Madden was a writer and one of the founders of the Dublin Society, later the Royal Dublin Society.

3 National Archives of Ireland (NAI), M.2533, W. Henry, 'Hints Towards a National, Typographical [*sic*] History of Counties Sligo, Donegal, Fermanagh and Lough Erne'. Hazelwood was built in 1731 to designs by Richard Castle for Owen Wynne, MP for Co. Sligo.

4 Trinity College Dublin (TCD), MS 4036, Mary Beaufort, 'Tour from Upton to Killarney and Limerick, on to Dublin, 1810', f. 17. This eighteenth-century house, demolished in the late 1830s, was located 500 metres north of the present Muckross House, designed by the Edinburgh architect William Burn and built 1839–43.

5 TCD, MS 4035, Mary Beaufort, 'A Journal of Our Tour to the Westward to Inspect the Charter Schools 1808', f. 113.

6 The east pavilion was where the family schoolroom was located. Hamwood was built in 1775. The nineteenth-century chatelaine, Caroline Hamilton, explained: 'It was then in such a bleak, cold situation that the corridors were built to put the hall door at a distance from the sitting rooms.' Jeremy Musson, 'Hamwood, Co Meath', *Country Life*, 23 February 2006, 70–5.

7 James Lewis, *Original Designs in Architecture Consisting of Plans, Elevations and Sections for Villas, Mansions, Town-houses etc. and a New Design for a Theatre* (London, 1797), Book II, plates xxix and xxx, 'Plans for Coole House in the Co. of Galway, seat of Robt. Gregory esq.'. This is annotated 'the hall is one and a half storeys high with half columns and four niches'.

8 Other elliptical halls are at Bear Forest, Co. Cork and Kilpeacon, Co. Limerick.

9 TCD, MS 4034, Louisa Beaufort, 'Journal of a Tour to the North, 1807', f. 10.

10 Walpole coined the word 'gloomth' in 1753 in a letter describing his house, Strawberry Hill, 'with all its painted glass and gloomth' (*Oxford English Dictionary* (*OED*)). The edition of the *OED* used throughout this book is the compact second edition in two volumes (Oxford, 1971).

11 'Living room' is an unusual room name at this date (1822) and does not appear on any other of the plans under discussion. It is also interesting to note here the variety and the ambiguity in room names.

12 A fire in 1974 destroyed the interior of the house, leaving it a roofless shell. It was rebuilt as a retail venue and opened in 1996.

13 The saloon was on the first floor, above the hall, together with the main reception rooms.

14 William Chambers, *A Treatise on Civil Architecture* (London, 1759), 82.

15 Isaac Ware, *A Complete Body of Architecture* (London, 1756), 335–6.

16 Christopher Hussey, *Early Georgian 1715–1760* (2nd edn, London, 1965), 17.

17 See discussion on dating for Beaulieu in Christine Casey and Alistair Rowan, *The Buildings of Ireland: North Leinster* (Harmondsworth, 1993), 154–6.

18 In a letter to the English poet William Shenstone in 1748, Lady Luxborough tells him that, when her brother decorated his villa near Uxbridge, 'which he chose to call a Farm', he had 'all the implements of husbandry placed in the manner one sees or might see arms and trophies in some General's hall; and it had an effect that pleased every body', Henrietta Knight, Baroness Luxborough, *Letters Written by the Late Right Honourable Lady Luxborough to William Shenstone, Esq.* (Dublin, 1776), letter ix from Barrells, 28 April 1748; Edward McParland, *Public Architecture in Ireland* (New Haven and London, 2001), 54–6.

19 Having the main staircase leading to the first floor only is common practice.

20 John Cornforth, *Early Georgian Interiors* (New Haven and London, 2004), 30.

21 The staircase at Castletown was admired by C.R. Cockerell (1788–1863), who cited 'the geometrical steps the boldest, lightest and best I believe to have seen. The brass balustrade completes the whole giving an effect of elegance quite new to me.' Brass banisters can be seen on the Townley Hall staircase by Francis Johnston (from 1794). They became popular in Ireland in the early nineteenth century through Richard Morrison, and Cockerell used them in England and at Kinturk, Castlepollard, Co. Meath. John Harris, 'C. R. Cockerell's *Ichnographica Domestica*', *Architectural History*, 14 (1971), 5–29.

22 Mark Bence-Jones, *A Guide to Irish Country Houses* (rev. edn, London, 1988), 255.

23 It is difficult to know from the drawing whether, like Beaulieu, the upper level has windows within the arches, or if these were the windows behind the staircase itself.

24 The staircase hall in the Old Library at Trinity College is also rusticated. Although built by

Burgh, both it and the hall were finished by Richard Castle. Also at Trinity College, the hall, inner hall and staircase hall of the Provost's House (1759) are rusticated, as are the staircase halls of Lord Powerscourt's houses in Wicklow and Dublin.

25 Bence-Jones, *Guide to Irish Country Houses*, 18, 107; Irish Architectural Archive (IAA), McParland Notebooks, 1.52.

26 Others were Carton (1762), Headfort (1765), Lucan, Mount Kennedy, Castle Coole (1789 and 1790), Carriglas, Ballycurry and Castle Dillon. The word 'saloon' (or 'sallon' or 'salon') was in use from about 1715, according to the *OED*. Castletown's plan is not annotated; no plan for Beaulieu has yet to come to light.

27 Headfort, seat of Sir Thomas Taylour, later 1st earl of Bective, was built to designs by George Semple. Plans for the building were made by Richard Castle, John Ensor and Sir William Chambers, all of which were unexecuted.

28 TCD, MS 4034, Louisa Beaufort, 'Journal of Charter School Tour 1808', f. 75; TCD, MS 4033, D.A. Beaufort, 'Observations in the Course of Visiting Charter Schools 1808', f. 88.

29 Ware recommended that the staircase 'should present itself immediately beyond the hall'. Ware, *Complete Body of Architecture*, 325.

30 John O'Connell and Rolf Loeber, 'Eyrecourt Castle, Co. Galway', *Irish Arts Review Yearbook*, 1988, 40–8. The stairs eventually found its way to the Detroit Institute of Art, where it now languishes.

31 Richard Morrison, *Useful and Ornamental Designs in Architecture* (Dublin, 1793), nos. 9 and 10.

32 Heaney, *A Scottish Whig*, 281.

33 *Ibid.*, 284. The progression of spaces at Rockingham is similar to that at Ballyfin, mentioned earlier.

34 IAA, McParland Notebooks, 1.4, 4.4, 3.5.

35 Ann Martha Rowan (ed.), *The Architecture of Richard Morrison and William Vitruvius Morrison* (Dublin, 1989), 93, 127.

36 The word 'corridor' was sufficiently novel in 1716 for Vanbrugh to explain its meaning in a letter to the duchess of Marlborough: ' The word Corridore Madam is foreign, and signifys in plain English, no more than a Passage, it is now however generally us'd as an English word.' Charles Saumarez Smith, *The Building of Castle Howard* (London, 1997), 54.

37 This refers back to Roger Pratt's double-pile Coleshill of the 1660s, where the house is divided on its long axis by a spinal wall or corridor, and the central element of the plan, the hall and saloon, are next to each other on the short axis, flanked by the staircases. Hussey, *Early Georgian*, 14.

38   The earliest mention of a vestibule among the inventories in this survey is in the 1783 estimate for Caledon (*see* List of Inventories) possibly from Mayhew & Ince, who subsequently invoiced James Alexander for furniture in 1785. The hall at Ardbraccan is annotated 'Vestibule' in a plan dating to *c*.1776. The earliest lobbies are listed among the Ormonde inventories at Clonmel (1685), Dublin Castle (1678) and Kilkenny Castle (1684), in Jane Fenlon, *Goods and Chattels: A Survey of Early Household Inventories in Ireland* (Kilkenny, 2003), 85, 102, 104; and, among the plans, on Richard Castle's for Carton, *c*.1739: Howard Colvin and John Newman (eds), *Of Building: Roger North's Writings on Architecture* (Oxford, 1981), 126.

39   Castletown, Russborough, Co. Wicklow, Seafield and Newbridge in Co. Dublin, Powerscourt, Dublin and Sir William Chambers's plan for Headfort. Seafield has the benefit of a portico in antis, which might have helped.

40   It is possible that the hall to the rear of the house referred to here might have been intended to be a saloon. John Aheron, in a builders' dictionary appended to his treatise on architecture defines a saloon as 'a Kind of Hall in the Middle of a House, or . . . a large Apartment, which ought to have a Symmetry on all sides'. *A General Treatise of Architecture in Five Books . . . By John Aheron, Architect* (Dublin 1754), Book iii, 'Builder's Dictionary' (unpaginated).

41   Colvin and Newman, *Of Building*, 129.

42   IAA, Murray Collection of drawings, Killeen Castle.

43   Aheron, *General Treatise of Architecture*, 'Builder's Dictionary'.

44   Morrison, *Useful and Ornamental Designs*, nos. 5–8.

45   NLI, Mahon of Castlegar Papers, MS 24,593.

46   IAA, Townley Hall Drawings Collection, 85/156.1. The drawing may be by Anne Maria Balfour, sister of the owner of the Hall, Blayney Townley Balfour.

47   It will be seen that the lobby is not confined to country houses. John Cornforth, 'Castle Coole, Co. Fermanagh', *Country Life*, 17 December 1992, 28–31; John Cornforth, 'Mount Kennedy – II', *Country Life*, 11 November 1965, 1256–9.

48   Heaney, *A Scottish Whig*, 290.

49   Henry, 'Hints Towards a National, Typographical History'.

50   Rowan, *Architecture of Richard Morrison*, 131.

51   Quoted in Maurice Craig, *Classic Irish Houses of the Middle Size* (London, 1976), 41.

52   Ware, *Complete Body of Architecture*, 335.

53   *The Diary of Anne, Countess Dowager of Roden from 6 August 1797 to 11 April 1802* (Dublin, 1870).

54   Dorothea's mother was the youngest daughter of the first Lord Desart. *Retrospections of Dorothea Herbert 1770–1806* (rev. edn, Dublin, 2004), 23.

55   Angélique Day (ed.), *Letters from Georgian Ireland: The Correspondence of Mary Delany, 1731–1768* (Belfast, 1991), 122, quoted in Cornforth, *Early Georgian Interiors*, 38.

56   Day, *Letters from Georgian Ireland*, 142.

57   K. Mullaney-Dignam, 'Music, Dancing and Social Life at Glin Castle', *Irish Architectural and Decorative Studies*, 14 (2011), 17–37.

58   George Mott, 'Eating and Drinking Habits in Ireland Two Hundred Years Ago', *Irish Ancestor*, 5, no. 1 (1973), 7–11.

59   Conversation with John Cornforth, October 2001; Cornforth, *Early Georgian Interiors*, 37–8.

60   Stephen R. Penny, *Smythe of Barbavilla: The History of an Anglo-Irish Family* (privately published, 1974), 40. My thanks to Kevin Mulligan for this.

61   My thanks to Alec and Hugh Cobbe for a print-out of the Newbridge inventory.

62   Edward MacLysaght, *Irish Life in the Seventeenth Century* (Dublin, 1979), 111n, quotes the following example: 'you shall not find a house of any account without one or two . . . [harps] and they always keep a harper to play for them at their meals'.

63   My thanks to the Knight of Glin for a photocopy of this.

64   Lady Morgan (Sydney Owenson), *The Wild Irish Girl: A National Tale*, ed. C. Connolly and S. Copley (London, 2000), 189–90.

65   Day, *Letters from Georgian Ireland*, 259.

66   F. Elrington Ball, *Howth and Its Owners* (Dublin, 1917), 16.

67   The *OED* defines a canterbury in the sense of furniture as 'a stand with light partitions to hold music-portfolios and the like', so it can probably be assumed that a 'dinner canterbury' was such a piece adapted to the requirements of dining.

68   For the scagliola table at Russborough, see http://russboroughhouse.ie/index.php/history/restoration-of-scagliola-table-at-russborough, accessed 12 November 2015.

69   *Dublin Evening Post*, 25 April 1835.

70   In Carton's fairly comprehensive inventory there is little listed under 'Inside Hall and Stairs', which is the only mention of a hall; the list of items under the heading 'Billiard Room' will therefore be used to describe this dual-purpose room.

71   Burton Hall's inventory of 1686 shows thirty-six 'cain bottom'd chairs' divided between the hall and the parlour. Cane-seated chairs became popular in England after the Restoration, being sought-after 'for their Durable, Lightness, and Cleanness from Dust, Worms and Moths

which inseparably attend Turkey-work, Serge and other stuff chairs and couches, to the spoiling of them and all furniture near them'. Rush-seated chairs (sometimes called 'Dutch chairs') were being made in Flanders from the beginning of the seventeenth century, and possibly in England by the end of the century. Peter Thornton, *Seventeenth-century Interior Decoration in England, France and Holland* (New Haven and London, 1983), 202, 206.

72   The four Howth Castle inventories date from 1746 to 1752. A compilation of these is to be found in Elrington Ball, *Howth and Its Owners*, 164–6.

73   See List of Inventories under Caledon House. Other correspondence indicates that this estimate was from the firm of Mayhew & Ince, London. Alexander was created Baron Caledon in 1790, Viscount in 1797 and 1st earl in 1800.

74   Wyatt also designed a set of four tripod atheniennes for this room, as well as dining room furniture. Illustrated in The Knight of Glin and James Peill, *Irish Furniture* (New Haven and London, 2007), 186–8.

75   See the List of Inventories for this invoice.

76   Ware, *Complete Body of Architecture*, 408.

77   Quoted in Linda Kelly, *Richard Brinsley Sheridan: A Life* (London, 1998), 178.

78   Often spelt 'forme', meaning a long seat without a back, according to the *OED*; Fenlon, *Goods and Chattels*, 85.

79   It is not clear whether these were chairs or benches.

80   This estimate is not dated, but was presumably sent in 1791 when M. Morgan of Henry Street supplied drawings of furniture arrangements for the oval room and the drawing room at Castlegar. MS notes from Mahon Family Papers concerning furnishings, seen and extracted by Edward McParland at Castlegar in 1973 now in the *IAA*. My thanks to him.

81   Historical Manuscripts Commission, Ormonde MSS NS 3, 16 February 1668/9, 441.

82   Ophelia Field, *The Favourite: Sarah, Duchess of Marlborough* (London, 2002), 301.

83   Craig, *Classic Irish Houses*, 36.

84   Quoted in P. Fagan, *The Second City: Portrait of Dublin 1700–1760* (Dublin, 1986), 96.

85   Quoted in Constantia Maxwell, *Country and Town in Ireland under the Georges* (rev. edn, Dundalk, 1949), 95.

86   Frances Power Cobbe, *Life of Frances Power Cobbe. By Herself*, 2 vols (3rd edn, London, 1894), I, 8.

87   Knight of Glin, 'Tarbert House, Co. Kerry', *Irish Arts Review*, Autumn 2006, 106–9. There are similar bayonet-holders over doors in the hall at Glin Castle.

88   Note that at Killeen Castle the hall is referred to as 'Lobby', a name that Francis Johnston uses

in this space in a plan of 1802/3 (IAA, Murray Collection).

89 James Lees-Milne, *Earls of Creation: Five Great Patrons of Eighteenth-century Art* (rev. edn, London, 1986), 71.

90 It is not clear from the manuscript if the latter locations were painted the same colour, but such a shade would have been suitable for those areas. NAI, Bolger MS IA 58 125. My thanks to Edward McParland for his transcript.

91 My thanks to Patrick Walsh for this information.

92 Jane Fawcett, 'Palaces, Public Buildings, Houses and Villas: Tile Mosaic, Stone and Marble Floors, Parquetry, Carpets and Painted Floors', in Jane Fawcett (ed.), *Historic Floors: Their History and Conservation* (Oxford, 1998), 129–63.

93 David Griffin and Caroline Pegum, *Leinster House, 1744–2000: An Architectural History* (Dublin, 2000), 27, plate 42.

94 NLI, Dept of Prints and Drawings, Mount Kennedy drawings, AD 3568(52m).

95 Desmond Guinness, 'Leixlip Castle, Co. Kildare', undated pamphlet, 4. It is likely that there were a number of painted floors, or borders of floors, in houses throughout the country during this period. Painted and stencilled floors were more popular in Scotland than in England but, while they were well documented from the seventeenth century on, few have survived. Fawcett, 'Palaces'; Glin, 'Tarbert House'.

96 Killadoon Papers. Draft by Anthony Malcomson of the papers in the NLI. My thanks to Edward McParland for a copy.

97 Kevin V Mulligan, *Ballyfin: The Restoration of an Irish House and Demesne* (Tralee, 2011), 97.

98 Richard Morrison was a subscriber to the Irish artist James Cavanah Murphy's book of engravings of Iberian antiquities, *Batalha* (1795), and used many of the designs from this and Murphy's *Arabian Antiquities of Spain* (1815) at Ballyfin. Mulligan, *Ballyfin*, 54, 109.

99 Ware, *Complete Body of Architecture*, 123. Information on stucco floors in Ireland has not as yet come to hand.

100 Peter Thornton, *Authentic Décor: The Domestic Interior, 1620–1920* (London, 1984), 99.

101 Fawcett, 'Palaces'.

102 C.C. Ellison, 'Remembering Dr. Beaufort', *Quarterly Bulletin of the Irish Georgian Society*, 18, no. 1 (January–March 1975), 1–36.

103 TCD, MS 4030, D.A. Beaufort, 'Journal of a Tour 3 July–17 September 1788', f. 2v.

104 Fawcett, 'Palaces'.

105 John Fowler and John Cornforth, *English Decoration in the Eighteenth Century* (London, 1974), 216.

106 NLI, Bellew of Mount Bellew Papers, MS 31,994(2), invoice to Boylan, 1810.

107 The Countess of Essex's seat in the chapel at Dublin Castle had 'fflowering [flooring] of cloath' (Glin and Peill, *Irish Furniture*, 25) and 'Persia carpetts' are mentioned in the Ormonde inventory of Dublin Castle (1678) as part of the furniture of the ducal couple's seats in the same chapel (Fenlon, *Goods and Chattels*, 103).

108 Ware, *Complete Body of Architecture*, 123.

109 Mahon Papers, seen at Castlegar in 1973 by Edward McParland.

110 See List of Inventories under Caledon House.

111 Mairead Dunlevy, 'Dublin in the Early Nineteenth Century: Domestic Evidence', in Raymond Gillespie and Brian P. Kennedy (eds), *Ireland: Art into History* (Dublin, 1994), 185–206.

112 The Killadoon inventories, with summary notes taken by Christopher Moore and Sally Clements, to whom I am grateful.

113 Mahon Papers, seen at Castlegar in 1973 by Edward McParland.

114 NLI, Doneraile Papers, MS 34,106(6).

115 Quoted in Glin and Peill, *Irish Furniture*, 62.

116 Patricia McCarthy, 'Decorative Painting 1600–1900', in Nicola Figgis (ed.), *Art and Architecture of Ireland, Volume II: Painting 1600–1900* (Dublin, London and New Haven, 2014), 67–71.

117 R. Armstrong, 'Mellifont Abbey', *Dublin Penny Journal*, vol. 1, no. 32 (2 February 1833).

3   Dining

1 John Cornforth, *Early Georgian Interiors* (New Haven and London, 2004), 38.

2 Isaac Ware uses the term 'waiting room' for the space to right or left of the hall that is usually referred to as a parlour. Isaac Ware, *A Complete Body of Architecture* (London, 1756), 408. This is in addition to 'common parlour' on plans.

3 James Macauley, *The Classical Country House in Scotland 1660–1800* (London, 1987), 80; Henry Grey Graham, *The Social Life of Scotland in the Eighteenth Century* (5th edn, London, 1969; first published 1899), 8. Macauley is of the opinion that, in William Adam's House of Dun, 'the day to day routine of living must have been in the linked parlour and family bedroom' (80).

4 Howard Colvin and John Newman (eds), *Of Building: Roger North's Writings on Architecture* (Oxford, 1981), 137–8.

5 A 1783 estimate for furniture at Caledon House from Mayhew & Ince (see the list of inventories) and an invoice from them to James Alexander Esq. in 1785, both refer to furniture for a 'Common Parlour'. It is not clear whether

Alexander used the term at Caledon or if it was assumed by the firm. Public Record Office of Northern Ireland (PRONI), Caledon Papers D/2433/A/2/3/9.

6 Bere, the steward at Carton, Co. Kildare, and the steward at Baronscourt, Co. Tyrone each had his own parlour. Stella Tillyard, *Aristocrats: Caroline, Emily, Louisa and Sarah Lennox, 1750–1832* (London, 1994), 213; John H. Gebbie (ed.), *An Introduction to the Abercorn Letters (as Relating to Ireland, 1736–1816)* (Omagh, 1972), 7.

7 'Autobiography of Pole Cosby, of Stradbally, Queen's Co., 1703–1737(?)', *Journal of the County Kildare Archaeological Society*, 5 (1906–8), 79–99.

8 Cornforth, *Early Georgian Interiors*, 40.

9 It should be noted that corner fireplaces in parlours appeared in Old Castle Coole (1709) in the Lesser Parlour (but not in the Grand Parlour) and at Dromoland (1730s) in the Parlour (but not the Great Parlour); illustrated in Toby Barnard, *Making the Grand Figure: Lives and Possessions in Ireland, 1641–1770* (New Haven and London, 2004), 67.

10 The three adjoining rooms to the north of the house, the Parlour, Dressing Room and Servants' Waiting Room (to the front of the house), had become the Supper Room by 1759.

11 Together with the two parlours already mentioned at Leinster House, there was a room called the Common Eating Room in the family quarters at the south end of the house.

12 It must be said that there were not many saloons on plans in the first half of the century.

13 Richard Morrison, *Useful and Ornamental Designs in Architecture* (Dublin, 1793), nos. 7–10.

14 Cornforth, *Early Georgian Interiors*, 40, 42.

15 Jane Austen, *Persuasion*, in *Jane Austen: The Complete Novels* (London, 1984), 948. As the reference was too early for Victorian clutter (*Persuasion* was published in 1817), Austen seems to be implying a casual approach to order in the house.

16 A 'spinett' is listed in St Sepulchre's, Dublin in the 'Little Parlour' in *c*.1730, and a piano in the 'Breakfast Parlour' at Clogrenane, Co. Carlow, *c*.1810.

17 The odours of food could lodge in wall hangings, tapestries and curtains. Cornforth, *Early Georgian Interiors*, 40.

18 Christopher Hussey, *Early Georgian 1715–1760* (2nd edn, London, 1965), 14.

19 Angélique Day (ed.), *Letters from Georgian Ireland: The Correspondence of Mary Delany, 1731–1768* (Belfast, 1991), 162.

20 Rush- and cane-bottomed chairs, sometimes with backs of the same material, became known as those most commonly used in

parlours, though in Ireland leather-covered chairs were also very popular.

21 Quoted in Valerie Pakenham, *The Big House in Ireland* (London, 2000), 46.

22 See the List of Inventories for this estimate.

23 Linda Kelly, *Richard Brinsley Sheridan: A Life* (London, 1998), 3.

24 'A Pilgrimage to Quilca'.

25 Other eighteenth-century breakfast parlours/rooms among the inventories include No. 10 Henrietta Street, Dublin (1772), Baronscourt (1782) and Gaulston, Co. Westmeath (1787).

26 Richard Castle died in 1751; John Ensor, who had worked with him, took over his practice.

27 Gervase Jackson-Stops, *The Country House in Perspective* (London, 1990), 115–16.

28 A passageway from the Dining Room leads to the kitchen wing.

29 There was an alternative route to the dining room here. Brook Lodge was built in 1776 to designs by William Leeson. He provided plans for its extension in 1786 that included 'a large room' (probably the dining room), with the breakfast room linking the 'large room' to the original house. Patricia McCarthy and Kevin V. Mulligan, 'Unfulfilled Mediocrity: The Hapless Career of Dominick Madden in the West of Ireland', *Irish Architectural and Decorative Studies*, 9 (2006), 98–149.

30 Other eighteenth-century plans with breakfast rooms include: Lucan House (1770s) by the stuccadore Michael Stapleton, who refers to what was the Common Parlour as the Breakfast Parlour; a villa among the Mount Kennedy drawings by Thomas Cooley (*c*.1781); and Johnston's and Wyatt's drawings for Castle Coole (1789 and 1790 respectively).

31 Irish Architectural Archive (IAA), Mitchell Crichton drawings, Townley Hall Collection, M2, 'unnamed, possibly Townley Hall or Rokeby', according to a note by Edward McParland on his sketch of the plan.

32 This unusual, ten-sided, spacious room has a doorway that leads directly into the elliptical bedroom, which is flanked by separate dressing rooms for the couple.

33 Illustrated in Patricia McCarthy and Kevin V. Mulligan, 'New Light on Ballyfin', *Irish Architectural and Decorative Studies*, 8 (2005), fig. 22.

34 Lady Morgan (Sydney Owenson), *O'Donnel*, 3 vols (London and New York, 1979; first published 1814), II, 231.

35 This is the earliest breakfast table mentioned in the inventories.

36 Indecipherable on the inventory: 'I . . . oven'.

37 Information from Peter Marson, with thanks.

38 And, later still, in the boudoir.

39 Peter Thornton, *Authentic Décor: The Domestic Interior, 1620–1920* (London, 1984), 51.

40 Nicholas Cooper, *Houses of the Gentry 1480–1680* (New Haven and London, 1999), 287.

41 The Knight of Glin and James Peill, *Irish Furniture* (New Haven and London, 2007), 15; Kilkenny Castle inventory of 1639, in Jane Fenlon, *Goods and Chattels: A Survey of Early Household Inventories in Ireland* (Kilkenny, 2003), 30, 32, 39. Other examples in Fenlon's book are on pp. 53 and 80, both part of the Ormonde inventories.

42 Gervase Jackson-Stops and J. Pipkin, *The English Country House: A Grand Tour* (London, 1984), 122; Cornforth, *Early Georgian Interiors*, 43.

43 *Dublin Intelligence*, 2 June 1711.

44 Quoted in Rosemary Baird, *Mistress of the House: Great Ladies and Grand Houses 1670–1830* (London, 2003), 57, where it is noted as describing Delville in 1746.

45 Mark Girouard, *Life in the English Country House* (New Haven and London, 1978), 203; Ware, *Complete Body of Architecture*, 416.

46 In a survey of 500 Paris inventories for the second half of the eighteenth century it was found that only 14 per cent of houses had dining rooms; and even up to 1770 they were encountered only among society's elite. Annik Pardailhe-Galabrun, *The Birth of Intimacy: Privacy and Domestic Life in Early Modern Paris*, trans. Jocelyn Phelps (Oxford, 1991), 61.

47 Robert Oresko (ed.), *The Works in Architecture of Robert and James Adam* (London, 1975), 48.

48 Thornton, *Authentic Décor*, 57. Numerous gilt leather hangings are to be found in the Ormonde Inventories in Fenlon, *Goods and Chattels*.

49 Quoted in Jane Fenlon, 'The Ormonde Inventories 1675–1717: A State Apartment at Kilkenny Castle', in Agnes Bernelle (ed.), *Decantations: A Tribute to Maurice Craig* (Dublin, 1992), 29–37.

50 Letter to the author, 16 October 2002.

51 Cornforth, *Early Georgian Interiors*, 39–41.

52 Quoted in Glin and Peill, *Irish Furniture*, 61.

53 Quoted in Constantia Maxwell, *The Stranger in Ireland from the Reign of Elizabeth to the Great Famine* (Dublin, 1979; first published 1954), 150–1.

54 John McVeagh (ed.), *Richard Pococke's Irish Tours* (Dublin, 1995), 168.

55 'A Pilgrimage to Quilca in the Year 1852 in a Letter to Anthony Poplar Esq.', *Dublin University Magazine*, 40, no. 239 (November 1852), 509–46.

56 Ware, *Complete Body of Architecture*, 433.

57 Macauley, *Classical Country House in Scotland*, 101.

58 RIA, Caldwell Collection, 12 R 41/160, letter from Thomas Percy, Bishop of Dromore, Dromore House, to Andrew Caldwell, 25 November 1793. My thanks to Jane Meredith.

59 Canon C.C. Ellison, 'Remembering Dr. Beaufort', *Quarterly Bulletin of the Irish Georgian Society*, 18, no. 1 (January–March 1975), 1–36. Other sizeable dining rooms were in Ballyfin and Adare Manor, both 40 × 24 feet, and Rockingham at 39 × 26 feet.

60 David J. Griffin, 'Castletown, Co Kildare: The Contribution of James, 1st Duke of Leinster', *Irish Architectural and Decorative Studies*, 1 (1998), 120–45.

61 Christopher Moore, 'Lady Louisa Conolly: Mistress of Castletown 1759–1821', in Jane Fenlon, Nicola Figgis and Catherine Marshall (eds), *New Perspectives: Studies in Art History* (Dublin, 1987), 123–41.

62 Of the ninety-six annotated ground-floor plans to hand, thirty-six dining rooms were located to the front of the house and fifty-five to the rear; of those to the front, twenty-two were to the right of the hall and fourteen to the left. Other dining rooms were between rooms to the side.

63 TCD, MS 4034, Louisa Beaufort, 'Journal of a Tour to the North, 1807', ff. 18–19. Mark Bence-Jones, *A Guide to Irish Country Houses* (rev. edn, London, 1988), 188, in his description of the house, calls the octagonal rooms a drawing room and a dining room.

64 Among these latter were the Grand Parlour at Old Castle Coole (1709), Lucan (1770s), Carriglas, Co. Longford (1790s), Ballycurry, Co. Wicklow (1807 and 1808) and the asymmetrical Castle Bernard, Co. Offaly, where there was a convoluted route across the vestibule.

65 Thornton, *Authentic Décor*, 94.

66 Frances Gerard, *Some Celebrated Irish Beauties of the Last Century* (London, 1895), Introduction, xvii, footnote.

67 Stephen R. Penny, *Smythe of Barbavilla: The History of an Anglo-Irish Family* (privately published, 1974), 40.

68 On none of the plans in this study is the saloon at Carton called a dining room; it apparently became one in the second half of the eighteenth century, until the Morrison alterations and additions in 1815.

69 The Lafranchinis were paid £501 in 1739 for this work. The drops were copied on the remaining walls in the later nineteenth century. Joseph McDonnell, *Irish Eighteenth-century Stuccowork and its European Sources* (Dublin, 1991), 18.

70 David Griffin and Caroline Pegum, *Leinster House, 1744–2000: An Architectural History* (Dublin, 2000), plates 61–2; 52–3, plate 92.

71 Similar examples are also to be found at No. 17 St Stephen's Green, Dublin.

72 June Eiffe, 'Lyons, Co. Kildare', *Quarterly Bulletin of the Irish Georgian Society*, 27 (1984), 1–37.

73 Christine Casey, 'Boiseries, Bankers and Bills: A Tale of Charlemont and Whaley', in Michael McCarthy (ed.), *Lord Charlemont and His Circle* (Dublin, 2001), 47–59.

74 Isaac Ware produced a design (not executed) in the French rococo style for Lady Kildare's dressing room in Leinster House *c.*1759. Griffin and Pegum, *Leinster House*, plate 108.

75 Maurice Craig, *Classic Irish Houses of the Middle Size* (London, 1976), 13–14. Christopher Wren visited Vaux-le-Vicomte in 1665, and Vanbrugh, with whom Craig associates the bow, may have seen it in the late seventeenth century. In 1699 William Talman made designs for Castle Howard that included a bow, dismissed by Vanbrugh later as no more than 'two or three little trifleing drawings as big as his hand' (quoted in Charles Saumarez Smith, *The Building of Castle Howard* (London, 1997), 34), and in the first years of the eighteenth century, Thomas Archer placed a bow on the north façade of Chatsworth. Pierre de la Ruffiniere du Prey, 'The *Bombé*-fronted Country House from Talman to Soane', in Gervase Jackson-Stops et al., *The Fashioning and the Functioning of the British Country House* (Hanover, NH and London, 1989), 29–49.

76 Of unknown nationality, Cramillion was brought to Ireland by Bartholomew Mosse in 1755 to decorate the chapel of the Lying-in Hospital (Rotunda) in Dublin.

77 Dawson Court was later replaced by a new house on a nearby site, built by John Dawson, 1st earl of Portarlington: known as Emo Court, it was designed by James Gandon in *c.*1790

78 Bowood Archives, extracts from the diary of Sophia, countess of Shelburne, vol. 5, 1769–70. My thanks to the Knight of Glin for a typescript of this.

79 Day, *Letters from Georgian Ireland*, 158.

80 Cornforth, *Early Georgian Interiors*, 44–5.

81 There is a similar screen in the dining room at The Hall, Mountcharles, Co. Donegal, which probably dates to about 1740. IAA, McParland Notebooks, 3.24.

82 Morrison, *Useful and Ornamental Designs*, nos. 7 and 8.

83 Ann Martha Rowan (ed.), *The Architecture of Richard Morrison and William Vitruvius Morrison* (Dublin, 1989), 92–7.

84 As noted in Chapter 1, Alicia resided in their Dublin house at Kevin Street with a governess/companion. Marie-Louise Legg (ed.), *The Synge Letters: Bishop Edward Synge to His Daughter Alicia Roscommon to Dublin 1746–1752* (Dublin, 1996), letter 80, 29 September 1749; letter 176, 15 October 1751.

85 Jackson-Stops and Pipkin, *English Country House*, 123; Legg, *Synge Letters*, letter 14. The Synges had a walled garden with at least one greenhouse at their house in Kevin Street. From the 1790s the silver epergne, holding fruit, sweetmeats and flowers, replaced the pyramid and its individual dishes, and was brought to the table. Sara Paston-Williams, *The Art of Dining: A History of Cooking and Eating* (London, 1993), 260–1.

86 According to the *OED*, 'beaufette' is a variation of 'buffet', commonly spelt 'beau-' in the eighteenth century ('the cause of which is not apparent'), and it is defined as 'a sideboard or side-table, often ornamental, for the disposition of china, plate etc'. The word 'dessert' has an interesting etymology, according to Girouard, that goes 'back to the mediaeval ceremony of the void'. It was 'a collation of sweet wine and spices . . . eaten standing while the table was being cleared or "voided" after a meal'. In the later seventeenth century, when the use of French words became fashionable, 'void' was replaced by 'dessert', a word with a similar meaning. Sometimes 'dessert', by then supplemented or replaced by fruit, would be served in a separate room or even in a garden building. Girouard, *Life in the English Country House*, 104–5.

87 In an inventory for what seems to be a town house in Cork, dating to 1763, a 'Buffett' and a 'China Buffet' are listed as spaces, apparently at ground-floor level (the front parlour is the formal dining space, the dining room being used as a dressing room). The value of the silver (and glass) listed in the Buffett is almost three times as much as the value of the furniture in the front parlour, the most expensively furnished room in the house. TCD, MS 2010–2015/395, 'Inventory, Laurence Delamain Late of the City of Corke, Gent Deceased, taken 20th January 1763'.

88 It is interesting that Belmore retained Johnston's name for this room, though he used Wyatt's plans for the house. Information from Peter Marson, with my thanks.

89 A 'Confectioner's Office' is similarly mentioned in an inventory of Dublin Castle in 1677. Fenlon, *Goods and Chattels*, 97.

90 Baird, *Mistress of the House*, 126, 129.

91 Quoted in *ibid.*, 128.

92 Quoted in Cornforth, *Early Georgian Interiors*, 120. Mrs Delany advised her sister about hanging wallpaper in 1750: 'the best way is to have it pasted on the bare wall: when lined with canvass it always shrinks from the edges'. Day, *Letters from Georgian Ireland*, 162. At Cavendish Row, Dublin, the colour scheme was also blue but, despite the room being called 'Dineing Room', the furniture indicates its use as a sitting/drawing room.

93 *Retrospections of Dorothea Herbert 1770–1806* (rev. edn, Dublin, 2004), 327.

94 In 2004, Headfort was selected by the World Monuments Fund for inclusion in its List of 100 Most Endangered Sites, owing to its Robert Adam interiors and the threat to these by water ingress. With funding from the WMF, the Headfort Trust, the Irish government and other bodies, a conservation programme was put in place under the direction of Richard Ireland that has revealed some unexpected decorative details.

95 Photocopy of 1782 inventory and other material transcribed by Gervase Jackson-Stops from the Abercorn Papers in PRONI, D/623. My thanks to Edward McParland.

96 PRONI, Caledon Papers, D/2433/A/2/4/1–19, 'Painting Executed for Lord Viscount Caledon at Caledon Hill Including the House, Offices & Garden by S. Stroker, August 1799'.

97 *Dublin Evening Post*, 25 April 1835. My thanks to Aidan O'Boyle for this reference.

98 Quoted in Eiffe, 'Lyons, Co. Kildare'.

99 To which must be added the green rooms at Carrick, Baronscourt and Caledon already mentioned.

100 Yellow was to be found in two dining rooms, while there was one room each of blue, drab, dove and grey.

101 Steven Parissien, *The Georgian House* (London, 1999), 43.

102 According to the *OED*, moreen or morine was 'a stout woollen or woollen and cotton material, either plain or watered'; Peter Thornton, *Seventeenth-century Interior Decoration in England, France and Holland* (New Haven and London, 1983), 112, describes caffoy or caffa as 'a woollen velvet fabric; according to the *OED*, calamanco was 'a woollen stuff of Flanders, glossy on the surface and woven with a satin twill and chequered in the warp, so that the checks are seen on one side only'.

103 NLI, De Vesci Papers MS 38,929/1, 31 October 1808. The price quoted was £85 6s. 3d.

104 There is mention of a bed in the Dining Room in the St Stephen's Green house of the Balfour family in March 1741/2. The room hung with tapestry, was probably used as a bedroom, as the Back Parlour was used as a formal dining room. Incidentally, at Killeen Castle as late as 1735/6 the only rooms not to contain a bed were the dining room, the kitchen and the Tea Room.

105 According to chair descriptions in inventories, out of a total of forty-six, forty were 'stuff'd' (including fourteen leather-covered chairs) and six were cane-bottomed.

106 NLI, Rockingham Papers, MS 8810(4) Part 8, August 1814; IAA, McParland Notebooks, 5.13.

107 PRONI, Caledon Papers D/2433/A/2/3/9.

108 Day, *Letters from Georgian Ireland*, 53.

109 Cornforth, *Early Georgian Interiors*, 49.

110 PRONI, Caledon Papers, D/2433/A/2/3/9. Also mentioned here are eight and a quarter yards of 'fine green Broad cloth for covers for dining tables'.

111 At Knapton, Co. Laois (1763) there were two dining tables in the Hall, none in the 'Big' Parlour; and at Gaulston, Co. Westmeath (1787) there were 3 mahogany oval tables in the Breakfast Parlour that may have been moved to the dining room when necessary. A note on Jackson-Stops's transcription of the Dining Room furniture in the Baronscourt inventory (1782) reads '(2 mahog. Dining tables & 2 mahog. Circular tables . . .kept in Hall outside)'.

112 Quoted in Paston-Williams, *The Art of Dining*, 247.

113 The inventory of Antrim House, Merrion Square, Dublin (dem.) was made after the death of the marchioness of Antrim in 1801. At that stage the house appears to have been divided between her two daughters, Anne Catherine, Countess of Antrim, who married Sir Henry Vane-Tempest, and Charlotte, who married Lord Mark Kerr.

114 F. Erlington Ball, *Howth and Its Owners* (Dublin, 1917), 133.

115 Benson Earle Hill, *Recollections of an Artillery Officer*, 2 vols (London, 1836), I, 110.

116 NLI, MS 741, Account returned by Sheriff of Co. Monaghan of sale at Dawson Grove, 1827.

117 Paston-Williams, *The Art of Dining*, 262.

118 Christopher Christie, *The British Country House in the Eighteenth Century* (Manchester, 2000), 257.

119 J.D. Herbert, *Irish Varieties for the Last Fifty Years* (London, 1836), 159.

120 It may also have been a cupboard, built-in or otherwise. In a Cork City inventory a 'Buffett' and a 'China Buffet' are mentioned, and they are both listed separately from the dining room or the front or back parlours. See above, n. 90.

121 Might these have been the '2 tables for holding plate covered with Crimson' in a later (c.1840) inventory added to the 1782 manuscript? In 1844 John Ynyr Burges mentioned a single sideboard: he remarked on Baronscourt's dining room where 'a colossal shield of arms enriched the wall where the mighty sideboard rested, glittering with plate'. PRONI, T/1282, 'Diaries of John Ynyr Burges', 4 vols, I, 95–6, 24 January 1844.

122 Letter from Robert Woodgate, Baronscourt to Marquis of Abercorn, London, 16 (6?) March 1793. Photocopy of abstract from PRONI, T.2541/IA1/19/24.

123 Peter Marson, *Belmore: The Lowry Corrys of Castle Coole 1646–1913* (Belfast, 2007), 74; Glin and Peill, *Irish Furniture*, 185–8 and fig. 253. Marson states that the joiners on-site at Castle Coole made a dining table, a sarcophagus, pedestals and pier tables for the dining room (73), while Glin and Peill note that four pier tables, a sarcophagus and the sideboard, complete with urns and pedestals, were made by John Stewart of Montgomery Street, Dublin. This does not preclude the possibility that Stewart or his workshop made the items on-site, as Stewart does not appear in any directory.

124 NLI, De Vesci Papers, MS 38,929/1, Invoice from Tatham & Bailey, upholsterers, dated October 1809; Edward McParland, MS notes from Mahon Papers, seen at Castlegar in 1973.

125 See the list of inventories for this estimate. By 1829 the tin plate warmer at Ashfield had been replaced by one that was 'Japanned', according to a note on the 1808 inventory.

126 NLI, Doneraile Papers, MS 34,106(6), 'Invoice to Rt Hon. Viscount Doneraile, from Pryer & Mackenzie, Upholsterers & Cabinet Makers, 30, Bridges Street, Strand, London, 28th April, 1821'.

127 Ian Gow, '"An Architect's Melancholy": Furniture by W.H. Playfair for an Irish House', *Irish Arts Review Yearbook*, 14 (1998), 57–61.

128 Might this have been a type of drinking table (akin to the horseshoe table), or for supper, in the absence of servants?

129 Linda Pollock, 'Living on the Stage of the World: The Concept of Privacy Among the Elite of Early Modern England', in A. Wilson (ed.), *Rethinking Social History: English Society 1570–1920 and Its Interpretation* (Manchester, 1993), 78–96.

130 In David Garrick's farce *Bon Ton: Or High Life Above Stairs* (produced 1775), Colonel Tivy is hidden behind a chimney board to avoid a confrontation. Wedgwood & Bentley made vases for the fireplace, but were particular about the type: Wedgwood wrote in 1772, 'Vases are furniture for a chimney piece, bough pots for a hearth . . . I think they can never be used one instead of the other.' A bough pot can be seen behind Samuel Richardson in his portrait by Joseph Highmore (1692–1780) in the National Portrait Gallery, London. James Ayres, *Domestic Interiors: The British Tradition 1500–1850* (New Haven and London, 2003), 33–4.

131 John Trusler, *The London Adviser and Guide: containing every instruction and information useful and necessary to persons living in London and coming to reside there* (London, 1790), 5.

132 TCD, MS 4026(II), D.A. Beaufort, 'Journal of a Tour Through Part of Ireland Begun August 26, 1787', ff. 77–8.

133 They appear in inventories for Howth Castle (1746–52), Woodville (1797), the Street Parlour in Antrim House (1801), North Great George's Street (1805), Killadoon (1807 and again, as '2 pieces under sideboard', in 1812), Shelton House (1816) Newbridge (1821, covering the hearth) and Doneraile Court (c.1830).

134 At Saltram in Devon the Axminster carpet was designed by Robert Adam, following the design of the ceiling. It was not intended at the time (1780–1) that this design would be covered with furniture on a permanent basis: such an arrangement became fashionable only c.1810. Jackson-Stops and Pipkin, *English Country House*, 131.

135 M.B. Harvey, *A Journal of a Voyage from Philadelphia to Cork in the Year of Our Lord 1809 Together with a Description of a Sojourn in Ireland* (Philadelphia, 1915), 35.

136 McParland, MS notes from Mahon Papers, *NLI*, now missing.

137 PRONI, Abercorn Papers, T2541/IA1/19/24, Letter from Robert Woodgate, Baronscourt to the Marquis of Abercorn, London, 16 (6?) March 1793.

138 Ada K. Longfield, 'History of Carpet-making in Ireland in the 18th Century', *Journal of the Royal Society of Antiquaries of Ireland*, 70 (1940), 63–88. This is quite interesting as, according to Longfield's research, from 1741 the Dublin Society offered premiums to encourage the industry. Richard Hogarth of Chamber's Street, Dublin won the premium in 1742 and 1743 for his 'Turkey Carpets'. Owing to lack of competition, the next premium was awarded in 1749 to Benjamin Bowes of Marybone Lane, Dublin and William Hoggart for 'the two best carpets woven on a loom', and in 1754 Bowes won for his 'Wilton or Tournay work'. Turkey carpet-making was slow in getting off the ground, as few were prepared to take the risk of investing in the broad loom necessary for their manufacture. Prior to 1750 there was little carpet-making in Ireland but between 1755 and 1775 the situation improved.

139 Quoted in Cornforth, *Early Georgian Interiors*, 49.

140 Colvin and Newman, *Of Building*, 55.

141 PRONI, Abercorn Papers, T2541/IA1/19/24, Letter from Woodgate to Lord Abercorn.

142 The Georgian Group, *The Georgian Group Guides, No. 14: Curtains and Blinds* (London, 1992). Venetian blinds were in the dining rooms at Caledon in 1785 and Killadoon in 1807.

143 PRONI, Caledon Papers, D/2433/A/2/3/9, Invoice from Mayhew & Ince for Caledon House, 1785.

144 Henry Heaney (ed.), *A Scottish Whig in Ireland 1835–38: The Irish Journals of Robert Graham of Redgorton* (Dublin, 1999), 231.

145 Quoted in Gow, 'An Architect's Melancholy'.

146 Glin and Peill, *Irish Furniture*, 149. This though Longueville was the house of a viscount!

147 Begun to Roger Morris's design in 1745; decorated in the 1780s in the Louis Seize style, associated with Carlton House, London. Cornforth, *Early Georgian Interiors*, 10.

148 Quoted in Glin and Peill, *Irish Furniture*, 191.

4   Public Rooms

1   Isaac Ware, *A Complete Body of Architecture* (London, 1756), 328.

2   The royal visit to Castle Coole did not materialise, as George IV preferred to remain in the company of his mistress, Lady Conyngham, at Slane Castle, Co. Meath.

3   Jane Fenlon, 'Episodes of Magnificence: The Material Worlds of the Dukes of Ormonde', in Toby Barnard and Jane Fenlon (eds), *The Dukes of Ormonde, 1610–1745* (Woodbridge, 2000), 137–59.

4   Floor levels vary somewhat between the towers. Jane Fenlon, 'The Ormonde Inventories 1675–1717: A State Apartment at Kilkenny Castle', in Agnes Bernelle (ed.), *Decantations: A Tribute to Maurice Craig* (Dublin, 1992), 29–37.

5   This collection, created mostly between 1660 and 1684, was the largest formed by Irish patrons, consisting of some 500 pictures. See Jane Fenlon, 'The Ormonde Picture Collection', *Irish Arts Review Yearbook*, 16 (2000) 142–9.

6   Jane Fenlon, 'Her Grace's Closet: Paintings in the Duchess of Ormonde's Closet at Kilkenny Castle', *Bulletin of the Irish Georgian Society*, 36 (1994), 30–47.

7   In the second half of the century Robert Adam advocated having the drawing room on the garden side of the house and the dining room to the front, apparently to remove the ladies from the sometimes raucous behaviour and conversation of the men as they remained in the dining room. Eileen Harris, *The Genius of Robert Adam* (New Haven and London, 2001), 6.

8   Angélique Day (ed.), *Letters from Georgian Ireland: The Correspondence of Mary Delany, 1731–1768* (Belfast, 1991), 222.

9   T.U. Sadleir, 'The Diary of Anne Cooke', *Journal of the Co. Kildare Archaeological Society*, 8 (1915–17), 205–19.

10 John Cornforth, 'Newbridge, Co. Dublin – I', *Country Life*, 20 June 1985, 1732–7.

11 Trinity College Dublin (TCD), MS 4028, D.A. Beaufort, 'Journal of a Tour Through Part of Ireland Begun August 26, 1787', f. 45. Owing to weather conditions in the northern tip of Ireland, this was unlikely to have been a temporary structure, and was either an early example

of architectural salvage where a room interior could be moved in panels from elsewhere, or an interior designed and supplied for a specific space. An 'almost complete carved room from the Great Dining Parlour' was one item in an eleven-day auction of lots after the demolition of Canons, Wiltshire in 1787, just forty years after it was built. John Harris, *Moving Rooms* (New Haven and London, 2007), 16. It is also of note that a wooden bridge for the city of Derry was pre-fabricated and sent over, together with workmen, from the U.S. in 1790.

12 John Cornforth, *Early Georgian Interiors* (New Haven and London, 2004), 58.

13 Harris, *Genius of Robert Adam*, 5.

14 Quoted in Annik Pardailhe-Galabrun, *The Birth of Intimacy: Privacy and Domestic Life in Early Modern Paris*, trans. Jocelyn Phelps (Oxford, 1991), 65.

15 *Ibid.*

16 Howard Colvin and John Newman (eds), *Of Building: Roger North's Writings on Architecture* (Oxford, 1981), 132.

17 Carton, Dromoland and Killeen Castle are each counted twice because of major refurbishing and rebuilding that they underwent: other houses are Leinster House, Samuel Chearnley's drawing, Headfort, Slane Castle (a reconstructed drawing), Charleville Forest, Woodville, Mount Kennedy, Straffan House, Farnham House, Markree Castle, Rockingham, Lough Glynn House, Castle Bernard, Lissadell, Ballyfin, Emo Court and Ballycurry.

18 Castle had already been dead for four years when Johnson's dictionary was published, and Aheron's plans are dated prior to 1750.

19 At Dromoland (1740s) and Charleville Forest (1789) and on Chearnley's plan (1746) the anterooms serve bedrooms.

20 Quoted in Cynthia O'Connor, *The Pleasing Hours: James Caulfeild, First Earl of Charlemont 1728–99* (Cork, 1999), 207.

21 *Ibid.*, 217.

22 J.P. Neale, *Views of the Seats of Noblemen and Gentlemen in England, Wales, Scotland and Ireland*, 6 vols (London, 1818–28), III (not paginated).

23 Bowood Archives, extracts from the diary of Sophia, countess of Shelburne, vol. 5, 1769–70, transcribed by the Knight of Glin.

24 François de la Rochefoucauld, *A Frenchman in England 1784* (Cambridge, 1933), 41.

25 Brian FitzGerald, *Correspondence of Emily, Duchess of Leinster 1731–1814*, 3 vols (Dublin, 1949–67), I, 149–50, letter from marchioness of Kildare to her husband, 9 December [1762].

26 In both houses the ante-room itself is off-axis.

27 Various changes of mind are noted in the plans for Ballyfin, where an 'Anti Chamber and Billiards' appear to the rear, but the space to the

left of the hall (where it could relate to both the hall and the library) is called 'Music Room or Anti Room'.

28 Ware, *Complete Body of Architecture*, 337.

29 William Chambers, *A Treatise on Civil Architecture* (London, 1759), 82.

30 Pardailhe-Galabrun, *Birth of Intimacy*, 62.

31 Gervase Jackson-Stops and J. Pipkin, *The English Country House: A Grand Tour* (London, 1984), 82, 142f.

32 Rolf Loeber and Magda Stouthamer-Loeber, 'Dublin and its Vicinity in 1797', *Irish Geography*, 35 (2002), 133–55.

33 James Macauley, *The Classical Country House in Scotland 1660–1800* (London, 1987), 79–80.

34 Mark Girouard, *Life in the English Country House* (New Haven and London, 1978), 162.

35 However, in 1815, the measurer Bryan Bolger referred to it as the 'Saloon and Musick Room'. National Archives of Ireland (NAI), 58 125 (Carton insert).

36 An account of the funeral of the earl of Bellamont's only son is in *Faulkners Dublin Journal*, 18 May 1786, quoted in Brian FitzGerald, *Lady Louisa Conolly, 1743–1821* (London, 1950), 141.

37 Five plans are for Headfort, and one is by Samuel Chearnley.

38 There are plans for a total of twenty-two houses during the period 1750–1800.

39 Morrison, *Useful and Ornamental Designs*, 'No. 9 and 10, A Design for a Villa'.

40 Powerscourt, Co. Wicklow is included here in the plan by Daniel Robertson dated 1843, as there are no original plans for the house.

41 TCD, Muniments, P4 59(6), Invoice from J.S. Cranfield, 30 November 1790; P4 183(24), 'Valuation of Sundry Articles of Household Furniture, the Property of the Rt Revd Lord Bishop of Limerick in the Provost's House 27 October 1820'; TCD, Muniments (uncatalogued), 'An Inventory of Furniture &c Belonging to T.C.D., in the Provost's House', [1852] 'drawn up by Upholsterer, Mr Durham', in which is a note received from the bishop of Limerick dated 12 October 1820 listing 'Heirlooms in the Provosts House'.

42 *The Georgian Society Records of Eighteenth Century Domestic Architecture and Decoration in Ireland*, vol. 5 (Dublin, 1913), 33.

43 David Griffin and Caroline Pegum, *Leinster House, 1744–2000: An Architectural History* (Dublin, 2000), 52–3.

44 The Farnham Drawings, which contain this plan, are now in a private collection.

45 Also at Ballyhaise in Co. Cavan. Mark Bence-Jones, *A Guide to Irish Country Houses* (rev. edn, London, 1988), 22.

46 Arthur Young describes the saloon at Headfort as being of the same dimensions as the hall, i.e.

31.5 feet × 24 feet × 17 feet. Arthur Young, *A Tour in Ireland with General Observations on the Present State of That Kingdom Made in the Years 1776, 1777 and 1778*, 2 vols (Dublin, 1780), I, 453.

47 At Adare Manor (1834), the saloon (located between the drawing and dining rooms) measures 31 feet × 26 feet, while the rooms flanking it measure 40 feet × 24 feet.

48 A late use of it is to be found at Ballyfin, where its role is that of an ante-room.

49 Christopher Hussey, *Early Georgian 1715–1760* (2nd edn, London, 1965), 17.

50 Letter from Horace Walpole to John Chute, connoisseur and amateur architect, 22 August 1758, http://images.library.yale.edu/hwcorrespondence/browse.asp?type=Letters&ns=1758, accessed 6 September 2013.

51 David Griffin, 'Richard Castle's Egyptian Hall at Powerscourt, Co. Wicklow', *Georgian Group Journal*, 5 (1995), 119–24; Cornforth, *Early Georgian Interiors*, 60. According to Bence-Jones, *Guide to Irish Country Houses*, 234–5, Powerscourt was built between 1731 and 1740.

52 NAI, M.2533, W. Henry, 'Hints Towards a Natural, Topographical [*sic*] History of Counties Sligo, Donegal, Fermanagh and Lough Erne', 464–5.

53 The date for this room is given in *Georgian Society Records*, V, 33, as the 1760s; The Knight of Glin and James Peill, *Irish Furniture* (New Haven and London, 2007), 95, suggest the 1740s.

54 See the List of Inventories for this invoice.

55 George Mott, 'Castle Coole, Co. Fermanagh', *Irish Arts Review*, 1989/90, 83–90.

56 The valuation was carried out at the end of the term of office of Provost Thomas Elrington (later bishop of Limerick). TCD, Muniments (uncatalogued).

57 TCD, Muniments, P4 187(43).

58 This number includes the three windows that make up the Serliana window. TCD, Muniments, P4 214(30), 'Invoice from Jones & Sons, Upholsterers & Cabinet Makers, 134 [St] Stephen's Green, 19th February 1838'.

59 In August 1821 Morgans rehung them after cleaning, and in 1837 George Gillington of Abbey Street dyed, retrimmed and replaced them (TCD, Muniments, P4 187(43) and P4 214(18)).

60 TCD, Muniments, P4 234(107).

61 Glin and Peill, *Irish Furniture*, 177.

62 Girouard, *Life in the English Country House*, 94. The point is also made that the term 'bed-chamber' came into use in the mid-sixteenth century, to underline the fact that the room was used mainly for sleeping in, and not as a sitting room (*ibid.*, 99).

63 In other early inventories listed in Jane Fenlon, *Goods and Chattels: A Survey of Early Household Inventories in Ireland* (Kilkenny, 2003), 'drawing chambers' are mentioned in Kilkenny Castle in 1630 (27) and possibly Dunmore House or Ormonde Castle in 1639 (31); by 1675 the Kilkenny inventories call it a 'Drawing Room'. Inventories for Dublin Castle of 1677 and 1678 mention 'The King's with Drawing Roome' (92, 100) with few contents, but the latter also lists rich furnishings for 'The Draweing roome' (101).

64 John Cornforth, 'The Key to the Drawing Room', *Country Life*, 11 December 2003, 44–7.

65 Old Castle Coole (one); Carton (four); Dromoland (one); Charleville Forest (one); Mr Barnet's (two drawing rooms on one plan); Chearnley's drawing (one); Leinster House (two); Headfort House (four).

66 The four drawings for Headfort vary in size between 20 feet square and 28 × 25 feet.

67 Old Townley Hall (one); Carton (one); Newbridge House (one); Headfort (one); Lucan House (one); Ardbraccan (three); Woodville (one); Mount Kennedy (five); Slane (one); Prospect (one); Charleville Forest (one); Castle Coole (two); Morrison drawings (two); Townley Hall (four); Carriglas (one); Killeen Castle (one); Garvey House (one).

68 The elliptical examples are Lucan, Mount Kennedy and Carriglas.

69 Bence-Jones, *Guide to Irish Country Houses*, 72–3, refers to it as a 'saloon' or 'ballroom'.

70 Young, *Tour in Ireland*, II, 46.

71 Castlegar (two); Cloncarneel (one); Corbalton Hall (one); Farnham (one); Headfort (one); Killeen Castle (three); Markree Castle (one); Polacton (one); Ballycurry (one); Straffan House (one); Rockingham (one); Castle Howard (one); Carton (one); Mount Bellew (one); Pakenham Hall (Tullynally) (two); Ballyfin (four); Emo (two); Howth Castle (three); Dromoland (two); Brook Lodge (one); Durrow Abbey (one); Lough Glynn (one); Old Adare House (one); Adare Manor (one); Lissadell (one); Crom Castle (one); Castle Bernard (one); Carriglas (one); Roxborough (one); Castle Dillon (one); Powerscourt, Co. Wicklow (one).

72 Carton's saloon has become the drawing room in this plan by Richard Morrison (1815). The drawing room at Castle Freke, Co. Cork was described in Neale, *Views of the Seats*, III, as 'in the gallery style, 50 feet × 20 feet'.

73 Cangort Park, Co. Offaly, attributed to Richard Morrison (1807), also has a semi elliptical bay. Irish Architectural Archive (IAA), McParland Notebooks, 1.68; Ann Martha Rowan (ed.), *The Architecture of Richard Morrison and William Vitruvius Morrison* (Dublin, 1989), 45.

74 Bowood Archives, extracts from the diary of Sophia, countess of Shelburne, vol. 5, 1769–70, 17 August 1765.

75 Rowan (ed.), *Architecture of Richard Morrison*, 65–6.

76 Representative Church Body Library, Dublin, MS 49/3–4, 'Beaufort's Journal of Irish Travels 1806', vol. 4, f. 84.

77 TCD, MS 4034, Louisa Beaufort, 'Journal of a Tour to the North, 1807', f. 9.

78 Steven Parissien, *The Georgian House* (London, 1999), 43.

79 Neale, *Views of the Seats*, III.

80 Cornforth, 'Key to the Drawing Room'.

81 IAA, McParland Notebooks, 1.41, 5.8, 1.9; John Cornforth, 'Castle Coole, Co. Fermanagh', *Country Life*, 17 December 1992, 28–31.

82 This space was called the 'gallery' while it was being built (Public Record Office of Northern Ireland (PRONI), Abercorn Papers T/2541/IAI/18/33, letter from James Hamilton Jr, Strabane to Marquis of Abercorn, Grosvenor Square, London, 14 May 1791). It is referred to as a 'saloon' in Alistair Rowan, *The Buildings of Ireland: North-West Ulster* (Harmondsworth, 1979), 131, and as a 'drawing room' in Rowan, *Architecture of Richard Morrison*, 27.

83 Rowan, *Architecture of Richard Morrison*, 24–8, 17, 92–3, 115–16.

84 Desmond FitzGerald and Donough Cahill, 'Vernon Mount', *Irish Arts Review*, 24, no. 4 (Winter 2007), 13–35.

85 FitzGerald, *Correspondence of Emily, Duchess of Leinster*, II, 152–4.

86 Quoted in Brian FitzGerald, 'Carton II', *Country Life*, 14 November 1936, 514–19. It might be surprising that Lady Kildare did not opt for the French rococo design by Isaac Ware for her dressing room in Leinster House, but chose instead one in the Palladian manner, in line with the other rooms in the house.

87 Cornforth, *Early Georgian Interiors*, 55.

88 See Christine Casey, 'Boiseries, Bankers and Bills: A Tale of Charlemont and Whaley', in Michael McCarthy (ed.), *Lord Charlemont and His Circle* (Dublin, 2001). The room at Charlemont House is called the 'dining room or French room'; at No. 86 St Stephen's Green the French room is a front parlour; at Dunsandle, Co. Galway it is a saloon; at Dowth Hall it is the dining room; and there is a design for a 'boudoir' or dressing room at Leinster House.

89 Henry Heaney (ed.), *A Scottish Whig in Ireland 1835–38: The Irish Journals of Robert Graham of Redgorton* (Dublin, 1999), 284.

90 Rowan, *Architecture of Richard Morrison*, 115.

91 M. Carey, 'Ballyfin, from "Condensed History" of the Queen's Co. and Co. of Kildare' (pamphlet, published 1903). The decoration of the drawing room at Ballyfin was either undertaken or changed in 1848 by the London firm of Gillows and Conefed, though the house was completed in 1826. Kevin V. Mulligan,

'Ballyfin, Co. Laois, *Architectural History*, February 2002', unpublished report, 56.

92 Similarly, Mrs Delany's bedroom at Delville was hung with crimson damask, the same material used for both furnishings and curtains.

93 Fenlon, *Goods and Chattels*, 101, 104.

94 Throughout the seventeenth century, other fabrics, such as silk damask and plain velvet, were used for hangings. Mohair was to be found in the last two decades of the century. Peter Thornton, *Seventeenth-century Interior Decoration in England, France and Holland* (New Haven and London, 1983), 133.

95 There is no mention of damask fabric in the Damask room, but it contained five pieces of tapestry hangings that had been removed from the 'Castleroom' and three pieces from the 'old drawing room', together with four white serge window curtains, 'all brought out of the room over the Damask room'.

96 J. Sheridan Le Fanu, *The Cock and Anchor*, 3 vols (Dublin, 1845), I, 52.

97 Day, *Letters from Georgian Ireland*, 158.

98 The earliest surviving wallpaper in Ireland is dated to *c.*1680–1700, found pasted to the back of a door in the Royal Hospital, Kilmainham during restoration in the 1970s. David Skinner, 'Irish Period Wallpapers', *Irish Arts Review*, 1997, 53–61.

99 Ada K. Longfield, 'History of the Dublin Wallpaper Industry in the 18th Century', *Journal of the Royal Society of Antiquaries of Ireland*, 77 (1947), 100–20.

100 *Pue's Occurrences*, 17 June 1746.

101 NLI, Edgeworth Papers, MS 1518.

102 Toby Barnard, *Making the Grand Figure: Lives and Possessions in Ireland, 1641–1770* (New Haven and London, 2004), 95.

103 Quoted in John Cornforth, 'A Georgian Patchwork', in Gervase Jackson-Stops et al., *The Fashioning and the Functioning of the British Country House* (Hanover, NH and London, 1989), 155–74.

104 FitzGerald, *Correspondence of Emily, Duchess of Leinster*, II, 153.

105 Bowood Archives, extracts from the diary of Sophia, countess of Shelburne, vol. 5, 1769–70.

106 Amanda Vickery, *Behind Closed Doors: At Home in Georgian England* (New Haven and London, 2009), 168.

107 Cornforth, 'A Georgian Patchwork'. Bishop Synge extended this economy to wallpaper, advising his daughter not to paper behind large pieces of furniture. Barnard, *Making the Grand Figure*, 95.

108 Cornforth, 'A Georgian Patchwork'.

109 Francis Haskell, 'The British as Collectors', in Gervase Jackson-Stops (ed.), *The Treasure Houses of Britain: Five Hundred Years of Private Patronage and Art Collecting* (New Haven and London, 1985), 50–9, fig. 4.

110 The drawing room at Dromana was 'commonly called the Picture Room', according to the 1755 inventory.

111 Glin and Peill, *Irish Furniture*, 131, illus. 177.

112 Anne Crookshank and the Knight of Glin, *Ireland's Painters 1600–1940* (New Haven and London, 2002), pl. 218.

113 Ware, *Complete Body of Architecture*, 469.

114 Cornforth, 'A Georgian Patchwork'.

115 The claim that this room was a drawing room is made in Rosemary ffolliott, 'Household Stuff', *Irish Ancestor*, 1, no. 1 (1969), 43–51. No other drawing room in the inventories contained a bed.

116 PRONI, Caledon Papers, D/2433/A/2/3/9, Invoice from Mayhew & Ince, 1785.

117 Glin and Peill, *Irish Furniture*, 97; John Cornforth, 'Killadoon, Co Kildare – 1', *Country Life*, 15 January 2004, 46–51.

118 The inventory states that the gilt chairs had 'cotton velvet covers', but no colour is mentioned.

119 Cornforth, 'Killadoon'.

120 Frances Power Cobbe, *Life of Frances Power Cobbe. By Herself*, 2 vols (3rd edn, London, 1894), I, 10; Julius Bryant, 'The Newbridge Drawing Room: A Picture Gallery for a Georgian Villa', in Alastair Laing (ed.), *Clerics and Connoisseurs: The Rev. Matthew Pilkington, the Cobbe Family and the Fortunes of an Irish Art Collection Through Three Centuries* (London, 2001), 63–72.

121 *Pue's Occurrences*, 20–23 November 1736.

122 NLI, Rockingham Papers, MS 8810 Part 7 (4).

123 This is the earliest mention in Irish country houses of an ottoman – a seat that is similar to a sofa, but without back or arms, known since 1806, according to the *OED*; NLI, Rockingham Papers, MS 8810 Part 8 (1).

124 Edward McParland extracted details from the Mahon Papers at Castlegar in 1973. These include the furniture plans mentioned, two for the drawing room and, it appears, one for the 'oval room', formerly the hall. My search through some of the material, which is now in the National Library of Ireland, did not produce them, and there is no mention of them in the Calendar. My thanks to him for photocopies of his drawings.

125 Barbavilla (1742), Dromana (1755), Henrietta Street (1772), Baronscourt (1782), Gaulston (1787), Denmark Street (1793), Antrim House (1801), Killadoon (1807 and 1844), Doneraile Court (1830s), Brownlow House (1848) and Mount Stewart (1821).

126 Cornforth, *Early Georgian Interiors*, 244.

127 'The Cooper Penrose Collection', http://www.crawfordartgallery.ie/Cooperpenrose/ CooperPenrose02.html, accessed 2 February 2012; M.B. Harvey, *A Journal of a Voyage from Philadelphia to Cork in the Year of Our Lord 1809 Together with a Description of a Sojourn in Ireland* (Philadelphia, 1915).

128 NLI, Wicklow Papers, MS 38/599, 1, letter from Hugh Howard to William Howard at Chancery Lane, Dublin, 21 May 1726.

129 Gaulston (1787), Prospect (later Ardgillan, 1795), Killadoon (1807), Convoy, Co. Donegal (*c.*1844) and Brownlow House (1848).

130 Jonathan Swift, *Directions to Servants* (London, 1745), 82–3.

131 Lady Morgan (Sydney Owenson), *Dramatic Scenes from Real Life*, 2 vols (London, 1979; first published 1833), II, 89.

132 Green wallpaper is listed at Killeen Castle in the Green Room also.

133 A rectangular table with a black and gold Chinese lacquer top from Killeen Castle, dated to *c.*1750, is illustrated in Glin and Peill, *Irish Furniture*, 241, cat. no. 156.

134 ffolliott, 'Household Stuff'.

135 Toby Barnard reckons that 'tea-drinking as a ritual was known among the elite by the end of the seventeenth century', though imports of tea to Ireland were recorded only in the second decade of the eighteenth century. Toby Barnard, 'The Political, Material and Mental Culture of the Cork Settlers, *c.*1650–1700', in P. O'Flanagan and C.G. Buttimer (eds), *Cork History and Society* (Dublin, 1993), 309–65; IAA, photocopy of the Dromoland Album from the NLI, f. 56v.

136 TCD, MS 4028, D.A. Beaufort, 'Journal of a Tour . . . 1787', f. 44.

137 Quoted in John Cornforth, *London Interiors from the Archives of Country Life* (London, 2000), 89.

138 Quoted in Alison Ardburgham, *Silver Fork Society* (London, 1983), 205.

139 Cornforth, 'Key to the Drawing Room'.

140 PRONI, T1282/1, 'Diaries of John Ynyr Burges', vol. 1, 4–6.

141 The three rooms shown on Castle's plan (parlour, dressing room and servants' waiting room) were built, but the walls dividing them had been removed by 1759, when the space was referred to as the 'great' or 'long' room, which later became known as the Supper Room.

142 Griffin and Pegum, *Leinster House*, 30, 49.

143 By 1775, the bedroom and dressing room would probably not have been part of the formal rooms.

144 The use of the library before dinner was noted by Robert Graham on a visit to Carton in 1835, when he remarked that 'gentlemen were already in the library where they meet before dinner'. Heaney, *A Scottish Whig*, 46.

145 The gallery was also intended to be used as a ballroom, according to notes by the architect, Francis Goodwin, quoted in Josslyn Gore-Booth, 'Lissadell', *Irish Arts Review*, Summer 2003, 112–19.

146 Lady Morgan (Sydney Owenson), *The Wild Irish Girl: A National Tale*, ed. C. Connolly and S. Copley (London, 2000), 188.

147 *Personal Sketches of His Own Times by Sir Jonah Barrington*, 2 vols (London, 1827), I, 320.

148 Quoted in Desmond Guinness and William Ryan, *Irish Houses and Castles* (London, 1971), 301.

149 The Maunsell seat was Oakly Park, Celbridge, Co. Kildare. The Maunsell Papers are in the National Library of Ireland.

150 Day, *Letters from Georgian Ireland*, 174.

151 Sara Paston-Williams, *The Art of Dining: A History of Cooking and Eating* (London, 1993), 249.

152 Eric Gillett (ed.), *Elizabeth Ham by Herself, 1723–1820* (London, 1945?), 75.

153 Quoted in Paston-Williams, *The Art of Dining*, 262. An example of a Scottish-made sideboard has, in a central compartment under the drawer, sliding doors that part to reveal the chamber pot. It can be seen at the National Trust's Georgian House at Charlotte Square, Edinburgh.

154 *Pückler's Progress: The Adventures of Prince Pückler-Muskau in England, Wales and Ireland as Told in Letters to His Former Wife 1826–9*, trans. Flora Brennan (London, 1987), 86.

155 Day, *Letters from Georgian Ireland*, 53, 146. In Britain in the late eighteenth to early nineteenth century, lunch was gradually introduced to fill the long gap between meals, according to Jackson-Stops, though Paston-Williams dates this development to the 1830s. Jackson-Stops and Pipkin, *English Country House*, 124; Paston-Williams, *The Art of Dining*, 244.

156 Cobbe, *Life of Frances Power Cobbe*, I, 16.

157 Rosemary Baird, *Mistress of the House: Great Ladies and Grand Houses 1670–1830* (London, 2003), 36.

158 Day, *Letters from Georgian Ireland*, 262; abstract of NLI, Killadoon Papers, 89–90.

159 Cornforth, *Early Georgian Interiors*, 49.

160 Barnard, *Making the Grand Figure*, 139; Elise Taylor, 'Silver for a Countess's Levée: The Kildare Toilet Service', *Irish Arts Review Yearbook*, 1998, 115–24: no date is given for the dinner service.

161 Barnard, *Making the Grand Figure*, 139.

162 *Ibid.*, 139.

163 Part of the Milltown Collection now in the National Gallery of Ireland. Desmond FitzGerald, 'Some Thoughts on Russborough', *Irish Arts Review*, Winter 2005, 124–5.

164 Barnard, *Making the Grand Figure*, 139.

165 Grania O'Brien, *These My Friends and Forebears: The O'Briens at Dromoland* (Whitegate, Co. Clare, 1991), 111–12.

166 W.A. Maguire, *Living Like a Lord: The Second Marquis of Donegall, 1769–1844* (Belfast, 1984), 30.

167 Cobbe, *Life of Frances Power Cobbe*, I, 19.

168 Quoted in Parissien, *Georgian House*, 43.

169 Mrs Godfrey Clark (ed.), *Gleanings from an Old Portfolio, Containing Some Correspondence Between Lady Louisa Stuart and Her Sister Caroline, Countess of Portarlington*, 3 vols (Edinburgh, 1895–8), I, 56–7.

170 Quoted in G.E. Mingay, *English Landed Society in the Eighteenth Century* (London, 1963), 147.

171 PRONI, T1282/1, 'Diaries of John Ynyr Burges', vol. 1, 19.

172 *The Irish Guardian: A Pathetic Story in Two Volumes, by a Lady* (Dublin, 1776), II, 220.

173 Edward Wakefield, *An Account of Ireland, Statistical and Political*, 2 vols (London, 1812), II, 787.

174 R.L. Edgeworth and Maria Edgeworth, *Memoirs of Richard Lovell Edgeworth*, 2 vols (Shannon, 1969; first published 1820), II, 375.

175 Quoted in Girouard, *Life in the English Country House*, 204.

176 Morgan, *Dramatic Scenes from Real Life*, II, 58–60.

177 Day, *Letters from Georgian Ireland*, 53, 146.

178 'Copy of a poem on a country dinner party. Written by Mrs Hamilton at Rossana, 1805. From Mrs Hamilton's Ms'. My thanks to the Knight of Glin for a photocopy of this document.

179 Edgeworth, *Memoirs*, II, 375–6. The tyranny of incessant card-playing after dinner was challenged somewhat by the introduction of the 'circle' for conversation among (mostly) women. Mrs Vesey, the wife of the builder of Lucan House, was the first to hold such a 'conversation', as early as the 1750s, in an effort to unite the literary and social worlds. She, together with a number of her friends became known as 'bluestockings'. However, she did not agree with the placing of chairs in a circle, a fashion that came later; instead she arranged her chairs and sofas in small clusters in her London home, with the idea that people could move from one to another.

180 Gillett, *Elizabeth Ham*, 75.

181 Maria Edgeworth, *Ormond* (reprint of 1st edn, London 1972), 1.

182 Alnwick Archives 121/11 [number unclear], Reference SEP.OCT 1763, Diary of the duchess of Northumberland, 20 October 1763.

183 PRONI, T2855/1, volume entitled 'Miscellaneous observations on Ireland, 1759–60' by Lord Chief Baron Willes.

184 Cobbe, *Life of Frances Power Cobbe*, I, 18.

185 Mrs G.H. Bell (ed.), *The Hamwood Papers of the Ladies of Llangollen and Caroline Hamilton* (London, 1930), 9.

186 NLI, Smythe of Barbavilla Papers, MS 41,577/1–5, letter from Mrs Jones to Mrs Bonnell, 16 October [1733?].

187 Barnard, *Making the Grand Figure*, 75.

188 NLI, Smythe of Barbavilla Papers, MS 41,577/1–5, letter from Mrs Jones to Mrs Bonnell, 11 May [1734?].

189 Day, *Letters from Georgian Ireland*, 53.

190 FitzGerald, *Correspondence of Emily, Duchess of Leinster*, I, letter dated 1 March [1760], 277.

191 Clark, *Gleanings*, I, 84.

192 Edgeworth, *Ormond*, 352–3.

193 T.M. MacKenzie, *Dromana: The Memoirs of an Irish Family* (Dublin, [1906?]), 188, 203, 210.

194 R. Bayne Powell, *Housekeeping in the Eighteenth Century* (London, 1956), 102.

195 PRONI, T1282/1, 'Diaries of John Ynyr Burges', vol. 1, 20.

196 *Pückler's Progress*, 183.

197 John H. Gebbie (ed.), *An Introduction to the Abercorn Letters (as Relating to Ireland, 1736–1816)* (Omagh, 1972), letter from James Hamilton Jr to the Marquess of Abercorn, 15 May 1793.

198 Between 1715 and the 1780s, Parliament met in Dublin usually every second winter, for five to eight months.

199 Quoted in Frances Gerard, *Some Celebrated Irish Beauties of the Last Century* (London, 1895), xix. A version of this section was previously published as Patricia McCarthy, 'Private Theatricals in Irish Houses, 1730–1815', *Irish Architectural and Decorative Studies*, 16 (2013), 12–49.

200 W.H. Grattan Flood, *A History of Irish Music* (Dublin, 1905) 271.

201 Day, *Letters from Georgian Ireland*, 255; Robert Hitchcock, *An Historical View of the Irish Stage* (Dublin 1788), 75; Edward McParland, *Public Architecture in Ireland* (New Haven and London, 2001), 101.

202 John Greene, 'The Repertory of The Dublin Theatres, 1720–1745', *Eighteenth-century Ireland/Iris dá chultúr* 2 (1987), 133–48.

203 Tighernan Mooney and Fiona White, 'The Gentry's Winter Season', in David Dickson (ed.), *Dublin: The Gorgeous Mask* (Dublin, 1987), 1–16.

204 *London Post*, 5 November 1776, quoted in Sybil Rosenfeld, *Temples of Thespis: Some Private Theatres and Theatricals in England and Wales, 1700–1820* (London, 1978), 11.

205 Linda Kelly, *Richard Brinsley Sheridan: A Life* (London, 1997), 3.

206 Knight of Glin and John Cornforth, 'Killruddery, Co. Wicklow – I', *Country Life*, 14 July 1977, 78–81.

207 The original house must have been called 'Lurgan'. Brownlow House was built from 1836. Bence-Jones, *Guide to Irish Country Houses*, 49. Kane O'Hara (1722–82) also wrote *The Two Misers, Tom Thumb: A Burletta* and *Tom the Great*, a burlesque tragedy in two acts, the latter two being adaptations. There is a portrait etching of him by Edmund Dorrell dated 1802 in the National Portrait Gallery in London. He was a friend of Garret Wesley, the future earl of Mornington, with whom he founded the Academy of Music in 1757. Grattan Flood, *History of Irish Music*, 296, 299.

208 IAA, Bunbury Letters 94/136 Box 1, letter from Louisa Conolly at Carton to her sister Sarah, 30 December 1790.

209 FitzGerald, *Correspondence of Emily, Duchess of Leinster*, 138–9.

210 Finola O'Kane, *Landscape Design in Eighteenth-century Ireland* (Cork, 2004), 146–7.

211 IAA, Bunbury Letters, letter from Louisa Conolly to her sister Sarah, 24 September 1771.

212 IAA, Bunbury Letters, letter from Louisa Conolly to Sarah, 24 September and 19 August 1771.

213 Presumably Edmund Malone, the Shakespearian scholar, friend of Robert Jephson. FitzGerald, *Correspondence of Emily, Duchess of Leinster*, III, 112, letter from Lady Louisa Conolly to duchess of Leinster, 8 January 1775.

214 Gerard, *Some Celebrated Irish Beauties*, 177.

215 *Hibernian Magazine*, January 1778, 62.

216 James Kelly, *Henry Flood: Patriot and Politician in Eighteenth-century Ireland* (Dublin, 1998), 176.

217 TCD MS 4028, D.A. Beaufort, 'Journal of a Tour . . . 1787', f. 44.

218 Bence-Jones, *Guide to Irish Country Houses*; Charles Topham Bowden, *A Tour Through Ireland* (Dublin, 1791), 235.

219 William Smith Clark, *The Irish Stage in the County Towns, 1720 to 1800* (Oxford, 1965), 240.

220 While it was not a domestic theatre in one sense, there are fascinating drawings executed by the architect James Lewis (c.1751–1820) in 1788 for a theatre (unexecuted) in Limerick City next to the Assembly Rooms, on ground donated by John Prendergast Smyth, MP for the city (1785–97) and later 1st Viscount Gort. Rather lavish living accommodation was provided within the building for Smyth that included private access to his own box; while the public gained access to the theatre either from the rear of the building or through the Assembly Rooms, his entrance was from the front. James Lewis, *Original Designs in Architecture Consisting of Plays, Elevations and Sections for Villas, Mansions, Town-houses etc. and a New Design for a Theatre*, 2 vols (London, 1780–97), I, plates xxi–xxiv.

221 Aidan O'Boyle, 'Aldborough House: A Construction History', *Irish Architectural and Decorative Studies*, 4 (2001), 102–41, fig. 10. References to the building of this theatre are taken from this article.

222 Ethel M. Richardson, *Long Forgotten Days (Leading to Waterloo)* (London, 1928), 323.

223 *Ibid.*, 321; J.S. Dodd, *The Traveller's Director through Ireland* (Dublin, 1801), 50.

224 *Retrospections of Dorothea Herbert 1770–1806* (rev. edn, Dublin, 2004), 70.

225 Shevawn Lynam, *Humanity Dick: A Biography of Richard Martin, MP, 1754–1834* (London, 1975) 47, 49–50. My thanks to Aidan O'Boyle for this reference.

226 *Faulkner's Dublin Journal*, 14 July 1795. My thanks to Charles Benson for this reference.

227 A.J.C. Hare (ed.), *Life and Letters of Maria Edgeworth*, 2 vols (London, 1894), I, 62.

228 Richard Cumberland, quoted in Rosenfeld, *Temples of Thespis*, 14.

229 *Private Theatricals: Being a Practical Guide for the Home Stage. By an Old Stager* (London, 1882); Henry J. Dakin, *The Stage in the Drawing Room: Amateur Acting for Amateur Actors* (London, [1883]).

230 Lady Morgan (Sydney Owenson), *O'Donnel*, 3 vols (London and New York, 1979; first published 1814), III, 38.

231 Information on Rash and the theatricals held there is taken from R.R. Madden, *The Literary Life and Correspondence of the Countess of Blessington*, 3 vols (London, 1855), I, i.

232 John Coleman, 'Luke Gardiner (1745–98), an Irish Dillettante', *Irish Arts Review Yearbook*, 1999, 161–8.

233 Rosenfeld, *Temples of Thespis*, 154.

234 PRONI, Abercorn Papers D623/A/167/9, letters from Lord Mountjoy to Lord Abercorn, July and August 1811. Lord Abercorn held theatricals at his seat in Middlesex, Bentley Priory, where he built a theatre in 1805, though he did not act in the productions mounted there. Rosenfeld, *Temples of Thespis*, 159.

235 Coleman, 'Luke Gardiner'.

236 Rosenfeld, *Temples of Thespis*, 168.

237 Kenneth Garlick (ed.), *The Diary of Joseph Farington*, 16 vols (New Haven, 1979), VII, 2745, 3 May 1806

5 Family Spaces

1 M. Pollard, *Dublin's Trade in Books 1550–1800* (Oxford, 1989), v.

2 *Ibid.*, 70.

3 Quoted in Charles Benson, 'Printers and Booksellers in Dublin 1800–1850', in Robin Myers and Michael Harris (eds), *Spreading the Word: The Distribution Network of Print 1550–1850* (Winchester, 1990), 47–59.

4 Pollard, *Dublin's Trade in Books*, 211.

5 John Cornforth, 'Books Do Furnish a Living Room', *Country Life*, 13 December 2001, 56–9. A library was not included in the original plan of Blenheim, and it was not until 1744 that the house got its library.

6 Jane Fenlon, *Goods and Chattels: A Survey of Early Household Inventories in Ireland* (Kilkenny, 2003), 40, 120.

7 National Library of Ireland (NLI), Wicklow Papers, MS 38,598/5, letter from Robert Howard, bishop of Killala, to his brother Hugh Howard, 18 September and 5 October 1729.

8 T.C. Barnard, *A New Anatomy of Ireland: The Irish Protestants, 1649–1770* (New Haven and London, 2003), 81; J. Dallaway (ed.), *Letters of the Late Thomas Rundle LL.D . . . to Mrs Barbara Sandys* (Dublin, 1789), cxxxv–cxli.

9 Angélique Day (ed.), *Letters from Georgian Ireland: The Correspondence of Mary Delany, 1731–1768* (Belfast, 1991), 159, 161.

10 Irish Architectural Archive (IAA), Elton Hall Drawings Collection, 'Stillorgan Album'.

11 Illustrated in David Griffin and Caroline Pegum, *Leinster House, 1744–2000: An Architectural History* (Dublin, 2000), 43–4, plates 74–6.

12 John Cornforth, *Early Georgian Interiors* (New Haven and London, 2004), 69; IAA, Charleville Forest Drawings collection.

13 William Laffan (ed.), *Miscelanea Structura Curiosa by Samuel Chearnley* (Tralee, 2005), plate 75.

14 Trinity College Dublin (TCD), MS 4035, Mary Beaufort, 'A Journal of Our Tour to the Westward to Inspect the Charter Schools 1808', f. 117; J.B. Trotter, *Walks Through Ireland in the Years 1812, 1814 and 1817* (London, 1819), 561. The library at Borris House, Co. Carlow is also on an upper floor.

15 [Philip Luckcombe], *The Compleat Irish Traveller*, 2 vols (London, 1788), I, 33; Rolf Loeber and Magda Stouthamer-Loeber, in *18th–19th Century Irish Fiction Newsletter*, no. 9 (September 1998), unpaginated, endnote 4.

16 According to the drawing this is in addition to his bow-windowed library.

17 J. Binns, *The Miseries and Beauties of Ireland*, 2 vols (London, 1837), I, 334.

18 Arthur Young, *A Tour in Ireland with General Observations on the Present State of That Kingdom Made in the Years 1776, 1777 and 1778*, 2 vols (Dublin, 1780), I, 3. Young described the main library as measuring 'about 40 × 30'.

19 The medals were kept in a medal cabinet designed by William Chambers for Charlemont, now in the Courtauld Institute, London.

20 Sean O'Reilly, 'Charlemont House: A Critical History', in Elizabeth Mayes and Paula Murphy (eds), *Images and Insights: Hugh Lane Municipal Gallery of Modern Art* (Dublin, 1994), 43–54.

21 RIA/12 R 41/149, Caldwell of New Grange Letters & Papers, vol. 3: 1704–1793, letter from Lord Charlemont, London, to Andrew Caldwell, 16 January 1773. My thanks to Jane Meredith for this information.

22 Quoted in Cynthia O'Connor, *The Pleasing Hours: James Caulfeild, First Earl of Charlemont 1728–99: Traveller, Connoisseur, and Patron of the Arts in Ireland* (Cork, 1999), 213.

23 In the 1686 inventory of Burton Hall, Co. Cork, 500 books ('of all sorts, great and small') are listed in Sir John Percival's study; on a plan for Ballyfin, the bow-windowed library is annotated 'Library and Living Room' (1822). At Holkham Hall, Norfolk, Kent's library (1741) has always been what we would now call the 'family room', and part of Lord Leicester's private apartments. Gervase Jackson-Stops and J. Pipkin, *The English Country House: A Grand Tour* (London, 1984), 200–1.

24 Quoted in Constantia Maxwell, *Country and Town in Ireland under the Georges* (rev. edn, Dundalk, 1949), 95.

25 Cornforth, 'Books Do Furnish a Living Room'.

26 Loeber and Stouthamer-Loeber, *Irish Fiction Newsletter*, no. 9, [p. 3].

27 C. Bruyn Andrews (ed.), *The Torrington Diaries*, 4 vols (London, 1934–8), I, 129.

28 Lady Morgan (Sydney Owenson), *O'Donnel*, 3 vols (London, 1979; first published 1814), II, 174–5.

29 *The Irish Guardian: A Pathetic Story in Two Volumes, by a Lady* (Dublin, 1776), I, 6.

30 Loeber and Stouthamer-Loeber, *Irish Fiction Newsletter*, no. 9, [p. 2], n. 6. It is interesting to note that the library must have been kept locked.

31 Other libraries mentioned by Edgeworth are Ballynahinch, Co. Galway, where she admired the 'two book-rooms opening into one another, and an excellent sitting room beyond', and Moore Hall, Co. Mayo, 'a most livable and elegant literary room – papered with a sort of gothic paper representing a colonade of pillars and fretwork arches above and all manner of tables and armchairs and low and highbacks'. Loeber and Stouthamer-Loeber, *Irish Fiction Newsletter*, no. 9, [p. 2], nn. 12 and 14.

32 A.J.C. Hare (ed.), *Life and Letters of Maria Edgeworth*, 2 vols (London, 1894), I, 82.

33 Quoted in F.G. James, *Lords of the Ascendancy: The Irish House of Lords and Its Members, 1600–1800* (Dublin, 1995), 154.

34 Loeber and Stouthamer-Loeber, *Irish Fiction Newsletter*, no. 9, [p. 2], n. 15.

35 Edward Wakefield, *An Account of Ireland, Statistical and Political*, 2 vols (London, 1812), II, 784.

36 TCD, MS 4035, Mary Beaufort, 'Journal of our Tour to the Westward . . . 1808'.

37 Quoted in Loeber and Stouthamer-Loeber, *Irish Fiction Newsletter*, no. 9, [p. 4].

38 'Two Tours in Ireland, in the years 1792 and 1793 . . . By George Hardinge, Esq, MA. FRS. FSA, Chief Justice of the Counties of Brecon Glamorgan and Radnor'. Transcript by Edward McParland from the Shirley Papers at Lough Fea, Co. Monaghan.

39 E. Ledwich, *The Antiquities of Ireland* (Dublin, 1790), 415.

40 See the list of inventories for this estimate.

41 John Cornforth, 'Killadoon, Co Kildare – II', *Country Life*, 22 January 2004, 54–7.

42 Eliza Pakenham, *Tom, Ned and Kitty: An Intimate Portrait of an Irish Family* (London, 2007), 74.

43 Knight of Glin, David J. Griffin and N.K. Robinson, *Vanishing Country Houses of Ireland* (Dublin, 1989), 23. A Dublin couple, Elizabeth and Thomas Russell, were among the first paper-stainers to advertise the 'new and much admired architect, gothic and landskip papers' in an Irish newspaper in 1761. David Skinner, *Wallpaper in Ireland 1700–1900* (Tralee, 2014), 52.

44 Public Record Office of Northern Ireland, Londonderry Papers D.654/H1/4, invoice, 18 February 1805; NLI, Bellew Papers, MS 27,477(5), July 1811 and May 1812, estimates from Lewis & Anthony Morgan, Cabinet Makers & Upholders, 21 Henry Street, Dublin; Karen J. Harvey, *The Bellews of Mount Bellew: A Catholic Gentry Family in Eighteenth-century Ireland* (Dublin, 1998), 77.

45 Clive Everton, *The History of Snooker and Billiards* (Haywards Heath, West Sussex, 1986), 8.

46 Toby Barnard, 'The Political, Material and Mental Culture of the Cork Settlers, *c.*1650–1700', in P. O'Flanagan and C.G. Buttimer (eds), *Cork: History and Society* (Dublin, 1993), 309–65, n. 64.

47 Laffan, *Miscelanea Structura Curiosa*, plate 75.

48 John Cornforth, 'Mount Kennedy, Co. Wicklow – I', *Country Life*, 28 October 1965, 1129–31. NLI, Mount Kennedy drawings, AD 3568(52f), 'Bed Chamber Story', drawing by Thomas Cooley, November 1781.

49 Similar alcoves are in the bedrooms at Russborough, Co. Wicklow.

50 Personal communication from David Griffin, director of the Irish Architectural Archive.

51 One has a powdering closet between the study and bedroom.

52 Mark Girouard, *Life in the English Country House* (New Haven and London, 1978), 231, 286.

53 *Retrospections of Dorothea Herbert 1770–1806* (Dublin, 2004 edn), 102.

54 Ethel M. Richardson, *Long Forgotten Days (Leading to Waterloo)* (London, 1928), 308.

55 Peter Somerville-Large, *The Irish Country House: A Social History* (London, 1995), 244.

56 Girouard, *Life in the English Country House*, 150. Lord and Lady Kildare enjoyed them too, at their Dublin house, as has been seen.

57 Maria Edgeworth, *Ormond* (reprint of 1st edn, London 1972), 339.

58 Howard Colvin and John Newman (eds), *Of Building: Roger North's Writings on Architecture* (Oxford, 1981), 134–5.

59 Belvoir Castle muniment room, Add. MS 43, 'Letters from Charles 4th Duke of Rutland to his wife . . . 1775–1787'.

60 Upon installing herself at the Hôtel Carnavalet, Paris, Mme de Sévigné was pleased to find close to her room 'a fairly adequate little private staircase; it will also be the morning stairs for my servants, my workpeople and my creditors'. Quoted in Michel Gallet, *Paris Domestic Architecture of the Eighteenth Century* (London, 1972), 80.

61 Girouard, *Life in the English Country House*, 286.

62 Mrs Godfrey Clark (ed.), *Gleanings from an Old Portfolio, Containing Some Correspondence Between Lady Louisa Stuart and Her Sister Caroline, Countess of Portarlington*, 3 vols (Edinburgh, 1895–8), II, 167–8, letter from Lady Portarlington to her sister, Lady Louisa Stuart, 10 January 1791. The correspondence of the countess of Kildare (from 1766, the duchess of Leinster) from as early as the 1760s is full of references to her expanding number of children. She espoused Rousseau's principles on the education of children, even asking him to be their tutor, an offer he declined. She acquired Frescati in Co. Dublin as a seaside home where her children enjoyed a healthy and balanced lifestyle under the direction of their tutor, William Ogilvie. See, generally, Brian FitzGerald, *Correspondence of Emily, Duchess of Leinster 1731–1814*, 3 vols (Dublin, 1949–67).

63 *Ibid.*, I, 83.

64 Cornforth, 'Killadoon II'.

65 Girouard, *Life in the English Country House*, 54, 150; Fenlon, *Goods and Chattels*, 40. The contents of Lord Kildare's room were '1 Great Lookinglasse, 1 Still, 1 Great presse wch is my Lord of Corkes' (the countess's father).

66 Girouard, *Life in the English Country House*, 150; the *OED* defines the closet as a 'room for privacy or retirement' and quotes as early examples Chaucer (*c.*1374), 'In a closet for to avyse her

better, She went alone' and Caxton (1490) 'In her closet she hideth herself sore sighying'.

67 Peter Thornton, *Authentic Décor: The Domestic Interior, 1620–1920* (London, 1984), 25.

68 Peter Thornton, *Seventeenth-century Interior Decoration in England, France and Holland* (New Haven and London, 1983), 302–3. A silver gilt toilette service was given by the 19th earl of Kildare to his wife as a wedding present in 1709; it is illustrated in Gervase Jackson-Stops (ed.), *The Treasure Houses of Britain: Five Hundred Years of Private Patronage and Art Collecting* (New Haven and London, 1985), cat. no. 124. A list with details of Lady Grandison's toilette service ('My Lady's Dressing Plate') at Dromana is among the Villiers-Stuart Papers at PRONI, T/3131/F/2/18.

69 Quoted in John Bold, 'Privacy and the Plan', in John Bold and Edward Chaney (eds), *English Architecture: Public and Private: Essays for Kerry Downes* (London, 1993), 107–19.

70 *OED*, under 'dressing room'.

71 Eileen Harris, *The Genius of Robert Adam* (New Haven and London, 2001), 7.

72 *Faulkner's Dublin Journal*, 26 January 1765, quoted in Ada Longfield, 'Up for Sale', *Irish Ancestor*, 17, no. 1 (1985), 30–4.

73 John Cornforth, 'More Than a Dressing Room', *Country Life*, 16 April 1992, 112–15.

74 Harris, *Genius of Robert Adam*, 265.

75 IAA, Photograph collection, Ballyfin, Co. Laois; NLI, AD 2674, Thomas Penrose plan of Bedchamber story at Woodville, 1779; IAA, Murray Collection, Killeen Castle bedchamber floor, Francis Johnston, 1802.

76 Griffin and Pegum, *Leinster House*, 31; other bow-shaped dressing rooms as formal rooms were at Headfort, Co. Meath (William Chambers, 1765), at Brook Lodge, Co Galway (Peter Madden, 1836, National Archives of Ireland (NAI), Ballyglunin Papers M6932/63) and at Antrim House, Merrion Square, Dublin in 1801.

77 TCD, MS 4027, D.A. Beaufort, 'Journal of a Tour through part of Ireland begun August 26th 1787', f. 34.

78 At Powerscourt, Co. Wicklow a dressing room connects with the octagonal library, but neither is part of the formal rooms.

79 A writing desk, or *scriptoire*, was a common item in dressing rooms on both sides of the Irish Sea. Maria Edgeworth observed, when she stayed with a family in England in 1813, that there was one in each dressing room, together with 'a table with everything that could be wanted for writing', Christina Colvin (ed.), *Maria Edgeworth: Letters from England 1813–1844* (Oxford, 1971), 25.

80 Elizabeth Kowaleski-Wallace, *Consuming Subjects: Women, Shopping and Business in the Eighteenth Century* (New York, 1997), 55.

81 Lorna Weatherill, *Consumer Behaviour and Material Culture in Britain, 1660–1770* (Cambridge, 1988), 31.

82 Jane Fenlon 'Her Grace's Closet: Paintings in the Duchess of Ormonde's Closet at Kilkenny Castle', *Bulletin of the Irish Georgian Society*, 36 (1994), 30–47.

83 Thornton, *Authentic Décor*, 49.

84 See Lorna Weatherill, 'A Possession of One's Own: Women and Consumer Behavior in England, 1660–1740', *Journal of British Studies*, 25 (1986), 131–56; Kowalski-Wallace, *Consuming Subjects*, 57–8.

85 http://www.crawfordartgallery.ie/ Cooperpenrose/CooperPenrose02.html, accessed 2 February 2012.

86 David S. Howard, 'Chinese Armorial Porcelain for Ireland', *Bulletin of the Irish Georgian Society*, 29, nos. 3 and 4 (July–December 1986), 3–24.

87 IAA, Bunbury Letters, 94/136, letter from Lady Louisa Conolly to her sister Lady Sarah Lennox, 17 September 1760.

88 Stella Tillyard, *Aristocrats: Caroline, Emily, Louisa and Sarah Lennox, 1750–1832* (London, 1994), 148.

89 FitzGerald, *Correspondence of Emily, Duchess of Leinster*, I, 158–9, letter from Lady Kildare to her husband, 17 December [1762].

90 Bowood Archives, vol. 5, 1769–70, extracts from the diary of Sophia, Countess of Shelburne, 1 August 1769. My thanks to the Knight of Glin for the transcription.

91 Quoted in Bold, 'Privacy and the Plan'.

92 Philip Dormer Stanhope, earl of Chesterfield, *Lord Chesterfield's Advice to His Son, on Men and Manners; Containing the Principles of Politeness* (Edinburgh, 1787; first published 1742), 63.

93 IAA, Bunbury Letters, Typescript 97/84, 10 June 1769.

94 Clark, *Gleanings*, I, 184, letter from Lady Carlow to Lady Louis Stuart, 14 January 1782.

95 Hare, *Life and Letters of Maria Edgeworth*, I, 258.

96 J Sheridan Le Fanu, *The Cock and Anchor*, 3 vols (Dublin, 1845), III, 40–1, 55.

97 Quoted in Ed Lilley, 'The Name of the Boudoir', *Journal of the Society of Architectural Historians*, 53 (June 1994), 193–8.

98 *Ibid.*

99 *Ibid.*

100 Quoted in Thornton, *Authentic Décor*, 101.

101 Quoted in Lilley, 'The Name of the Boudoir'.

102 Thornton, *Authentic Décor*, 146.

103 Frederick Scheffer [i.e. William King], *The Toast: An Heroick Poem in Four Books* (reissued, Dublin, 1747), xiii–xvi, verse 56. Latin notes translated into English by Oscar Timoney. My thanks to Edward McParland

for use of these notes. Edward McParland, *Public Architecture in Ireland* (New Haven and London, 2001), 180.

104 Thornton, *Authentic Décor*, 146.

105 IAA, Townley Hall Drawings, M14, attributed to Blayney and Anne Balfour.

106 Mr Balfour had his 'Own Room' and dressing room on the other side of the house.

107 IAA, Murray Collection of drawings, Killeen Castle, plan of tower house; TCD, MS 4035, Mary Beaufort, 'Journal of our Tour to the Westward . . . 1808', f. 117.

108 Mark Girouard, 'Charleville Forest, Co. Offaly, Eire', *Country Life*, 27 September 1962, 710–14.

109 Drawings also in IAA, Photograph collection, Castle Bernard, Co. Offaly.

110 IAA, Murray Drawings Collection, Crom Castle, no. 289, Survey of Castle, ground-floor plan, drawn by the architect William Murray in the late 1830s. The castle was accidentally burnt down in 1841, but was later rebuilt.

111 The only inventory in the survey that lists a boudoir is Mount Stewart, but it is a private room.

112 Quoted in Tita Chico, *Designing Women: The Dressing Room in Eighteenth-century English Literature and Culture* (Lewisburg, PA, 2005), 219–20.

113 Thornton, *Authentic Décor*, 21.

114 Cornforth, 'More Than a Dressing Room'.

115 Thornton, *Seventeenth-century Interior Decoration*, 302.

116 FitzGerald, *Correspondence of Emily, Duchess of Leinster*, III, 23, letter from Lady Louisa Conolly to the countess of Kildare, 28 July 1759.

117 IAA, Bunbury Letters, 94/136, letters from Lady Louisa Conolly to Lady Sarah Lennox (later Bunbury), 28 April 1761, 22 May 1762, 16 December 1760 and 14 February 1768.

118 Bowood Archives, vol. 5, 1769–70, extracts from the diary of Sophia, Countess of Shelburne, 1 August 1769.

119 Rosemary Baird, *Mistress of the House: Great Ladies and Grand Houses 1670–1830* (London, 2003), 105; IAA, Bunbury Letters, 94/136, letter from Lady Louisa Conolly to Lady Sarah Bunbury, 2 August 1768.

120 Clark, *Gleanings*, II, 39–40, letter from Lady Carlow to Lady Louisa Stuart, 4 September 1785.

121 Marie-Louise Legg (ed.), *The Synge Letters: Bishop Edward Synge to His Daughter Alicia Roscommon to Dublin 1746–1752* (Dublin, 1996), 84, 126 and 154, letters dated 9 September 1747, 4 July 1749 and 18 August 1749.

122 Toby Barnard, *Making the Grand Figure: Lives and Possessions in Ireland, 1641–1770* (New Haven and London, 2004), 94.

123 Day, *Letters from Georgian Ireland*, 164, 171.

124 Isaac Ware, *A Complete Body of Architecture* (London, 1756), 432.

125 Brian FitzGerald, *Lady Louisa Conolly, 1743–1821* (London, 1950), 25.

126 Thornton, *Authentic Décor*, 25 and 52, indicates that the 'study' as a room name was established by the end of the seventeenth century. Ware, *A Complete Body of Architecture*, 324, recommended an eastern situation 'most proper for a study, for the morning is the time for resorting thither'.

127 Thornton, *Seventeenth-century Interior Decoration*, 303; Thornton, *Authentic Décor*, 25, 52. 'The Earl of Corke's study' in Cork House, Dublin (1645) and at the earl of Kildare's Dublin house (1656), both in Fenlon, *Goods and Chattels*, 33, 40. Burton Hall, Co. Cork (1686) in Rosemary ffolliott and Brian de Breffny, 'The Contents of Burton Hall, Co. Cork in 1686', *Irish Ancestor*, 5, no. 2 (1973), 104–13.

128 IAA, Mitchell/Crichton collection, Townley Hall, Principal Floor, June 1794; NLI, AD 2499.

129 William Makepeace Thackeray, *Vanity Fair* (London, 1848), 260.

130 'Caffoy' is described in the *OED* as 'some kind of fabric, imported in the 18th c', but quotes Mrs Delany using a caffoy paper with a 'pattern like damask'.

131 Neither boudoir had a bed at Crom Castle.

132 Lord Powerscourt had a 'Green Paragon Couch Bed' in his closet at Powerscourt (1728/9); field beds appear in dressing rooms at Killeen Castle (1735/6) and the old bishop's palace at Elphin (1740); there were oak table beds at Killeen Castle and at Barbavilla (1742/3), and settee beds at Ashfield House (1808), Clogrenan, Co. Carlow (c.1810) and Lord Howth's house at St Mary's Abbey, Dublin (1748). At Killadoon (1807) and at Judge Vandaleur's property at Furry Park, Raheny (1834) were sofa beds; the Carton inventory (1818) lists a 'wardrobe bed with red check curtains', a 'couch bed with green furniture' and a 'bookcase bedstead' in the Summer, Spring and Winter Dressing Rooms respectively; and tent bedsteads appear at Mount Stewart (1821). As well as bed steps, beds usually had pieces of carpet either to step out upon or to go around them. At Carton most beds were surrounded by 'Venitian Bedround' carpets: Mrs Delany made one for her bed in 1752.

133 *Dublin Evening Post*, 30 June 1834, 'Sale of the late Judge Vandeleur's property at Furry Park near Raheny'.

134 Quoted in Norma Clarke, 'Refining Tastes: Literacy and Consumerism in the Eighteenth Century', *Gender and History*, 6, no. 2 (August 1994), 275–80.

135 Richard Twiss, *A Tour of Ireland in 1775* (London, 1776).

136 'Port If You Please', *Dublin Review of Books*, http://www.drb.ie/blog/dublin-stories/2012/11/10/port-if-you-please, accessed 3 November 2015.

137 Chimney or fire boards fitted the opening of the fireplace exactly. Some were decoratively painted; others were covered by wallpaper purchased from a warehouse such as McCormick and Benn, located opposite the piazzas in Essex Street, who advertised their paper 'for hanging Rooms, Staircases, Ceiling and Chimney Boards' in the *Dublin Journal*, 7–10 June 1766.

138 Frances Power Cobbe, *Life of Frances Power Cobbe. By Herself*, 2 vols (3rd edn, London, 1894), I, 10, writes that her father kept 'a few' pistols, 'two or three blunderbusses, sundry guns of various kinds' and his regimental sword, all of which hung in his study.

139 John Ainsworth (ed.), *The Inchiquin Manuscripts* (Dublin, 1961), 525.

140 Bootjacks are mentioned in the dressing room of Lord Doneraile at Doneraile Court (c.1830s), the Eagle Dressing Room at Killadoon (1807), and the Autumn Dressing Room and Dressing Room adjoining Study at Carton (1818).

141 Fenlon, *Goods and Chattels*, 130–4.

142 Vaulted stables designed by Castle can be seen at Gill Hall, Co. Down, Strokestown Park, Co. Roscommon and Bellinter, Co. Meath, as well as in an unexecuted plan for Headfort, Co. Meath and in plans for Leinster House, Dublin.

143 Giles Worsley, *The British Stable* (New Haven and London, 2004), 149.

144 Patricia McCarthy, 'Stables and Horses in Ireland c. 1630–1840', in *The Provost's House Stables: Building & Environs, Trinity College Dublin* (Dublin, 2008), 28–71.

145 Mrs Delany (when she was Mrs Pendarves) said of Sir Arthur Gore of Newton Gore, Co. Mayo in 1732 that his 'dogs and horses are as dear to him as his children'. Quoted in Constantia Maxwell, *The Stranger in Ireland from the Reign of Elizabeth to the Great Famine* (Dublin, 1979; first published 1954), 141.

146 Quoted in Clare Hogan and Livia Hurley, *Report on The Huntsman's Lodge & Dog Kennels, Fota Island* (Cork, 2003). My thanks to Livia Hurley for her help.

147 Barnard, 'Political, Material and Mental Culture of the Cork Settlers'.

148 Quoted in *ibid*.

149 J Greig (ed.), *The Diaries of a Duchess: Extracts from the Diaries of the First Duchess of Northumberland 1716–76* (London, 1926), entry dated 27 September 1771.

150 Quoted in Leo F. McNamara, 'Some Matters Touching Dromoland: Letters of Father and Son, 1758–59', *North Munster Antiquarian Journal*, 28 (1986), 62–70.

151 Barnard, *Making the Grand Figure*, 231–2.

152 Thomas U. Sadleir, 'Letter from Edward, 2nd Earl of Aldborough, to His Agent at Belan', *Journal of the County Kildare Archaeological Society*, 7 (1912–14), 333–4.

153 NLI, Doneraile Papers, MS 34,112(7), Invoice to The Right Honble Lord Doneraile from John Wright & Co. London, 5 October 1775.

154 NLI, Doneraile Papers, MS 34,120, Accounts for household and personal, gardens and livery, 1837–9.

155 *Retrospections of Dorothea Herbert* (Dublin, 1988 edn), 217–18.

156 Legg, *Synge Letters*, letter 20, 11 July 1747.

157 Part of the footman's duty was to ride on the outside of the coach. Alnwick Castle Archives, MS 670, 'Rules for the government of the Marquis of Kildare's (Duke of Leinster's) household 1763–1773', f. 69.

158 Peter Somerville-Large, *The Irish Country House* (London, 1995), 230.

159 PRONI, Shannon Papers, D2707/B15.

160 Kildare House, Dublin, was called Leinster House after the dukedom was conferred on Lord Kildare in 1766. Alnwick Castle Archives, MS 670, 'Rules for the government', ff. 27–30; Patricia McCarthy, 'Vails and Travails: How Lord Kildare Kept His Household in Order', *Irish Architectural and Decorative Studies*, 6 (2003), 120–39.

161 These servants were sometimes referred to as 'running' footmen, because their duties included running errands, often of great distances, taking short cuts across the countryside. They would also run before the carriage to prepare an inn or lodging for the arrival of their master. E.S. Turner, *What the Butler Saw* (London, 1972), 30–1.

162 Gallet, *Paris Domestic Architecture*, 120.

163 Thornton, *Authentic Décor*, 50.

164 Quoted in Valerie Pakenham, *The Big House in Ireland* (London, 2000), 56.

165 Lawrence Wright, *Clean and Decent: The Fascinating History of the Bathroom and the Water Closet* (London, 1966; first published 1960), 114–15.

166 The 'commode' originally referred to a piece of furniture with drawers. The 'night stool' or 'night table' with the hidden chamber pot became known as a 'night commode', then simply a 'commode'. *Ibid.*, 118; for the Eggleso invoice, see the list of inventories.

167 According to Wright, the bidet originated in France in the early eighteenth century and was

advertised in Paris from 1739: 'To the English the bidet has always carried a certain aura of Continental impropriety, and has never quite been accepted. It is found in bathroom designs of the naughty nineties, but then only in the most palatial, made for a sophisticated and well-travelled few, and there it has its discreet upboard' (*ibid.*, 115).

168 Victoria Percy and Gervase Jackson-Stops, 'The Travel Journals of the 1st Duchess of Northumberland, I', *Country Life*, 31 January 1974, 192–5.

169 Gallet, *Paris Domestic Architecture*, 120.

170 *Ibid.*, 215, 216.

171 A.P.W. Malcomson, *Archbishop Charles Agar: Churchmanship and Politics in Eighteenth-century Ireland, 1760–1810* (Dublin, 2002), 58, 354.

172 'Regency Hygiene: The Bourdaloue', https://janeaustensworld.wordpress.com/2012/07/16/regency-hygiene-the-bourdaloue/, accessed 3 November 2015.

173 Girouard, *Life in the English Country House*, 256, plate 161.

174 Hardyment, *Behind the Scenes*, 205.

175 Christine Hiskey, 'The Building of Holkham Hall', *Architectural History*, 40 (1997), 152.

176 Gordon Wheeler, 'John Nash and the Building of Rockingham Co Roscommon', in Terence Reeves-Smyth and Richard Oram (eds), *Avenues to the Past: Essays Presented to Sir Charles Brett on His 75th Year* (Belfast, 2003), 169–95.

177 Hardyment *Behind the Scenes*, 205.

178 'Woodstock', http://tottenham.name/Places_Woodstock.html, accessed 27 April 2012.

6   Servants and Privacy

1 Arthur Young, *A Tour in Ireland with General Observations on the Present State of That Kingdom Made in the Years 1776, 1777 and 1778*, 2 vols (Dublin, 1780), I, 108.

2 S. Madden, *Reflections and Resolutions Proper for the Gentlemen of Ireland* (Dublin, 1738), quoted in Constantia Maxwell, *Dublin under the Georges* (Dublin, 1997; first published 1936), 104.

3 Mrs Godfrey Clark (ed.), *Gleanings from an Old Portfolio, Containing Some Correspondence Between Lady Louisa Stuart and Her Sister Caroline, Countess of Portarlington*, 3 vols (Edinburgh, 1895–8), I, 81; J.D. Herbert, *Irish Varieties for the Last Fifty Years* (London, 1836), 159. No date is given for the latter reference, but it must have been between 1786 and 1795.

4 Angélique Day (ed.), *Letters from Georgian Ireland: The Correspondence of Mary Delany, 1731–1768* (Belfast, 1991), 203, letter dated 20 May 1745.

5 Samuel Madden, quoted in T.C. Barnard, *A New Anatomy of Ireland: The Irish Protestants, 1649–1770* (New Haven and London, 2003), 302.

6 *Ibid.*, 295.

7 Isaac Ware, *A Complete Body of Architecture* (London, 1756), 346–7.

8 Brian FitzGerald, *Correspondence of Emily, Duchess of Leinster 1731–1814*, 3 vols (Dublin, 1949–67), II, 150, letter from Lady Sarah Bunbury to the duchess of Leinster, Castletown, 10 September 1775.

9 'Autobiography of Pole Cosby of Stradbally, Queen's Co., 1703–1737(?)', *Journal of the County Kildare Archaeological Society*, 5 (1906–8), 79–99, 164–84, 253–73, 311–24, 423–36.

10 In 1813 Lord Lorton's agent wrote to him about Mr Murphy, the upholsterer, who had informed him that 'good oat straw will make better palliasses for the servants where there is no feather bed than wheat and I think so too as it will be much softer'. NLI, Rockingham Papers, MS 8810 Part 7(1), 28 November 1813. According to R. Bayne Powell, *Housekeeping in the Eighteenth Century* (London, 1956), 42, palliasses could be filled with 'bog-moss, willow catkins, cotton-grass and flock and chopped straw'. They were often put under feather mattresses to preserve the latter.

11 Christina Hardyment, *Behind the Scenes: Domestic Arrangements in Historic Houses* (London, 1997), 43; E. Dillon, *Wild Geese* (New York, 1980), 49.

12 J.P. Mahaffy, 'Society in Georgian Dublin', in *The Georgian Society: Records of Eighteenth Century Domestic Architecture and Decoration in Dublin*, vol. 3 (Dublin, 1911), 28.

13 The bed at Antrim House was listed together with a chest containing old livery clothes. Formerly known as Clown, Cloncarneel was remodelled in 1801 by Francis Johnston. Mark Bence-Jones, *A Guide to Irish Country Houses* (rev. edn, London, 1988), 88.

14 William Hepworth Dixon (ed.), *Lady Morgan's Memoirs* (rev. edn, London, 1863), 169n.

15 *Pückler's Progress: The Adventures of Prince Pückler-Muskau in England, Wales and Ireland as Told in Letters to His Former Wife 1826–9*, trans. Flora Brennan (London, 1987), 85.

16 See the list of inventories, under Brooke Lodge.

17 *Retrospections of Dorothea Herbert 1770–1806* (Dublin, 1988 edn), 68.

18 Christine Casey mentions some decorated attic rooms in Dublin. At No. 22 Merrion Street there is a three-bay rear room with a coved early rococo ceiling with birds, strapwork motifs and acanthus scrolls in its central panel; and at No. 11 Parnell Square the bow-windowed rear room is also bowed on its inner wall, making an elongated oval with similar plasterwork on its ceiling.

Christine Casey, *The Buildings of Ireland: Dublin* (New Haven and London, 2005), 591, 225.

19 John Fowler and John Cornforth, *English Decoration in the Eighteenth Century* (London, 1974), 76.

20 Chevalier de Latocnaye (trans. J. Stevenson), *A Frenchman's Walk Through Ireland, 1796–7* (facsimile edn, Belfast, 1984), 187.

21 McCarthy, 'Vails and Travails: How Lord Kildare Kept His House in Order', *Irish Architectural and Decorative Studies*, 6 (2003), 120–39.

22 Accommodation for 'strangers' servants' occurs quite rarely on plans/inventories. There are four rooms at Killeen Castle (1790), and one in the servants' wing on Daniel Robertson's plans for Carriglas, Co. Longford (1837–8) at first-floor level. In Richard Castle's plan for Carton there is a 'Room for a second table' to facilitate visiting servants.

23 An early plan of Ballyfin shows a 'Maids Sitting Room' in the service block.

24 Stewards generally had a house of their own on the estate. The parlour in the main house would have been for estate business.

25 Powdering rooms for gentlemen appear on plans for Mount Kennedy (1781) and Ardbraccan (1794), and in inventories for Caledon (1783) and Prospect (1795).

26 In another plan Castle replaces the housekeeper's room (to the rear) with one for the steward.

27 The servants' hall and other service rooms were presumably in the kitchen pavilion.

28 Another plan by Johnston for Townley Hall is annotated 'Hot & Cold baths'. Irish Architectural Archive (IAA), Murray Collection, M18.

29 NLI, Domville Papers, MS 11,297.

30 Quoted in Valerie Pakenham, *The Big House in Ireland* (London, 2000), 58.

31 A 'Confectionary' is listed in the Powerscourt, Co. Wicklow inventory (1729) as a space in which were '2 Oak presses for Sweet-Meats', a bed and other furniture.

32 The basement plan calls the staircase 'Stairs to ye Servants Hall'.

33 This room, together with the two rooms behind it, was converted into what became known later in the eighteenth century as the Supper Room. David Griffin and Caroline Pegum, *Leinster House, 1744–2000: An Architectural History* (Dublin, 2000), 31.

34 There is also a 'Postman's Room' on the plan of Powerscourt, Co. Wicklow. Carton was turned back to front at about this time, to a design (it is suggested) by Johnston. Ann Martha Rowan (ed.), *The Architecture of Richard Morrison and William Vitruvius Morrison* (Dublin, 1989), 53.

35 James Lewis, *Original Designs in Architecture Consisting of Plays, Elevations and Sections for*

Villas, Mansions, Town-houses etc. and a New
Design for a Theatre, 2 vols (London, 1780–97),
II, plates xxix and xxxi.

36 Rolf Loeber and Magda Stouthamer-Loeber, in
18th–19th Century Irish Fiction Newsletter, no. 9,
(September 1998), unpaginated, endnote 7.

37 John Ainsworth (ed.), *The Inchiquin
Manuscripts* (Dublin, 1961), 525, doc. 1511, Will
of Sir Edward O'Brien of Dromoland, Bt, 26
August 1765.

38 Quoted in Kathy Trant, *The Blessington Estate
1667–1908* (Dublin, 2004), 51.

39 According to the *OED*, board wages were
'wages allowed to servants to keep themselves
in victual'.

40 Alnwick Castle Archives, MS 670, 'Rules for
the government of the Marquis of Kildare's
(Duke of Leinster's) household 1763–1773',
ff. 88, 15.

41 J.J. Hecht, *The Domestic Servant Class in
Eighteenth-century England* (London, 1956), 155.

42 John Stevenson, *Two Centuries of Life in Down*
(Belfast, 1990; first published 1920), 439.

43 NLI, Pakenham–Mahon Papers, MS 10,136,
Account of clothes given to servants 1844. It
should be noted that the pantry and kitchen
boys might also have been postilions when required.

44 Marie-Louise Legg (ed.), *The Synge Letters:
Bishop Edward Synge to His Daughter Alicia
Roscommon to Dublin 1746–1752* (Dublin,
1996), 83, Letter 37 from Bishop Edward
Synge, Elphin, 9 September 1747.

45 NLI, Powerscourt Papers, MS 43,066/2,
Probate of the will of Dorothy Beresford, 1
viscountess, née Rowley, 1 August 1785.

46 When a member of the royal family died,
prominent families, particularly those connected with the church or the parliament, put
their servants into mourning. Three months'
full mourning meant dress in matt black; this
was followed by second mourning, when dress
could be lightened somewhat. Legg, *Synge
Letters*, 276, Letter 133 from Synge, Elphin, 24
May 1751, n. 12; L. Taylor, *Mourning Dress: A
Costume or Social History* (London, 1983), 104.

47 Ainsworth, *Inchiquin Manuscripts*, 525.

48 Jonathan Swift, *Directions to Servants* (London,
1745), 33–4.

49 D. Marshall, 'The Domestic Servants of the
Eighteenth Century', *Economica*, 9 (April
1929), 15–40.

50 Hecht, *Domestic Servant Class*, 168.

51 Swift, *Directions to Servants*, 34; Marshall,
'Domestic Servants'.

52 Marshall, 'Domestic Servants'.

53 Bridget Hill, *Servants: English Domestics in the
Eighteenth Century* (Oxford, 1996), 77.

54 Horace Walpole's house, Strawberry Hill, in
England was so popular that he joked that he

could recoup some of the money laid out on
the house by marrying his housekeeper there
as she made so much money. Hecht, *Domestic
Servant Class*, 171.

55 Benson Earle Hill, *Recollections of an Artillery
Officer*, 2 vols (London, 1836), I, 55–6.

56 R. and E. Griffith, *A Series of Genuine Letters
Between Henry and Frances*, 4 vols (3rd edn,
London, 1770), IV, 142–3, letter dxii.

57 Quoted in Marshall, 'Domestic Servants'.

58 Swift, *Directions to Servants*, 33, 14.

59 Marshall, 'Domestic Servants'. Two footmen at
the court of Queen Anne, Fortnum and Mason,
used this perquisite as capital to begin their
grocery business in London. *Country House
Lighting 1660–1890*, Temple Newsam Country
House Series No. 4 (Leeds, 1992).

60 Hill, *Servants*, 76–7.

61 Daniel Defoe wrote *The Behaviour of Servants*
and *Everybody's Business is Nobody's Business* in
1725.

62 Quoted in Hill, *Servants*, 77.

63 *Anthologia Hibernica*, I (May 1793), 357. No date
is given for this account, but 'Grand George'
Mathew, who died in 1737, was the man described, who was host to Jonathan Swift at
Thomastown in the 1720s, a visit described
by Thomas Sheridan in *A Life of the Rev. Dr.
Jonathan Swift* (Dublin, 1785).

64 Marshall, 'Domestic Servants'.

65 Griffith, *Series of Genuine Letters*, IV, 142–3,
footnote to letter dxii: 'An Agreement entered
into among the Gentlemen of several Counties
in Ireland, not to give Vails to Servants'.

66 Alnwick Castle Archives, MS 670, 'Rules for
the government', ff. 56–7.

67 Philip Ariès (trans. Robert Baldick), *Centuries
of Childhood: A Social History of Family Life*
(New York, 1962 edn), 390–1.

68 Quoted in Linda Pollock, 'Living on the
Stage of the World: The Concept of Privacy
Among the Elite of Early Modern England',
in A. Wilson (ed.), *Rethinking Social History:
English Society 1570–1920 and Its Interpretation*
(Manchester, 1993), 78–96.

69 *Ibid*.

70 Tim Meldrum, *Domestic Service and Gender
1660–1750: Life and Work in the London
Household* (Harlow, 2000), 125.

71 McCarthy, 'Vails and Travails'. Samuel Johnson,
Dictionary of the English Language (London,
1755) defined 'family' as 'those who live in the
same house'.

72 Legg, *Synge Letters*, 383, letter 175.

73 Quoted in McCarthy, 'Vails and Travails'.

74 Thomas U. Sadleir and Page L. Dickinson,
Georgian Mansions in Ireland (Dublin, 1915),
84–5.

75 Gillian Russell, *The Theatres of War:
Performances, Politics and Society 1793–1815*

(Oxford, 1995), 124. At a masquerade in the
assembly rooms in Fishamble Street, Dublin
in 1778, Lord Jocelyn dressed as a housemaid
and Lady Ely as a washerwoman. *Hibernian
Magazine*, April 1778, 189–90.

76 Ita M. Hogan, *Anglo-Irish Music 1780–1830*
(Cork, 1966), 30.

77 Toby Barnard, 'Public and Private Uses of
Wealth in Ireland, *c.*1660–1760', in J. Hill and
C. Lennon (eds), *Historical Studies*, 21 (Dublin,
1999), 66–85.

78 William M. Thackeray, *The Irish Sketch Book
1842* (Belfast, 1985 edn), 209–10.

79 Madden, *Reflections and Resolutions*, 62.

80 John Scott, 1st earl of Clonmell, 'Life in the
Irish Country House', *Quarterly Bulletin of
the Irish Georgian Society*, 7, nos. 2–4 (April–
December 1964), 68–70.

81 Clark, *Gleanings*, I, 166–7, letter from Lady
Portarlington to Lady Louisa Stuart, November
1781.

82 Barnard, *New Anatomy of Ireland*, 302–3.

83 IAA, Bunbury Letters, letter from Lady Louisa
Conolly, Carton, to Lady Sarah Bunbury, 11
September 1766.

84 FitzGerald, *Correspondence of Emily, Duchess of
Leinster*, I, 61 and 151, letters from the countess
of Kildare to the earl, Carton, 17 April 1759 and
10 [December 1762].

85 IAA, Bunbury Letters, in box marked 'bits &
undated', letter from Lady Louisa Conolly, to
Lady Sarah Bunbury, 29 September.

List of Inventories

ANTRIM HOUSE, DUBLIN, 1801
Public Record Office of Northern Ireland (PRONI), Antrim Papers, D/2977/5/1/7/2 'An Inventory of the Furniture &c. of Antrim house taken by Mr S[. . .] & Michl. Campbell, this 19th day of August 1801'.

ASHFIELD, CO. CAVAN, 1808, 1829
Trinity College Dublin (TCD), Clements Papers, MS 7344/34, 'A List of Furniture in Ashfield Lodge House July 1829', added to inventory for same house of 1808.

ASHFIELD, CO. CAVAN, 1843
TCD, Clements Papers, MS 7279, 'Inventory and valuation of Farming, Stock, Crop, Farming and Garden Utensils etc. the Property of the late Henry John Clements, Esq MP of Ashfield. Dated 28 Jany 1843'.

MR BALFOUR'S HOUSE, DUBLIN
See St Stephen's Green (Mr Balfour's house).

BARBAVILLA, CO. WESTMEATH, 1742–3
Rosemary ffolliott, 'The Furnishings of a Palladian House in 1742–3: Barbavilla, Co. Westmeath', *Irish Ancestor*, 11, no. 2 (1979), 86–95.

BARONSCOURT, CO. TYRONE, 1782
Public Record Office of Northern Ireland (PRONI), D/623/D/4/1, Abercorn Papers, 'Inventory of Household Furniture at Baron's Court 1782'.

BISHOP'S PALACE, ELPHIN, CO. ROSCOMMON, 1740
National Library of Ireland (NLI), Wicklow Papers, MS 38,597/22, 'An Inventory of the Household Goods Belonging to Doctor Robert Howard Late Lord Bishop of Elphin Taken This 21st Day of June 1740'.

BROOK LODGE, CO. GALWAY, 1808
NAI, Ballyglunin Papers M 6933, Parcel 20 (57b), 'Invoice from Eggleso's Upholstery & Cabinet Ware House, 12 Abbey Street, Dublin to Mr Thomas Hynes, bought of Henry Eggleso, 29 June 1808, for Brook Lodge'.

BROWNLOW HOUSE, CO. ARMAGH, 1848
PRONI, D/1928/H/9, Brownlow Papers, 'Inventory and valuation of Furniture and Plate in Brownlow House, Co Armagh made by Robert Pasley of Bachelors Walk, Dublin and James Dowell of George St, Edinburgh, Upholsterers & valuators appointed to make such valuation by order of 11 November 1848'.

BURTON HALL, CO. CORK, 1686
Rosemary ffolliott and Brian de Breffny, 'The Contents of Burton Hall, Co. Cork in 1686', *Irish Ancestor*, 5, no. 2 (1973), 104–13.

CALEDON HOUSE, CO. TYRONE, 1783
PRONI, Caledon Papers D/2433/A/2/4/1–19, 'London 1st May 1783, Estimate of Furniture for My Caledon House', headed 'Estimate to James Alexander Esq. for Furnishing the Principal Story in Caledon House', probably from Mayhew & Ince, London.

CARTON HOUSE, CO. KILDARE, 1818
'Inventory of furniture &c of Carton House, January 1st, 1818'.
By kind permission of Patrick Guinness.

CASTLE COOLE, CO. FERMANAGH, 1802
Belmore: The Lowry Corrys of Castle Coole, 1646–1913 (Belfast, 2007).
My thanks to Peter Marson for allowing me to view a draft of this
work before publication.

NO. 10 CAVENDISH ROW, DUBLIN, 1763
British Library, Cockburn Papers, MS Add. 48314.

CLOGRENAN LODGE, CO. CARLOW, c.1810
NLI, Rochfort Papers, MS 8682(3), 'Inventory of the Furniture of
Clogrenan Lodge', undated but early nineteenth century.

CLONMEL, CO. TIPPERARY, 1675
NLI, MS 2527, ff. 78–83; Jane Fenlon, *Goods and Chattels: A Survey
of Early Household Inventories in Ireland* (Kilkenny, 2003), 80–6.

CONVOY HOUSE, CO. DONEGAL, c.1844
TCD, MS 11258, 'Inventory for Convoy House, Co. Donegal, c.1844'.
With thanks to Professor Anne Crookshank and Edward McParland.

CONYNGHAM HALL, CO. MEATH, 1710
Irish Architectural Archive (IAA), Castletown Deposit, Section F,
Box 4, 'Inventory of Goods in Dispute at Conyngham Hall, Slane,
[Co. Meath] 1710'. My thanks to Livia Hurley for this reference.

CORK HOUSE, DUBLIN, 1645
Chatsworth House, Lismore Papers, vol. 28, no. 4; Fenlon,
Goods and Chattels, 32–4.

COROFIN HOUSE, CO. CLARE, 1718
NLI, Inchiquin Papers, MS 1804; Fenlon, *Goods and Chattels*, 127–9.

CROM CASTLE, CO. FERMANAGH, 1860s
PRONI, Erne Papers, D/1939/27/26, undated inventory, possibly
c.1860.

DAWSON GROVE, CO. MONAGHAN, 1827
NLI, MS 741, Account returned by Sheriff of Co. Monaghan of sale
at Dawson Grove, 1827.

LAURENCE DELAMAIN'S HOUSE, CORK, 1763
TCD, MS 2010–2015/395, 'Inventory, Laurence Delamain Late of
the City of Corke, Gent Deceased, taken 20th January 1763'.

DENMARK STREET, DUBLIN, 1793
PRONI, Erne Papers, D/1939/24/11/2, 'Schedule of furniture attached to lease of house from Earl of Rosse to David Courtney, Esq.,
18 December 1793'.

DONERAILE COURT, CO. CORK, c.1830s
NLI, Doneraile Papers, MS 34,104(5), 'Inventory of Furniture Room
by Room in Doneraile Court', n.d. but probably c.1830s.

DROMANA, CO. WATERFORD, 1755
PRONI, T/3131/F/2/17, Villiers Stuart Papers, 'An Inventory of the
Houshold . . . at Dromana Belonging to the Right Honourable Earl
Grandison, Taken August 12, 1755'.

DROMOLAND HOUSE, CO. CLARE, 1753
NLI, MS 14,786; Fenlon, *Goods and Chattels*, 130.

DRUMCONDRA HOUSE, CO. DUBLIN, 1773
Trinity College Irish Art Research Centre (TRIARC), Crookshank-
Glin Archive, TRIARC/1/13, photocopy of Alexander de Lapere

Kirkpatrick, *Chronicles of the Kirkpatrick Family* (privately printed,
n.d.).

DRUMCONDRA HOUSE, CO. DUBLIN, 1689
NLI, De Vesci Papers, MS 38,777, 'Inventory of Giles Martin, late of
Drumcondrah in the Co. of Dublin Esq. Appraised 25 June 1689'.

DUBLIN CASTLE, 1677
NLI, MS 2,528; Fenlon, *Goods and Chattels*, 87–98.

DUBLIN CASTLE, 1678
NLI, MS 2,554; Fenlon, *Goods and Chattels*, 99–103.

DUNMORE HOUSE, CO. CORK (OR ORMOND CASTLE OR KILKENNY
CASTLE), 1639
NLI, MS 2,552, ff. 19v–20; Fenlon, *Goods and Chattels*, 30–1.

DUNMORE HOUSE, CO. CORK, 1684
NLI, MS 2,554; Fenlon, *Goods and Chattels*, 123–6.

FURRY PARK, CO. DUBLIN, 1834
Dublin Evening Post, 30 June 1834, 'Sale of the late Judge Vandeleur's
property at Furry Park near Raheny'.

GAULSTON, CO. WESTMEATH, 1787
Private Collection, 'Inventory of Furniture in Galston House, Taken
December 1787'. This inventory was given to me by the Knight of
Glin, who received it from Lord Kilmaine.

GEASHILL, CO. OFFALY, 1628
BL Add. MS, Charter 13,340; NLI Microfilm No. 1965, p. 1492;
Fenlon, *Goods and Chattels*, 20–3.

HENRIETTA STREET, DUBLIN, 1772
NLI, Gardiner Papers, MS 36,617/1, 'List of the goods at Henrietta
Street House which did belong to the late Luke Gardiner Esq taken
and valued by Joseph Ellis and J Kirchhoffer Novr. 9, 1772'.

HOWTH CASTLE, CO. DUBLIN, 1746–52
F. Elrington Ball, *Howth and Its Owners* (Dublin, 1917), 164–6.

LORD HOWTH'S DUBLIN HOUSE, ST MARY'S ABBEY, 1751
J.P. Mahaffy, 'The Furnishing of Georgian Houses in Dublin in
the Earlier Part of the Century', *The Georgian Society Records of
Eighteenth Century Domestic Architecture and Decoration in Dublin*,
5 vols (Shannon, 1969), IV, 1–10.

INGOLDSBY HOUSE, MARY STREET, DUBLIN, 1731
NLI, Smythe of Barbavilla Papers, MS 41,581/8, 'A catalogue of
the Household Goods, Of the late Henry Ingoldsby, Esq: Deceas'd.
to be sold by Auction in Mary's-street, on Monday the 29th day of
November, 1731, and to continue until the end of the Week'.

EARL OF KILDARE'S HOUSE, DUBLIN, 1656
NLI, MS 18,996; Fenlon, *Goods and Chattels*, 39–40.

KILKENNY CASTLE, CO. KILKENNY, 1630
NLI, MS 2,552; Fenlon, *Goods and Chattels*, 26–9.

KILKENNY CASTLE, CO. KILKENNY, 1639
See Dunmore House, 1639.

KILKENNY CASTLE, CO. KILKENNY, 1684
NLI, MS 2,554; Fenlon, *Goods and Chattels*, 104–22.

KILKENNY CASTLE, CO. KILKENNY, 1675–1717
Jane Fenlon, 'The Ormonde Inventories 1675–1717:
A State Apartment at Kilkenny Castle', in Agnes Bernelle (ed.),
Decantations: A Tribute to Maurice Craig (Dublin, 1992), 29–37.

Killadoon, Co. Mayo, 1807, 1812, 1830, 1836, 1844 and 1855
  Private Collection. Summary notes taken by Christopher Moore and Sally Clements, to whom I am grateful.

Killeen Castle, Co. Meath, 1735/6
  NLI, Fingall Papers, MS 1678, 'An Inventory of the Rt Honble Earl of Fingall's Goods in the Castle of Killeen, March 23rd 1735/6'.

Killeen Castle, Co. Meath, 1790
  NLI, Fingall Papers, MS 1678, 'Furniture belonging to the Earl & Countess of Fingall in Killeen Castle taken 15th June 1790'.

Kilrush, Co. Kilkenny, c.1750
  TCD, St George MSS, Misc. photocopy 175/17, 'An Account of the Goods and particulars belonging to Gen.ll St George in his house at Kilrush', [1750].

Knapton, Co. Laois, 1763
  NLI, De Vesci Papers, MS 38,905, 'An Inventory and Valuation of the Furniture, Cattle, Corn, Hay and Brewing Eutencils of George Pigott Esq. at Knapton Sept 9 1763'.

Moore Abbey, Co. Kildare, 1826
  NLI, Drogheda Papers, MS 9743, 'Sale by Auction of Furniture, House, Linen, Books &c. at Moore Abbey, Co Kildare on 29, 30, 31st March . . . 1826'.

Mount Stewart, Co. Down, 1821
  PRONI, D/654/S1/1, Londonderry Papers, 'An Inventory of the Household Furniture Belonging to the Most Noble the Marquis of Londonderry Taken at Mount Stewart Septr 1821'.

Neptune (later Temple Hill House), Co. Dublin, 1789
  'A Schedule or Inventry of the fixtures household Goods furniture and other Articles . . . contained in the House and premis of Neptune', 14 May 1789. Copy in the Irish Art Research Centre (TRIARC), ref. TRIARC/1/13.

Newbridge House, Co. Dublin, 1821
  Private Collection.

North Great George's Street, Dublin, 1705
  TCD, MS 7344/32, 'Valuation of Furniture in Nth Gt Georges St Dublin: Property of Mrs Clements in Her Late Dwelling House, April 17, 1805'.

Ormond Castle, Co. Tipperary, 1639
  See Dunmore House.

Ormonde inventories (covering Kilkenny Castle, Dunmore House, Dublin Castle), 1667–1753
  NLI, Ormonde Inventories, MSS 2527–9, 2521–5, 2552–5.

Powerscourt, Dublin, 1728/9
  NLI, POS 6071, 'A Catalogue of the Goods & Stock of the Late Edward Wingfield, Esq. at Powerscourt, & at His House in Dublin, to Be Sold by Auction. 25 Feb 1728–9 and to Continue'.

Powerscourt, Co. Wicklow, 1728/9
  NLI, POS 6071, 'A Catalogue of the Goods & Stock of the Late Edward Wingfield, Esq. at Powerscourt, & at His House in Dublin, to Be Sold by Auction. 25 Feb 1728–9 and to Continue'.

Prospect (later Ardgillan Castle), Co. Dublin, 1795
  NAI, Taylor Documents, M.7069(195), 'Inventory of the Furniture in Prospect Castle Taken 25 Sept 1795'.

Provost's House, Dublin, 1820
  TCD, Muniments, P4 183(24), 'Valuation of Sundry Articles of Household Furniture, the Property of the Rt Revd Lord Bishop of Limerick in the Provost's House 27 October 1820'.

Provost's House, Dublin, 1852
  TCD, Muniments (uncatalogued), 'An Inventory of Furniture &c Belonging to T.C.D., in the Provost's House', [1852], 'drawn up by Upholsterer, Mr Durham'.

Rathcline, Co. Longford, 1688
  NLI, MS 8644(5), 'An Inventory of Goods, Pictures & houshold stuffe belonging to the Rt Honble the Lord Viscount Lanesborough . . . in his Lordps. House at Rathcline dated this tenth day of April 1688'.

St Sepulchre's, Dublin, c.1730
  TCD, MS 1995-2008/2438, 'Inventory for Revd Mr Robert Dougatt executor of his late Grace, Dr William King' of the Palace of St Sepulchre.

St Stephen's Green (Mr Balfour's house), Dublin, c.1741
  NLI, Balfour Papers, MS 10,279, 'An acct of the Late Capt. Belfourt [Balfour?], Hous, Goods, Plate, China, Linnin &c sold by Auction March 15th 1741/2'; MS 9534, 'An inventory of Mrs Balfour's goods in her house at Stephen's Green', c.1741.

Shelton House, Co. Wicklow, 1816
  NLI, Wicklow Papers, MS 38,574/20, 'Inventory and Valuation of the Furniture in Shelton House, Co. Wicklow. Taken by L. & A. Morgan, January 4th 1816'.

Stackallen, Co. Meath, 1757
  NAI, Stackallen Inventory, M.1148/5/3

Strokestown Park, Co. Roscommon, c.1806
  NLI, Pakenham–Mahon Papers, MS 10,139, 'A List of the Furniture of the late Luke Mahon Esq as valued by Maurice Mahon Esq and Mr Harry West', n.d. but probably c.1806.

Townley Hall, Co. Louth, 1773
  NLI, Townley Hall Papers, MS 9349, 'List of Townley Hall Furniture, 1773'.

Woodville, Co. Dublin, c.1797
  TCD, Clements Papers MS 7344/30, 'Sale of the late Rt Hon. Theophilus Clements household furniture &c. at Woodville, November 25 & succeeding days', c.1797.

Glossary

AEDICULE   Used in classical architecture to describe the unit formed by a pair of columns or pilasters, an entablature and (usually) a pediment, placed against a wall to frame an opening.

ARCADE   A series of arches supported by piers or columns. *See also* COLONNADE.

ARCHITRAVE   A formalised lintel, the lowest member of the entablature in classical architecture. Also the moulded frame of a door or window.

ATTIC   A small top storey within a roof. Also the storey above the main entablature of a classical façade.

BAIZE   A coarse fabric (usually wool), napped to resemble felt.

BAROQUE   A European architectural style, at its height in the seventeenth and early eighteenth centuries, derived from Renaissance architecture. Characteristically theatrical and extravagant, it employed convex and concave flowing curves and ornate detail, and delighted in large-scale sweeping vistas.

BAWN   Literally an ox fold. A defensive walled enclosure attached to or near an Irish tower house or Plantation castle.

BOISERIES   Panelling or other fitted interior woodwork with elaborate decoration of foliage, etc. Particularly common in seventeenth–nineteenth-century France.

BOW WINDOW   A window of one or more storeys projecting from the face of a building at ground level, and curved in plan. A *canted* bay window has a straight front and angled sides.

BROCADE   A richly decorative silk fabric, woven with a raised pattern of figures, flowers and other ornaments.

BROCATELLE   A type of coarse brocade, used mainly for tapestry.

BUCRANIUM (plural: BUCRANIA)   An ox skull used decoratively in friezes on classical buildings, especially those of the Doric order.

CAFFOY PAPER   A type of flock paper used for covering walls in the eighteenth century.

CALICO   Cotton cloth with patterns printed in one or more colours.

CALIMANCO   A thin fabric of worsted wool yarn which could come in a variety of weaves. The surface was glazed or calendered (pressed through hot rollers).

CANTILEVER   A horizontal projection (e.g. a step or a canopy) supported at one end only.

CAPITAL   The head or top part of a column.

CHINTZ   Printed or painted calico.

CLOSE-STOOL   A chamber pot enclosed in a box (originally a wooden stool). In the eighteenth century sometimes built into a chair. Also known as a 'deception commode'.

COFFERING   An arrangement of sunken panels (coffers), square or polygonal, decorating a ceiling, vault or arch.

COLONNADE   A range of columns supporting an entablature, without arches. *See also* ARCADE.

CORINTHIAN   The most slender and ornate of the three main classical orders. It has a basket-shaped capital ornamented with acanthus leaves.

CORNICE   A horizontal moulded projection along the top of a building or feature, in particular the uppermost member of the classical entablature. Also the ornamental moulding in the angle between wall and ceiling.

DADO   The finishing (often with panelling) of the lower part of a wall, usually in a classical interior. In origin, a formalised continuous pedestal.

DADO RAIL   The moulding along the top of the dado.

DAMASK   A rich silk fabric, normally from India, Genoa or Nassau, woven with elaborate designs and figures.

DEMESNE   Land belonging to a manor house or estate which is retained by the owner for their own use.

DORIC   The oldest and simplest of the three main classical orders, featuring a sturdy column shaft and a frieze with triglyphs and metopes. A Greek Doric column has no base, a shaft, normally fluted, which narrows in diameter towards the top, and a thin convex capital. A Roman Doric column consists of a base, a shaft (plain or fluted) with more slender proportions than in Greek Doric, and a simple round capital.

DRAB   Dull light brown or yellowish-brown.

DRUM   An evening assembly of fashionable people at a private house. Popular in the late eighteenth and early nineteenth centuries.

DUMB WAITER   An article of dining room furniture designed to dispense with servants at the table, usually wheeled in at the end of dinner, laden with sweetmeats, fruit, cheese and wines, and placed by the table for the diners to help themselves.

ELLWIDE   A measure of length varying in different countries. The English ell measured 45 inches, the Flemish ell 27 inches.

EMPIRE STYLE   The neo-classical style of decoration and interior design that evolved in the Napoleonic period in France in the first fifteen years of the nineteenth century. Largely the creation of the architects Percier and Fontaine.

ENFILADE   Rooms in a formal series, usually with all the doorways on axis.

ENGAGED COLUMN   A column that is partly merged into a wall or pier.

ENTABLATURE   In classical architecture, the collective name for the three horizontal members (architrave, frieze and cornice) carried by a wall.

ESCUTCHEON   A shield for a coat of arms or other heraldic display.

GIRANDOLE   An ornamental branched candleholder.

GOTHIC   The architectural style of the Middle Ages from the later twelfth century to the Renaissance; it coincided with Renaissance style into the seventeenth century in certain forms. Sometimes called Pointed style, reflecting its defining feature, the pointed arch. It is also characterised by window-tracery, pointed rib-vaults and deep buttresses.

GOTHIC REVIVAL   The self-conscious and often scrupulously accurate use of Gothic architecture for its historical or religious associations. It began in the seventeenth century and reached its peak in the nineteenth century.

GOTHICK   An early phase of the Gothic Revival, at its peak *c.*1730–80, marked by thin, delicate forms used without much concern for archaeological accuracy or structural logic.

GRISAILLE   Monochrome painting, especially on walls or glass.

HOLLAND   A linen fabric from the Netherlands. When unbleached called 'brown Holland'.

IMPERIAL STAIR   A stair rising in one flight and returning at right angles in two.

IONIC   One of the three main classical orders, identifiable by the curling spirals (volutes) on the capital of the column.

JIB DOOR   A concealed door that is flush with the wall and treated to resemble it. Sometimes spelled GIB DOOR.

KIDDERMINSTER   A type of carpet originally manufactured at Kidderminster in Worcestershire.

LIVERY   A special uniform provided for servants.

LUNETTE   A semicircular window. Also a semicircular or crescent-shaped surface.

LUTESTRING   A plain-weave silk with glossy finish, popular for summer wear.

MOREEN   A heavy fabric of wool or wool and cotton, watered or with embossed figures, used for curtains and upholstery.

MUSLIN   A very fine, semi-transparent cotton.

ORIEL WINDOW   A window that projects on corbels or brackets from an upper floor.

OVERDOOR   The painting or relief above an internal door.

OVERMANTEL   An ornamented or painted feature above a fireplace.

PALLADIAN   A classical style derived from the work of the Italian architect Andrea Palladio (1508–80), who in turn derived it from Roman architecture. Palladio's work, including his buildings and publications, had great influence on Western architecture, with revivals in the seventeenth and eighteenth centuries, and continuing into the twentieth century.

PAVILION   A terminating feature of a wing projecting from a larger structure, common in Palladian architecture. Also an ornamental building for occasional use in a garden, park, etc..

PEDIMENT   In classical architecture, a formalised gable derived from that of a temple. Also used over doors, windows, etc..

PEMBROKE TABLE   A table that is supported by four fixed legs, having two hinged side-flaps which can be spread out horizontally and supported on legs connected with the central part by joints.

PERQUISITE   Something that has served its primary use and to which a subordinate or employee has a customary right.

PIANO NOBILE   The principal storey of a classical building, containing the reception rooms, located over a ground floor or basement and usually taller than other storeys.

PICTURESQUE   A style of architecture based on the eighteenth-century picturesque aesthetic theory, which was primarily concerned with landscape. In architecture it is characterised by compositions of irregular forms and textures that were thought to be pleasing to the eye, and in planning by asymmetrical layouts in which particular views are highlighted

PILASTER   A flat representation of a classical column which projects slightly from a wall.

PORTE-COCHÈRE   A porch large enough to admit wheeled vehicles.

PORTICO   A porch with the roof (and frequently a pediment) supported by a row of columns.

ROCOCO   A style of eighteenth-century decoration characterised by asymmetrical ornament, often in C- or S-shapes, usually derived from foliage or shells. It began in France, flourishing most fully there and in Germany and Central Europe. It is sometimes associated with the imitation Chinese style known as *chinoiserie*, and, in the British Isles, with the phase of the Gothic Revival known as Gothick.

ROTUNDA   A building or room that is circular in plan.

ROUT   A fashionable gathering or assembly; a large evening party or reception. Popular in the late eighteenth and early nineteenth centuries.

RUSTICATION   Treatment of joints and/or faces of masonry to give an effect of strength. In the most usual kind, the joints are recessed by a V-section chamfering or square-section channelling.

SARCOPHAGUS   A coffin of stone or other durable material, often decorated with relief sculpture or inscriptions.

SARSANET   A fine soft fabric, often of silk, made in plain or twill weave and used especially for linings.

SCAGLIOLA   A polished composition covering giving the effect of (usually coloured) marble, made of plaster with glues and dyes. Deriving from Italy, it was used especially on columns from the mid-eighteenth century to the early nineteenth.

SERGE   A hard-wearing twilled worsted.

SGABELLO   An Italian Renaissance side chair, usually made of walnut, with a variety of carvings and turned elements. Armless, it had a thin back on which the family coat of arms was carved, and an octagonal seat. It was not designed for comfortable seating and was usually to be found in hallways.

STUCCO   A durable lime plaster, sometimes incorporating marble dust. It can be shaped into ornamental or architectural features, or used externally as a protective coating.

TABBY   A thick silk/taffeta fabric woven with a slight nap, passed in folds under a hot cylinder, which produced an uneven or moire effect on the surface of the material.

TAMMY   A twilled worsted fabric.

TERM   A pedestal or pilaster tapering downwards, usually with the upper part of a human figure growing out of it. Sometimes called a terminal figure.

TESSELLATED PAVEMENT   Mosaic flooring, particularly Roman, made of tesserae, i.e. small cubes of glass, stone or brick.

TÔLE   Lacquered or enamelled metalware, from the French word for sheet metal. Popular in the eighteenth century.

TORCHÈRE   A tall stand for a candelabrum.

TOWER HOUSE   A compact fortified house in Ireland and Scotland with the main hall raised above the ground and at least one more storey above that. The type continued well into the seventeenth century in its modified forms: L-plan, with a jamb or wing at one corner; Z-plan, with a jamb or wing at each diagonally opposite corner.

TROMPE L'ŒIL   Literally a deception or trick of the eye, it is usually a two-dimensional painting or decoration in which objects are represented three-dimensionally. Often used to suggest architectural elements, or painted representations of marble, grained wood, etc.

VAILS   A tip or gratuity.

VENETIAN WINDOW   In classical architecture, a window, door or other opening consisting of an arched central opening with two lower and narrower flat-topped openings each side. Also called a Palladian or Serliana window (having been popularised by Sebastiano Serlio (1475–c.1554)).

WAINSCOT   A wooden lining to interior walls. Also called panelling.

WYATT WINDOW   A large tripartite sash window with narrower side lights and a segmental arch above. Made popular by the Wyatt family of architects in the late eighteenth century.

Index

Photographic Credits

Failte Ireland: 89, 122

Courtesy of Carton House: 92, 129

The Alfred Beit Foundation: 93, 131

Courtesy of the Brennan family: 95

Courtesy of Fairfax House, York, England: 97

Photograph courtesy of Richard Ireland: 98, 99

Courtesy of Ronald Phillips Ltd: 104

© National Trust Images, Andreas von Einsiedel: 106, 124

Photograph Kevin McFeely by kind permission of Fingal County Council: 113

© James Fennell (Christopher Moore): 120

National Museums Northern Ireland: 132

Patrick Guinness Collection, Irish Architectural Archive: 137, 186

© Christie's Images: 140

Private collection, image courtesy of the National Gallery of Ireland: 142

Deputy Keeper of Records, Public Record Office of Northern Ireland: 145

Image courtesy of the Victoria and Albert Museum, London: 147

Courtesy of Frederick O'Dwyer: 150

Courtesy of the Royal Irish Academy: 151

Photo © National Gallery of Ireland NGI.4312: 154

© National Museums Northern Ireland: Collection Ulster Museum: 164

San Antonio Museum of Art, bequest of John V. Rowan, Jr., 2004.13.154.a–p; photography by Peggy Tenison; courtesy of the San Antonio Museum of Art: 175

Courtesy of Anne and Bernard Gray: 178

The J. Paul Getty Museum: 180

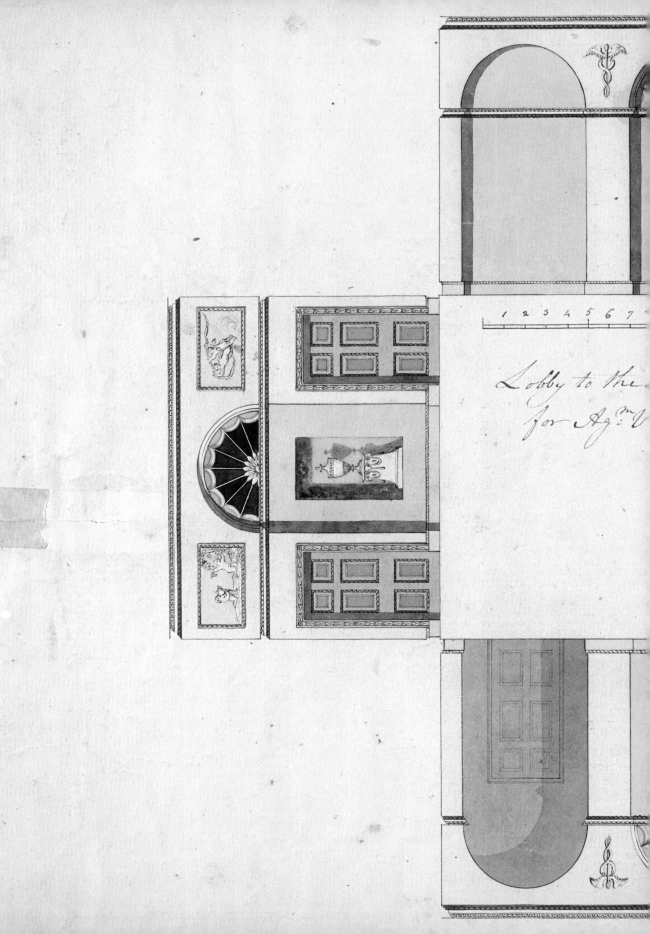

1 2 3 4 5 6 7

Lobby to the
for Ag.ᵐ.